T0351802

Measuring Wealth and Financial Intermediation and Their Links to the Real Economy

Studies in Income and Wealth
Volume 73

National Bureau of Economic Research
Conference on Research in Income and Wealth

Measuring Wealth and Financial Intermediation and Their Links to the Real Economy

Edited by **Charles R. Hulten and Marshall B. Reinsdorf**

The University of Chicago Press

Chicago and London

CHARLES R. HULTEN is professor in the Department of Economics at the University of Maryland. He is a research associate of the National Bureau of Economic Research and chairman of the National Bureau of Economic Research's Conference on Research in Income and Wealth. MARSHALL REINSDORF is senior economist in the Statistics Department at the International Monetary Fund. He is the former chief of the National Economics Accounts Research Group at the Bureau of Economic Analysis.

The University of Chicago Press, Chicago 60637
The University of Chicago Press, Ltd., London
© 2015 by the National Bureau of Economic Research
All rights reserved. Published 2015.
Printed in the United States of America

24 23 22 21 20 19 18 17 16 15   1 2 3 4 5
ISBN-13: 978-0-226-20426-0 (cloth)
ISBN-13: 978-0-226-20443-7 (e-book)
DOI: 10.7208/chicago/9780226204437.001.0001

Library of Congress Cataloging-in-Publication Data

Hulten, Charles R., author.
    Measuring wealth and financial intermediation and their links to the real economy / Charles R. Hulten and Marshall B. Reinsdorf.
    pages cm — (Studies in income and wealth ; volume 73)
    Includes index.
    ISBN 978-0-226-20426-0 (cloth : alk. paper) — ISBN 978-0-226-20443-7 (e-book) 1. Global Financial Crisis, 2008-2009. 2. United States—Economic conditions—2001-2009. 3. Intermediation (Finance) 4. Investments, Foreign. I. Reinsdorf, Marshall B., author. II. Title. III. Series: Studies in income and wealth ; v. 73.
    HB37172008 .H85 2015
    332—dc23
                                                            2014020869

♾ This paper meets the requirements of ANSI/NISO Z39.48-1992 (Permanence of Paper).

Relation of the Directors to the
Work and Publications of the
National Bureau of Economic Research

1. The object of the NBER is to ascertain and present to the economics profession, and to the public more generally, important economic facts and their interpretation in a scientific manner without policy recommendations. The Board of Directors is charged with the responsibility of ensuring that the work of the NBER is carried on in strict conformity with this object.

2. The President shall establish an internal review process to ensure that book manuscripts proposed for publication DO NOT contain policy recommendations. This shall apply both to the proceedings of conferences and to manuscripts by a single author or by one or more co-authors but shall not apply to authors of comments at NBER conferences who are not NBER affiliates.

3. No book manuscript reporting research shall be published by the NBER until the President has sent to each member of the Board a notice that a manuscript is recommended for publication and that in the President's opinion it is suitable for publication in accordance with the above principles of the NBER. Such notification will include a table of contents and an abstract or summary of the manuscript's content, a list of contributors if applicable, and a response form for use by Directors who desire a copy of the manuscript for review. Each manuscript shall contain a summary drawing attention to the nature and treatment of the problem studied and the main conclusions reached.

4. No volume shall be published until forty-five days have elapsed from the above notification of intention to publish it. During this period a copy shall be sent to any Director requesting it, and if any Director objects to publication on the grounds that the manuscript contains policy recommendations, the objection will be presented to the author(s) or editor(s). In case of dispute, all members of the Board shall be notified, and the President shall appoint an ad hoc committee of the Board to decide the matter; thirty days additional shall be granted for this purpose.

5. The President shall present annually to the Board a report describing the internal manuscript review process, any objections made by Directors before publication or by anyone after publication, any disputes about such matters, and how they were handled.

6. Publications of the NBER issued for informational purposes concerning the work of the Bureau, or issued to inform the public of the activities at the Bureau, including but not limited to the NBER Digest and Reporter, shall be consistent with the object stated in paragraph 1. They shall contain a specific disclaimer noting that they have not passed through the review procedures required in this resolution. The Executive Committee of the Board is charged with the review of all such publications from time to time.

7. NBER working papers and manuscripts distributed on the Bureau's web site are not deemed to be publications for the purpose of this resolution, but they shall be consistent with the object stated in paragraph 1. Working papers shall contain a specific disclaimer noting that they have not passed through the review procedures required in this resolution. The NBER's web site shall contain a similar disclaimer. The President shall establish an internal review process to ensure that the working papers and the web site do not contain policy recommendations, and shall report annually to the Board on this process and any concerns raised in connection with it.

8. Unless otherwise determined by the Board or exempted by the terms of paragraphs 6 and 7, a copy of this resolution shall be printed in each NBER publication as described in paragraph 2 above.

Contents

Prefatory Note

This volume contains revised versions of most of the papers and discussions presented at the Conference on Research in Income and Wealth entitled "Wealth, Financial Intermediation and the Real Economy," held in Washington, DC, on November 12–13, 2010. We thank the Board of Governors of the Federal Reserve System for graciously hosting the conference.

We gratefully acknowledge the financial support for this conference provided by the Bureau of Economic Analysis. Support for the general activities of the Conference on Research in Income and Wealth is provided by the following agencies: Bureau of Economic Analysis, Bureau of Labor Statistics, Census Bureau, Board of Governors of the Federal Reserve System, Internal Revenue Service, and Statistics Canada.

We thank Charles R. Hulten and Marshall B. Reinsdorf, who served as editors of the volume, as well as Michael Palumbo, who served as a conference organizer along with the editors.

Introduction

Charles R. Hulten and Marshall B. Reinsdorf

On the eve of the financial crisis of 2007–2008, few observers of the economy were pessimistic about the future, in part because the magnitude of the approaching financial crisis and Great Recession was not apparent in the data commonly used to inform economic policy. In retrospect, however, the data trails left by the crisis are all too apparent. For example, the Case-Shiller twenty-city index of housing prices rose from a base of 100 in 2000 to over 200 in mid-2006, stabilized for about a year, then plummeted to 140 in April 2009. Propelled in part by housing prices, household net worth rose by about $25 trillion between 2000 and mid-2007. Half of these gains then vanished over the next two years, a loss of wealth equivalent to a year's worth of pretax income. Meanwhile, in the real economy, eight million jobs were lost and the unemployment rate rose from 5 to 10 percent. These patterns invite the questions: How could the approach of an economic event of this magnitude have been so little noticed? And what, if anything, can be done so that our data will reveal a developing future problem of this magnitude?

These questions were the subject of a conference held in Washington, DC, on November 12–13, 2010, at the Board of Governors of the Federal Reserve System (FRB), organized by Charles Hulten, Michael Palumbo, and Marshall Reinsdorf. This volume contains a collection of eleven chapters from the conference, grouped into three sets. The first set of five chapters

Charles R. Hulten is professor of economics at the University of Maryland and a research associate of the National Bureau of Economic Research. Marshall B. Reinsdorf was chief of the National Economic Accounts research group at the Bureau of Economic Analysis when this chapter was written. He is now a senior economist at the International Monetary Fund.

Opinions and interpretations are the sole responsibility of the authors, and should not be attributed to any organization with which they are associated. For acknowledgments, sources of research support, and disclosure of the authors' material financial relationships, if any, please see http://www.nber.org/chapters/c12517.ack.

is organized around the measurement problems associated with the financial crisis and identification of changes in macro- and micro-based measurement procedures needed to deal with future crises. Next is a set of three chapters that advance the measurement of specific areas of financial activity, including pension plans and cross-border finance. A final set of chapters examines the effects of the financial crisis and the associated recession on households and on Main Street using microdata on consumers, companies, detailed industries, and stock market returns.

The chapters are summarized in detail in the following section. By way of an editorial overview, we note that the financial crisis originated in a relatively small segment of the housing mortgage market (e.g., Alt-A and subprime). When the housing bubble burst, the shock was transmitted from this segment to the market as a whole, and then to the real economy. To invoke the old saw about searching for the lost keys under the lamppost at night, the financial intermediation sector is the logical place to start looking for crisis-related metrics, though the search is inhibited by the dimness of the light in some parts of the sector, most notably in the shadow banking system.

Part of the visibility problem arises from the fact that the decades before the onset of the financial crisis were a period of significant innovation and structural change. The possibilities introduced by the information technology (IT) revolution transformed the way stocks were traded and financial markets were organized. They also facilitated innovations in the areas of securitized lending and financial derivatives, which grew dramatically. The organization of the financial intermediation industry also changed as some activities migrated to unregulated industries with few data-reporting requirements.

The rapid evolution of financial intermediation products and processes posed significant challenges to policy analysts and regulators, as well as to the statisticians who sought to measure them. New financial instruments and arrangements take time to understand and incorporate into existing frameworks. Furthermore, large-scale macrodata systems have requirements of consistency over time and among cross sections of interdependent variables, which can slow the introduction of the new measures needed to keep up with an evolving economy. Moreover, macroeconomic statistics have other inherent limitations as leading indicators of emerging risks to financial stability. Their economy-wide perspective means that *breadth of coverage* is emphasized over depth of detail, and this bias is reinforced by the need to suppress much of the underlying detail in order to keep the databases manageable. In the process, important crisis-related microeconomic information may be buried in the statistical aggregates. For example, a mean rate of return can be calculated for an aggregate, but not the sort of statistics that would give insight into the distribution of returns.

Important changes in the *composition* of a data aggregate may also be concealed by the aggregation process. The characteristics of the mortgage assets held by financial intermediaries, for example, shifted to include more mortgage-backed securities and other asset-backed securities. The characteristics of the loans being bundled into mortgage-backed securities (MBS) and asset-backed securities (ABS), and each institutional sector's holdings of MBSs and ABSs, would have been valuable information before and during the crisis. Household debt service costs are another example. These costs were growing faster than household income and balance sheet leverage was rising, but the aggregate debt service ratio did not convey the growing concentration of debt in segments of the population that lacked the income to service it, nor did the aggregate leverage ratio convey the highly leveraged position of a growing subset of households who had bought or refinanced a home. The aggregate debt statistics thus gave, at best, a muted warning of the growing imbalances compared to what detailed distributional statistics would have revealed.

These considerations suggest that macrodata sets should not be regarded as the first line of defense in predicting emerging financial crises. Risk assessments by policy analysts and economic researchers based on macroeconomic statistics are ultimately a back-up system against emerging threats. It is the agencies responsible for regulating the financial sector that are the true front line. They are the ones in direct contact with the protagonists in an emerging crisis and are the best positioned to collect and interpret information that could reveal problems like rising risk taking in individual institutions and in the system as a whole. Much information is already obtained as part of the regulatory process, some of it quantitative and some qualitative, but one lesson from the financial crisis is that gaps exist in this information that need to be addressed. These gaps exist in a number of dimensions: in the scope of institutions included (e.g., systemically relevant unregulated financial entities), in the scope of instruments covered (e.g., derivatives and bilateral repurchase agreements), and in valuation (gross and net amounts of positions, and mark-to-market versus hold-to-maturity values where relevant). Improvements are underway, but confidentiality constraints limit their general use.

While the regulatory process and associated data are the front line of defense, existing macrodata sets do have a role to play in crisis detection and management. They connect the financial sector to the economy as a whole and may help reveal unsustainable imbalances as they emerge.[1] They are also publically available so that external policy analysts can provide inde-

---

1. For example, in the period before the crisis the integrated macroeconomic accounts for the household sector did show some troubling patterns. These included unprecedented highs in ratios of debt and debt service costs to income, nearly unprecedented lows in the saving rate, an anomalous reversal in the normal flow of net lending from households to businesses, and a breakdown in the normal relationship between households' net mortgage borrowing and their gross investment in new residential assets, with the household sector borrowing as much as $1.91 for every dollar it invested (Yamashita 2013).

pendent assessments. In order for the macrodata to play this role, however, an improvement in the organization and scope of the financial data would have to be translated into corresponding changes the macrodata. This is a major task, even apart from the confidentiality issue and the qualitative, even impressionistic, nature of some of the data. However, part of the process was underway before the financial crisis, with the introduction of the integrated macroeconomic accounts (IMAs) in 2007 based on research in Teplin et al. (2006). The IMAs bring together the BEA's National Income and Product Accounts with the Flow of Funds Accounts ([FFA]s, recently renamed the Financial Accounts of the United States), and contain data on lending net of borrowing, income, investment, and balance sheets for the major sectors of the US economy.

A further step in the direction established by the IMAs would be to organize publically available regulatory statistics, expanded in scope as indicated above, into a database that can be linked to the FFAs. Forging the link between a detailed financial database and aggregate macrodata presents many challenges. They include: breaking existing aggregates of asset holdings into finer categories (e.g., along such dimensions as issuer type and maturity); adjusting classifications to accommodate new instruments, new types of information (e.g., the collateral posted by derivatives traders [McDonald 2014]); and extending coverage to previously uncovered financial institutions. Positions might also be shown on a gross rather than a net basis. A more ambitious goal would be to construct a detailed financial input-output table for financial intermediaries. This might take the form of a "risk map" developed along the lines discussed by Cecchetti, Fender, and McGuire (2011), though some of the relevant microdata may not fit into this kind of framework because they concern developments that are too new to have a place in slowly adapting statistical databases, or because they are incomplete or qualitatively inferior. Such data might, however, be offered in a series of satellite accounts or supplementary tables.

Most of these points are discussed in greater detail in the chapters reviewed below. In sum, improvements in measurement practice in both financial and aggregate macrodata are possible and are a partial response to the question posed at the outset: How could the approach of the financial crisis have been so little noticed? Filling existing gaps and adding "dots" where needed are almost certainly necessary steps toward an information system capable of anticipating financial crises, but there is still the open question of whether they are sufficient. Answering the key question is not just a matter of a richer sets of dots, it also depends on the ability to see the right connections. How the data are used matters, and in this regard, the forecasting record of macroeconomic models and analysts has not been good, particularly in the run-up to the financial crisis and during the aftermath. Better data may help with this problem, but they are not a substitute for better analysis.

The Chapters in This Volume

The chapters in this volume identify areas in which technical improvements in measurement procedures are needed in order to better understand developments in finance and their effects on households, Main Street businesses, and the international financial situation of the US economy. They also use new methods to measure and analyze defined-benefit pension plans and international financial flows. Finally, they use specialized microdata sets to examine how households and businesses fared in the financial crisis. Among their themes are the data gaps revealed by the financial crisis, the development of financial and economic data and statistics, and approaches to data collection and analysis that will help us to see, understand, and manage potential sources of systemic risk, disequilibria, and poor economic performance.

Advancing Economic and Financial Measurement Practice:
Lessons from the Financial Crisis

The first of the chapters that focus on statistics for monitoring macroeconomic and financial stability is "Integrating the Economic Accounts: Lessons from the Crisis" by Barry Bosworth. Bosworth observes that the emergence and subsequent collapse of the subprime mortgage industry is a major lesson about the failure to document and analyze large innovations within the financial system. He also identifies some important gaps in the data needed to assess risks to financial stability and to understand economic conditions during recoveries that became evident in the financial crisis and its aftermath. The modern view of financial intermediaries emphasizes their role in transforming financial claims in the dimensions of liquidity, maturity, and credit risk, but these transformations are not well captured by the IMAs and Flow of Funds Accounts. This helped to obscure the emergence of a shadow banking sector characterized by maturity mismatches and excessive leverage as a major provider of financial intermediation. Furthermore, the rise of the subprime mortgage industry on the back of financing made possible by new types of asset-backed securities and credit derivatives was not visible in the FFAs. The FFAs do not distinguish subprime from prime mortgages, nor do they distinguish asset-backed securities from standard corporate bonds when looking at the holders of these securities, nor do they have information on derivatives. Finally, turning to our macrostatistics on the real economy, Bosworth finds that our understanding of the behavior of employment and of the current account deficit after the crisis was hindered by weaknesses in GDP and employment data.

Besides filling these data gaps, Bosworth suggests that the IMAs might also include balance sheets for subsectors of financial business, along with the net worth measures needed for conventional measures of their leverage.

Data on the roles of prices and quantities in value changes would also help to improve the usefulness of the FFAs and IMAs for monitoring financial stability. Finally, the financial crisis highlighted the need for better analysis of financial stability and showed that the financial regulators cannot themselves be relied upon to identify emerging risks, so Bosworth sees an important role for academics and other independent researchers. To promote independent research on systemic risk and financial developments, outside researchers should have as much access to detailed data as can be arranged without violating confidentiality constraints.

Another perspective on the performance of the IMAs and on changes in data and methods needed for monitoring financial stability is provided by "Financial Statistics for the United States and the Crisis: What Did They Get Right, What Did They Miss, and How Could They Change?" by Matthew Eichner, Donald L. Kohn, and Michael G. Palumbo. Eichner, Kohn, and Palumbo identify some patterns that could be seen in the IMAs that might have warned of growing risk or unsustainability. Financial intermediaries normally channel funds made available through household saving to finance the investment needs of businesses, but as households' saving began to fall short of their housing investment this flow reversed direction and business saving began to be used for lending to households. Also, the proportion of disposable income needed to service households' debts rose over the decade preceding the crisis. Nevertheless, major developments that raised systemic risk in the middle of the first decade of the twenty-first century, such as the deterioration in underwriting standards for mortgage debt and the growth of maturity transformation outside of the traditional banking sector, were invisible to the statistical system.

Looking at the longer historical record, some elements of financial crises that remain the same can be identified. Among these are excessive leverage and risk taking and heavy reliance on short-term sources of funding to finance long-term illiquid positions. Yet the particulars of the instruments and institutions tend to evolve in ways that require constant updating of risk metrics. Eichner, Kohn, and Palumbo therefore emphasize that the organization of finance and the instruments that it trades are too dynamic for any static or predefined set of measures of risk to maintain their relevance. An illustration of this point comes from the failure in 1990 of Drexel Burnham Lambert, whose unsecured short-term funding could not be rolled over when funders lost confidence. Secured funding was not affected by the loss of confidence, so the episode suggested that secured funding could be regarded as safe and collateralization became the norm. Yet, as securitized lending grew, the assets used as collateral changed from being predominantly Treasury bonds to include many asset-backed securities whose value would be quite uncertain in a crisis. The risk metric that treated secured funding as not vulnerable to crises of confidence therefore began to be misleading.

In light of the constant evolution and complexity of financial markets, the authors conclude that work on expanding the public-use data and work on frameworks for analysis of more specialized data will be most effective if they proceed in tandem. More complete macroeconomic and financial data are only part of the process of developing an early warning system. More fundamental is the need to use data in a way that integrates analyses to identify areas of special interest with the development of specialized information to illuminate those areas.

The next chapter, "Durable Financial Regulation: Monitoring Financial Instruments as a Counterpart to Regulating Financial Institutions" by Leonard Nakamura, proposes a strategy that would help to facilitate the sort of detailed analytical research advocated by Eichner, Kohn, and Palumbo and that would fill in some key data gaps. Of particular note, it would reveal changes in the characteristics of instruments that affect their riskiness and allow risks to be tracked as they migrate to parts of the shadow banking system that would otherwise be obscure. The strategy features a linked macro-micro database that would be available to government agencies involved in systemic financial regulation, but Nakamura recommends that a mechanism be developed to give visiting researchers access as well, subject to confidentiality restrictions.

The underlying framework for the macro-micro database is an extended version of the Flow of Funds Accounts, with satellite accounts showing the details of the stocks and flows shown in the core FFAs. One of these satellite accounts provides a decomposition of the net change in mortgage liabilities of households into gross flows by tracking originations, repayments, defaults, and revaluations.[2] Some others provide information on prices, including mark-to-market prices of exchange-traded instruments.

The next step in the database design is to link key macroaggregates in the extended FFAs to microdata containing samples of the instruments that they comprise. The variables in the data sets will provide detailed characteristics of these instruments. Such a sample of mortgages that were securitized might, for example, have revealed the deteriorating lending standards and inflated appraisals that emerged in the period before the financial crisis. Furthermore, when particular instruments migrate out of the heavily regulated parts of the financial system to special purpose entities, hedge funds, insurance companies, or other unregulated entities, they become indistinguishable from other kinds of assets, making them effectively invisible in the existing macrostatistical system. By tracking instruments by ownership, the database will be able to illuminate those parts of the financial system and to provide a good picture of the holders of risky assets.

In the next chapter the topic turns from identifying data gaps that helped to hide the activities of the shadow banking system to asking what kind of

---

2. This bears a striking similarity to an idea discussed by Mendelson (1962) and Denison (1962) at an earlier CRIW conference on the Flow of Funds Accounts.

picture of this system can be constructed from the data that are already available. In "Shadow Banking and the Funding of the Nonfinancial Sector," Joshua Gallin constructs measures of the size of the shadow banking system and its importance to the real economy by synthesizing data from different tables of the FFAs. The process involves tracing the long-term financing used by households and nonfinancial businesses along intermediation chains to terminal funders outside of the traditional banking and shadow banking systems. Gallin's measure of the shadow banking system adds up the short-term liabilities to terminal funders that directly or indirectly support illiquid long-term lending to households and nonfinancial business. The reason to focus on these liabilities is their vulnerability to runs in the event of a loss of confidence; indeed, many of them did experience a run during the financial crisis. One direct kind of terminal funder is money market mutual funds; in 2006, they held 2.4 percent of the outstanding debt of nonfinancial sectors. The funding routed through intermediaries such as government-sponsored enterprises (GSEs) and issuers of private-label ABS was larger. In 2006, they provided 28 percent of the funding for the nonfinancial sector debt and they obtained 16.4 percent of their funding from runnable short-term sources. These short-term liabilities therefore supported an additional 4.6 percent of the nonfinancial sector's long-term borrowing.

Gallin's definition based on runnable liabilities to terminal funders results in a smaller measure of the size of the shadow banking system than other definitions in the literature. Although the shadow banking system seems too small for its activities to have mattered, its volatile growth means that it was, in fact, quite important for credit availability to the real economy. Over the two years ending in the fourth quarter of 2008, the shadow banking system contributed +4.3 percentage points to the two-year growth rate of nonfinancial sector debt, but over the next years it contributed −3.7 percentage points. Overall, the growth rate of nonfinancial sector debt fell by 8 percentage points between these periods, so the change in the growth contribution of the shadow banking system was on a par with the change in the overall growth rate of nonfinancial sector debt.

The final chapter focusing on macroeconomic accounts and the financial crisis is "Financial Intermediation in the National Accounts: Asset Valuation, Intermediation, and Tobin's q," by Carol A. Corrado and Charles R. Hulten. The chapter argues that the centrality of financial intermediation for the functioning of the economy has not been properly recognized in our macroeconomic accounting framework. To illuminate the role of financial intermediaries in linking nonfinancial businesses and households, the authors amend the familiar circular flow diagram to include a capital market. In this market, funds saved by households are transformed into financing for investment needs of businesses in exchange for claims on the income generated by the businesses. The pricing of the financial assets created in this process has the potential to imply a value for the capital stock that differs from the present value of the income stream that the capital stock earns as an input into production or the cost of replacing the capital stock. Complex intermediation chains increase the chances of such valuation inconsistencies.

To measure the relationship between the value of the capital stock implied by financial markets and the value implied by the investment needed to replace the capital stock, the authors construct aggregate measures of Tobin's q. Although influences from cyclical factors could potentially make these measures a weak statistic for detecting asset-pricing bubbles, they do seem to perform well in practice. The estimates of Tobin's q diverge from the theoretical equilibrium value of 1 on three occasions. In first episode of divergence, from 1974 to 1985, the capital stock was valued at less than its replacement cost, but in the run-up to the dot-com crash of the stock market and again in the run-up to the financial crisis, the estimates of Tobin's q are above 1.

The authors also construct leverage ratios for major sectors based on the data in the IMAs. For financial business, this ratio provides no indication of rising risk before the financial crisis, but in the cases of homeowners and noncorporate, nonfinancial business, the leverage ratio does exhibit a rising trend before the crisis.

Advances in Measuring Wealth and Financial Flows

The next group of chapters presents some practical advances in measuring and analyzing wealth and financial flows in the areas of defined-benefit pension plans and cross-border investment. In "Adding Actuarial Estimates of Defined-Benefit Pension Plans to National Accounts," Dominique Durant, David Lenze, and Marshall B. Reinsdorf develop new actuarial measures of the income and wealth accrued by households through participation in defined-benefit (DB) pension plans. The DB plans set benefit levels based on a formula involving factors like career length and final pay. Until now, national accounts have measured these plans on a cash basis. Although this approach avoids the need for assumptions, employers may not time their cash contributions to DB plans to correspond to when claims to benefits are accrued, and a plan's assets may differ greatly from amount needed to cover the benefits due to the plan participants. Another impetus for this change in methods is that the international guidelines for national accounts set forth in the 2008 System of National Accounts (SNA) contained a new recommendation that households' pension wealth from DB plans be measured by the actuarial value of benefit entitlements.

Durant, Lenze, and Reinsdorf modify the framework that is recommended in the 2008 SNA to include an imputed interest expense for employers that have underfunded their plans and to recognize that holding gains on plan assets can reduce the amount of funding that must come from employers. The results on the DB plans of the United States help to explain why the measured personal saving rate has been so low—the cash measures of DB pension plans underestimated the personal saving rate by an average of 1.7 percentage points in the period from 2000 to 2007. The higher estimates of income received by households also imply higher estimates of expenses for employers. Notably, the newly recognized pension expenses for state and local government exceed $100 billion in each of the years after 2002, changing the picture of the fiscal situation of state and local governments from one of balanced budgets to one of significant deficits.

The new treatment of pensions in the 2008 SNA also addresses the problem of institutional differences between countries in trying to construct meaningful international comparisons of retirement saving and wealth. In the core national accounts, government-sponsored pension plans, which predominate in most countries, are grouped with social security and accounted for in a different way from employer-sponsored DB plans. The new SNA has a supplementary table where actuarial measures of government-sponsored plans and social security that are comparable to the measures for employer-sponsored plans are reported alongside the figures for employer-sponsored plans.

In France, DB pension plans are largely government sponsored, while in the United States—leaving aside railroad retirement—they are employer sponsored. A comparison of these countries is therefore a good test of the usefulness of the supplementary table. Durant, Lenze, and Reinsdorf find that substituting actuarial measures for cash measures of employer-sponsored pension plans raises the estimate of saving by US households by enough to narrow the large gap between the official household saving rates of the United States and France substantially. Yet the size of the gap returns to almost its original level once accruals of benefit entitlements in government-sponsored plans and social security are added. These benefit entitlements are much larger in France, even after deducting the funding gap of social security. Taking social security wealth into account, French households have net wealth equal to 8.6 years' worth of disposable income compared to 6.5 years for American ones.

The group of chapters on recent measurement advances is rounded out with two chapters on cross-border financial flows and investment positions. A longstanding puzzle in the US balance of payments is how the United States can enjoy persistently positive net cross-border receipts of investment income while having a negative net international investment position. In "The Return on US Direct Investment at Home and Abroad," Stephanie E. Curcuru and Charles P. Thomas attempt to solve this mystery and to answer the related question of whether the US balance of payments is sustainable. Their first step is to locate the source of the investment income surplus. The average rate of return on US direct investment abroad (USDIA) turns out to be far above the rate of return on foreign direct investment in the United States (FDIUS). Next, the authors use a benchmark rate of return for domestic operations of US firms (USIUS) to analyze the gap between rates of return, and find that USDIA has a much higher rate of return than USIUS, while FDIUS has a lower rate of return.

The gap between the average return on USDIA and the average return on tangible assets for USIUS over the entire sample from 1983 to 2010 is 330 basis points. Over half of this gap disappears, however, once allowance is made for the taxes that US parents must pay on their foreign direct investment (FDI) income. Curcuru and Thomas estimate the risk premium needed to compensate investors for the greater riskiness of the investments in the countries receiving US FDI and find that it can explain much of the remaining gap between returns on USDIA and tangible asset returns on USIUS. The rest of the gap is, they argue, explained by the risk premium needed to compensate the investors in USDIA for the higher amounts of sunk costs.

The low rate of return on FDIUS compared to USIUS also needs to be explained. To do this, Curcuru and Thomas construct measures of the average age of FDIUS compared with USIUS, and fit models of how age of investment affects returns. They find that younger investments earn lower returns and that the average age of FDIUS was comparatively young over much of the time period covered by their data. Young ages of FDIUS investments account for 150 of the 230 basis points separating the average rate of return on tangible assets for USIUS and the average rate of return on FDIUS over 1983–2010. This effect comes mostly from the years before 2002, however. The age gap between FDIUS and USIUS closes after 2002, and if the rate of return denominator for USIUS is changed from just tangible assets to tangible and financial assets (with the interest from the financial assets included in returns), it vanishes.

The implications for the sustainability on the US balance of payments are generally optimistic. The net income paradox is not caused by errors in the data, but by differences in rates of return between USDIA and FDIUS that are mostly due to stable factors such taxes and risk premia. Nevertheless, the favorable gap in investment returns between USDIA and USIUS is likely to become smaller in the future because of the maturing of FDIUS.

Further evidence on US receipts international investment income and rates of return on USDIA and FDIUS is provided in Christopher A. Gohrband and Kristy L. Howell's chapter on "US International Financial Flows and the US Net Investment Position: New Perspectives Arising from New International Standards." The chapter begins by presenting a new way to organize the financial account in the US balance of payments (BOP) tables and in the US international investment position (IIP) tables to classify international flows and positions by purpose (such as FDI) rather than by sector. Gohrband and Howell also develop more detailed estimates of the composition of the flows shown in the primary income and financial account sections of the main BOP table. The portfolio investment detail reveals that net foreign purchases of long-term debt issued by GSEs and of mortgage-backed securities were very large in the years leading up to the financial crisis, amounting to almost $800 billion in 2006. Foreign portfolio investment seems, therefore, to have helped to fuel the housing price bubble. When the bubble burst and the crisis began, foreigners became net sellers of mortgage-related securities and turned instead to short-term and long-term Treasury securities, buying $712 billion worth of them in 2008.

The chapter also provides for the first time a detailed decomposition of the sources of change in the value of international investment positions into income flows, price changes, exchange rate movements, and other changes. The "other changes" component reflects statistical discontinuities and should not be included in a measure of investment returns, so this new decomposition allows returns to be measured more accurately than was possible before. For the period 1990–2005, excluding the other changes from investment returns makes the gap between the average rate of return on USDIA and the average rate of return on FDIUS even bigger than it is using the measure in Curcuru and Thomas (chapter 7, this volume). Nevertheless, Curcuru and Thomas's result that the excess return earned by US investors abroad compared to foreign investors in the United States comes from the direct investment component holds up in this more detailed analysis.

How Did the Financial Crisis Affect Households and Businesses?

Two chapters from the conference develop empirical evidence on how households fared during the financial crisis and subsequent recession, while a third develops evidence of whether gaining access to external sources of the funding and liquidity was a serious problem for nonfinancial businesses. The first chapter on households' experiences is "Household Debt and Saving during the 2007 Recession," by Rajashri Chakrabarti, Donghoon Lee, Wilbert van der Klaauw, and Basit Zafar. These authors had access to some unique microdata, including the Federal Reserve Bank of New York (FRBNY) Consumer Credit Panel sample of credit report records, a household survey collected by RAND in November 2008 to assess the impact of the financial crisis, and an FRBNY household survey on saving conducted from October 2009 to January 2010. These data can be used to analyze changes in households' financial position and behavior in the recession that began in 2007.

The RAND and FRBNY surveys show that about a third of households experienced some type of financial distress, and the effects of the financial crisis were felt by all segments of the population. Different age, income, and education groups suffered in different ways, however. When labor market conditions deteriorated, younger and less educated households were relatively more likely to lose their jobs or suffer a reduction in pay or benefits. Older and more educated households were less affected by bad labor market conditions, but they lost substantial fractions of their wealth as their home equity and retirement savings fell. Looking at all households combined, in the FRBNY survey 7 percent of respondents were unemployed at the time of survey, 8 percent reported that their spouse had lost a job in the past 12 months, 15 percent reported that they had incurred a pay cut, and 19 percent reported that their household's pretax income had declined by 10 percent or more. Over 9 percent of households had negative equity in their home.

Along with falling income or wealth, the recession also brought about a tightening of credit conditions. Low down payments, defined as under 10 percent, fell to a share of just 7 percent of new mortgage originations. In the FRBNY survey, 13 percent of respondents had had a credit card account closed by the bank, and 19 percent had had their credit limit cut.

Yet the contraction in the supply of credit was not the only driver of declines in debt and open lines of credit: a more conservative approach to borrowing on the part of households also meant that there was less demand for credit. For example, over a postcrisis period in which the number of open credit card accounts fell by over 20 percent, credit card accounts were closed more frequently by consumers than by banks. The microdata from the FRBNY household survey also suggest that this changed attitude toward credit was behind the rise in personal saving that started in 2008 in the macroeconomic data of the national accounts. In particular, households did not, on balance, start to put more money into retirement accounts and savings accounts. Instead, they reduced borrowing and began to pay down loan balances. This is further confirmed by data from the FRBNY Consumer Credit Panel. The authors use those data to estimate the change in household debt, excluding the effects of write-offs by banks and home purchase transactions. Before 2008, cash-out refinancing, second mortgages, and home equity lines of credit gave rise to more new debt than was extinguished by principal repayments on existing mortgages, so that the household sector's net pay-down of mortgage debt was negative. It became positive in 2008, however, and in 2009 a net amount of 140 billion dollars of mortgage debt was retired.

Finally, the RAND survey of November 2008 provides some insight into the strong increase in personal saving in the fourth quarter of 2008. In this survey, 75 percent of respondents reported that they had reduced their spending between October 1 and the interview date, with a median cut of about $200 per month. This seems to be a response to a very uncertain economic environment: the period from mid-September to mid-November 2008 saw the Lehman Brothers bankruptcy, failures of some major commercial banks and thrifts, a run on money market funds, and a large drop in the stock market.

Microdata on households during the recession are also analyzed in "Drowning or Weathering the Storm? Changes in Family Finances from 2007 to 2009" by Jesse Bricker, Brian Bucks, Arthur Kennickell, Traci Mach, and Kevin Moore. These data were available to the authors because participants in the 2007 FRB Survey of Consumer Finances (SCF) were reinterviewed in the last half of 2009 to find out how they were coping in a time when the unemployment rate was nearing 10 percent.

Consistent with the macrodata for these years, mean family wealth was down by 20 percent in the 2009 wave of the panel. Nonetheless, the macrodata could not reveal how much variation there really was in how families were faring. Analyzing the data from the SCF panel, the authors find that a quarter of families had *increases* in wealth of 25 percent or more. Some of the variation can be related to families' income, debt, or employment circumstances. Over 70 percent of the families in the top income decile in 2007 had a fall in wealth, but for families in the lower three income quintiles the probability of a decline in wealth was only around 60 percent. Also, families with high debt payments relative to their income in 2007 were more likely than average to move far down in the wealth distribution, while families with high debt balances relative to assets were unusually likely to have a large move up in the distribution. Wealth declines were much more common among families where the respondent or spouse became unemployed, while large upward moves in the wealth distribution were more likely in families where the respondent or spouse had exited unemployment.

The responses from the SCF panel also suggested that aggregate spending by consumers was going to remain depressed. Families' desired levels of precautionary savings were higher in 2009 than in 2007, and their reported willingness to take risks was lower. Also, about 60 percent of households reported that they would curtail spending if they experienced a decline in the value of their assets, whereas only around 20 percent said that they would increase spending if their assets were to go up in value. If households actually responded in such an asymmetric way, very little of the cuts in spending by families that had falls in the value of their assets would have been offset by increases in spending by families with rising asset values.[3]

In the closing chapter in the volume, "The Misfortune of Nonfinancial Firms in a Financial Crisis: Disentangling Finance and Demand Shocks" by Hui Tong and Shang-Jin Wei, the focus changes to how businesses fared in the crisis period. The prospect of falling customer spending was not the only problem that businesses had to cope with as the subprime mortgage problems began to reach a crisis stage in mid-2007. They also faced more restricted access to external finance as lenders became weakened and investors became less tolerant of risk. Nevertheless, whether the loss of access to financing would have serious effects was not obvious because nonfinancial businesses held record amounts of cash. Indeed, they even had negative average net debt (debt minus cash on hand).

A challenge in measuring the effect of access to external finance is dis-

---

3. On the other hand, many older households may have buffered their cuts spending by changing their retirement plans—a significant number of respondents said that they were planning to delay retirement.

entangling it from the effect of falling demand. To identify financing constraint effects separately from demand destruction effects, Tong and Wei take advantage of heterogeneity across nonfinancial firms in their ex ante vulnerability to these two types of shock. The terrorist attack of 2001 caused a demand shock but not a financing access shock, so they use stock price behavior just after the terrorist attack to construct a demand shock sensitivity variable. They also use a model fitted by previous researchers to construct a financial constraint (or liquidity constraint) index for firms that reflects their ease of access to outside finance. Finally, as an alternative to this financial constraint index, they also construct a measure of the intrinsic dependence on external finance of about 400 detailed (four-digit SIC) industries. (Airlines, defense, and finance sectors are excluded because these industries were directly affected by the terrorist attack or the subprime crisis.)

The results show that both the firms that were sensitive to a demand contraction and the firms that were liquidity constrained had greater than average declines in their stock price during the subprime crisis. Yet the impact of the liquidity constraint was larger than the demand contraction effect, and was discounted more quickly into stock prices. Intrinsic dependence on external finance is also associated with an above average decline in stock price during the crisis, and the combination of a high financial constraint index and dependence on external finance measures is associated with an even larger stock price decline than either of these variables on its own. As a robustness check, Tong and Wei test a number of alternative specifications of the model and confirm their main findings.

In assessing the implications of their results, Tong and Wei conclude that policy measures aimed at relaxing liquidity and financing constraints faced by nonfinancial firms were essential if the goal was to help the real economy to recover from the financial crisis; policies aimed only at increasing demand would be insufficient. In the case of the recovery from the financial crisis, the financial market in the center of Corrado and Hulten's amended circular flow diagram seems to be more critical for economic stability than the product markets of the traditional circular flow diagram.

References

Cecchetti, Stephen G., Ingo Fender, and Patrick McGuire. 2011. "Toward a Global Risk Map." In *Central Bank Statistics: What did the Financial Crisis Change?* Proceedings of the European Central Bank conference, 2010, 73–100. Frankfurt: European Central Bank. https://www.ecb.europa.eu/pub/pdf/other/centralbank statistics201102en.pdf.

Denison, Edward F. 1962. "Comment." In *The Flow of Funds Approach to Social Accounting*, Studies in Income and Wealth, vol. 26, 425–30. Princeton, NJ: Princeton University Press.

McDonald, Robert L. 2014. "Measuring Margin." In *Risk Topography: Systemic Risk and Macro Modeling*, edited by Markus Brunnermeier and Arvind Krishnamurthy. Chicago: University of Chicago Press.

Mendelson, Morris. 1962. "The Optimum of Grossness in the Flow-of-Funds Accounts." In *The Flow of Funds Approach to Social Accounting*, Studies in Income and Wealth, vol. 26, 411–25. Princeton, NJ: Princeton University Press.

Teplin, Albert, Rochelle Antoniewicz, Susan Hume McIntosh, Michael Palumbo, Genevieve Solomon, Charles Ian Mead, Karin Moses, and Brent Moulton. 2006. "Integrated Macroeconomic Accounts for the United States: Draft SNA-USA." In *A New Architecture for the US National Accounts*, Studies in Income and Wealth, vol. 66, edited by Dale Jorgenson, J. Steven Landefeld, and William Nordhaus, 471–539. Chicago: University of Chicago Press.

Yamashita, Takashi. 2013. "A Guide to the Integrated Macroeconomic Accounts." *Survey of Current Business* 93 (April): 12–27.

I

Advancing Economic and Financial Measurement Practice: Lessons from the Financial Crisis

1

Integrating the Economic Accounts
Lessons from the Crisis

Barry Bosworth

In recent times, we have benefitted from a wealth of interesting articles and research on the institutional changes and other innovations within the financial system that contributed to the 2008–2009 crisis. Unfortunately, nearly all of that work postdates the crisis itself. It is disappointing and puzzling that so little evaluation of those changes was undertaken in earlier years. Our profession did not perform well in anticipating the risks created by many of the financial innovations. Yet, with the benefit of hindsight, many economists have written very lucid descriptions that suggest that the dangers were obvious. Many of us will comfort ourselves with the phrase, "If only I had known what they were doing . . . ." Hence the topic of this conference on what can be done to provide a better flow of information to help prevent similar crises in the future.

However, the crisis was not so much a failure of information as it was an analytical failure to draw the appropriate conclusions. We knew what the individual agents were doing, but did not understand the linkages and the chain of reactions that would lead the system to spiral out of control. Policymakers became excessive advocates for financial innovation and placed far too much confidence in the incentives and discipline of private markets to restrain participants from excessive risk taking. Our ability with hindsight to identify the failures that led to the past crises can also create a false optimism about our ability to prevent future crises. In effect, the inability to

Barry Bosworth is a senior fellow in the Economic Studies Program (the Robert V. Roosa Chair in International Economics) at The Brookings Institution.

I am indebted to Charles Schultze for helpful discussions and Sveta Milusheva and Maria Ramrath for research assistance. For acknowledgments, sources of research support, and disclosure of the author's material financial relationships, if any, please see http://www.nber.org /chapters/c12520.ack.

conduct laboratory experiments to explore directly the implications of various reforms to the system leads to an overemphasis on explaining the past rather than thinking about how various innovations might affect the future. The focus of this chapter is on designing a flexible and robust statistical framework that could monitor an evolving financial system and assist regulators in controlling the risks. While that is an important objective, let me begin with some doubts that a new regulatory process can reduce the risks to an acceptable level; perhaps we should also consider the alternative of moving further in the direction of a plain-vanilla financial system that forgoes some of the gains from financial innovation in return for reduced risk. James Tobin was fond of observing that "It takes a heap of Harberger triangles to fill one Okun Gap." (Tobin 1977, 468). His perspective seems particularly appropriate in the present context when we try to balance the gains from financial innovations in the United States and Europe against the costs of a mistake to an even wider global economy. Our neighbor, Canada, is an example of that alternative: while the menu of financial products is more restricted and the prices for some services are higher, Canada did avoid the direct effects of the financial crisis. It suffered only through the channel of reduced trade and its position as a major trading partner of the United States.

For too long, the financial sector has been a poor cousin within the statistical system. Just as the national accounts provide the macroeconomic framework for a variety of real sector analyses, the flow of funds should be the starting point for analysis of financial developments. Traditionally, the Federal Reserve has had the major responsibility for the collection of financial statistics and construction of the Flow of Funds Accounts, but for many years the flow of funds was a neglected element, and the Federal Reserve was reluctant to devote a significant amount of resources to developing the data system. More recently, the Bureau of Economic Analysis and the Federal Reserve have made a major effort to expand the financial accounts and integrate them with the sector income and outlay statements of the national accounts.[1] The integrated macroeconomic accounts bring the United States more in line with the international System of National Accounts (SNA) in which economic agents are organized into five major sectors (nonfinancial corporations, financial corporations, government, nonprofit institutions serving households and households). There is also a consistent set of accounts that flow from production, income and outlay, capital, financial, and ultimately a net balance sheet for each sector.

The Flow of Funds Accounts played a more significant role in financial analysis during the 1960s and 1970s, relative to recent decades. In part,

---

1. Additional details are available in Bond et al. (2007). There are still some significant inconsistencies because the national accounts rely on information from tax returns and firms are classified on the basis of principle line of business. In the flow of funds, financial subsidiaries are split off from nonfinancial parent companies.

the reasons might reflect the more restricted nature of the earlier financial system where various interest-rate ceilings and other restrictions created some nonlinearities in the system that created a need to observe changes in different types of credit. As those restrictions were eliminated, financial markets seemed more homogeneous, and many credit instruments were viewed as highly substitutable for one another. Interest shifted away from the composition of credit toward a greater focus on aggregates and the price of credit. There may be some shift back toward an interest in the composition of credit because of the severity of the disruptions of the past few years and a realization that they did not impact equally on all forms of credit.

The integrated accounts are an advance in providing an improved system-wide framework for analyzing macroeconomic flows and the links between the real and financial sectors, but they provide surprisingly little insight into the causes of financial crises. The traditional view of financial institutions emphasized their role in intermediating the flow of resources between savers and investors. While it is true that financial institutions continue to fulfill that function, a modern interpretation places greater emphasis on their activities in transforming financial claims in the dimensions of liquidity, maturity, and credit risk. These dimensions are not captured in the aggregate accounts because the accounts rely on purely deterministic measures of value and cannot reflect the accumulation and transmission of risk exposures. To measure these variables, the system needs to incorporate measures of the risk and volatility of key balance sheet items, and to integrate prices and quantities in the financial accounts. At the same time, the emphasis on balance sheets at the sector level highlights the role of counterparty risk in a system in which the assets of one sector are the liabilities of others. As conventionally presented, however, the accounts are too deterministic and too aggregated to serve that goal.

The primary purpose of this chapter is to review the need for new types of economic statistics in the light of the financial crisis. There has been—and will be even more—discussion of the need for an expanded reporting system to meet the needs of the financial regulators. The focus herein is more on the public side of the statistical system. It reflects a nervousness about relying on internal confidential channels of information between private firms and their regulators. While there is a need to balance the needs for a public information flow and legitimate private concerns about confidential business strategies, there may be substantial returns to outside scholars accessing the kind of data that would permit the analysis and construction of indicators that will provide realistic evaluations of the consequences of future financial innovations. Part of the argument is that the statistical system of the federal government has not evolved at a pace that matches the changes in the economy and the new technologies that can be used to monitor it. It is most apparent with respect to the financial system where the reporting structure has remained largely frozen in time despite a drastic change of financial structure. The later portions of the chapter also examine the effects of financial crises on the real economy and whether there are major gaps in the reporting system outside of the financial accounts.

1.1   Data Challenges in the Financial Sector

The Flow of Funds Accounts (the financial side of the integrated accounts) have the appearance of a well-defined system that facilitates tracing out the flow of credit and the distribution of financial assets and liabilities throughout the economy, but they are not particularly useful to identify the distribution of financial risks, and in some respects they describe a system that no longer exists. The US system has been complicated by the emergence of a shadow banking system that operates in parallel with the traditional system of commercial banks. Problems within the shadow banking system during the crisis highlighted three specific areas in which information was lacking and limited the usefulness of the aggregate financial accounts: the maturity structure of the underlying financial claims (liquidity), the lack of information on the use of leverage to support the claim structure, and the shifting of returns and risks away from the reported holders of the claims through the growth of credit derivatives. They all relate to establishing some measure of the underlying quality or risk of the financial assets and institutions. Either the economic accounts need to be expanded to incorporate increased detail or the individual entries need to be accompanied by some index or alternative measure of their risk and volatility.

1.1.1   Shadow Banking

The shadow banking system is essentially the collection of financial companies who do not have access to central bank liquidity or the government guarantees of normal banks, but who provide bank-like services. It includes money market funds, investment banks, finance companies, hedge funds, and various asset guarantors. The major funding instruments include commercial paper, repurchase agreements, and various derivatives. A significant portion of the system's growth is motivated by regulatory arbitrage, but there may be some broader economic benefits in the form of gains from specialization (Pozsar et al. 2010). The bulk of their funds are provided through short-term lenders, such as money market funds, which expect their funds to be available on demand and at par. Despite its similarity to commercial banking, shadow banking lacks deposit insurance and the ultimate backing of the state to protect itself against a run. Absent such a backstop, a general crisis of confidence can be expected to trigger a run on the system. That is what happened in the recent crisis and it resulted in a near complete, albeit temporary, government guarantee.

The official statistics have failed to adapt in the face of this change in the structure of the financial system. They maintained a focus on the com-

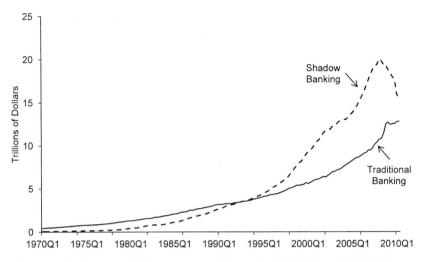

Fig. 1.1   Shadow bank liabilities versus traditional bank liabilities (1970–2010)
Source: Flow of Funds L.109, L.121, L.126, L.130, L.207, L.208, Federal Reserve Board Release of September 17, 2010.

mercial banking system while an increasing proportion of the activity was being conducted through other venues. Surveys of nonregulated institutions, such as finance companies, are of questionable quality—relying on voluntary participation. Information on pension funds is incomplete and subject to large revisions. The basic elements of the shadow banking system are included within the flow of funds and the integrated economic accounts. One study (Pozsar et al. 2010) used that data to estimate the size of the shadow banking system, and suggested that it exceeded the commercial banking system beginning in 1995 and peaked at $20 trillion in 2008 (figure 1.1).[2] However, the individual elements are not grouped in a fashion that emphasizes their interrelationships. In addition, the accounts do not directly measure the activities of hedge funds, which are largely allocated to the residual household sector. The hedge funds have a big impact on the market for liquidity because they rely on short-term credit to enhance their investment strategies.

1.1.2   Maturity Structure

A major feature of the buildup to the crisis was a heavy reliance on short-term borrowing to finance long-term lending. It has also been a key element in the majority of past financial crises and is always listed among the major

---

2. They provide a listing of the included elements of the Flow of Funds Accounts, but by combining information from the accounts by instrument and by sector, they may have introduced some double counting.

lessons of every postmortem; yet, somehow, those lessons are quickly forgotten. Maturity mismatches in the collapse of commercial banks in the 1930s led to the introduction of deposit insurance and an expanded regulatory system. Yet, a similar crisis emerged within the saving and loan industry in the 1980s and ultimately led to the bankruptcy of that industry. The growth of the S&L industry was a reflection of efforts to avoid the constraints of the regulated sector. In the current episode, the problem began within the shadow banking system with its emphasis on repos, but it ultimately spread to the larger commercial banks through the interbank markets.[3]

The statistics can be expanded to differentiate among financial liabilities of varying maturity, but in the absence of explicit insurance, this form of maturity transformation is inherently unstable and subject to runs. Thus, liquidity can vanish overnight. It is particularly true when so much of the short-term lending is dependent on high-frequency repo agreements. It would help if the statistical system could measure the magnitude of the maturity mismatches and the exposures, but information is not a solution to the fundamental instability.

1.1.3   Leverage

Extensive reliance on leverage, particularly within the shadow banking system, was another important contributor to the liquidity crisis that developed in late 2008. Some firms were financing their activities with liabilities more than fifty times their own capital. Doubts about the quality of the assets being put up as collateral for short-term financing forced the sale of assets at distressed prices and quickly wiped out the firms' net worth.

A traditional measure of leverage focused on the extent to which a firm uses fixed debt to finance its activities because the highly leveraged firm would, in the absence of other factors, have a more volatile stream of income after deducting its interest expenses. In notional accounting, leverage is simply total assets divided by total assets less liabilities (net worth). In an economic context, however, the concern is more with the volatility of net worth relative to the volatility in the underlying asset values. Thus, economic leverage might be much lower than the notional level because the valuations of the assets and liabilities share a positive covariance. These computed leverage measures, however, depend upon the accuracy of the underlying model assumptions. In a regulatory context, leverage became a particularly ambiguous concept when regulators attempted to place different risk ratings on various asset classes and use those ratings in the computation of an overall leverage rate.[4]

---

3. Repos are asset sales in which the seller agrees to repurchase the asset at a fixed future date. It is effectively a collateralized loan.

4. Internationally, Basel I was an example of such an approach to measuring risk. Basel II was to rely on the internal risk-management systems of large banks that were largely untested. The role of capital requirements in an international context is elaborated on in Tarullo (2008).

As pointed out in Greenlaw et al. (2008), many of the examples of excessive leverage were outside the regulated commercial banking sector. The leverage rate for commercial banks was about 10, compared to 24 for the government sponsored enterprises, 25 for brokers and hedge funds, 19 for Citibank, and over 50 for some foreign banks like Deutsche Bank and UBS.

Currently, the Flow of Funds Accounts have an incomplete treatment of leverage in that the notional measure is available for only a few sectors, such as households and nonfinancial corporations. In the integrated macroeconomic accounts, the balance sheet framework is extended to the total of all financial institutions, but we still have no balance sheet with net worth measures for subsectors of financial business.[5] In any case, the flow of funds does not include the measures of volatility that would be needed to compute an aggregate measure of economic leverage.

1.1.4   Credit Derivatives

Much of the puzzlement about financial developments in 2006–2009 centered on the role of credit derivatives, especially the mortgage-related credit derivatives that were developed early in the first decade of the twenty-first century. Derivatives were initially designed to reduce price-related risks of financial instruments (asset prices, the price of foreign currencies, and interest rates.) The pricing of those derivatives is relatively transparent and they are marketable. The extensions of these instruments to hedge other risks, such as credit default swaps (CDS) and other more qualitative outcomes, are harder to price and have thinner markets or are traded over the counter (OTC).[6] The contracts were designed by the participants to avoid the oversight of the various regulatory agencies, and, until recently, CDS trades were neither reported to, nor effectively overseen by any public authority. The fundamental problem with these risk markets is that the risks are only redistributed, not eliminated; it is not clear that all participants understand that. What began as a tool for hedging risks has spread to become an important market for speculation. Many of the OTC contracts are very complex and it can become nearly impossible to measure the net exposure of an individual firm or group of firms. They are often a means of transferring risk off of a bank's balance sheet, enabling it to expand its loan portfolio.

Despite their heightened role, credit derivatives are largely excluded from the Flow of Funds Accounts. At the global level, the notional value of CDS contracts was reported by the Bank for International Settlements at $32 tril-

---

5. It is not evident that the net worth of the total financial sector is a particularly useful measure since it was usually negative even before the crisis. The balance sheets are largely an aggregate of financial instruments, rather than individual firms. Thus, many nonconventional claims are excluded.

6. The two dominant forms of credit derivatives are credit default swaps and total return swaps. The former is equivalent to an insurance contract against default. In a total return swap, one party contracts to receive any income inclusive of the capital gain/loss without actually owning the asset.

lion at the end of 2009 (down from $58 trillion at the end of 2007), but the gross market value was a far smaller $1.8 trillion.[7] Because of their volume, often far exceeding the magnitude of the underlying reference asset, their inclusion on a gross notional basis seems inappropriate, but they do have a major effect on the actual distribution of the risks and returns in contrast to an accounting system that focuses only on holders of the underlying securities. And though they were created to manage risk in primary markets, as OTC instruments, they can create their own liquidity and settlement risks. The Federal Reserve is in the process of expanding its survey of derivatives, but it does not publically divulge the results.

1.2   Subprime Mortgage Crisis

The collapse of the subprime mortgage market was an important initiating force behind the crisis in the broader financial system. Subprime mortgages were loans made to borrowers who were perceived to have high credit risk, often because they lacked a strong credit history or had other characteristics that are associated with high probabilities of default. At least initially, the risks were offset by a higher interest rate and were manageable within a diversified portfolio. Subprime mortgage lending grew to become a significant activity in the late 1990s, spurred in large part by innovations that reduced the costs of assessing and pricing risks. Technological advances made it easier to collect and disseminate information on the creditworthiness of prospective borrowers (credit scoring), and lenders developed new techniques for using this information to establish underwriting standards, set interest rates, and manage their risks. Loan standards were significantly easier than for conforming loans of the government-sponsored enterprises (GSEs). About half of subprime mortgages were used for refinancing and the rest for home purchase. The phenomena had a relatively short life as originations of subprime mortgages grew very rapidly after 2000, peaked in 2006, and largely disappeared by 2008 (see figure 1.2).

The emergence of a subprime crisis can be traced to a combination of factors. The loosening of lending standards within the subprime market greatly expanded the pool of potential borrowers, and together with low borrowing rates it fueled a major run-up of housing prices that far exceeded the growth in income and other measures of affordability. The extent of the bubble in housing prices seems obvious in figure 1.3, which compares an index of home prices with the growth in average family incomes; yet, its existence was controversial among real estate economists as late as 2005 (Himmelberg, Mayer, and Sinai 2005; Shiller 2005). There was a further deterioration of

---

7. Notional value is a measure of the value of the underlying asset for which insurance is purchased. Market value is the price at which the contract could be exchanged in a market or an estimate of its value if no market exists.

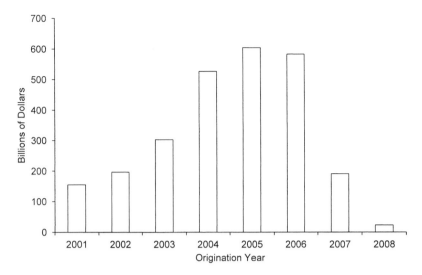

Fig. 1.2 Subprime mortgage originations (2001–2008)
Source: Inside Mortgage Finance, 2008 Mortgage Market Statistical Annual and 2008 HMDA data.

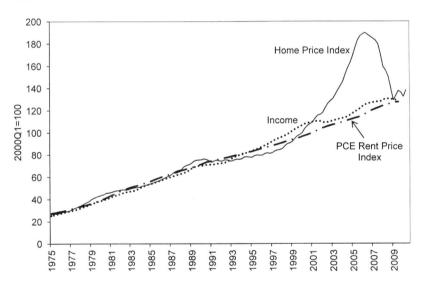

Fig. 1.3 Growth of home prices versus household mean income and rent (1975–2010Q2)
Note: The home price index extends the Case-Shiller national price index backward from 1986 to 1975 using the Office of Federal Housing Enterprise Oversight (OFHEO) home price index. Quarterly mean household (HH) income is linearly interpolated from census annual data and then adjusted so that the average over four quarters equals annual income. Indexes of income and rent are created and then adjusted so that the ratio of housing prices to income and to rent averages 1.0 over the years 1975–2001. The personal consumption expenditure (PCE) "rent" is rent of owner-occupied dwellings from the Bureau of Economic Analysis (BEA).

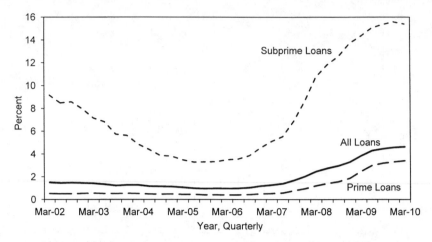

Fig. 1.4   Foreclosure inventory at end of quarter by loan type, 2002–2010
Source: Mortgage Bankers Association.

loan standards after the boom in refinancing ended in 2004, as originators sought to maintain volume by lowering loan standards. They were relatively unconcerned about loan defaults as long as home prices continued to rise, since owners could always refinance or sell the property.

Home prices began to level out and decline in early 2006. Lower prices quickly wiped out the limited equity of many borrowers and the percent of loans in foreclosure began to rise rapidly, from 3.6 percent in mid-2006 to 8.7 percent by the end of 2007, and 15.4 percent in early 2010 (figure 1.4). Foreclosure rates for conforming mortgages have remained far below those of subprimes, but they too accelerated as the overall market worsened. The effects of declining home values were compounded in the later years by rising rates of unemployment. According to the data in figure 1.3, home values have now declined back to a historical norm, but there is still a large inventory of homes awaiting sale or foreclosure.

While the reasons for the collapse of the subprime market now seem evident, it is surprising that the breakdown of a portion of the mortgage market could trigger a wider financial crisis of such magnitude and global consequence. The explanation must include the development of a private securitization industry, paralleling that of the GSEs in conforming mortgages but based on subprime mortgages.[8] Private securitization of mortgages and other consumer loans fueled much of the growth in the shadow

---

8. While the GSEs did not directly participate in the securitization of subprime mortgages, they did purchase large volumes of such assets to hold on their own balance sheet. They arbitraged their position as a near-government entity to take advantage of their low borrowing rate and leverage to invest in assets that were riskier than those that would qualify for their own securitization programs.

banking system.[9] Pools of subprime mortgages were securitized through mortgage-backed securities (MBSs) and divided into tranches in which the most senior tranches are paid first, and each tranche was assigned a credit rating by rating agencies. Through this credit enhancement process, a large proportion of the MBSs could obtain investment-grade status even though the underlying collateral was of poor quality.

In the early years of private securitization, loan standards and risk were kept under control by the active role of bond insurers and institutional investors who focused on the characteristics of the underlying loans. In 2004–2005, however, subprime MBSs emerged as a principle asset backing for collateralized debt obligations (CDOs). Off-balance sheet entities of commercial and investment banks repackaged the lower tranches of MBSs into CDOs and tranched them again to obtain higher ratings for the senior portions. What emerged was a highly complex set of investments that were very difficult to value and an environment in which CDO managers were less concerned with the underlying loan quality. As CDOs came to dominate the market for subprime MBSs in 2006 and 2007, the discipline on primary market originators was lost with a consequent large reduction in loan quality.

In addition, the complexity of the CDO market created enormous uncertainty about their dependency on subprime valuations and questions about the distribution of the CDOs and their associated risk exposure. It was no longer possible to work backward from a specific CDO to the underlying bonds to determine the extent of subprime exposure. In early 2006, the introduction of traded ABX indexes made it possible for participants to express their view of the value of the underlying assets, but it did not answer the question of who held them.[10] The deterioration of the subprime securitization market during 2007 is evident in table 1.1. In some respect, the ABX indexes worsened that crisis by making clear the extent of the collapse of subprime mortgage value, but without any knowledge about the location of the risk—who was exposed to the loss. The uncertainty drastically curtailed the market for all CDOs and other structured products, and without a measure of market value, the repo market collapsed.

Ultimately, the whole episode reflected a dramatic failure by regulators, analysts, and participants in the CDO market to appreciate the sensitivity of the whole chain of value to changes in home prices. When home prices began to decline in 2006, the whole structure unraveled.

The subprime debacle is probably a one-time event and many parts of

9. Growth in the market for subprime loans and their use in structured assets are explained in Ashcraft and Schuermann (2008) and Gorton (2008). See, in particular, Gorton's summary of the chain of subprime risk in his table 19.
10. The ABX index was a credit derivative based on an underlying set of MBS tranches. Individual subindexes were created for bonds of different risk levels from AAA to BBB–. Four vintages of the ABX were created at six-month intervals covering issues of the prior six months, beginning in January of 2006. There is no new index after 2007.

Table 1.1   Price indexes of Markit ABX.HE (CDS based on subprime residential
                 mortgage-backed securities) by tranche, vintage, and date

TRANCHE	VINTAGE	Jan. 2006	Jan. 2007	Dec. 2007	Sep. 18, 2008	Nov. 20, 2008	Mar. 3, 2009	Oct. 27, 2010
AAA	06-1	100	100	94	89	66	85	87
	06-2		100	89	70	40	61	80
	07-1		100	79	47	28	36	60
	07-2			78	46	28	31	50
AA	06-1	100	100	88	52	26	22	50
	06-2			70	24	11	11	18
	07-1			51	11	5	5	6
	07-2			48	12	5	5	6

Source: Compiled by Charles Schultze from periodic press releases of Markit.com.
Note: Four vintages were issued by Markit, each vintage was based on RMBSs assembled over the prior six months. The price was 100 on the day of issue.

the process have disappeared. However, it is interesting to note that most of the episode was invisible within the government statistical system. In the flow of funds, all mortgages are equal with no distinctions by quality. Some elements of the subprime network are reflected in the flow of funds table on issuers of asset-backed securities (figure 1.5), but the vast bulk of their liabilities were simply classified in the general category of corporate bonds, with no information on ownership of the ABSs. There was also far too little available information on the prices of the new financial instruments. Most were traded over the counter and only a few firms were aware of how prices were changing over time. With the introduction of the ABX indices, there was a much wider—perhaps exaggerated—awareness of the problems in the subprime markets.

Substantial amounts of data were available from private sources but at prices that can be afforded only by the government regulators, the large private-market players, and experts connected with them. Information on subprime mortgage originations, default rates, and ABX indices are all collected and sold by private firms. Such a system excludes large numbers of smaller players like academic researchers and the general public. Particularly within the financial sector, nearly all of the recent growth in statistical information has been generated by for-profit private firms. Perhaps a wider dissemination of the underlying information about the growth in the shadow banking system and the new products that were being innovated would not have made a difference, but a larger forum has been helpful in understanding and evaluating other issues of public economic policy. A system that relies on an expanded flow of information to the regulatory agencies may not be adequate: there have been too many examples of regulators being captured by those that they were meant to regulate.

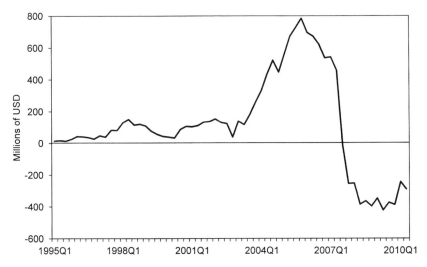

Fig. 1.5   Issuers of asset-backed securities: Flow of total mortgages, 1995–2010
Source: Flow of funds F.126, Federal Reserve Board Release of September 17, 2010.

1.3   Impacts on the Real Economy

The historical experience is that the US economy recovers very rapidly from recessions, and to some extent, the deeper the recession the faster the recovery. However, there is also evidence, as reported in a recent IMF study involving a number of advanced economies, that financial crises are not like other recessions and that the recovery phase is much longer and drawn out (IMF 2009, 109–19). The primary reason given for such outcomes is the extent of deleveraging that takes place within the financial system and the need for private sector actors to rebuild their balance sheets.

Thus far, the United States appears to be following the path of past financial crises (figure 1.6). The top line of the chart shows the projected growth in potential output as estimated by the Congressional Budget Office (CBO). They incorporate a pronounced slowing in the contribution of capital due to lower rates of investment and a small negative effect on total factor productivity. The result is a projected annual growth in potential output of only 2.1 percent over the next five years. The second line reports the average rate of gross domestic product (GDP) growth from the trough of the past eight recessions. On that basis, the United States would expect to be back at full employment by the end of 2012. The third line shows the actual growth in GDP to date and a projection based on the forecast of the CBO. There is only a modest closing of the gap between actual and potential by the end of 2012.

At present, the United States has an output gap of about 6 percent of potential output, and it is increasingly evident that recovery will be very slow and it will require a rebalancing of the economy away from its recent reliance

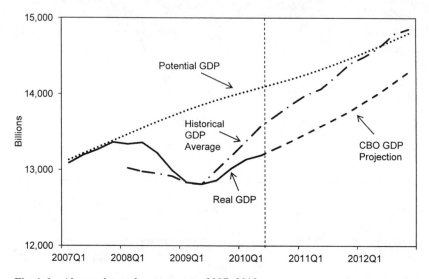

Fig. 1.6   Alternative paths to recovery, 2007–2012
Source: The CBO and authors' calculations as explained in text.

on domestic consumption toward a greater effort to expand exports to the rest of the world. The effort to rebuild household balance sheets will lead to increased saving and lower consumption and the government cannot afford to support household disposable income indefinitely through deficit financing. On the investment side, the collapse of the real estate sector suggests that private investment will remain well below prior rates for several years.

1.3.1   Excess Unemployment

One early puzzle about the recession phase of the crisis involved the speed and magnitude of the rise in unemployment. It appeared to be much larger than would have been anticipated from an application of Okun's law to the reported decline in GDP. Past experience suggested that the unemployment rate would peak in the neighborhood of 8–8.5 percent, rather than the observed 10 percent that it reached in the household survey in late 2009.[11] The employment losses are even more striking in the payroll survey; payroll employment fell by 8 million between December of 2007 and September 2009, compared with 6.5 million in the household survey. A discrepancy between the two major employment surveys also emerged a decade earlier (figure 1.7), but in that case, the payroll survey showed a faster rate of growth in the expansion of the late 1990s and then slowed relative to the household survey in 2002–2003. Despite an extensive round of research, the Bureau

11. The major discrepancy in the relationship between output and employment in 2008–2009 can be traced in part to an initial underestimate of the decline of GDP in the national accounts.

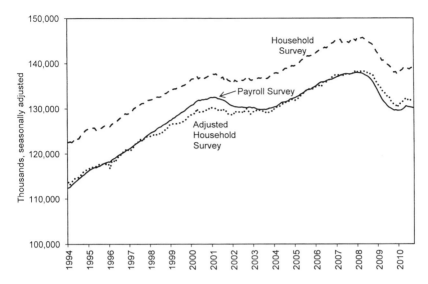

Fig. 1.7   Household and payroll survey employment, 1994–2010
Source: Bureau of Labor Statistics, October 8, 2010.

of Labor Statistics (BLS) has been unable to identify the reason for the emergence of the discrepancy in the late 1990s.[12]

In the current episode, a large portion of the gap between the payroll and adjusted household surveys emerged after the March 2009 annual benchmark adjustment of the payroll employment to the state unemployment insurance records. The revision resulted in a downward revision of 900,000 workers. An additional downward revision of 366,000 will be implemented for the March 2010 reference month. The magnitude of the benchmark revision is a recurring problem because in some years it represents a major proportion of the annual change.

The drop in payroll employment has also translated into a surprising rise in labor productivity that contrasts with much of the modern economic discussion, which emphasizes the procyclical behavior of productivity and attributes to it a major causal role in business cycles. As documented by Gordon (2010), it is difficult to find a consistent cyclical behavior in recent decades, but it is also apparent in figure 1.8 that the current recession actually had two phases. If we accept the NBER dating that the recession began in the fourth quarter of 2007, the recession was initially marked by small employment losses and a significant slowing of productivity, but the intensification of the recession in early 2009 led to an acceleration of the job losses

12. Using a linked microdata set, Abraham et al. (2009) traced the discrepancies early in the first decade of the twenty-first century to differences in the reported employment status of individual workers in the two surveys, with the most serious problems in the reports for more marginal workers and jobs.

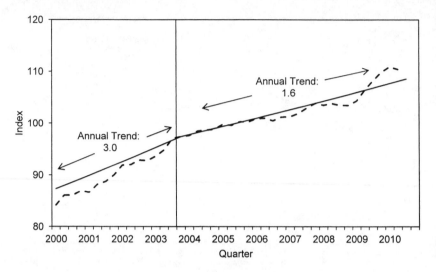

Fig. 1.8   Nonfarm labor productivity, 2000–2010:2
Source: Bureau of Labor Statistics. The trends are estimated for 1994:4–2003:4 and 2003:4–2007:4.

that continued in the last half of the year. In that respect, the 2009 job losses look like the response to a panic.

Another study by Alan Krueger and others at the Treasury used data from the BLS Job Opening and Labor Turnover Survey (JOLTS) to examine differences in new hires and layoffs among large and small firms (Krueger 2010). They found that the large firms were more likely to make the adjustment to the financial crisis by freezing new hires, whereas the small firms responded with a more aggressive pattern of layoffs of existing workers. They interpreted this evidence as suggesting that the small firms were more severely impacted by the curtailment of credit during the crisis. That is a much different explanation than that of Gordon (2010), who stressed the role of excessive cost cutting by corporate executives. Some of these puzzles in the employment data are long standing, but they illustrate the value of having more employment and firm data that distinguishes small- and medium-sized enterprises by industry.

1.3.2   External Sector

The economic crisis has had a strikingly large effect on global trade. A decline in global GDP of 2–2.5 percent in 2009 was sufficient to reduce global merchandise trade flows by 23 percent from $16 to $12 trillion. It was the trade channel, as much as financial linkages, that was responsible for the global dimension of the crisis. The surprise for the United States, however, is that the collapse of trade was recorded as having a stabilizing influence on the economy: initially, goods imports were 165 percent of exports, but the percentage decline in merchandise imports was significantly larger than that for exports (–26 versus –18 percent). The current account deficit fell from a peak of 6.6 percent of national income to 3.1 percent in 2009, and gains in the net trade balance offset 40 percent of the decline in GDP. Unfortunately, the recovery of trade is now having an even larger negative effect on GDP growth in 2010—the net contribution of trade offset more than half of an otherwise robust 4.6 percent annual rate of domestic demand growth in the second and third quarters.

It is becoming increasingly evident that the external trade sector will occupy a major role in the recovery from the recession. The United States cannot continue to support a large external deficit. In partial recognition of this fact, the president established a goal of doubling US exports over five years, and the G-20 has taken up a discussion of means for reducing global trade imbalances. All of this suggests the desirability of a close monitoring of the trade sector. While not a necessity in an economy of high unemployment, the United Sates will ultimately have to restructure its own economy by raising the level of saving to finance more of its investment out of domestic resources. There is an elementary accounting identity that relates the external balance (the current account) to the difference between domestic saving and investment. In that context, we would like to be able to trace out the domestic factors that led to the prior large imbalance and how the economy was able to accommodate the large improvement in the current account in 2009.

Unfortunately, the statistical discrepancy has played a large role in the efforts to account on the domestic side for large adjustments in the external imbalance. As shown in figure 1.9, both the domestic and external measures capture the broad pattern of the changes over time, but the statistical

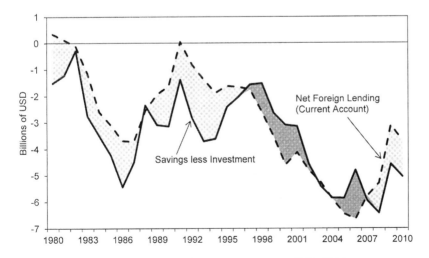

Fig. 1.9   Saving less investment and the current account, 1980–2010
Source: Bureau of Economic Analysis website, National Income Accounts, tables 1.7.5 and 5.1.

discrepancy is a large portion of the explanation in some periods of major change, such as 2005 to 2010. Thus, it is hard to see much of an adjustment on the domestic side.

1.4   Conclusion

This chapter has focused on the adequacy of the statistical system in light of the financial crisis. While I believe that the crisis was primarily reflective of a failure of analysis rather than a lack of data, there is evidence that the statistical system—particularly on the financial side—has failed to evolve in a fashion that would capture the implications of several major financial innovations. The emergence of the subprime mortgage industry took place within a surprisingly short period and many of its elements may only be of historical interest as it now fades away, but it was a major lesson about the failure to document and analyze large innovations within the financial system. In particular, the flow of funds could be expanded to provide more detail on the nonbank financial institutions and finer maturity breakdowns to evaluate liquidity risks. Furthermore, the accounts are reported almost exclusively in nominal terms with little or no distinction between changes in asset prices and their quantities. To a lesser extent, we were also left with uncertainty about how the disruption of credit flows would affect the real economy.

References

Abraham, Katharine, John Haltiwanger, Kristin Sandusky, and James Spletzer. 2009. "Exploring Differences in Employment between Household and Establishment Data." NBER Working Paper no. 14805, Cambridge, MA.

Ashcraft, Adam, and Til Schuermann. 2008. "Understanding the Securitization Of Subprime Mortgage Credit." Staff Report no. 318, New York, Federal Reserve Bank of New York.

Bond, Charlotte Anne, Teran Martin, Susan Hume McIntosh, and Charles Ian Mead. 2007. "Integrated Macroeconomic Accounts for the United States." *Survey of Current Business* (February):14–31.

Gordon, Robert. 2010. "The Demise of Okun's Law and of Procyclical Fluctuations in Conventional and Unconventional Measures of Productivity." Paper presented at the 2010 NBER Summer Institute, July.

Gorton, Gary. 2008. "The Panic of 2007." In *Maintaining Stability in a Changing Financial System*, Proceedings of the 2008 Jackson Hole Conference, Federal Reserve Bank of Kansas City.

Greenlaw, David, Jan Hatzius, Anil Kashyap, and Hyun Song Shin. 2008. "Leveraged Losses: Lessons from the Mortgage Market Meltdown." US Monetary Policy Forum Report no. 2. http://research.chicagobooth.edu/igm/docs/USMPF_FINAL_Print.pdf.

Himmelberg, Charles, Christopher Mayer, and Todd Sinai. 2005. "Assessing High

House Prices: Bubbles, Fundamentals and Misperceptions." *Journal of Economic Perspectives* 19 (4): 67–92.

International Monetary Fund (IMF). 2009. *World Economic Outlook: Crisis and Recovery.* April. http://www.imf.org/external/pubs/ft/weo/2009/01/.

Krueger, Alan. 2010. "Written Statement before the Joint Economic Committee." May 5.

Pozsar, Zoltan, Tobias Adrian, Adam Ashcraft, and Hayley Boesky. 2010. "Shadow Banking." Federal Reserve Bank of New York, Staff Report no. 458, July.

Shiller, Robert J. 2005. *Irrational Exuberance*, 2nd ed. Princeton, NJ: Princeton University Press.

Tarullo, Daniel K. 2008. *Banking on Basel: The Future of International Financial Regulation.* Washington, DC: Peterson Institute for International Economics.

Tobin, James. 1977. "How Dead is Keynes?" *Economic Inquiry* 15 (4): 459–68.

Financial Statistics for the United States and the Crisis
What Did They Get Right, What Did They Miss, and How Could They Change?

Matthew J. Eichner, Donald L. Kohn, and Michael G. Palumbo

2.1 Introduction

Although the instruments most closely associated with the financial crisis of 2008 and 2009, including option adjustable-rate mortgages, structured investment vehicles (SIVs), and "CDO squareds," were novel, the underlying themes were familiar from previous episodes: Competitive dynamics resulted in excessive leverage and risk taking by large, interconnected firms, in heavy reliance on short-term sources of funding to finance long-term and ultimately terribly illiquid positions, and in common exposures of many major financial institutions to specific credit and liquidity risks. Understandably, in the wake of the crisis, financial supervisors and policymakers want to expand and improve the information infrastructure to obtain better and earlier indications regarding these critical, and apparently recurring, core vulnerabilities in the financial system. One expression of this appetite to collect more data is the belief that had the community of policymakers, analysts, and investors had such data in "real time," the vulnerabilities amassing in

Matthew J. Eichner is deputy director of the Division of Research and Statistics of the Board of Governors of the Federal Reserve System. Donald L. Kohn is a senior fellow at The Brookings Institution and former vice chairman of the Board of Governors of the Federal Reserve System. Michael G. Palumbo is associate director of the Division of Research and Statistics of the Board of Governors of the Federal Reserve System.

This chapter was prepared for the Fifth ECB Conference on Central Bank Statistics, Frankfurt, April 22–23, 2010. We appreciate receiving helpful comments from Dan Covitz, Josh Gallin, and Nellie Liang and excellent research assistance from Allison Cassing. The views expressed in this chapter are those of the authors and do not necessarily reflect the views of the Board of Governors of the Federal Reserve System or other members of its staff. For acknowledgments, sources of research support, and disclosure of the authors' material financial relationships, if any, please see http://www.nber.org/chapters/c12518.ack.

the years before the crisis may have been recognized and possibly diffused before the systemic crisis took hold.

Being empirical economists by training, we are hugely sympathetic to the desire for more and better real-time data, and we are optimistic about the development of models that will allow those data to be put to use in highlighting emerging imbalances of potentially systemic effect. Indeed, we emphasize in this chapter that gauging vulnerabilities in the financial system requires targeted analysis by specialized research teams with expertise and data tailored to particular areas (such as specific financial instruments and transaction types) that might be identified by unusual trends observed in aggregate statistics.

That said, we harbor no illusions about the difficulty of collecting all the "right" data in a timely fashion, particularly because the dynamic nature of our financial system implies that the relevant set of data is a moving target. Major data collection projects naturally take quite a while to design and implement, and, more importantly, are generally predicated on the proposition that the systems being analyzed remain fairly stable over time.

Moreover, standard approaches to aggregate data collection and analysis may simply not be consistent with the dynamism of the financial system, particularly in light of the tendency of innovation to continually shift outside of the areas to which analysis and scrutiny are most directed. Indeed, a key point we make later in this chapter is that many of the products most closely identified with the recent crisis and the near collapse of the financial system—including ABSs and CDOs (asset-backed securities and collateralized debt obligations), SIVs, and subprime securitizations relying on excess spread and overcollateralization—scarcely existed just a few years ago and now cease to exist again (except as "legacy" positions).

We would not want to push the point too far, but we note that the assemblage of relationship that stood at the center of the crisis was termed the "*shadow* banking system"—a moniker that was coined after the crisis began. Gaps in data and analysis, in a sense, defined the shadows in which this system grew and prevented the building vulnerabilities from being recognized.

Thus, in this chapter, we emphasize that, while very important, collecting more data is only part of the process of developing early warning systems. More fundamental, in our view, is the need to use data in a different way—in a way that can deliver more flexibility in targeting than static data collection can allow.

As we will describe, certain aggregate data collected through processes well established prior to the crisis sent signals suggesting material changes in the nature of flows between different parts of the US economy. Yet fully understanding the implications of these developments and associated risks required a tactical approach that not only used the aggregate data as signals of where to look, but expanded to include granular and specialized information that may have been collected for purposes other than financial stability analysis or even microprudential supervision. Although such an idiosyncratic approach is not customarily part of the empirical economics toolkit—and would have been foreign to our more academically oriented colleagues—it may have offered the best chance to highlight in real time what later proved to be misplaced confidence on the part of a wide range of market participants in the efficacy of risk-transfer mechanisms. For example, data collected and sold for very specialized commercial purposes, notably targeting solicitations to borrowers, provided the best, and possibly the only, way to understand the rapid decline of underwriting standards for US residential mortgages subsequent to 2004. But these data probably did not exist and probably would not have appeared worth examining in detail, prior to 2004.

To resort to a metaphor, the information delivered by expanded and improved, but essentially static, aggregate data can be relied on for signals akin to grainy images captured by reconnaissance satellites: images that are suggestive, but not dispositive. Improved data collections can provide the greatest value by highlighting changes and inconsistencies that bear further investigation using other, more-focused tools mobilized to deal with a particular anomaly. A key challenge, of course, is that the appropriate tools cannot generally be specified ahead of time but must be designed in response to the particular signals teased from the aggregate data. In fact, we are concerned that specifying the tools suited for this second stage generically and prior to considering the first-stage signals will not be fruitful: We can easily imagine specifying ex ante a program of data collection that would look for vulnerabilities in the wrong place, particularly if the actual act of looking by macro- or microprudential supervisors causes the locus of activity to shift into a new shadow somewhere else.

In the following pages, we flesh out these ideas. We begin by reviewing macroeconomic data from the System of National Accounts developed in recent years to better illuminate high-level financial flows among different sectors of the US economy. These aggregate data backtest fairly well against the recent crisis, sending discernible but grainy signals of substantial shifts in flows across sectors that preceded the crisis.

Subsequently, we offer several examples highlighting why collection of formal time series may fail to bring these grainy signals into better focus, and could possibly turn out to be counterproductive. We argue that the focus on a fixed set of metrics changes behavior in a way that diminishes the usefulness of the indicators. Given the dynamic nature of the financial system, the process of specifying these metrics inevitably leads to active management of these metrics, at which time they cease to fully reflect the risks that they were intended to capture. Finally, we conclude with some comments about the shape of a more dynamic process of analysis that we argue is more likely to bring into clearer focus the signals sent by more aggregated data. In a recent paper, Adrian, Covitz, and Liang (2013) describe a practical approach to financial stability monitoring that is very much in the spirit of the broad framework we consider.

2.2   What Did Financial Statistics for the United States Get Right in the Prelude to the Crisis?

In this section, we present information about the US economy that is drawn from an innovative set of macroeconomic accounts that integrates data on real and financial economic activity from distinct primary sources using the System of National Accounts (SNA).[1] In particular, we present data from the Integrated Macroeconomic Accounts for the United States (US-SNA)—an implementation of SNA for the US economy resulting from joint research by staff at the Bureau of Economic Analysis (BEA) and the Federal Reserve Board (FRB). Data in the US-SNA are constructed primarily from information reported in the National Income and Product Accounts (NIPA), which measure the production of, use of, and income generated by newly produced goods and services, and the Flow of Funds Accounts (FFA), which measure net flows and balances of financial and certain tangible assets for the major sectors of the US economy.[2]

We use data from the US-SNA to document certain important trends and developments in the period leading up to and during the financial crisis that began in 2007 and severe recession of 2008 and 2009. First, we track the secular and recent changes in saving, financial investment, and real investment through the capital and current accounts for the household and other SNA sectors of the US economy. In the period leading up to the financial crisis, the macroeconomic data showed large increases in household-sector leverage brought about by rapid increases in mortgage debt and financed, in large part, with funds obtained from the rest of the world.[3] But, while certainly suggestive, these signals provided only limited aid to anyone seeking to distinguish among hypotheses regarding the causes of the trends carrying very different implications for financial stability analysis. We emphasize, though, that the aggregate nature of data in the national financial and real statistical accounts left them unsuited for illuminating the extent of vulnerability that had evolved in the US financial system. In particular, data in the national accounts did not illuminate substantial increases in the underlying riskiness of mortgage loans in the years leading up to the financial crisis,

1. Commission of the European Communities, International Monetary Fund, Organization for Economic Cooperation and Development, United Nations, and the World Bank (1993).

2. For details about the SNA data for the United States—and how they relate to information provided in the FFA and the NIPA—please see Teplin et al. (2006). In this chapter, we report annual data from the integrated macroeconomic accounts from 1960 through 2008 (using information as of March 15, 2010; the data can be found at www.bea.gov/national/nipaweb /Ni_FedBeaSna/Index.asp). We also report some financial data that are available through 2009.

3. This section is primarily an update of analysis originally presented by Palumbo and Parker (2009).

nor did they convey the extent to which maturity transformation was being undertaken by the shadow financial system.

2.2.1   Some Background on the US-SNA Data

Compared with the NIPA and the FFA, the US-SNA data have two principal advantages: First, they contain a full set of macroeconomic information broken down to correspond to sectors of the economy that are economic units of interest—households (including nonprofit organizations serving households); nonfinancial noncorporate businesses (sole proprietorships and limited partnerships); nonfinancial corporate businesses; financial businesses; federal government; state and local governments; and the rest of the world (foreign governments and businesses that engage in trade or financial transactions with domestic counterparts). Second, the US-SNA integrates financial and real information. For each sector, US-SNA follows a current account that tracks the flows of production/income and consumption; a capital account that tracks saving and capital formation; a financial account that tracks net acquisition of financial assets and net incurrence of debts; a revaluation account that tracks gains and losses on tangible and financial assets; and a balance sheet account that tracks the outstanding stocks of tangible assets, financial assets, and liabilities.

A novel aspect of US-SNA is its focus on sectoral net lending or borrowing, which, for each sector of the macroeconomy, is presented in both the capital account and the financial account. In the NIPA-based capital account, a sector's net lending or borrowing position is defined as the difference between its net saving—disposable income less current spending—and its net investment (gross purchases of physical capital less depreciation on its existing capital stock). Sectors that invest on net more than they save out of current income are net borrowers. In the FFA-based financial account, a sector's net lending or borrowing position is defined as the difference between its net acquisition of financial assets and its net incurrence of debt. Except for statistical discrepancies—actual measurement differences coming from the independently constructed capital and financial accounts in the United States—each sector's net lending or borrowing position should be the same, whether measured from its capital account or its financial account.

2.2.2   Key Trends in the Household Sector of the US-SNA
Leading up to and during the Financial Crisis

Data in the US-SNA clearly document the considerable rise in household-sector leverage in the years leading up to the financial crisis and they also show the extent to which leverage has dropped back during the crisis and recession of 2008 and 2009. The solid line in figure 2.1 shows the well-known fact that, after having fluctuated in the neighborhood of 9 percent from the early 1960s through the mid-1980s, the household saving rate dropped sharply and averaged only about 2 percent in the middle of the first decade

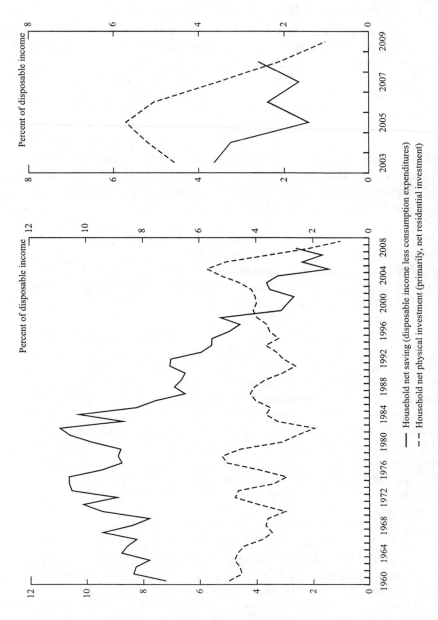

Percent of disposable income

Percent of disposable income

— Household net saving (disposable income less consumption expenditures)
-- Household net physical investment (primarily, net residential investment)

Fig. 2.1 Household sector net saving and investment in the SNA capital account, 1960 to 2009

of the twenty-first century. The household saving rate increased some in 2008 and, based on the personal saving rate in the national income accounts, appears to have risen further last year. What is perhaps more interesting is that households' net physical investment, plotted as the dotted line in figure 2.1, did not decline along with the saving rate—either in the earlier period of declining saving (from the late 1980s through the late 1990s) or in the more recent period when the saving rate was consistently very low (from 2000 through 2007). Indeed, during the recent boom years of the US housing market (2002 through 2006), the household sector's rate of net tangible investment, mainly comprising net residential investment, actually increased from about 4 percent of disposable personal income to nearly 6 percent at the peak. The downturn in the US housing market has certainly left its imprint on the rate of households' net investment—the dotted line dropped sharply in 2007 and 2008, and the net investment rate is estimated to have fallen again last year.

Figure 2.1 shows that the boom years leading up to the financial crisis represented the first time since the early 1960s (and before, we think) that the household sector's rate of net tangible investment (dotted line) exceeded its rate of saving (solid line). Thus, as can be seen in figure 2.2, the boom years of the housing market were the first in which the US household sector was in a net borrowing position with respect to the other domestic sectors and the rest of the world, on balance. The lighter shaded region shows that from the early 1960s through the early 1990s, the household sector typically was in the position of lending about 4 percent of its income to help finance investment by other domestic sectors and the rest of the world. From 2003 through 2007, however, the US household sector, on net, borrowed at an average rate of nearly 3 percent (of disposable income) to finance the excess of net tangible investment over its net saving. During the financial crisis and recession, the household sector swung back to a slight net lending position in 2008, and last year household-sector lending appears to have risen to a level more typical of the average pace from the 1960s through the 1990s.

Because of its substantial detail regarding each sector's net acquisition of financial assets and net incurrence of debts, the US-SNA provide much more information about household-sector trends before and during the financial crisis. A key element was that the decline in household saving and, thus, a sizable portion of the consequent rise in net household borrowing reflected a rapid increase in new residential mortgages; indeed, borrowing in the form of other types of consumer credit (auto loans, credit card loans, and other consumer loans) was relatively light in the years leading up to the financial crisis, in part because home equity loans and cash-out mortgage refinancing provided a cheaper source of funding for consumers. The upper-right panel of figure 2.3 shows the rapid growth of overall household debt from 2002 through 2006 (the dotted line) and the relatively small contribution to the growth rate that was accounted for by (nonmortgage) consumer credit (the

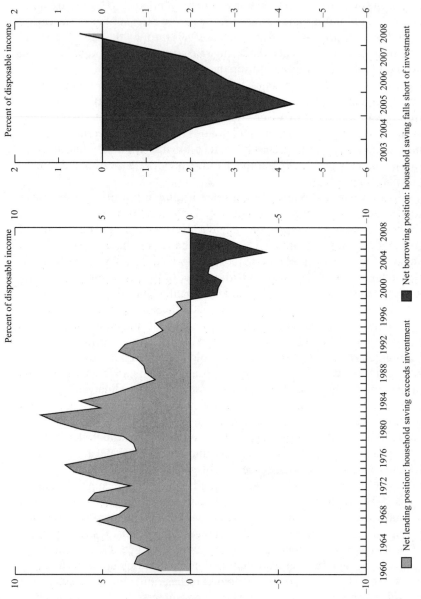

Fig. 2.2   Net lending (+) or borrowing (−) by US households in the SNA capital account, 1960 to 2008

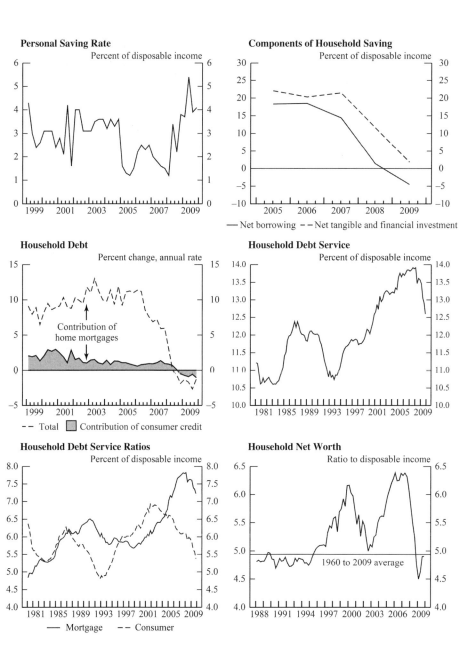

Fig. 2.3 Personal saving rate/components of household saving

Sources: Personal saving rate, Bureau of Economic Analysis; all other series, Federal Reserve Board.

shaded region). Analogously, the area between the dotted line and shaded region shows that the substantial deceleration in household borrowing since 2006—and the outright decline in household debt that occurred for much of 2008 and 2009—was due to changes in mortgage borrowing, rather than consumer credit.

The lower-left panel of figure 2.3 plots a key indicator of leverage in the household sector—the ratio of debt service payments (principal and interest) to disposable income.[4] Even though interest rates on home mortgages and consumer loans were generally low by historical standards from 2002 through 2007, growth of household debt exceeded growth of income by enough to drive up the measured share of disposable income needed to service debt. Over this period, the share of aggregate disposable income needed to service consumer credit was actually trending down significantly, meaning that more and more income was needed to cover principal and interest on home mortgages. The sharp deceleration in borrowing in recent years—and the outright contraction in debt seen for much of 2008 and 2009—resulted in a significant deleveraging for the household sector and, by the end of last year, is estimated to have brought down the aggregate debt service ratio to a level not seen since late 2000.

It is noteworthy that even as the debt service ratio—and its mortgage debt component—surged to indicate greater household leverage in the years leading to the financial crisis and recession, measures of *balance sheet* leverage did not signal imminent problem—in fact, even during the years of rapid household borrowing, typical indicators of balance sheet leverage did not rise much at all, on net. The bottom-right panel shows that the ratio of aggregate household net worth to disposable personal income climbed from 2002 through 2007, as the arithmetic contribution to wealth from rising home prices and equity prices far outstripped increases in households' disposable income. Meanwhile, measures of housing leverage—such as the ratio of homeowners' equity (aggregate home values less mortgage debt outstanding) to home value—fluctuated in a fairly high, very narrow range from 2000 through 2005. However, as home prices in many parts of the United States began to fall in 2006—and as they subsequently fell almost everywhere in the country in 2007 and 2008—housing leverage and balance sheet leverage turned down severely. In 2009, home values stabilized and corporate equity values rose markedly, raising the ratio of household net worth to disposable income to about its longer-run average level. That said, homeowners' equity ratio remained far below any value registered before 2007.

Figure 2.4 puts into a historical context the size of the revaluations of

4. Data on debt service payments are not directly provided in the US-SNA. However, the quarterly estimates shown in figure 2.3 are produced at the Federal Reserve Board (based on outstanding debt levels reported in the board's FFA, disposable personal income in the BEA's NIPA, and other sources); for more information, see www.federalreserve.gov/Releases/housedebt. For analyses of the causes and consequences of secular increases in debt across the distribution of households, see Dynan and Kohn (2007) and Dynan (2009).

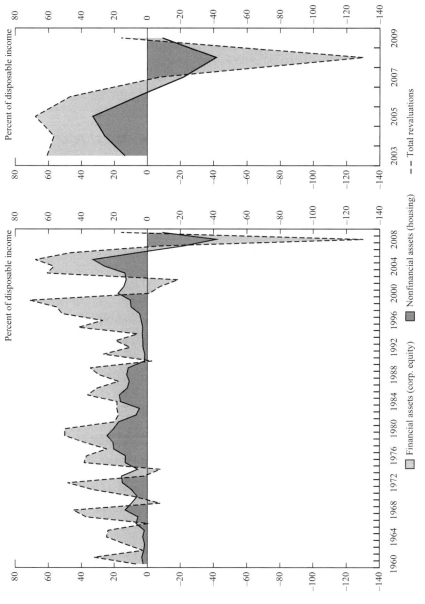

Fig. 2.4   Revaluations of household assets, 1960 to 2009

household assets experienced in the years leading up to the financial crisis and during 2008 and 2009. The figure shows that from 2003 through 2006, the combination of rising equity prices (which show through to the lighter-shaded region) and rising home prices (affecting the darker-shaded region) added to aggregate household net worth on the order of 50 to 60 percent of disposable income each year. However, equity prices were unchanged over 2007 while home prices fell significantly that year, so that, arithmetically, asset revaluations subtracted from net worth at a rate of about 25 percent of income. Of course, the situation worsened substantially in 2008: a further drop in equity prices cut into household net worth by about 40 percent of income, while plunging home prices contributed more than 80 percentage points (of income) to the decrease in net worth.[5] Although asset revaluations typically result in large swings in household net worth—very large in relation to personal income or saving—the 2008 realizations were unmatched in the postwar period (flow of funds data extend back to 1947).

2.2.3   Sectoral Net Lending and Borrowing, 1960 to 2009

Table 2.1 reports data from the US-SNA capital account to document where the funds came from to finance the sizable net borrowing by US households, as well as borrowing by the other nonfinancial domestic sectors during the years of the mortgage credit and housing boom. In particular, table 2.1 compares net lending or borrowing across all the major sectors of the US-SNA from 2000 to 2007 with patterns from the earlier decades (1960 to 1979 and 1980 to 1989); it also shows the extent to which sectoral net lending and borrowing had reversed course in 2008 and 2009.[6] Note that, except for the statistical discrepancy (line 9), net lending and borrowing across all sectors (lines 1 through 8) sum to zero each period.

Table 2.1 shows that in the 1960s and 1970s, the two nonfinancial business sectors (lines 3 and 4), the two government sectors (lines 6 and 7), and the rest of the world were, on average (and, according to the underlying annual data, consistently from year to year until the late 1970s), net borrowers, meaning that their rates of investment typically exceeded their rates of saving. In those decades, the household and the financial business sectors served as net lenders to the others.

The key sectoral development that occurred over the course of the 1980s and 1990s was that the rest of the world sector shifted from a net borrowing position vis-à-vis the US domestic sectors to a net lending position. On average over the 1980s and 1990s, real net borrowing by the federal government and the nonfinancial business sectors rose so much that even a larger real volume of net lending by the US household sector ($199 billion per year

---

5. For a detailed analysis of changes in net worth across the distribution of American households in the past three recessions, see Moore and Palumbo (2010).
6. As noted in the table, we have made rough estimates for the US capital account in 2009 based on incomplete information available in the FFA and the NIPA.

Table 2.1   **SNA-based sectoral net lending and borrowing in the United States (capital account data, 1960 through 2009)**

	1960–1979	1980–1999	2000–2007	2008–2009*
Net lending (+) or borrowing (–) by sector (billions of $2005)				
1 All US sectors	–16	–110	–522	–679
2 Households	127	199	–189	209
3 Nonfinancial, noncorporate businesses	–57	–66	–48	–5
4 Nonfinancial corporations	–31	–40	–30	83
5 Financial businesses	15	–9	66	190
6 Federal government	–56	–185	–228	–1030
7 Municipal governments	–15	–10	–94	–126
8 Rest of the world	–14	54	594	519
9 Statistical discrepancy	30	56	–73	–159

Note: Current-dollar estimates have been converted to 2005 dollars using the BEA's GDP deflator.
*Figures for 2009 are rough estimates based on the available (but incomplete) data in the financial and capital accounts.

in the 1980s and 1990s compared with $127 billion in the 1960s and 1970s) was not enough to provide funding, on average; the difference, thus, was funded by foreign official and private-sector entities (to $54 billion per year in the 1980s and 1990s, from negative $14 billion in the prior two decades).

From 2000 to 2007, net lending to the domestic sectors of the economy by the rest of the world ballooned to $594 billion per year. Even though, in real terms, the average pace of net borrowing by the nonfinancial business sectors (lines 3 and 4) decreased in the first decade of the twenty-first century while net lending by financial businesses picked up (line 5), these developments only partly offset the very large real increases in borrowing by the federal and municipal governments (lines 6 and 7). Meanwhile, on average, the US household sector shifted from having lent an average of almost $200 billion per year, on net, over the 1980s and 1990s to borrowing an average of almost $190 billion per year from 2000 through 2007.

In sum, the years leading up to the financial crisis and recession were characterized by an increase in net investment by the US household sector that was funded by borrowing rather than saving. The household sector's shift from its role from the 1960s through the 1990s as a net funding source for other sectors' investment to a net borrowing position is something that appears to have been unprecedented in the US postwar period.

2.3   What Elements of the Crisis Did the Aggregate Financial Statistics Not Convey?

Although financial statistics for the US economy conveyed some important information about rising household leverage more or less in real time, their aggregate nature masked the buildup of important underlying risk factors and did not convey the overall vulnerability of the financial system to a reversal of the flows that had supported economic activity and promoted liquidity and financial risk taking during the credit expansion. In this section, we highlight two key elements that contributed to the severity of the financial crisis that were not conveyed in aggregate financial statistics for the US economy: First, a material increase in the underlying credit risk associated with the rapid growth of home mortgages and a consequent increase in the vulnerability of borrowers to a downturn in home prices or incomes, and second, the growth of maturity transformation outside the traditional banking sector (where a significant proportion of the funding comes from insured deposits held at institutions having explicit access to external liquidity support)—that is, a greater reliance on short-term funding for longer-term financial instruments—that left the financial system highly vulnerable to a withdrawal of liquidity.

2.3.1   Mounting Credit Risk during the Mortgage Boom

As home mortgage debt was expanding at double-digit rates in the middle of the first decade of the twenty-first century, the composition of mortgage lending began to shift markedly, with subprime borrowers and loans with nontraditional terms ("alt-A" loans) becoming more and more prevalent and with loans containing "multiple layers of risk" over time. It now seems fairly clear that loans were being increasingly originated without full regard to borrowers' underlying ability to repay their loans from household income; rather, while home prices were marching up and underwriting was becoming easier, borrowers were generally able to refinance into new loans before encountering problems making their monthly payments.[7]

For example, Mayer, Pence, and Sherlund (2009) note that the overwhelming majority (more than 75 percent) of subprime mortgages originated from 2003 to 2007 were "short-term hybrid" loans, in which the initial interest rate was usually fixed for a two- or three-year period, then became adjustable and tied to market interest rates thereafter (with a substantial rate margin). The initial rate on these subprime loans was often referred to as a "teaser" rate because it was held a few percentage points below the "fully indexed rate" during the initial, fixed-rate term of the contract. The idea behind this underwriting appeared to be to extend loans to homeowners who might not currently qualify for a "prime" or traditional mortgage, but who could refinance into such mortgages after having established a record of making on-time payments for a couple of years and after their homes had appreciated in value, raising their equity positions. Meanwhile, the expansion of so-called alt-A mortgages that was occurring at roughly the same time as

7. For a thorough description of characteristics of mortgage borrowers and loan terms during the credit boom in the United States, as well as a thorough analysis of the factors behind the rise in mortgage defaults, see Mayer, Pence, and Sherlund (2009).

the subprime lending boom was also associated with a significant shift in the underlying risk characteristics of those loans. In particular, the growth of alt-A mortgages was disproportionate in the "floating rate" category of loans, including interest-only mortgages (in which borrowers did not have to make payments to reduce their loan balance during the first several years of the contract) and negatively amortizing mortgages (in which not even the "minimum payments" to cover interest were required). Although this type of alt-A mortgage was very rare through 2003, it grew to compose about one-quarter of originations in 2005 and 2006.

One indication—albeit an indirect one—that mortgage origination was expanding without sufficient regard to a borrowers' underlying ability to repay their loans or afford their homes is that the median loan for purchased homes (as opposed to refinanced loans) in subprime mortgage pools from 2005 through the first half of 2007 carried a combined loan-to-value ratio of 100 percent; for loans for purchased homes in alt-A pools, the median combined loan-to-value ratio was 95 percent in 2006 and the first half of 2007 (up slightly from 90 percent in the prior three years; Mayer, Pence, and Sherlund [2009], table 2.B). Mayer, Pence, and Sherlund (2009, figures 1 and 2) report two other indications of how the latest vintage of borrowers in subprime and alt-A mortgage pools very soon ran into trouble making their monthly mortgage payments. First, they show how later vintages of loans in subprime mortgage pools experienced larger frequencies of "early payment defaults"—which reached about 8 percent for the 2007 vintage—where borrowers had fallen ninety days or more delinquent in their monthly mortgage payments less than one year after receiving their loan. Second, they show how later vintages of borrowers with option adjustable-rate mortgages—interest-only loans in which borrowers have the option of making less than the "minimum" monthly payment and rolling the unpaid interest into their loan balance (for a period of time)—took the option: within six months of having taken out an option adjustable-rate mortgage that was securitized in an alt-A mortgage pool in 2007, almost 95 percent of borrowers had exercised their option to pay less than the monthly interest on their mortgage.

Thus, while the SNA clearly signaled the household sector's transformation from a net supplier to a net user of credit, the aggregate measures of housing leverage (such as homeowners' equity to home values) and balance sheet leverage (households' debt service ratio) did not clearly signal imminent mortgage credit risks. In particular, these aggregate time-series data simply could not capture the fundamental transformation of the mortgage market that is described above, with the increasing prevalence of instruments that embedded a reliance on increasing real estate values. While there was anecdotal information regarding changes in mortgage products (and while the shift in mortgage funding to so-called private-label mortgage-backed securities [MBS] was also recognized), a point we emphasize later is that disaggregated information derived specifically from the mortgage origination process was needed to understand more fully the extent to which underwriting standards had deteriorated and, thus, the extent to which a drop in home prices and a shift back to more restrictive underwriting could amplify the initial effects.

2.3.2   Funding Mechanisms that Amplified and Propagated the "Mortgage Credit Shock" through the Financial System

The decline in underwriting standards and proliferation of new instruments was predicated on the ability of borrowers to refinance as their equity increased with home prices was one significant driver of the growth in mortgage credit in the years prior to the crisis. Another, which proved to be of great importance as conditions deteriorated, was the widespread availability of low-cost funding for mortgages from vehicles that engaged in significant amounts of maturity transformation. While underwriting was deteriorating, the funding available for these loans was increasing through expansion of securitization channels and, in part, more complex and more opaque financial products structured to appeal to short-term, risk-averse investors. Effectively, a significant fraction of the longer-term securitized mortgages was held by vehicles that obtained a considerable share of their funding from short-term sources, and those sources were quickly withdrawn when confidence disappeared.

A new form of asset-backed commercial paper (ABCP) conduit called a structured investment vehicle (SIV) became the "poster child" for the type of maturity transformation just discussed that developed outside the traditional banking sector. The SIVs issued short-term debt (as well as medium-term and capital notes) and used the proceeds to purchase residential MBS, among other structured financial products and primary debt. However, unlike other ABCP conduits, SIVs had only limited contractual liquidity support, meaning that SIVs would need to sell assets to repay investors if they ran into difficulties placing (or "rolling over") their commercial paper. At the onset of the financial crisis in August and September of 2007, investors lost confidence in the values of subprime and alt-A MBS that were held by SIVs, leaving them unable to roll over their commercial paper and leaving them short of funding.[8] The flight of short-term, risk-averse investors resulted in pressure on sponsor institutions to support SIVs and other ABCP programs, even in the absence of explicit legal obligations to do so, and thus contributed to growing doubts about the condition of the commercial and investment banks at the center of the financial system. Aggregate data—including those presented in the FFA and the US-SNA, plotted in figure 2.5—documented the rapid expansion of ABCP that occurred between 2004 and 2007 and the withdrawal of $350 billion from the ABCP market

---

8. Covitz, Liang, and Suarez (2009) and Acharya, Schnabl, and Suarez (2010) discuss ABCP in the context of the recent financial crisis.

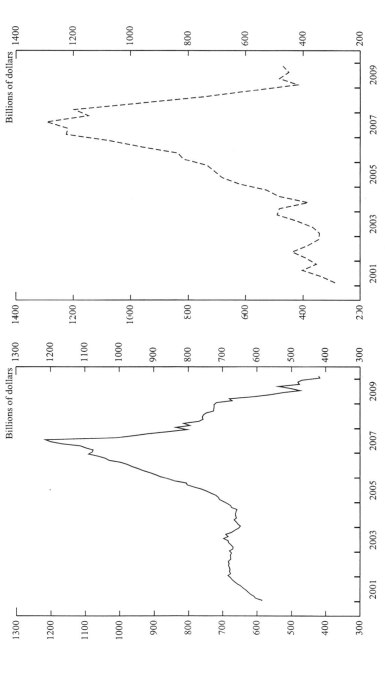

Fig. 2.5 Selected short-term collateralized debt instruments, 2001 to 2010

Source: Left panel, commercial paper rates and outstanding, the Federal Reserve Board. Right panel, Flow of Funds Accounts of the United States, the Federal Reserve Board.

——— Asset-backed commercial paper outstanding in the U.S.   – – – – Net repurchase agreements: liabilities outstanding of U.S. brokers and dealers that occurred from August to December 2007.[9] However, the aggregate data did not illuminate (or provide any indication of) the more subtle shift in the funding strategies of ABCP conduits that were, for example, associated with the development of SIVs (in the extreme case; see Covitz, Liang, and Suarez [2009]). Nor were the aggregate data capable of (or at all designed to) document material shifts in the underlying collateral purchased by ABCP conduits. Of course, the years in which ABCP was growing rapidly were also the years in which mortgage lending and issuance of residential MBS were soaring, and there is reason to believe those trends were related. That is, while ABCP was becoming more prevalent, the underlying collateral funded through ABCP conduits was shifting from more traditional assets (such as trade receivables and "standard" ABS) to newer and riskier securities (such as senior tranches of ABS CDOs collateralized by mezzanine tranches of subprime and alt-A MBS; again, see Covitz, Liang, and Suarez [2009]). A key point is that, as in the case of residential mortgages, ongoing shifts in ABCP structures that were material to their systemic vulnerability could not be gleaned from the aggregate data.

Despite the considerable attention paid to SIVs and other ABCP programs in many narratives of the crisis, SIVs actually had quite a small footprint relative to the size of the money markets as a whole. Rather, a much more important source of short-term funding for MBS (as well as many other classes of structured financial products) in the years preceding the crisis was the market for repurchase agreements (repos). Repos serve as a collateralized source of short-term lending and borrowing that began as a way for institutional investors and broker-dealers to earn small returns by lending Treasury and agency securities on a short-term basis. But, as we describe in more detail below, in the years preceding the financial crisis, the repo market evolved slowly, but substantially, to become a major funding source for structured financial products, including some of the more complex and systemically risky instruments (such as senior tranches of ABS CDOs).

As emphasized by Brunnermeier (2009) and Gorton and Metrick (2009), repo funding was a major factor behind the expansion of the shadow banking system prior to the financial crisis and the sudden withdrawal of repo funding—and a pullback in repo transactions with certain counterparties (including Bear Stearns in March 2008), against specific collateral classes (ABS CDOs), and a rise in repo haircuts played a major role in propagating the subprime/alt-A mortgage shock throughout the financial system.

Aggregate financial statistics, such as the FFA and (to a lesser extent) the US-SNA, contain some information about repo transaction volumes. As can be seen in the right-hand panel of figure 2.5, these aggregate data indeed show rapid increases in the net liability positions of US brokers and dealers

---

9. From the end of July 2007 through February 2010, ABCP outstanding in the United States contracted by almost $775 billion, from $1.19 trillion to $415 billion.

through repo agreements in the years preceding the financial crisis and the severe drop that occurred in 2008.[10] As dramatic as the movements in the aggregate series are, they materially understate the actual level of activity (and risk) in the repo market because the individual firms report to the Securities and Exchange Commission repo positions that have been netted with respect to counterparties and security types. In times of normal market functioning, it makes sense for brokers and dealers to net such positions in their financial statements and regulatory reports. However, in times of stress, information about gross positions, and thus about the overall volume of outstanding short-term funding trades, are more relevant for sizing the potential market frictions that could become destabilizing, amplifying and propagating even small disturbances (Brunnermeier 2009; Gorton and Metrick 2009). Hordahl and King (2008) cite a figure of about $10 trillion of gross repos outstanding in the US market at the end of 2007, roughly twice the size of the market five years earlier and more than seven times the net aggregate position reported in the FFA. Finally, as we describe below, the period of rapidly rising repo volumes was associated with a material shift in the underlying collateral away from the most stable government and agency securities that tend to rise in price and liquidity during periods of market turmoil and toward a more heterogeneous mix that included a range of structured financial products.

2.4   Beyond Augmented Financial Statistics—Or, What Other Analytic Approaches Are Called For, and What Additional Lessons from the Crisis Are Critical for Future Financial Stability Analyses?

The growth of nontraditional mortgages and novel funding vehicles did not go unnoticed during the period preceding the crisis. However, enormous comfort was taken by both policymakers and market participants in the degree to which the associated risks were broadly dispersed through various transfer mechanisms. Of course, the crisis revealed that far more of the exposure remained in the core financial sector than was apparent to most observers beforehand. To better understand the failure of risk mitigation and transfer mechanisms, specialized data were required about mortgage contracts and underwriting criteria and about the maturity transformation that became ubiquitous outside of the traditional banking sector.

In the wake of the financial crisis, there is understandable appetite to fill those gaps and collect more information about activities that might place large institutions and, ultimately, the broader economy at risk. Without dis-

---

10. The data plotted in figure 2.5 are from table L.129 of the Flow of Funds Accounts of the United States; the underlying source data come from two reports from the Securities and Exchange Commission: Financial and Operational Combined Uniform Single Report (of securities brokers and dealers; [FOCUS]) and Report on Finances and Operations of Government Securities Brokers and Dealers (FOGS).

counting the importance of such efforts, we emphasize the need to proceed in a manner that also recognizes that the remedy is not merely to collect data going forward on mortgage origination standards and the prevalence of certain funding vehicles. Rather, to diminish the likelihood of future crisis, we must change the way that we focus data collection for financial stability analysis. In fact, and as explained further below through several examples, a massive data collection effort focused on filling the gaps that became evident after the recent crisis will not only fail to make things better, measured against the goal of a more stable financial system, but can also arguably make things worse when data collections are static while financial markets are dynamic.

2.4.1   A First Example: Consequences of Drexel Burnham Lambert's Failure in 1990

Prior to the near-collapse of Bear Stearns in March 2008 and its sale to JP Morgan Chase, the lessons on the vulnerabilities of broker-dealer firms were mostly extracted from the Drexel failure in 1990. While other broker-dealers failed both before and after Drexel, these situations involved firms with limited involvement in the capital markets. With few exceptions, these failures had few effects other than on brokerage customers, whose assets and interests were protected by the actions of the Securities and Exchange Commission and Securities Investors Protection Corporation. Drexel, on the other hand, played a major role in the fixed-income markets, and in fact had been a pioneer in creating an active market for the debt of below-investment-grade issuers.

And, of the lessons drawn from the Drexel failure, none were more influential over the ensuing fifteen years than those related to funding. Post-mortems on Drexel revealed that the firm had relied very heavily on the use of short-term, confidence-sensitive commercial paper in funding its business. Further, much of that funding had been raised at the parent level and, in some instances, downstreamed into the broker-dealer entity in the form of equity, which then supported further leverage.

These lessons were quickly incorporated into the approaches taken by securities firms, by their supervisors, and by the community of equity analysts that follows securities firms. Firms began to carefully limit their use of unsecured short-term funds—commercial paper, in particular. Regulators tracked the use of short-term unsecured borrowings, and the firms themselves emphasized their minimal dependence on such funding in their public filings and touted their reliance on secured funding. For example, one firm included the following language in its 2006 10–K filing the statement:

> In financing its balance sheet, the Company attempts to maximize its use of secured funding where economically competitive. Short-term sources of cash consist principally of collateralized borrowings, including re-

purchase transactions, sell/buy arrangements, securities lending arrangements, and customer free credit balances. Short-term unsecured funding sources expose the Company to rollover risk, as providers of credit are not obligated to refinance the instruments at maturity. For this reason, the Company seeks to prudently manage its reliance on short-term unsecured borrowings by maintaining an adequate total capital base and extensive use of secured funding.[11]

Similar statements could be found in the annual reports of many other institutions that were active dealers in securities and over-the-counter derivatives.

But the comfort taken in this reliance on short-term secured funding, while explicitly rejecting short-term unsecured funding as highly confidence-sensitive and fickle, proved to be gravely misplaced during the crisis. At least two realities were not sufficiently appreciated by firms, their supervisors, and other observers before 2008. First, the composition of the collateral in the years leading up to the crisis changed slowly but steadily and fundamentally. When Drexel failed in 1990, the collateral that was funded through repos and other types of secured funding arrangements was almost exclusively US Treasury and agency securities. Such collateral embedded a "right way risk" in the sense that the collateral was likely to rise in value and liquidity during a flight to quality, at precisely the time when institutions lending against and borrowing against such collateral faced stress.

Over time, however, the repo collateral pool evolved to include a much wider range of instruments, many of which were not likely to benefit during a flight to quality. According to some estimates, by 2007, the fraction of the more pristine collateral types had fallen to about one-third of the overall funding market. Particularly insidious, of course, were structured products tied to mortgages. Not only were these instruments, it is now clear, less likely than debt issued by the Treasury or agencies to remain liquid during a stress scenario, but, because of the assumptions about default correlations that were fundamental to their design, they were particularly exposed precisely to the sort of systemic risk event that would also negatively affect financial institutions that were funding these instruments on a secured basis.

The other reality that was driven home by the crisis involved a fundamental disconnect between the perspective of secured lenders and secured borrowers, notably securities firms (including those affiliated with commercial banking organizations). As evidenced in the statement quoted earlier, secured borrowers financing positions for themselves and their customers viewed repos and other such transactions as asset-backed lending, where the comfort of the lender was tied exclusively to the presence and amount of collateral, meaning the degree to which a "haircut" reduced the amount financed below the market value of the collateral. Such asset-backed lending models were familiar to dealers and reflected their approach to conducting

11. Bear Stearns 2006 10–K.

business with, in particular, hedge funds. In such relationships, the dealers placed little reliance on the financial condition of the counterparty or its overall portfolio of positions. Rather, credit risk was managed by assuring that the amount of funding provided was always less, again by some haircut, than the amount of collateral held by the dealer, which the dealer could quickly liquidate if necessary. But, unfortunately, such a model was not consistent with the manner in which secured lenders, including money market mutual funds and other institutions, viewed and managed their credit exposure. As became clear in the course of the crisis, they drew comfort from the collateral, but also very much from the capacity of the counterparty, as reflected in market-based indicators like credit spreads and equity price as well as less-objective signals including market "noise." The effect of this sensitivity would also be amplified, of course, by the manner in which the composition of the collateral had evolved away from consisting exclusively of Treasury securities and other similar, highly liquid instruments.

2.4.2   A Second Example: Consequences of Losses on Collateralized Mortgage Obligations in the Early 1990s

If overconfidence in the reliance of secured funding was one recurrent theme in the crisis, the overconfidence in the capacity of pooling and tranching to manage default risk stood at the absolute epicenter. Here, too, lessons from previous adverse events made a lasting impression on the psyches of market participants, regulators, and analysts. This experience led to careful tracking of certain metrics, not only externally, as evidenced by the questions that rating agencies asked when reviewing financial institutions' ratings and by equity analysts on earnings calls, but internally as well. And, unfortunately, the tracking of these metrics, and their incorporation into the internal risk control systems of financial institutions, was not sufficiently resilient to the dynamic nature of the financial markets.

In the early 1990s, a number of financial institutions, including some investment banks like Salomon Brothers, experienced outsized losses related to holdings of certain tranches of mortgage-backed bonds known as collateralized mortgage obligations, or CMOs. More particularly, the losses were related to the holding of certain tranches that concentrated interest rate risk. This spate of losses followed an earlier incident in 1987 when a trader at Merrill Lynch lost the then-stunning sum of $377 million trading similar positions. In the years that followed, both internal and external watchdogs became very focused on these tranches. While creation of these bonds that concentrated exposure to certain risks was critical to bringing lucrative securitization deals to market, it was understood that not distributing these products to parties willing and able to bear these risks placed structuring banks in jeopardy of one sort or another: if the bonds were sold to unwitting or unsophisticated parties, there were clear reputational and compliance consequences. If the bonds were held by the firm, the consequences were potentially financial. As the securitization market grew and evolved, including by increasingly securitizing assets that entailed not only interest rate risk but also credit risk, the mantra remained that distribution of the most risky tranches must be carefully managed and monitored. And so they were, with management providing assurances and supporting metrics to regulators, rating agencies and, on a more limited scale, to the public through filings and commentary on conference calls.

However, the structures devised for securitizations are anything but static. The underlying assets generate finite cash flows that are distributed to purchasers of the asset-backed bonds. The design of a structure is an exercise in allocating those cash flows to different liability holders, with many different possible methodologies. If certain liabilities over time come to be referred to as "toxic waste," if their retention immediately raises red flags and if there are significant penalties for not distributing those instruments cleanly and promptly, market participants naturally respond by ensuring that those bonds find willing purchasers, typically by adopting allocation rules that pay potential holders generously.

Of course, where the underlying assets generate finite cash flows, making one tranche of liabilities richer must, by definition, make some other piece of the capital structure less attractive to hold. As market practices evolved over the past fifteen years, often the so-called *mezzanine* tranches became the key to getting securitizations done. Investors, such as hedge funds and other specialists, were paid generously to own the lowest pieces of the capital structure. The most senior securities, on the other hand, were attractive at moderate yields to any number of investors. The middle ranges often proved the most difficult to place, as these did not pay like the lower tranches, yet were clearly significantly more risky than the most senior liabilities.

As the pace of securitization activity continued to accelerate after the turn of the century, some institutions found it increasingly difficult to distribute the mezzanine bonds. Although free of the stigma accorded to the "residual" or "equity" tranches, there was enough sensitivity to any buildup of these marginally investment-grade instruments that pressure built for some solution, either developing new distribution channels or slowing the speed with which the factory was churning out product. Appetite to slow the factory was, of course, limited by the profitability of the enterprise. So, several institutions solved the problem in a different way that ultimately had very profound consequences for themselves and the broader financial system.

By relying not just once but also a second time on the pooling and tranching technology, mezzanine bonds could be resecuritized and thus supported by a new capital structure. As this process played out at the firms most affected, the lower tranches of the resecuritization were small in size and priced to move. The bulk of the liabilities from the resecuritization consisted of bonds receiving the highest possible rating. Not only was the normal diversification benefit from pooling assets relied on when assessing the likelihood that different parts of the capital structure would experience losses through defaults, but in many cases, additional diversification effects were recognized, as multiple pools of assets, or pools of different types of assets, were combined to back a single resecuritization deal. But, given the finite cash flows generated by the underlying assets, the need to direct cash flows with sufficient generosity to the lower tranches to ensure distribution, and the large proportion of senior bonds, the yields on the highly rated bonds produced through resecuritization were anemic.

The combination of high ratings and low yields turned out to be a very dangerous one for financial institutions. If the yields had been greater, more of the product would presumably have been sold to investors with the capacity to assess the relevant risks. If the ratings had been lower, the securities would have looked more like residual tranches, and a number of internal and external risk control processes would have likely engaged to quickly sound alarm bells at a dangerous buildup of undistributed product. But those systems were not as attuned to concentrations of highly rated instruments as they were to lower tranches in the capital structure. Financial controllers were less likely to aggressively force markdowns of highly rated product to levels at which sales would be possible to sophisticated investors. The regulatory capital signals were also muted, given the heavy reliance on ratings in most regulatory capital regimes. And risk managers, who carefully watched the balance sheet footings of traditional "residuals," were less alarmed by highly rated bonds. As a result, Citi, Merrill Lynch, and UBS ended up with tens of billions of dollars of super senior ABS CDO on their balance sheets, and large volumes of similar instruments held in less obvious ways—for example, in SIVs or conduits that were highly dependent on the secured funding discussed above.

2.4.3   Discussion

Through two examples, one focusing on secured funding and the other focusing on resecuritization, we have made the argument for a regulatory and supervisory analog to Heisenberg's Uncertainty Principle. In physics, the principle is rather remarkable, given that physical systems are generally stationary and invariant. It is therefore somewhat surprising that efforts to measure the movement of a particle actually changes its trajectory. In the world of finance, where institutions and markets are continually evolving and individuals are highly sensitive to incentives, it seems less shocking that focusing on certain metrics would erode their usefulness. Nor is it surprising that elements of the financial system should evolve such that risks migrate toward instruments and strategies less likely to sound alarms.

But these points should not constitute an argument against an empirical approach to understanding risks in the financial system or data collection exercises. It does, however, underscore the dangers of static data collection in an effort to understand a financial system that is highly dynamic. It also suggests that those wishing to understand the system need to imagine themselves less like the physicist, who has the luxury of dealing with a system that is not continuously changing and where measurements relevant in one decade will continue to shed light during the next decade, and more like the intelligence analyst who must combine a variety of signals to form a mosaic that sheds light on the plans of an adversary. Key to this latter methodology is a fundamental recognition that the system being considered is dynamic, and more attention devoted to any one signal increases the likelihood that this signal will cease to be relevant, or perhaps even mislead.[12]

This realization suggests a paradigm for expanding the use of data in financial stability analysis. We have argued that aggregate statistics usefully signal unusual patterns of financial flows across sectors and emerging imbalances that should stimulate targeted analysis reliant upon additional sources of information collected specifically to investigate anomalies that presumably differ each time and cannot be predicted in advance. Just like intelligence analysts who begin by staring at a grainy satellite image, but follow up by bringing other resources to bear to understand what they are seeing, changes in some of these aggregate measures could be impetus for further work that would elucidate what particular instruments and activities are driving the change. Thus, we suggest exploring ways to collect additional comprehensive and timely aggregate financial data. But given how quickly transactional forms evolve, particularly when they are tied to metrics against which firms or positions are judged, this approach must be complemented with a second stage of more-targeted analysis relying on less traditional sources of information that are specifically utilized to illuminate trends and potential anomalies visible in the aggregate data.

An approach that relies on these two distinct stages, expanded collection of aggregate data followed by collection of more-targeted and specialized information, could have been helpful in the period leading up to the recent crisis. In theory, such an approach could have identified signs in the aggregate data that credit provision to the nonfinancial sectors of the economy was growing rapidly. Likewise, aggregate data could have offered hints that the transfer of risk from the core financial system to other sectors was not growing commensurately with the increase in the securitization of assets. Such signals might have motivated earlier efforts, using specialized granular data, to drill down into the types of transactions that, over a short period of time, came to dominate the mortgage and secured-funding markets prior to the crisis.

The approach we describe might have allowed regulators and supervisors

---

12. In a sense, this idea is similar to the intuition behind Goodhart's Law (Goodhart 1975) or Chrystal and Mizen (2004), which posited that whatever monetary aggregate was targeted by a central bank would become less tied to market interest rates and less predictive for aggregate demand.

to develop a holistic understanding of the shadow banking system earlier. Although regulators and supervisors had a good understanding of some of its key elements, when confidence in this parallel system suddenly disappeared in August 2007, they generally lacked the perspective on the system as a whole—that is, how the various parts were linked together.

A better understanding of the shadow banking system, as it developed from, say, 2004 to 2007, was certainly not a sufficient condition for the crisis to have been averted. That would also have required timely judgments and forceful actions by policymakers, regulators, and financial institution executives, and surely the solution to a number of very difficult collective action problems as well. But, at the least, a better understanding of the shadow banking system could have played a critical role in effectively mitigating consequences of the crisis once it took hold.

2.5   Conclusions

The market turmoil of 2008 and 2009 demonstrated once again that, while the particular instruments and transactions are novel in each crisis, the underlying themes are recurring. In general, financial crises create and are then perpetuated by illiquidity: triggering "shocks" cause critical funding to be suddenly withdrawn from some institutions or activities, and concerns about liquidity rapidly become concerns about solvency. And only at this point does the degree to which major institutions share common exposures suddenly become clear. As market participants struggle to reduce leverage in an atmosphere of vanishing liquidity and correlated exposures, market participants become reluctant, even unwilling, to transact with one another. Pressures quickly spread through the financial system.

In the recent crisis, the evolution of the financial system away from traditional banking—portfolio lending funded heavily with insured deposits—toward a system dominated by a complex network of collateralized lending relationships served only to increase the primacy of liquidity. Once the spreading illiquidity of formerly highly liquid instruments called into question the value of the underlying collateral, as well as the strength of many counterparties, the shadow banking system proved extremely fragile.

The task at hand for supervisors and policymakers is to better understand future changes in the financial system and the associated vulnerabilities with the new institutional arrangements and transactional forms that are created. These efforts will in turn require expanded and improved measurement and analysis of financial activity—efforts that, we believe, should be structured around two basic principles: First, work on and analysis of aggregate data and more-specialized data must proceed in tandem. Much good work has been done, both before and after the onset of the crisis, but we believe that these efforts have not been sufficiently coordinated across analyses of macro-

and microdata. In fact, we believe that such coordination, with the analysis of aggregate data leading to the identification of those areas where work with more-specialized data should be targeted, should be a key aspect of the paradigm in future financial stability work. Second, and in a similar vein, we believe that the analysis of aggregate data should be structured to be neutral with regard to transactional form and focused instead on the recurring underlying themes associated with financial instability—competitive dynamics leading to greater leverage and risk taking, correlated exposures among interconnected firms, and maturity transformation that results in a critical vulnerability to sudden withdrawals of funding. That said, the targeted work must be organized around awareness of and expertise in the prevalent transactional forms and the specialized data needed to understand their subtleties and implications. Substantial efforts reflecting both of these principles, including projects aimed at assessing leverage and maturity transformation, are now under way at the Federal Reserve and other central banks.

In a recent paper, Adrian, Covitz, and Liang (2013) describe a practical approach to financial stability monitoring that is very much in the spirit of the framework we consider. They lay out a flexible and forward-looking monitoring program capable of covering developments and innovations in the financial system broadly. Their monitoring program focuses on identifying structural and cyclical vulnerabilities building in the financial system that can arise from a range of market failures and lead to excessive leverage, maturity transformation, interconnectedness of large financial firms, and evolving complexity of securities and transactions—key elements that we have also emphasized. The approach described by Adrian, Covitz, and Liang also recognizes—and, importantly, attempts to directly address—the challenges to monitoring posed by the natural tendency of the financial system to migrate activities outside the regulatory reach and official-sector safety net.

References

Acharya, Viral V., Philipp Schnabl, and Gustavo A. Suarez. 2010. "Securitization without Risk Transfer." NBER Working Paper no. 15730, Cambridge, MA.

Adrian, Tobias, Daniel Covitz, and Nellie Liang. 2013. "Financial Stability Monitoring." Finance and Economics Discussion Series no. 2013–21, Washington, DC, Federal Reserve Board. http://www.federalreserve.gov/pubs/feds/2013/201321/201321pap.pdf.

Brunnermeier, Markus K. 2009. "Deciphering the Liquidity and Credit Crunch of 2007–08." *Journal of Economic Perspectives* 23 (1): 77–100.

Chrystal, Alec, and Paul Mizen. 2004. "Goodhart's Law: Its Origins, Meaning and

Implications for Monetary Policy." In *Central Banking, Monetary Theory and Practice: Essays in Honour of Charles Goodhart, vol. 1*, edited by Paul Mizen, 221–43. Cheltenham, United Kingdom: Edward Elgar.

Commission of the European Communities, International Monetary Fund, Organization of Economic Cooperation and Development, United Nations, and the World Bank. 1993. *System of National Accounts*. Brussels/Luxembourg, New York, Paris, and Washington, DC.

Covitz, Daniel M., Nellie Liang, and Gustavo A. Suarez. 2009. "The Evolution of a Financial Crisis: Panic in the Asset-Backed Commercial Paper Market." Finance and Economic Discussion Series Paper no. 2009–36, Washington, DC, Federal Reserve Board. www.federalreserve.gov/pubs/feds/2009/200936/200936pap.pdf.

Dynan, Karen E. 2009. "Changing Household Financial Opportunities and Economic Security." *Journal of Economic Perspectives* 23 (2): 49–68.

Dynan, Karen E., and Donald L. Kohn. 2007. "The Rise in US Household Indebtedness: Causes and Consequences." Finance and Economic Discussion Series Paper no. 2007–37, Washington, DC, Federal Reserve Board. www.federalreserve.gov /pubs/feds/2007/200737/200737pap.pdf.

Goodhart, Charles A. E. 1975. "Monetary Relationships: A View from Threadneedle Street." In *Papers in Monetary Economics, Volume I*, 1–27. Sydney: Reserve Bank of Australia.

Gorton, Gary B., and Andrew Metrick. 2009. "Securitized Lending and the Run on Repo." NBER Working Paper no. 15223, Cambridge, MA.

Hordahl, Peter, and Michael R. King. 2008. "Developments in Repo Markets during the Financial Turmoil." *BIS Quarterly Review*, December. http://ssrn.com/abstract =1329903.

Mayer, Christopher, Karen Pence, and Shane M. Sherlund. 2009. "The Rise in Mortgage Defaults." *Journal of Economic Perspectives* 23 (1): 27–50.

Moore, Kevin B., and Michael G. Palumbo. 2010. "The Finances of American Households in the Past Three Recessions: Evidence from the Survey of Consumer Finances." Finance and Economics Discussion Series Paper no. 2010–06, Washington, DC, Federal Reserve Board. www.federalreserve.gov/pubs/feds/2010/201006 /201006pap.pdf.

Palumbo, Michael G., and Jonathan A. Parker. 2009. "The Integrated Financial and Real System of National Accounts for the United States: Does It Presage the Financial Crisis?" *American Economic Review* 99 (2): 80–86.

Teplin, Albert M., Rochelle Antoniewicz, Susan Hume McIntosh, Michael G. Palumbo, Genevieve Solomon, Charles Ian Meade, Karin Moses, and Brent Moulton. 2006. "Integrated Macroeconomic Accounts for the United States: Draft SNA-USA." In *A New Architecture for the US National Accounts*, edited by Dale W. Jorgenson, J. Steven Landefeld, and William D. Nordhaus, 471–540. Chicago: University of Chicago Press.

Durable Financial Regulation
Monitoring Financial Instruments as a Counterpart to Regulating Financial Institutions

Leonard Nakamura

3.1 Introduction: A Financial Regulatory Database for Durable Financial Regulation

In the wake of the recent financial crisis, an effort is underway to redesign the regulation of financial institutions. As part of the new regulatory structure, a new information framework may be desirable. In particular, I describe a system for monitoring financial *instruments* as a complement to the regulation of financial *institutions*. If a system of financial regulation is to be durable, it must evolve with the development of new institutions and instruments. This is one of the chapters in this volume that sets forth perspectives on frameworks for the analysis of systemic risk data collection. Here I discuss explicitly how to construct a macro-micro database that links our knowledge of sectoral financial assets, liabilities, and flows to underlying microdatabases with data on individual instruments and the holdings and liabilities of individual economic actors (households, firms, states). This database represents one way to implement the Squam Lake proposal for

Leonard Nakamura is vice president and economist at the Federal Reserve Bank of Philadelphia.

The views expressed here are those of the author and do not necessarily reflect those of the Federal Reserve Bank of Philadelphia or the Federal Reserve System. I would like to thank Viral Acharya, John Bell, Mitchell Berlin, Robert Bliss, John Bottega, Paul Calem, Satyajit Chatterjee, Larry Cordell, Ronel Elul, Jose Fillat, Jeff Fuhrer, Josh Gallin, Itay Goldstein, Chris Henderson, Chuck Hulten, Bob Hunt, Tor Jacobson, George Kauffman, Arthur Kennickell, Bill Lang, Jamie McAndrews, Susan McIntosh, Greg Nini, Marshall Reinsdorf, Kasper Roszbach, Tom Stark, Todd Vermilyea, Larry Wall, Christina Wang, two anonymous referees and participants in seminars at the Sveriges Riksbank and at the Federal Reserve Banks of Boston, New York, and Philadelphia, the Federal Reserve System Conference on Real-Time Policy Issues, and the System Committee on Financial Structure and Regulation for many helpful comments. For acknowledgments, sources of research support, and disclosure of the author's material financial relationships, if any, please see http://www.nber.org/chapters/c12521.ack.

a new information infrastructure for financial markets (French et al. 2010, chapter 3).

What is meant by such a macro-micro financial instrument database? The macro side of the database would have summary aggregate data on the nominal quantities of financial instruments and both the debtors and the current asset holders, by broad sector. I argue that this macro side is best understood as an extension of the Flow of Funds database already collected by the US Federal Reserve. The micro side of the database would have microdata samples of individual instruments and economic actors. The two sides of the database could then be interconnected so that the microdata can be interpreted as a (possibly weighted) sample of portions of the aggregates. The proposed macro-micro database would make it possible to detect, understand, and mitigate potential systemic risks.

In the 2007–2009 financial crisis, financial regulators were surprised both by the size of the potential losses and by the types of institutions that were affected. Regulators moved to protect investment banks, insurance companies, mutual funds, and government-sponsored enterprises, as well as traditional depository institutions. More detailed knowledge of the risks of financial instruments and the holders of these risks might have permitted regulators to move more aggressively in advance of the crisis and would have made regulators better informed once the crisis was at hand. I examine some of the risks that arose in the recent crisis and how we could have known more about them as they were beginning.

The database I describe is intended to be of substantial use to supervisors in identifying risk at regulated institutions. It would also be used to help them know when financial risks are being held by unregulated financial institutions, generating new systemic risks. United States and European regulators are already taking steps to improve data availability. The Eichner, Kohn, and Palumbo (chapter 2, this volume) argues that while macrodata may be useful for discerning trends in financial risks, it is valuable to have more specialized information to further illuminate them. My framework would take a step toward facilitating this side-by-side use of macro- and more specialized data.

An important consideration in any such database is that it create a cost-effective means of collecting and organizing the microdata, that is, the individual financial instruments, so that the evolution of the underlying risks can be followed. For this reason we consider how to best use and improve existing databases, as well as how to develop new ones. Just as the Flow of Funds Accounts permits us to observe how much the sectors own and owe by broad class of instruments, we also need links across the microdatabases that help us observe the distribution of individuals, firms, and agencies that own and owe, by individual instruments.

In this chapter I set forth a framework in which a US financial data office could be the central data keeper for information on US-originated financial instruments and could be active in making the data available to academic researchers as well as economists from regulatory agencies. Such an office has been provided for in the Dodd-Frank Act as the Office of Financial Research (OFR). The OFR would actively share data (within the limits of confidentiality) and research results on the risks of specific financial instruments with financial regulators, with risk managers within financial institutions, and with the academic community. It would thus strengthen financial institutions' ability to recognize and manage their own risk, conceivably reducing the burden on regulation.

The framework that I set forth here does not easily encompass cross-border risks. However, if foreign financial supervisory authorities set up similar frameworks in their jurisdictions, and if data can be shared among international supervisors, then some cross-border risks may be assimilated into a global framework. The paper by Cecchetti, Fender, and McGuire (2010) discusses the Bank for International Settlements (BIS) data and how the BIS's global financial statistics may be used as a framework for monitoring cross-border risks, using the prime example of the carry trade, which may increase volatility across international borders.

The chapter by Eichner, Kohn, and Palumbo, like this one, explores the development of both macro- and microanalyses of data. They argue, as I do, that during the recent financial crisis regulators lacked crucial disaggregated information about the changing risks in household balance sheets amid weakening underwriting standards. Their paper points to the observational paradox that is a central problem for regulation: that the problems that regulators are aware of are those that they place limitations on. Financial activity then naturally flows away from the known risks toward risks that are unknown to the regulators. Maintaining financial stability may then depend on how quickly regulators can inform themselves about the risks of new activities. By pursuing a variety of targeted microanalyses at the same time as macro indicators of risk, there is a greater likelihood that regulators can limit the damage from new risks created by the inevitable evolution of the financial system.

3.2   How Monitoring Financial Instruments Can Aid in the Regulation of Financial Institutions

The task I am describing has two central pieces: one is finding out who holds financial instruments and the other is measuring the risks of the instruments and of the holders. Before addressing precisely how these objectives could be achieved, let us use examples from the 2007–2009 financial crisis to consider further how this informational database will aid the systemic regulator and all financial regulators.

In this part, we make several points: (1) the database could aid in detecting buildups of systemic risk outside the regulated financial system; (2) it could reduce the opacity of institutional portfolios; (3) it could support studies of the changing risks of instruments, in particular, by permitting investigation of the actions of agents along the full life cycle of instrument creation, distribution, and servicing; (4) it could support pricing analysis that would bring financial, economic, and econometric theory to bear in the determination of potential systemic risk; (5) it could engage a broader, more creative, and potentially more objective community in systemic risk analysis; (6) it could enable regulators to observe counterparty risk and to undertake regular systemic stress testing; and (7) it could be used to improve estimation of long-term relationships across variables that may be useful in identifying potential asset bubbles.

Following the risk off-balance sheet. The US financial institutions are regulated piecemeal. This system avoids excessive concentration of regulatory power and provides avenues of regulatory competition: regulators who regulate efficiently can be rewarded. However, the system has weaknesses. One is that regulated financial entities may shop for weak regulators and, by choosing the most complaisant regulator, weaken the system as a whole. Another is that financial activities and instruments may be created or moved outside the purview of regulation.

A financial asset such as a mortgage can be created within a tightly regulated financial entity, such as a commercial bank, or a loosely regulated one, such as a mortgage subsidiary or a freestanding mortgage company. The regulatory treatment of the mortgage may depend on the form in which it is held. For example, the AAA tranche of a collateralized debt obligation may have much lower regulatory capital requirements than a mortgage loan held in portfolio. Depending on the relevant costs and benefits of the regulatory treatments and the risks of the assets, the form in which the asset is held may change, and this form may have little to do with underlying economic efficiency.

A mortgage asset can be moved off the originator's balance sheet by placing it in a separate legal entity, such as a special investment vehicle or an entity that issues asset-backed commercial paper. This vehicle may reproduce the characteristics of a financial intermediary, by issuing short-term liabilities that are money-like while it holds long-term instruments that are subject to some risk. These entities generally have standby lines of credit issued by the financial intermediary. If the entity's asset risk increases, the holders of its short-term liabilities may refuse to roll over the debt, creating a run on the entity and a drawdown on the standby line of credit. Thus, the risks from the vehicle can be easily transferred to the financial intermediary, while the capital of the financial intermediary may be inadequate, since these assets and liabilities were not on its books. The risks and consequences of asset-backed commercial paper are documented in Covitz et al. (2013).

This and other examples of the creation of a "shadow banking" system point out the value to financial regulators of continuing to monitor financial assets after they are removed from the balance sheets of closely regulated financial intermediaries. Note that such a system would permit innovation—it would not block new institutions or new instruments from arising. Rather, it would seek to monitor these novelties and perhaps bring them under regulation if they reach systemic importance.

As the case of AIG illustrates, the migration of systemic risk to a lightly regulated or unregulated entity contains the seeds of systemic financial crisis. To contain the 2007–2009 financial crisis, the regulatory process would have had to identify that AIG was a systemic risk, ascertain the quantitative scale of those risks, and bring AIG under greater regulatory discipline, including preparing a means for unwinding AIG with minimal systemic risk.

In their article on the central role of the repo market in the recent financial crisis, Gorton and Metrick (2012) are able to analyze the risks to that market posed by lightly regulated and unregulated cash pools and highlight the danger of regulators relying exclusively on data from regulated institutions. Adrian et al. (2014) discuss the mechanics of the market and data needs for adequate monitoring.

Opacity. An important aspect of the recent financial crisis was that many financial institutions themselves lost track of the total real estate exposure of their portfolios. This reflected, in part, the fact that regulation created incentives for opacity. To reduce capital requirements, an institution may change an instrument from a loan to one or more securities that it continues to hold, although no risk has been transferred. The resulting increase in opacity may cause an institution to lose track of its true vulnerabilities.

If financial instruments are opaque to the financial institution holding them, then they must be even more opaque to a regulator. To the extent that instruments can be finely categorized and characterized, and their risks more precisely measured, both regulators and internal risk monitors at financial institutions will be better able to avoid crises. Steps to reduce opacity are being taken to the extent that customized instruments that are not exchange traded will have higher risk capital requirements. To the extent that instruments are exchange traded, they will be easier to categorize and quantify, and measuring their risk will be easier.

To the extent that financial instruments and securities based on them are priced on exchanges, similar customized instruments and securities may be evaluated and priced based on a model of the values of their financial characteristics. When trades or acquisitions of such assets are observed, the quality of the mark-to-model pricing may be verified.

Derivative trading is also being made more transparent through creating risk penalties for derivaties that are not exchange traded. Derivatives are another avenue for both opacity and for transfer of risk; Acharya (2014) discusses the value of regulatory and public disclosure of derivative trading.

Following the full life cycle of instrument creation, distribution, and servic-

ing. There are many facets to the creation and maintenance of financial instruments. The characteristics of the financial instrument may be influenced by many institutions and agents. Actions of one set of agents may affect instruments so as to exacerbate systemic vulnerabilities. In the losses associated with the recent financial crisis, the actions of a panoply of agents were at work in increasing the risk of mortgages. The severity of the risks of real estate finance might have been recognized earlier if regulators had been more aware of changes taking place across a variety of institutions.

The risks of mortgages were compounded because a number of the agents were subject to uncorrected weaknesses, many of them well recognized by relevant players. For example, persistent and significant upward bias in home appraisals was recognized as early as the mid-1990s (Cho and Megbolugbe 1996). According to this analysis, some 95 percent of home purchase mortgages in the Fannie Mae mortgage database had appraisals at or above the sale price. Having been recognized, this bias was tracked through automated valuation models (AVMs) by Fannie Mae and Freddie Mac. It was well known among those actively using these AVMs that these biases were particularly strong for refinancing and for subprime lending. However, these biases were not widely known or understood outside this circle. In particular, many regulators were not aware of the risks thereby posed to mortgage refinancing, since upward appraisal bias resulted in understated loan-to-value ratios.

Upward biases in refinance appraisals would have the consequence of allowing homeowners to refinance with too small a cushion against the risk of home price decline. Unfortunately, the databases of the government-sponsored enterprises have not been available for study by academics; their information has been considered the intellectual property of these entities. The losses at these entities—which perhaps might have been mitigated if scholars and regulators had had better access to these databases—have far exceeded the value of the intellectual property of these entities. Moreover, it is by no means obvious that these entities should have exclusive rights to the data generated by government sponsorship.

Microdata have been used to analyze changes in subprime mortgage lending standards (Demyanyk and Van Hemert 2011; Brueckner, Calem, and Nakamura 2012), the behavior of securitizers (Elul 2009), and the behavior of mortgage brokers (Garmaise 2008; Keys et al. 2009).

Demyanyk and Van Hemert (2011) found that subprime mortgage lending standards—as measured ex post by delinquencies and foreclosures—deteriorated monotonically from 2001 to 2006. The decline in lending standards is revealed in differential performance rates detectable within a year of origination. However, aggregate default rates were somewhat masked by the rise of housing prices from 2003 to 2005. Brueckner, Calem, and Nakamura (2012) show that house price inflation momentum tended to drive the decline in lending standards in a vicious cycle in which house price inflation reduced the risk to mortgage lenders, who then reduced lending standards at the local level, and thus widened the effective demand for housing and further inflated house prices.

Elul (2009) finds that prime mortgage loans that were securitized were of lower quality than loans that were held in portfolio. He does not find a similar effect for subprime loans, but the vast majority of subprime loans were intended for securitization.

Garmaise (2008) presents evidence that mortgage brokers' lending standards deteriorated over time so that experienced mortgage brokers' loans performed worse. Keys et al. (2009) show that states with stricter regulation of mortgage brokers had better performing subprime loans.

We use these examples to illustrate the types of data that could have permitted regulators to detect changes in the risks of mortgages. That, in turn, we are arguing, could have resulted in an earlier and more appropriately calibrated response to the impending crisis.

Financial regulators and academic financial researchers are now assembling microdata sets for forensic reasons, to attempt to understand the causes, consequences, and the scale of the financial crisis. However, it is widely recognized that the data collected to date have serious weaknesses. In particular, commercial databases often have crucial identifiers missing or encoded so that associating observations across data sets has been difficult or impossible. In addition, financial institutions, servicers, and other parties whom the systemic regulator needs to be able to identify are often contractually anonymous within these databases. Permitting the database to obtain these identifiers may require regulatory action or possibly legislation.

In addition, certain agency problems appear to have worsened significantly as time passed. The rise of mortgages with very high combined (reported) loan-to-value ratios (100 percent or higher) was another warning sign of difficulties. These data were partially available in, for example, Loan-Performance microdata sets on second mortgages based on information gathered from mortgage servicers. But it was often difficult for the holders of first mortgage portfolios to know the extent to which second liens had made their mortgage assets riskier.

Systemic risk pricing in the market. Economic theory suggests that financial payoffs that will occur when the marginal utility of consumption is high have a greater present value than payoffs in periods when the marginal utility of consumption is low. Systemic risks involve low payoffs in bad economic states, when the marginal utility of consumption is high. Instruments with embedded systemic risks thus have lower value and require compensatingly higher rates of return in equilibrium.

Coval et al. (2009b) have pointed out that structured finance created strong incentives to concentrate systemic risks in financial instruments that otherwise were of very low risk. These financial instruments had inherently high expected returns because of the risks involved. As long as the systemic risks did not emerge, such instruments had a high rate of return and appeared to be earning excess returns. Coval et al. (2009a) then go on to develop a pricing kernel for structured finance instruments that have little idiosyncratic risk but high systemic risk and argue that, in fact, such economic catastrophe bonds that were issued in the period just before the financial crisis were overpriced. In this case, bonds appeared to be paying a high rate of return and thus represented a financial arbitrage opportunity with positive excess return, but in fact, they had a negative excess return and were fundamentally loss making to the holders.

These two papers show how data on financial instruments can reveal the existence of systemic risk and may be of help to regulators in requiring the holders of such assets to hold higher capital, offsetting the apparent reward to holding these assets. To the extent that the systemic regulator is held responsible for minimizing the likelihood of a systemic crisis, a paradox arises. As the likelihood of systemic risk declines, the price of holding the systemic risk will fall. This in turn encourages the creation of more instruments of this type, until a systemic crisis does occur. The consequence may be that the crisis, when it occurs, may be surprisingly large. Maintaining a watch over this potential dynamic will be an important task of the systemic regulator.

Engaging a broader and more objective community in monitoring. To the extent consistent with privacy considerations, permitting academics and investment advisors to access and analyze the financial database would enhance the capacity to identify cyclic and systemic risks within the US financial structure.

This broader community can bring new insights from financial research to bear on these issues and also offer a counterweight to the authority of the private financial institutions. One of the difficulties regulators have faced in the recent period is that employees at private financial institutions have been compensated on a scale with which public authorities cannot hope to compete. While higher compensation may not strictly imply higher marginal product, the possibility that it does so may cause less-well-paid regulators to sometimes defer to the judgment of extremely well-paid regulatees. (Indeed, part of the Basel II structure was constructed on the assumption that complex financial institutions were better positioned to measure their own risks compared with outside regulators.)

Moreover, internal risk managers are often in a similarly weak position, as risk management is a cost center, while the departments creating the risks are profit centers that can richly reward their employees. The regulatory database can provide empirical models of risk that enable bank supervisors and internal risk managers to more aggressively challenge the views of risk takers.

By opening up the measurement of risk in the financial database to a wider group, regulatory risk measurement can be done at the frontier of financial science. Indeed, the systemic regulator could have built into its structure a research steering group composed of leading academic experts, as well as funding for grants and conferences to identify the structure of risks underlying the database. In addition, if the systemic regulator should hire a full-time staff of research economists to undertake financial risk studies, this might well help in identifying data shortcomings, as these researchers would gain privileged, hands-on views of the data. If that knowledge can be freely shared with regulators, the regulators could ask the financial institutions originating the data to improve their data management processes as needed.

One potentially important first research task of the systemic regulator could be a full quantitative accounting of the sources of the financial crisis. One possibility would be to set up a contest for the best paper providing such a full quantitative accounting, to be judged by a prestigious academic panel with the reward being a substantial sum (say, $1 million). The academic panel could also be charged with assessing the weaknesses of the best paper, and additional, smaller awards would be given to subsequent papers that eliminated these shortcomings.

Counterparty risk and systemic stress testing. Simulating the impact of systemic risks on the financial system would be greatly facilitated by a clear view of which financial institutions are holding which financial instruments.

In a financial crisis, the identification of counterparty exposure comes to the fore. However, in the current complex financial environment, counterparty exposure has become far from transparent. Large complex financial institutions have hundreds, even thousands, of subsidiary institutions. Thus, in the recent crisis, financial institutions considering the possibility of a default by some threatened bankruptcy were unable to accurately estimate the size of their exposures. This is a problem that large financial institutions are now very aware of, and steps are being taken to link subsidiaries to their parents through institutional identifiers. A unique registry of legal entity identifiers is in the process of being adopted internationally—these will permit regulators and financial entities to identify the parties to a transaction with much greater certainty.[1]

More broadly, while tools for mapping the dynamic conditional correlations across financial instruments are being rapidly developed (e.g., Engle 2009), these correlations are being traced out by trades made by agents who themselves typically lack detailed knowledge of the dynamic interrelations of financial institutions. An important task of the systemic regulator will be to understand the volatile pattern of institutional relationships, as they are revealed in quarterly or daily snapshots of institutional cross-exposure.

Addressing bubble-like risks. The identification of financial bubbles remains a difficult art. It is often impossible to clearly identify a bubble in

1. More information about the international efforts to implement legal entity identifiers can be found at http://www.financialstabilityboard.org/publications/r_120608.pdf.

advance. While we can identify key historical ratios between measures of price and measures of return, for example, and historical mean-reverting relationships, it is very difficult to be sure that a structural change has not occurred. However, it is relatively easy to model the possibility that a bubble has been created and the consequences of the bubble bursting; that is, we can assume that historical averages will be maintained and that reversion to the mean occurs over some short period of time. For housing, ratios of rents to house prices appear to display a long-run equilibrium relationship that can be and was used to scale the likely size of the mean reversion—a relationship documented by Gallin (2008) and by Crone, Nakamura, and Voith (2010). We can then perform stress simulations under such scenarios using the database. These simulations could then be brought to the relevant financial regulators and internal risk monitors, and perhaps to Congress, if additional statutory authority appears necessary.

Such simulations are instructive stress tests in that the case of no structural change is hard to rule out, so placing very low weight on this case is generally unconvincing. In addition, outside researchers could be allowed to (or be paid to) conduct their own simulations, offering useful alternative scenarios to regulators.

3.3   Expanding the Flow of Funds Framework: The Macro Side of the Database

The macro side of the database helps regulators know, for example, which types of financial institutions are funding a given financial instrument. Because the totality of such transactions is so vast and variegated, it is vital to have an intellectual framework for organizing and aggregating them. I argue that the Flow of Funds Accounts provide such an intellectual framework.[2] Eichner, Kohn, and Palumbo (chapter 2) argue a similar point about the US-SNA, the overarching framework that encompasses the Flow of Funds and the National Income and Product Accounts.

How can we use the Flow of Funds Accounts as a framework for the envisioned database? Most fundamentally, the Flow of Funds Accounts provides an accounting framework that includes all the assets and liabilities of nonfinancial and financial institutions. The Flow of Funds (a part of the system of financial accounts that is compiled by the Federal Reserve System) establishes a framework that accounts for the financial assets and liabilities of all US parties (including households, nonprofits, firms, governments, and the rest of the world).[3] Furthermore, the Flow of Funds has a

2. An online guide to the Flow of Funds Accounts can be found at http://www.federalreserve.gov/apps/fof/. Additional detail on the housing finance accounts can be found at http://www.federalreserve.gov/releases/z1/about/kennedy-fof-20120628.pdf.
3. For a description of the Flow of Funds and its relationship to the national accounts, see Bond et al. (2007). Further discussion is in Teplin et al. (2006) and in Yamashita (2013).

fluid conceptual framework that can be expanded to reflect derivative and synthetic instruments. The US Flow of Funds is tied to the US National Accounts; individual sectors borrow and lend because of the national, sectoral, and individual imbalances between saving and investment. To the extent that financial instrument risk is tied to agents, sectors, and markets, this framework facilitates the economic analysis of risk.

Similar to the national income accounts, the Flow of Funds Accounts framework can accommodate a series of satellite accounts to extend the value of the framework. These, some of which are discussed below, could include mark-to-market or mark-to-model pricing, agents behind the scenes (such as exchanges and rating agencies), and measures of risk. Finally, the microdatabases and statistics that underlie the aggregate measures could be associated with the Flow of Funds as a linked library, in which the aggregate categories of the Flow of Funds organize the microdata as a set of reference headings.

The US Flow of Funds Accounts has two intimately related parts. One part is a set of flows representing net new borrowing and lending, and the other is a set of outstanding stocks of assets and liabilities.[4] These are presented as aggregates by sector (lenders and borrowers, such as banks, households, governments, and corporations) and by instrument (equity, mortgages, loans, commercial paper, consumer credit, and securities).

The Flow of Funds reflect the financial assets and liabilities and the financial activities of both financial and nonfinancial entities in the United States. It thus provides a natural framework from which a systemic regulator could observe the types of risks distributed across the financial system.

The first column in table 3.1 shows the credit market borrowing by nonfinancial sectors in 2008, taken from the Flow of Funds, Annual Flows, as published June 11, 2009. In this table, borrowings are organized by instrument, such as commercial paper and home mortgages, and by sector, such as household sector and nonfinancial corporate business. The table also shows borrowings by foreigners. The second and third columns show the debt levels owed by the nonfinancial sectors for the same instruments and sectors at year-end 2007 and 2008. Adding column one to column two gives column three; the net borrowing flow during 2008 added to the level of debt at the end of 2007 gives the level of debt at the end of 2008. Other summary tables in the Flow of Funds Accounts, not presented here, show financial sector borrowing and total liabilities and their relationship to total financial assets. Yet others relate the Flow of Funds to national savings and investment and the national income accounts.

---

4. The quarterly net flows are defined to be the difference in the quarterly level of outstanding stocks. In practice, however, the Flow of Funds Accounts levels are not always consistent and contain breaks resulting from incomplete or inconsistent underlying data. When there is a break, the quarterly flow is defined as the flow associated with a consistently defined level and may not be equal to the reported difference between quarterly levels.

Table 3.1   Credit market borrowing and debt owed by nonfinancial sectors, 2007 and 2008 (billions of dollars)

Annual flows and levels Tables F.2 and L.2	(1) Net borrowing 2008	(2) Year-end debt 2007	(3) Year-end debt 2008
Domestic	1,873.2	31,707.1	33,580.3
By instrument	1,873.2	31,707.1	33,580.3
Commercial paper	7.7	123.8	131.5
Treasury securities	1,239.0	5,099.2	6,338.2
Agency and GSE-backed securities	0.2	23.1	23.3
Municipal securities	63.2	2,618.9	2,682.1
Corporate bonds	204.6	3,558.9	3,763.5
Bank loans, n.e.c.	195.2	1,648.9	1,844.1
Other loans and advances	62.0	1,674.5	1,736.6
Mortgages	57.3	14,407.8	14,465.1
Home	−109.0	11,137.2	11,036.6
Multifamily residential	53.8	820.0	878.2
Commercial	109.3	2,342.8	2,439.2
Farm	3.3	107.8	111.1
Consumer Credit	44.0	2,551.9	2,595.9
By sector	1,873.2	31,707.1	33,580.3
Household sector	49.5	13,778.4	13,832.9
Nonfinancial business	544.1	10,614.5	11,153.7
Corporate	362.6	6,809.3	7,167.0
Nonfarm, noncorporate	170.2	3,591.2	3,761.4
Farm	11.3	214.0	225.3
State and local government	40.4	2,191.8	2,232.2
Federal government	1,239.2	5,122.3	6,361.5
Foreign credit market debt held in United States	−152.1	2,017.3	1,864.9
Commercial paper	−71.0	413.0	342.0
Bonds	−84.7	1,478.1	1,393.4
Bank loans n.e.c.	5.1	102.8	107.9
Other loans and advances	−1.6	23.4	21.5
Domestic and foreign	1,721.1	33,724.4	35,445.2

Through its ties to the National Income and Product Accounts, the Flow of Funds Accounts obtain a benchmark measure of the total borrowing and lending by a given sector necessary to balance net cash flows. This provides an indirect estimate of the completeness of direct measures of total borrowing and lending.

The efficiency of the borrowing and lending of the nonfinancial sector provides a prime economic rationale for the activities of the financial sector. An important rationale for systemic regulation is to ensure this two-way flow of financial transactions. It is of fundamental importance that the financial transactions of the nonfinancial sector come under the scrutiny of the systemic regulator. Table 3.1 presents a compact view of the total borrowing of the nonfinancial sector from the Flow of Funds Accounts, year-end 2007 and 2008.

Less aggregated tables in the Flow of Funds—as of this writing there are thirty-one sector tables and thirty-one instrument tables—show holdings of instruments by different sectors. In short, the Flow of Funds relates instruments to the assets and liabilities of institutions. The assets and liabilities of each individual agent are naturally organized within this flow of funds framework. Moreover, the databases in which samples or the universe of agent outstandings or flows are captured naturally map into this framework as well. For example, if an agency is using samples of a credit bureau's data on individuals and households, this database can be mapped into and benchmarked with the household balance sheet from the Flow of Funds Accounts.

3.4 What the Existing US Flow of Funds Accounts Lack: Creating an Expanded Framework with Satellite Accounts

In many cases, the existing US Flow of Funds Accounts lack crucial detail that would have been helpful to know during the financial crisis. For example, an important question was: Which sectors were holding the nonagency jumbo and subprime securitized mortgages? The table on residential mortgages does have an entry that shows the total quantity of home mortgages that were the assets of ABS issuers—nonagency pools of $2.2 trillion in 2007 (table L.218). However, the table on Issuers of Asset-Backed Securities (L.124) lists their assets as $4.5 trillion (including credit cards, commercial mortgages, and agency and GSE-backed securities) and lists liabilities divided into commercial paper ($0.6 trillion) and corporate bonds ($3.9 trillion). Corporate bonds are also in table L.212, Corporate and Foreign Bonds, which shows the holders of $11.4 trillion of bonds, of which $2.2 trillion are nonagency ABS. There, we can find the various sectors that hold corporate and foreign bonds, but we do not know which sectors are holding nonagency ABS. One significant exception is the account for US-chartered commercial banks, which divides corporate and foreign bonds into (1) private mortgage pass-through securities, (2) CMOs and other structured MBS, and (3) other. This allows us to see that banks and thrifts were holding about one-quarter of the nonagency ABS, while they held only 10 percent of other corporate and foreign bonds. But the other nonagency ABS holders could not be easily identified from the Flow of Funds Accounts, so it was difficult for regulators to estimate whether other holders of nonagency ABS posed a threat to financial stability—as it turned out, they did.

Satellite Accounts. National income accounts can be expanded in ways that may not easily be accommodated into the complete framework. For example, if quarterly data are not available for a set of statistics, or if, say, prices are not available, then a satellite account can be created. Similarly, it would be useful for an expanded macro-micro financial database to have a number of satellite accounts.

Net financial flows could be further decomposed into the sum of gross new originations, repayments, defaults, and revaluations, but these subelements are not shown separately within the Flow of Funds Accounts.[5] From a regulatory perspective, it would be preferable to track these subcomponents, particularly for longer-term debt. Doing so would facilitate tracking instruments by vintage and would also contribute to data quality. It would also help macroprudential supervisors, for example, to see to what extent nonfinancial balance sheets are being repaired through saving and to what extent through defaults. Gross flows may be tracked by and matched with microdata sets on loan originations, including regulatory data sets such as the Home Mortgage Disclosure Act (HMDA) data, financial industry data such as Fannie Mae and Freddie Mac data sets on agency securitizations or daily data on market transactions, and data collected by statistical agencies.

The aggregate stocks and the US Flow of Funds assets and liabilities could be matched with microdata on households (credit bureau, statistical agencies, regulatory data) and firms (Compustat, call reports, statistical agencies, SEC filings, Survey of Terms of Bank Lending). The matching of the aggregate statistics with historical and current microdata would permit regulators to examine the default risks associated with financial instruments as they evolve. Having measured variances and covariances of financial instruments, the systemic regulator can use the augmented Flow of Funds to identify the sectors in which the risks associated with the financial instruments are lodged. In turn, the microdata will aid the systemic regulator in examining the sectors and observing the distribution of risks across financial firms.

Another important satellite account would have prices. The national accounts framework can accommodate valuation changes, but the US National Income Accounts, by their very nature, capture flows of production and not capital gains. Similarly, the US Flow of Funds Accounts primarily carries assets and liabilities at nominal book value. For risk analysis, it is highly desirable to have the mark-to-market prices for exchange-traded instruments. It would also be useful to be able to mark-to-model instruments that are not frequently traded.

It is crucial for the systemic regulator to have a broad picture of the risks of the set of financial instruments and their consequences for the system of financial institutions. To support the database, one aspect of the new regulatory structure could be a requirement that financial institutions—regardless of their direct regulator—provide information to the systemic regulator to facilitate construction of the database. Indeed, the regulatory structure should have the provision of such information as part of the transparency requirement of all financial regulation. One example of missing data is the

---

5. Morris Mendelson (1962) and Edward Denison (1962) provide some useful early discussion of the difficulties and value of decomposing net flows in the Flow of Funds Accounts.

portfolios of hedge funds; these are not shown in the Flow of Funds separately because of a lack of data and are implicitly included in households. The US (and the worldwide) financial system is in constant flux due to innovations in the world economy and to financial innovations. Undeniably, many of these financial innovations have reduced the transactions and information costs associated with borrowing and lending and thus have improved the efficiency of consumption and investment. However, financial market participants, left to pursue their private interests, will not take fully into account the knock-on effects of their actions on others. In particular, financial markets include both sophisticated and unsophisticated borrowers and lenders and informed and uninformed borrowers and lenders. The information asymmetries have their beneficial aspect—it is valuable to have specialization. But financial agents may be tempted to use these information asymmetries for private, inefficient gain.[6] This is the motivation for regulation, which creates an ongoing temptation to escape regulatory burden. Profit-maximizing financial innovation can create socially desirable efficiencies, or it can be a socially undesirable means of evading regulatory constraints.

Financial regulators are typically called on to regulate financial institutions that are the sites of existing financial activity. New financial instruments and institutions may evolve outside the scope of regulation. By creating an evolving financial monitoring framework, regulatory agencies can bring these new instruments and institutions into view and, as necessary, under the regulatory umbrella. In particular, this monitoring system may limit the creation of unregulated intermediaries that pose systemic risk and whose rescue might become necessary in a financial crisis. For example, if an investment vehicle has assets that carry systemic risk (identifiable by covariance and possibly excess return) and short-term liabilities (e.g., AA commercial paper), then the investment vehicle prima facie is liable to runs and may transmit systemic risk to regulated entities if those regulated entities provide back-up lines of credit and/or credit risk insurance (Acharya and Richardson 2009). If the new combination of instruments reduces capital requirements, then capital requirements for the new entities may need to be increased. Another valuable step would be to require that whenever risk is removed from a regulated financial institution's balance sheet, that institution should be responsible for informing the systemic regulator of the counterparty that has taken on the risk. Such notification could have revealed to regulators the buildup of systemic risk at AIG's United Kingdom offices.

One concern about setting up a financial regulatory database is the increasingly global nature of finance. Debts originated in one country can

---

6. In taking advantage of these information asymmetries, the agents may not be aware that they are not acting in the interests of the principals. As we shall see, agents who took advantage of the apparent gains from holding "economic catastrophe" bonds may have thought they were simply doing efficient arbitrage between mispriced instruments.

be held on the other side of the world. Can we keep track of enough US financial assets to make a difference, beginning with US financial borrowings? Fortunately, the US financial structure is unusual in that a substantial proportion of US financial liabilities are held abroad (15 percent, 2008 year end), but only a relatively small proportion of US financial assets are owed by the rest of the world (4 percent, 2008). As seen in table 3.1, of the $35.4 trillion owed by the nonfinancial sector, only $1.9 trillion is owed by foreigners. Thus, most of the nonfinancial holdings of the US financial system can be understood based on microdata from US entities. This means that as a first approximation, financial instruments originating in the United States would be a reasonable starting point for understanding US nonfinancial risks. It would be of value, of course, if other countries carried out similar efforts to expand this macro-micro database across the globe. Other countries' financial regulatory databases can perhaps be more easily built once the US financial regulatory database is in place.

3.5   Drilling beneath the Flow of Funds Accounts to the Microdatabase

We envision a microdatabase that is attached to the Flow of Funds Accounts and its satellite accounts. Ideally, clicking on a given cell in the Flow of Funds Macro Accounts would reveal the underlying microdata that are used to create the aggregate, as well as databases linked to this primary sampling data. The Flow of Funds section of the Federal Reserve has already developed a prototype system for showing the data source for all the cells of the Flow of Funds Accounts. As these data sources themselves are typically based on microdata surveys, this is a first step in the direction we envision.

The microdata part of the database could be built up with existing databases, including existing academic, government, and commercial databases (e.g., CRSP, Compustat, LoanPerformance, Equifax, call reports, HMDA, Quarterly Terms of Bank Lending, Shared National Credit, Census, IRS, Fannie Mae and Freddie Mac), and data from existing depositories, exchanges, and registries (e.g., Depository Trust and Clearing Corporation, Federal Reserve Depository).

These databases collectively show that it is feasible to collect data and to aggregate them along a variety of dimensions. For existing databases, as argued above, each could be mapped to corresponding entries in the Flow of Funds Accounts.[7] For example, a microdata set of credit bureau data on households could be viewed as a sample of the universe of households, and the entries used to estimate the universe. The estimate of total mortgages could then be compared against the estimate of total mortgage borrowing by households in the Flow of Funds. Doing this across data sets will result

---

7. Begenau, Piazzesi, and Schneider (2014) discuss performing this mapping as well as concrete measures that can be used to summarize the microdata.

in a more reliable aggregate estimate of household mortgage borrowing and will allow researchers and decision makers to see relatively transparently how representative a given microdata set is and, therefore, how trustworthy results from analysis of the microdata are likely to be.

Record Linkage. A key improvement to these databases could be automated record linkage. The econometric studies discussed in section 3.2 rely on the econometrician's ability to track instruments and agents across data sets and over time, known generically as record linkage. There are now relatively standard computational techniques for optimizing record linkage (Herzog, Scheuren, and Winkler 2007), but these techniques have not been used in economic and financial studies.

For example, a mortgage origination in a credit bureau's data on a given household will permit the identification of other mortgages held by the same household, and thus may help to reveal the possibility that the home is actually a speculative investment and therefore its mortgage is not for an owner-occupied residence. However, to follow the ongoing current loan-to-value ratio of the mortgage, a key element in the evaluation of the credit risk of the mortgage, requires knowing the location of the home and home price inflation at that location since purchase, with a link to the local home price index. Depending on the regulator's concerns, it may be useful to know the broker, the appraisal value, the interest rate on the mortgage, the originator, whether the mortgage is held in portfolio or securitized, and the servicer. Each of these may be available from a different data set or within the same data set at a different point in time. Establishing procedures to automate these linkages would be of value to regulators and would facilitate new and updated econometric analyses of risks.

If individual financial instruments are given unique identifiers so that they can be linked from data set to data set, that would clearly facilitate cross-checks in financial monitoring. The CUSIP numbers (the American Bankers Association numbering system) perform this service for many financial instruments. A consistent form of instrument identification would be of aid to the financial industry itself, which would be better able to merge portfolios (as a consequence of mergers and acquisitions) while retaining a deep understanding of their characteristics. Linking permanent identifiers to financial instrument characteristics will facilitate bottom-up analysis of portfolios and permit complex stress test simulations. Establishment of a set of unique identifiers has apparently been hampered by coordination issues; in this situation, regulators can take a strong stance in favor of implementation and benefit both regulation and private parties.

All financial instruments that represent direct claims against nonfinancial institutions—firms, households, or other legal entities such as governments—could be registered, provided with a unique identifier, and accompanied by summary data on its characteristics, such as its legal form, the issuer or debtor, type of debt or equity, and so forth. These financial instruments are the fundamental financial instruments; their provision is an important rationale for concern about systemic risk. The summary data could be coded in a uniform system, following the experience of database providers and depositories. The American Securitization Forum's ASF LINC (Loan Identification Number Code) is a mechanism that seeks to provide unique identifiers for mortgages, credit cards, auto loans, and other retail debt. These unique identifiers would be linked to a database that would have characteristics of the instrument. The Enterprise Data Management Council, with the support of the financial industry and data management firms, has taken important steps toward developing a system that codes a wide variety of financial instruments, fundamental and otherwise.

A crucial step is to see where microdata are not yet available; in particular, it would be valuable to map out areas where the Flow of Funds aggregate data rely on estimates or where the underlying data are inadequately reported. For example, repo data are reported on a net basis rather than on a gross basis (Eichner, Kohn, and Palumbo, chapter 2).

To provide more transparency, it would be desirable to map the microdata geographically, to the extent possible. In the absence of unique identifiers and with data where identities of lender and borrower have been scrubbed, much can still be learned by associating microdata geographically. It is often possible for data managers to match, say, mortgage performance to credit ratings across data sets while maintaining anonymity of the underlying individuals. Even if that is not the goal or not possible, missing data (such as income in credit bureau data) can be usefully estimated using geography together with geocoded census information. To the extent that geocoded microdata can be obtained, this information provides a more detailed crosscheck on the accuracy and quality of data.

Measures of the quality of the data, both for aggregate estimates and for the microdata, could be integrated into metadata provided as a standard feature of the database. Quarterly vintages of the data, once vetted, could be archived, to create a real-time database.

One efficient form for gathering microdata is presented by the US Survey of Terms of Bank Lending, a quarterly survey that collects information on all loans granted by the surveyed banks in the first week in the middle month of each quarter. The survey draws voluntary responses on 30 to 40 thousand loans from 648 banks and, according to the Office of Management and Budget's Information Collection Review, requires 6,840 annual burden hours from respondents. (A limitation of this survey is that it collects information on loans only at origination and does not follow them over time.) Another efficient alternative may be to have a third-party registry collect data on financial instruments as the Depository Trust and Clearing Corporation does. Third-party vendors are also efficient providers of data; servicer data—for example, the First American LoanPerformance mortgage and home equity loan data sets—are another efficient way to collect data.

It should also be noted that sampled loan data are routinely used as part of bank examinations in the United States; the systematic compilation of loan data may impose little additional burden on banks.

An interesting pioneering step has been taken by the Sveriges Riksbank, the Swedish central bank, in collecting microdata on loans at Swedish banks together with credit bureau information. This data collection is discussed in Jacobson, Linde, and Roszbach (2006). Nakamura and Roszbach (2010) provide a methodology for comparing the quality of bank loan ratings to credit bureau ratings using this data set.

Another valuable and efficient regulatory data set is the US Shared National Credit. This covers all syndicated loans and loan commitments of more than $20 million that are shared pro rata across three or more unaffiliated federally supervised institutions—in all, $2.9 trillion in committed funds as of the end of 2009. This data set includes all the institutions holding the loans and the internal loan ratings of the supervised institutions. As Avery et al. (2014) demonstrate, the data can be used to evaluate the quality of bank loan monitoring and thus is a valuable adjunct to bank examination. Moreover, syndicated loans are risks that are shared across financial institutions and thereby provide direct estimates of systemic risk factors.

Derivative securities, including derivatives, options, exchange-traded funds, asset-backed securities, and the like should be provided with unique identifiers and accompanied with summary data on the fundamental financial instruments to which the derivative security is linked. As mentioned before, the Enterprise Data Management Council has been taking important steps in developing methodologies and semantics for these tasks.

Some difficult questions arise from intellectual property in databases and in unique identifiers. Private third-party collection of databases is an efficient method of collecting and organizing data. These databases, moreover, have the advantage of having already been created, so that their creation is a sunk cost and their profitability makes it likely that the data will be collected moving forward. However, such data have drawbacks as well. First, the databases are expensive, and regulatory use of the data, by validating them, may make them more valuable. Second, key attributes of the data—such as the entity providing the data—may not be available to the users of the database as a condition of the entity's participation. Third, the licenses to use the databases that are purchased typically come with restrictions on how the data may be used and shared. If regulators are to view these third-party vendors as providing a conduit by which a regulated entity fulfills part of its data-reporting requirements, then it would appear natural that some of these license restrictions should be annulled. And the databases could be required to be made available to the regulator on a marginal cost basis.

Regulated financial institutions that hold, acquire, or sell financial instruments or derivatives as assets could be required to ensure that the financial monitor is provided with quarterly information on the current holder of these assets and the current status of the instrument. Fulfilling this requirement would be facilitated by the use of depositories and exchanges. As time passes, the data received quarterly will become a historical microdatabase.

3.6   Access to the Data

Access to the microdata supporting the financial monitoring database would be made available to the staff of the financial monitor and to other regulators. It might also be made available to academic and government specialists who wish to use the data to make studies of risk characteristics of the instruments and of the holders of the instruments. Such studies would be made public, with public data screened for confidentiality, and would also be made available to financial regulators.

An academic advisory board composed of leading financial and economic professors and researchers could be established to advise the financial monitor and the regulatory community about the advisability of extensions to data collection and of extensions of regulation to additional institutions that are potential sources of systemic risk.

The academic advisory board could also designate studies to be conducted to measure alternative aspects of systemic risk. This would naturally be accompanied by open access of the database (conditional on strict confidentiality) to academic researchers who wish to investigate questions related to systemic risk. Finally, the systemic regulator could have a substantial research department of economic and finance researchers of the highest academic quality. This research department could devote most of its time to frontier research on finance and economics and also conduct policy studies on systemic risk. Having access to the database will help the research department attract top researchers.

These researchers would, as a byproduct of their research, analyze the quality of the data being supplied by regulated financial intermediaries and other data providers. It might be useful for the database office or the analytical group to have the authority and the responsibility to monitor the quality of the data. The systemic regulator and other regulators could be empowered to require that regulated financial intermediaries maintain high-quality data. This would help ensure that regulators and internal risk managers have access to the information they need to provide high-quality analysis.

3.7   Summary

I have discussed how to assemble and maintain a database of financial instruments and derivatives with both macro- and microcomponents. Such a database would have been of material aid to regulators and to financial institutions in measuring the accumulating risks that led up to the financial crisis of 2007–2009, and it would be designed to be of aid in enabling regulators to anticipate and mitigate future financial crises.

The US Office of Financial Research will have the authority to obtain data from financial institutions. An important element of this would be requiring that individual financial instruments and institutions have unique identifiers linked to machine-readable contract characteristics. The office could be responsible for establishing quality standards for the data obtained and would advise financial institution supervisors when institutions were failing to live up to those standards. It would be desirable from the standpoint of monitoring systemic risk to establish readily usable links across these data sets, a process that would be facilitated by efforts currently underway to standardize identifiers for instruments and entities, and to provide machine-readable contractual terms. It would also be useful in the long run to establish data links and methods to create accessible archival data that could be accessed from multiple secure data centers.

References

Acharya, Viral V. 2014. "A Transparency Standard for Derivatives." In *Risk Topography: Systemic Risk and Macro Modeling*, edited by Markus K. Brunnermeier and Arvind Krishnamurthy. Chicago: University of Chicago Press.

Acharya, Viral V., and Matthew Richardson, eds. 2009. *Restoring Financial Stability: How to Repair a Failed System*. New York: NYU Stern School of Business.

Adrian, Tobias, Brian Begalle, Adam Copeland, and Antoine Martin. 2014. "Repo and Securities Lending." In *Risk Topography: Systemic Risk and Macro Modeling*, edited by Markus K. Brunnermeier and Arvind Krishnamurthy. Chicago: University of Chicago Press.

Avery, Robert, Lewis Gaul, Leonard Nakamura, and Douglas Robertson. 2014. "Measuring the Quality of Bank Loan Monitoring: Evidence from US Syndicated Loans." Working Paper, Federal Reserve Bank of Philadelphia.

Begenau, Juliane, Monika Piazzesi, and Martin Schneider. 2014. "Remapping the Flow of Funds." In *Risk Topography: Systemic Risk and Macro Modeling*, edited by Markus K. Brunnermeier and Arvind Krishnamurthy. Chicago: University of Chicago Press.

Bond, Charlotte Ann, Teran Martin, Susan Hume McIntosh, and Charles Ian Mead. 2007. "Integrated Macroeconomic Accounts for the United States." *Survey of Current Business* February:14–31.

Brueckner, Jan, Paul Calem, and Leonard Nakamura. 2012. "Subprime Mortgages and the Housing Bubble." *Journal of Urban Economics* 71:230–43.

Cecchetti, Stephen G., Ingo Fender, and Patrick McGuire. 2010. "Toward a Global Risk Map." BIS Working Paper no. 309, Bank for International Settlements, May.

Cho, Man, and Isaac F. Megbolugbe. 1996. "An Empirical Analysis of Property Appraisal and Mortgage Redlining." *Journal of Real Estate Finance and Economics* 13:45–55.

Coval, Joshua, Jakub Jurek, and Erik Stafford. 2009a. "Economic Catastrophe Bonds." *American Economic Review* 99:628–66.

———. 2009b. "The Economics of Structured Finance." *Journal of Economic Perspectives* 23:3–25.

Covitz, Daniel M., Nellie Liang, and Gustavo Suarez. 2013. "The Evolution of a

Financial Crisis: Collapse of the Asset-Backed Commercial Paper Market." *Journal of Finance* 68:815–48.

Crone, Theodore M., Leonard I. Nakamura, and Richard Voith. 2010. "Rents Have Been Rising, Not Falling, in the Postwar Period." *Review of Economics and Statistics* 92:628–42.

Demyanyk, Yuliya, and Otto Van Hemert. 2011. "Understanding the Subprime Mortgage Crisis." *Review of Financial Studies* 24:1848–80.

Denison, Edward F. 1962. "Comment." In *The Flow of Funds Approach to Social Accounting*, Studies in Income and Wealth, vol. 26, 425–30. Princeton, NJ: Princeton University Press.

Elul, Ronel. 2009. "Securitization and Mortgage Default: Reputation vs. Adverse Selection." Federal Reserve Bank of Philadelphia Working Paper no. 09–21, September.

Engle, Robert. 2009. *Anticipating Correlations: A New Paradigm for Risk Management*. Princeton, NJ: Princeton University Press.

French, Kenneth, Martin N. Baily, John Y. Campbell, John H. Cochrane, Douglas W. Diamond, Darrell Duffie, Anil K. Kashyap, et al. 2010. *The Squam Lake Report: Fixing the Financial System*. Princeton, NJ: Princeton University Press.

Gallin, Joshua. 2008. "The Long-Run Relationship between House Prices and Rent." *Real Estate Economics* 36 (4): 635–58.

Garmaise, Mark. 2008. "After the Honeymoon: Relationship Dynamics between Mortgage Brokers and Banks." Working Paper, Anderson School of Management, UCLA.

Gorton, Gary B., and Andrew Metrick. 2012. "Who Ran On Repo?" NBER Working Paper no. 18455, Cambridge, MA.

Herzog, Thomas N., Fritz J. Scheuren, and William E. Winkler. 2007. *Data Quality and Record Linkage Techniques*. New York: Springer.

Jacobson, Tor, Jesper Linde, and Kasper Roszbach. 2006. "Internal Rating Systems, Implied Credit Risk, and the Consistency of Banks' Risk Classification Policies." *Journal of Banking and Finance* 30:1899–926.

Keys, Benjamin J., Tanmoy Mukherjee, Amit Seru, and Vikrant Vig. 2009. "Financial Regulation and Securitization: Evidence from Subprime Loans." *Journal of Monetary Economics* July:700–20.

Mendelson, Morris. 1962. "The Optimum of Grossness in the Flow-of-Funds Accounts." In *The Flow of Funds Approach to Social Accounting*, Studies in Income and Wealth, vol. 26, 411–25. Princeton, NJ: Princeton University Press.

Nakamura, Leonard, and Kasper Roszbach. 2010. "Credit Rating and Bank Monitoring Ability." Federal Reserve Bank of Philadelphia Working Paper no. 10–21, May.

Teplin, Albert, Rochelle Antoniewicz, Susan Hume McIntosh, Michael Palumbo, Genevieve Solomon, Charles Ian Mead, Karin Moses, and Brent Moulton. 2006. "Integrated Macroeconomic Accounts for the United States: Draft SNA-USA." In *A New Architecture for the US National Accounts*, Studies in Income and Wealth, vol. 66, edited by Dale Jorgenson, J. Steven Landefeld, and William Nordhaus, 471–539. Chicago: University of Chicago Press.

Yamashita, Takashi. 2013. "A Guide to the Integrated Macroeconomic Accounts." *Survey of Current Business* 93 (April): 12–27.

4

Shadow Banking and the Funding of the Nonfinancial Sector

Joshua Gallin

Introduction

The financial and economic upheaval of the past few years has provided a harsh reminder of the dangers of overreliance on short-term funding. The financial crisis also revealed how little regulators, supervisors, and market participants themselves know about the extent to which such funding was, and continues to be, provided by what is now commonly known as the shadow banking system. Recent research has improved our understanding of the role played by elements of the shadow banking system. Pozsar et al. (2010) gives an overview of the shadow banking system, Pozsar (2011) provides information on investors' pools of cash, and Ricks (2011) examines the growth of private money claims. Others have examined particular instruments used in shadow banking, such as repurchase agreements (Gorton and Metrick 2010), asset-backed commercial paper (Covitz, Liang, and Suarez 2009; Acharya, Schnabl, and Suarez 2011), auction rate securities and variable-rate demand notes (Han and Li 2010), and money market mutual funds (McCabe 2010).

In this chapter I describe a way to use data from the Financial Accounts of the United States[1] (FA) and other readily available sources to provide rough

Joshua Gallin is deputy associate director in the division of research and statistics at the Board of Governors of the Federal Reserve System.

The opinions expressed in this chapter are those of the author only. They do not necessarily reflect those of the governors of the Federal Reserve System or its staff. I would like to thank Dan Covitz, Patrick McCabe, Rebecca Zarutskie, Marshall Reinsdorf, and two anonymous referees. For acknowledgments, sources of research support, and disclosure of the author's material financial relationships, if any, please see http://www.nber.org/chapters/c12522.ack.

1. The Federal Reserve Board's Z.1 statistical release, previously named the Flow of Funds Accounts of the United States, was renamed the Financial Accounts of the United States for the June 2013 publication.

"top-down" measures of the size of the domestic shadow banking system.[2] In particular, I estimate the amount of debt financing of the *nonfinancial* sectors of the US economy that is dependent on the shadow banking system. I loosely define shadow-bank funding of the nonfinancial sector as funding provided to households, nonfinancial businesses, and federal, state, and local governments that have a "runnable" link in their intermediation chain. My definition of a runnable link is that the financial intermediary relies significantly on short-term funding that is not insured by the Federal Deposit Insurance Corporation (FDIC) and that the intermediary does not have direct access to the Federal Reserve's Discount Window.

I examine shadow-bank funding of the nonfinancial sector rather than the financial sector to focus on the direct effects on economic activity. A shadow banking system that is just a network of "side bets" with few direct links to the real economy or that primarily funds the traditional banking system might require very different supervision and regulation than one that is inextricably linked to real economic activity. Although it may be self evident to most that the rise and collapse of shadow banking had dire effects on real economic activity, there is actually little agreement on how best to measure the size of the shadow banking system. The purpose of this chapter is to add to our ability to measure this hard-to-measure sector.

The main results are as follows: In the lead-up to the financial crisis of 2008, the domestic shadow banking system was a significant, but not dominant supplier of funding to the nonfinancial sectors of the economy. For example, nonfinancial-sector debt stood at about $34 trillion in the fourth quarter of 2008. Of that debt, I estimate that about $10 trillion was provided by the traditional banking system (either as direct loans or through holdings of securities) and $12 trillion was provided through traditional nonbank sources such as insurance companies, pension funds, and long-term mutual funds—sources that are not typically thought of as runnable. In contrast, only about $4 trillion was provided through short-term funding outside the traditional banking system. Thus, despite the well-deserved notoriety garnered by the shadow banking system, it did not account for a particularly large portion of nonfinancial-sector funding.

My estimate of the size of the shadow banking system is much smaller than that provided by Pozsar et al. (2010). There are two main reasons for the difference. First, I focus on the net debt financing of the nonfinancial sector, and therefore ignore the "grossing up" of shadow banking liabilities that occurs in long intermediation chains. Second, I do not equate all nonbank intermediation, particularly that provided by the government-sponsored

---

2. For the remainder of the chapter I drop the word "domestic" when referring to the shadow banking system unless the distinction with the foreign shadow banking system is explicitly needed.

enterprises (GSEs) and issuers of private-label, asset-backed securities, with shadow banking.

Although I find that the shadow banking system was not large compared to traditional banking in terms of the level of financing extended to the nonfinancial sector, I do find that funding from the shadow banking system dropped significantly after 2008. This contraction was, at least in an arithmetic sense, the *entire* reason for the slowdown in the growth rate of nonfinancial-sector debt over this period. In other words, the sharp contraction of the shadow banking system had enormous effects on nonfinancial-sector debt, and thus presumably on real economic activity. These results are consistent with those in Krishnamurthy, Nagel, and Orlov (2014), but are more broad than their results, which focused specifically on repo and asset-backed commercial paper.

To estimate the size of the shadow banking system, I begin with the observation that every dollar of credit-market debt provided to the nonfinancial sector represents one end of a financial intermediation chain. My aim is to trace intermediation chains from nonfinancial-sector borrowers to what I call terminal funders. These are not the households and foreign entities that are the "ultimate" providers of funding (with the financial system as the intermediator). Rather, these terminal funders are one or two links away from such ultimate funders. I define five categories of terminal funders: traditional banks, which include commercial banks, credit unions, and thrifts that reside in the United States; foreign entities, which are entities that are not domiciled in the United States; long-term funders, which are domestic nonbank entities such as insurance companies and pension funds that are typically not runnable; the government, which includes federal, state, and local governments (including the Federal Reserve); and short-term funders, which are domestic and runnable nonbank-providers of short-term financing.

Short-term funders notionally include entities such as money market mutual funds (money funds), unregistered liquidity funds, local government investment pools, and cash-collateral reinvestment pools from securities lending programs. I also define intermediate funders such as broker-dealers, government-sponsored agencies, finance companies, and private securitizers that are links between terminal funders and nonfinancial-sector borrowers. I then use data from the FA to estimate each terminal funder's holdings of nonfinancial-sector debt. The calculations often require "drilling down" through layers of FA data to determine how various sectors themselves are funded. The decomposition of nonfinancial-sector debt into that which is held by the five terminal funders provides a new perspective on the relative size of the shadow banking system.

Because shadow banks can provide funding to traditional banks or foreign entities, my definition of short-term funders is narrower than those that include shadow-bank funding of other terminal funders. For example, money market funds, which are clearly runnable (McCabe 2010), provide significant funding to traditional commercial banks and foreign entities. To provide a very rough measure of shadow-bank funding of the traditional banking system, I use Call Report data to estimate the share of bank liabilities that are short term and uninsured, and therefore, potentially runnable.

Fender and McGuire (2010), McGuire and von Peter (2009), and Baba, McCauley, and Ramaswamy (2009) show that foreign financial institutions, especially those in Europe, faced a short-term dollar funding squeeze during 2008 and 2009, in part because they relied heavily on US money market mutual funds. Their work suggests that an important portion of foreign financing of the domestic nonfinancial sectors should also be attributed to the shadow banking system. However, a decomposition of financing provided by foreign entities to traditional and shadow banking is beyond the scope of this chapter.

The chapter ends with a brief discussion of how even an imperfect measure of the size of the shadow banking system could be useful as a tool for macroprudential supervision of the financial system. Macro measures could provide a perspective that can complement more microstudies, such as Covitz, Liang, and Suarez (2009) and McCabe (2010), that focus on the instruments and markets that make up the shadow banking system. To use a metaphor proposed by Eichner, Kohn, and Palumbo (2010), a macro measure of the shadow banking system can provide a "grainy satellite photo" that prompts market watchers to take a closer look at particular instruments or structures. For example, evidence that nonfinancial sectors are highly dependent on the shadow banking system for funding should raise warning flags about the risks to economic activity. Indeed, although funding from the shadow banking system to the nonfinancial sectors has dropped significantly since 2008, the fact that the shadow banking system remains an important provider of financing to households, nonfinancial businesses, and governments (not to mention domestic and foreign banks and broker-dealers) should raise warning flags about risks to economic activity that arise from reliance on this inherently fragile source of funding.

4.1   Defining and Measuring the Shadow Banking System in a Model Financial System

Figure 4.1 provides a highly stylized model of a financial system. The nonfinancial sector has borrowers with mortgage liabilities that are ultimately funded by savers in the nonfinancial sector. That is, the nonfinancial sector is the ultimate borrower and the ultimate lender, and the financial system provides the intermediation. The financial sector contains a traditional commercial bank, a mortgage securitizer, a broker-dealer, a pension fund, and a money fund. Arrows indicate financial obligations; the arrow heads indicate the direction of the obligation and the line style (solid, dotted, etc.) indicates

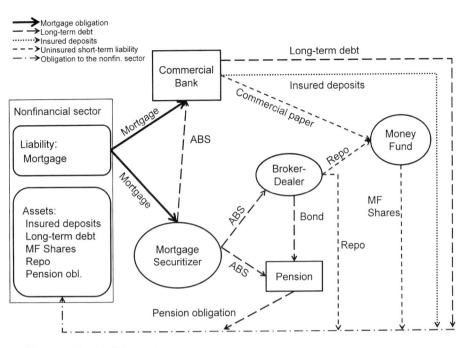

Fig. 4.1   A model financial system

type. For example, the nonfinancial sector has a mortgage loan that it owes to the traditional bank and to the mortgage securitizer (which need not have originated the mortgage); the broker-dealer has a short-term obligation (a security repurchase agreement, or repo) to the money fund and a long-term obligation (a bond) to the pension fund; and the money fund has a short-term obligation (money-fund shares) to the nonfinancial sector. Note that the use of derivatives is outside the scope of this chapter.

There are multiple ways to define and measure the shadow banking system, even in this simple model. Shadow banking is often defined as the conduct of maturity transformation outside the traditional banking system (Gorton and Metrick 2010; Gibson 2010; Ricks 2011). At least two measures of the shadow banking system could arguably satisfy this definition. First, one could interpret "outside the traditional banking system" as excluding any liabilities issued by a traditional bank. In this case, for the model in figure 4.1, one would add together the broker-dealer's repo and money-fund shares outstanding because the broker-dealer funds long-term bonds with short-term repo, the money fund finances short-term commercial paper and repo using potentially shorter-term shares, and neither the broker-dealer nor the money fund is a bank. Second, one could interpret "outside the traditional banking system" to mean excluding insured deposits. In this case, one would add bank commercial paper to the first measure.[3] Note that both these approaches involve some degree of double counting because the commercial paper and a portion of the repo back the money-fund shares.[4]

Others use broader definitions of the shadow banking system. For instance, in measuring the size of the shadow banking system, Pozsar et al. (2010) include all the asset-backed securities issued by the GSEs and private-label securitizers. In the context of the schematic in figure 4.1, this would entail including in a measure of the shadow banking system all the asset-backed securities (ABS) issued by the mortgage securitizer.[5]

The approach I take in this chapter differs subtly from those in the literature. I am interested in measuring the fraction of nonfinancial-sector debt that is funded by intermediation chains that are runnable. I call an intermediation chain runnable if it involves, at any link, short-term funding outside the traditional commercial banking system. However, I am not interested (in this chapter) in measuring the gross amount of shadow banking liabilities or the total liabilities of all entities that have some connection to the shadow banking system.[6] Rather, I seek to measure the amount of funding of the nonfinancial system that depends on a runnable source of funding. That is, I am interested in measuring the degree to which borrowing of nonfinancial entities depends quite directly on the inherently fragile shadow banking system.

If key information about counterparties and loan terms for the model financial system in figure 4.1 were recorded at issuance and resale, we could in principle follow intermediation chains with relative ease from the nonfinancial borrower to the terminal funder *and* identify the form, prevalence, and degree of maturity transformation in the traditional and shadow banking systems. Of course, such comprehensive data do not exist, and "tagging and tracking" all financial instruments is costly and currently politically infeasible.

Suppose instead that we had FA-like data for the simple financial system in figure 4.1. The actual FA are an integrated set of national financial

3. This is implicitly the approach Ricks (2011) uses to estimate "gross private money-claims outstanding."

4. Such double counting is more prevalent in a more complicated financial system (not shown) where, for example, the broker-dealer runs a matched-book in repo. In that case, the total amount of repo in the system would increase without any additional funding of the nonfinancial sector. Indeed, long intermediations chains or significant rehypothecation will increase some measures of the shadow banking system without resulting in more funding to the nonfinancial sector.

5. A paper by the Financial Stability Board (2011) points out that there is "no clear commonly agreed definition" of shadow banking. That paper suggests that monitoring of the shadow banking system should start with a very broad definition that includes all nonbank credit intermediation and then narrow the focus to nonbank intermediation that includes maturity or liquidity transformation.

6. Nor am I interested here in every type of nonbank maturity transformation. For example, five-year loans for very long-lived commercial real estate assets are a form of maturity transformation that is subject to significant roll-over or renewal risk, but is not runnable.

accounts and balance sheets. The accounts include measures of financial assets and liabilities for many broad sectors of the economy, which can be classified as either financial or nonfinancial. For each sector, the FA provide sector tables that show a sector's financial assets and liabilities broken out by the various financial instrument used. For each financial instrument, the FA have an instrument table that shows which financial and nonfinancial sectors use that instrument to borrow or lend.[7]

I start by defining what I call "terminal" and "intermediate" funders. The terminal funders are *not* the ultimate funders of nonfinancial debt—as mentioned, the ultimate funder is the nonfinancial sector itself. Rather, terminal funders are one or two links away from the ultimate funder on the intermediation chain. In this example, there are three types of terminal funders: the traditional bank, the long-term funder, and short-term funders. The traditional bank is this case is simply the commercial bank. The traditional bank has whole-loan mortgages and ABS as assets that it funds with a long-term liability to the nonfinancial sector, insured deposits held by the nonfinancial sector, and commercial paper held by the money fund. The pension fund is the long-term funder. Its assets are the ABS and the (unsecured) corporate bond, and its liabilities are the pension obligations to the nonfinancial sector. Of course, a pension fund may engage in frequent trades and may choose to quickly dump assets that it no longer wants. However, it is not typically thought of as being subject to runs.

The short-term funders are defined by activities rather than entities, and are therefore not depicted as a box in the figure. Rather, a short-term funder is any nonbank provider of financing using short-term, uninsured, and therefore runnable, methods. In this example, the financing from the short-term funders is the sum of the direct repo between the broker-dealer and the nonfinancial sector and the money fund shares. Alternatively, it can be thought of as the sum of all short-term, uninsured instruments in the financial system (the repo, the commercial paper, and the money fund shares) netted out to eliminate double counting.

The "intermediate" funders in this case are the mortgage securitizer and the broker-dealer. As intermediate funders, the holdings of nonfinancial-sector debt by the mortgage securitizer and the broker-dealer are apportioned to the terminal funders as described below, based on how these two entities are themselves funded.

In practical terms, my approach requires following intermediation chains in figure 4.1 from the nonfinancial borrower to a terminal funder, and stopping there; thus the name. The model financial system in figure 4.1 has ten intermediation chains. The individual chains are shown in figure 4.2, and can

---

7. The FA presents full balance sheets for the household and nonfinancial business sectors (corporate and noncorporate). The accounts do not contain full balance sheets for the financial sectors, and therefore lack estimates of financial-sector net worth or equity.

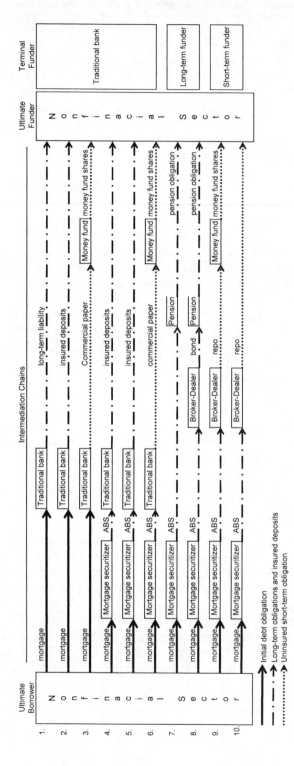

Fig. 4.2   Taxonomy of intermediation chains for the model financial system

be thought of as an unraveling of the intermediation chains shown in figure 4.1. The dollar amount of mortgage obligations held by the commercial bank is simply allocated to the traditional bank (figure 4.2, lines 1 through 3). Mortgage obligations held by the mortgage securitizer must be followed further along various intermediation chains. To do so, we would look at FA data on holders of ABS. The commercial bank's holdings of ABS are, of course, allocated to the traditional bank (figure 4.2, lines 4 through 6) and the pension-fund holding of ABS are allocated to the long-term funder (figure 4.2, line 7).

For the ABS held by the broker-dealer, we must continue along the intermediation chains. At this point we would look at the sector table in the FA for broker-dealers. To the extent that the broker-dealer funds its balance sheet using an (unsecured) corporate bond, we would allocate that amount to the long-term funder (figure 4.2, line 8). To the extent that the broker-dealer funds itself using repo, we would allocate that amount to the short-term funder (figure 4.2, lines 9 and 10). Thus, each dollar of nonfinancial debt gets allocated to one (and only one) of the three terminal funders.[8]

The method described above is designed to estimate how much debt of the nonfinancial sector is funded by each terminal funder regardless of how that terminal funder is, itself, funded. The portion attributed to the short-term funder is one measure of the importance of the shadow banking system, and can be compared directly to the portion attributed to the other terminal funders. However, the method ignores the extent to which traditional commercial banks are, themselves, funded by runnable sources. A question then is, should we include the intermediation chain depicted in line 6 of figure 4.2 in the traditional banking system or the shadow banking system?

There is no clear dividing line between the traditional and shadow banking systems. A traditional bank can raise funds through insured deposits or through noninsured "hot money," which includes short-term funding such as commercial paper and jumbo CDs that could be runnable. Moreover, banks can sponsor supposedly off-balance sheet entities such as asset-backed conduits and money market mutual funds that are runnable and whose assets and liabilities end up, in the event of a crisis, on the sponsor's balance sheet (Acharya, Schnabl, and Suarez 2011; McCabe 2010).[9] By allocating to my measure of the traditional bank funder all financing provided to the nonfinancial sector by the commercial banks, I make the division between shadow and traditional banking at the point where the commercial bank legal entity ends: all funding provided by the traditional bank is considered distinct from the shadow banking system and all funding provided

8. Note that the approach abstracts from equity.
9. Indeed, elements of the shadow banking system such as asset-backed conduits were arguably a form of regulatory arbitrage that allowed traditional commercial banks to increase their use of short-term funding without affecting how their balance sheet looked (Acharya, Schnabl, and Suarez 2011).

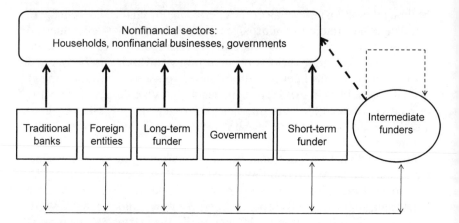

Fig. 4.3   Funding of nonfinancial-sector debt

by off-balance sheet entities is considered distinct from the traditional bank-ing system. Although my main focus here is on this narrow definition of the shadow banking system, I present supplemental results on a broader concept of shadow banking that includes hot money funding of traditional banks.

4.2   The Estimation Method Applied to the Actual Financial System

Figure 4.3 presents a schematic of the actual financial system that has more sectors but less detail. The nonfinancial sectors are households, nonfin-ancial businesses, and governments and are represented by the large box in the figure. In addition to the three terminal funders I defined in the previous section (the traditional bank, long-term funder, and short-term funder), I add two more: foreign entities, which includes entities domiciled abroad even if they are subsidiaries of US firms, and the government, which includes the federal and state and local governments and the Federal Reserve.[10]

I am interested in allocating all funding of the nonfinancial sector to the five terminal funders. Funding can be direct. For example, a household can owe a mortgage loan to the traditional bank, a nonfinancial firm could issue a long-term bond to a foreign entity or a long-term funder such as an insurance company, or a municipal government could issue a variable-rate demand obligation that is purchased by a short-term funder such as a money fund. This direct funding is represented by the thick arrows in figure 4.3. Funding of nonfinancial borrowers can be provided indirectly through intermediate funders (the thin arrows and then the thick dotted arrow). Con-sider an example in which a bank originates a mortgage and then sells it to

10. Domestic subsidiaries of foreign-owned firms are not considered foreign entities for the purposes of this chapter and government pension plans are classified as long-term funders.

Table 4.1   **Definitions of terminal and intermediate funders (for use in estimating direct funding in step 1)**

Funding source	Flow of Funds sector
Terminal funders	
Traditional banks	Commercial banks
	Savings institutions
	Credit unions
Government	Federal government
	Monetary authority
Foreign entities	Rest of the world
Long-term funders	Households and nonprofits
	Nonfinancial businesses
	Property-casualty insurance companies
	Life insurance companies
	Private pension funds
	State and local government employee retirement funds
	Federal government retirement funds
	Mutual funds
	Closed-end and exchange-traded funds
	State and local governments
Short-term funders[a]	Money market mutual funds
Intermediate funders	Government-sponsored enterprises
	Agency- and GSE-backed mortgage pools
	Private-label issuers of asset-backed securities
	Finance companies
	Real estate investment trusts
	Security brokers and dealers
	Funding corporations

[a]This designation is for the purpose of identifying direct funding in step 1. It does not mean that money market mutual funds are the only kind of short-term funder.

a private-label issuer of ABS. The ABS issuer funds the purchase by issuing a bond. Just as in the previous section, the portion of that bond issuance that is purchased by, say, a pension, is then said to come from a long-term funder, but through the intermediate funder.[11] The asset-backed bond could also be purchased by another intermediate funder such as a broker-dealer, and funded with a repurchase agreement made with a money fund. In that case, the funding comes from the short-term funder but through two intermediate funders.

The terminal funders are defined in table 4.1. The definitions for the traditional bank, government, and foreign entities are straightforward and are based on the FA's banking sectors, government sectors, and the rest-of-the-

11. I cannot literally determine which portion of each type of asset is funded by different types of liabilities. In most cases this is not even a sensible question. Rather, I assign shares based on the composition of a sector's liabilities.

world sector. However, choosing the sectors to be defined as long-term funders clearly requires judgment calls. I chose sectors such as insurers and pensions that typically do not reply upon short-term funding and are generally not considered runnable. Note that I included mutual funds (excluding money market mutual funds), closed end funds, and exchange-traded funds in the long-term funder category. Although these types of funds are highly liquid, their liabilities are not like money claims (Ricks 2011), and I therefore do not consider them runnable in the same sense as instruments such as commercial paper and repo.[12]

Note also that I include money funds in the short-term funder category. This does not mean that money funds are the only short-term funder. As I mentioned above, the short-term funder category is largely characterized by activities rather than by the entities themselves. The classification of money funds captures only the *direct* funding of the nonfinancial sector by the short-term funder. In practice, most financing from the short-term funder category comes indirectly through the runnable financing of intermediate funders.

As shown in line 1 of table 4.2, total credit market debt of the nonfinancial sector was $40 trillion in the fourth quarter of 2012. The upper part of the table shows the debt of the major nonfinancial sectors and the lower part of the table shows the instruments used to borrow funds.[13]

Given these definitions, the estimation procedure is as follows:

1. For each of the identified instruments in table 4.2, use the appropriate FA instrument table to calculate the share of the dollar amounts of each instrument to be allocated to each terminal funder and each intermediate funder. Apply those shares to the dollar amounts for that instrument to allocate funding to the terminal funders and the intermediate funders.

2. For each intermediate funder, use the liabilities structure reported in the appropriate FA sector table to estimate the share of the dollar amounts identified in (1) that should be allocated to each terminal funder and, if relevant, each intermediate funder. Apply those shares to the dollar amounts identified in (1) for intermediate funders to allocate funding to the intermediate funders and the terminal funders.

3. Repeat (2) as necessary. For private-label ABS issuers, real estate investment trusts (REITs), finance companies, broker-dealers, and funding corporations, use the liability structure reported in each sector's FA table to allocate funding to the five terminal funders.

12. Mutual funds, closed-end funds, and exchange-traded funds can employ leverage, some of which might create short-term liabilities, and other long-term funders such as insurance funds invest cash collateral from securities-lending programs. I leave a more complete treatment of these sectors to future work.
13. See appendix figures 4A.1 and 4A.2 for time series of the subcomponents.

Table 4.2   Credit market debt owed by domestic nonfinancial sectors (by debtor sector, end of period 2012:Q4)

	Billions of dollars	Percent
1. Total	40,098	—
By sector		
2. Households	12,831	32.0
3. Nonfinancial business	12,694	31.7
4. State and local governments	2,980	7.4
5. Federal government	11,594	28.9
By instrument		
6. Commercial paper	130	0.3
7. Treasury securities	11,569	28.9
8. Agency- and GSE-backed securities	25	0.1
9. Municipal securities	3,714	9.3
10. Corporate bonds	5,795	14.5
11. Depository loans n.e.c.	1,751	4.4
12. Other loans and advances	1,385	3.5
13. Mortgages	12,949	32.3
14. Nonmortgage consumer credit	2,779	6.9

Source: Financial Accounts of the United States.

The appendix provides a more detailed example for mortgages and the full set of data and calculations are available by request from the author.

To identify the extent to which traditional banks are funded using runnable sources, I use Call Reports data to define "short-term money" at banks as the sum of large-time deposits with maturity less than one year, federal funds purchased and securities sold under agreements to repurchase, deposits in foreign offices, trading liabilities (excluding revaluation losses on derivatives), accounts payable, dividends declared but not yet payable, and other borrowed money with maturity less than one year.[14]

Figure 4.4 shows uninsured short-term liabilities at traditional banks as a share of their total assets. This share provides an admittedly rough estimate of the share of traditional bank funding that is provided by runnable sources.[15] The product of this share and the estimate of traditional bank funding from step 1 provide an estimate of the shadow-bank funding that works through the traditional banking system. The remainder represents an estimate of traditional bank funding that is funded by insured deposits and long-term liabilities—that is, an estimate of the most traditional of traditional banking.

14. This measure excludes advances from Federal Home Loan Banks.
15. Note that even if all such funding were removed from a traditional commercial bank, the bank would still have access to financing from the discount window.

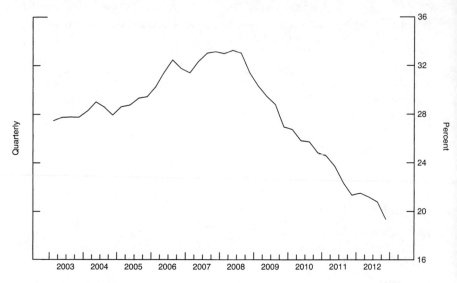

Fig. 4.4   Uninsured short-term liabilities as a share of bank assets
Source: Call Reports. The data are plotted through 2012:Q4.
Note: Uninsured short-term liabilities is the sum of: large-time deposits with maturity less than one year, federal funds purchased and securities sold under agreements to repurchase, deposits in foreign offices, trading liabilities (excluding revaluation losses on derivatives), accounts payable, dividends declared but not yet payable, and other borrowed money with maturity less than one year (not including FHLB advances).

4.3   Results

Table 4.3 summarizes step 1 of the estimation method by providing snapshots of total debt of the nonfinancial sectors and the holders of that debt in 2006, 2008, 2010, and 2012.[16] For these four years, two-thirds to three-quarters of nonfinancial-sector debt was held directly by one of the five terminal funders (line 2). The vast majority of that debt was held directly by traditional banks (line 3), foreign entities (line 4), and long-term funders (line 5).[17] Short-term funders (line 6) have historically not been important *direct* holders of debt issued by nonfinancial entities. This is not surprising given that shadow banking is typically characterized by long intermediation chains. To the extent that shadow banking funds nonfinancial-sector debt, we should expect that funding to run through the financial sectors that make up the intermediate funders. Taken together, these intermediate funders held about one-third of nonfinancial-sector debt (line 8). Of this portion, the majority was held by the GSEs (line 9) and issuers of private-label ABS

16. These dates were chosen to focus on the run-up to the financial crisis and the immediate aftermath. A more complete time series can be found in appendix figure 4A.3.
17. These direct holdings mainly took the form of whole loans, corporate bonds, and government securities.

Table 4.3   Holders of nonfinancial-sector debt (end of period, 2012:Q4)

		2006	2008	2010	2012
1.	**Grand total (billions of dollars)**	**30,059**	**34,528**	**36,913**	**40,098**
	Contributions (percent)				
2.	**Direct from a terminal funder**	**65.3**	**65.6**	**71.3**	**74.1**
3.	Traditional bank	25.9	24.3	22.3	21.8
4.	Foreign	10.4	12.6	15.5	17.2
5.	Long-term	20.7	19.6	24.5	24.8
6.	Short-term	2.4	3.8	2.4	2.4
7.	Government	6.0	5.3	6.6	7.9
8.	**From an intermediate funder**	**34.7**	**34.4**	**28.7**	**25.9**
9.	GSE	15.7	17.2	17.4	16.2
10.	Private-label ABS	12.3	10.6	5.8	4.2
11.	REIT	0.5	0.2	0.1	0.1
12.	Broker-dealer	0.5	1.0	0.7	0.9
13.	Finance company	5.6	4.7	3.8	3.3
14.	Funding corporation	0.1	0.8	0.9	1.1

Source: Financial Accounts of the United States.

(line 10), two intermediate funders that were implicated in the recent shadow banking debacle.

Table 4.4 shows the results of steps 2 and 3 of the estimation method for the GSEs and private-label ABS issuers.[18] The total amount of GSE securities outstanding increased substantially from 2006 through 2010 and edged up through 2012 (line 1). In 2006, most GSE securities were held by long-term funders (line 4), traditional banks (line 2), and foreign entities (line 3). Short-term funders were a decidedly minor source of funding for the GSEs in 2006, but had more than doubled their funding share by the end of 2008. That said, traditional banks, foreign entities, and long-term funders each financed more GSE securities in 2008 than did short-term funders. Following the financial crisis, short-term funders' role in funding the GSEs collapsed and the government's role expanded dramatically as the Federal Reserve began its Large Scale Asset Purchase program.

The lower panel of table 4.4 presents terminal funders' financing of private-label ABS. It is well known that much of the shadow banking system involved the purchase (often with significant leverage) of private-label ABS. My estimates indicate that short-term funders did indeed play a significant role in this sector (line 11). However, the results also indicate that most private-label securities, and therefore the underlying nonfinancial-sector debt, were actually funded by the other terminal funders. In other words, traditional banks, insurance companies, pension funds, and the like held significant quantities of private-label ABS.

18. See appendix figures 4A.4 through 4A.8 for a time series of the allocation shares.

Table 4.4   Terminal funders' holdings of GSE and private-label securities

	2006	2008	2010	2012
1. GSE securities (billions of dollars)	4,717	5,923	6,437	6,511
Percent allocation				
2. Traditional banks	24.9	20.7	24.1	26.7
3. Foreign entities	23.2	20.2	15.0	14.9
4. Long-term funders	38.5	37.8	30.2	31.7
5. Short-term funders	6.0	14.3	7.5	8.4
6. Government	7.3	7.0	23.2	18.4
7. Private-label securities (billions of dollars)	3,703	3,661	2,150	1,673
Percent allocation				
8. Traditional banks	16.9	22.5	20.7	25.1
9. Foreign entities	22.4	17.8	20.5	21.4
10. Long-term funders	31.2	32.0	34.7	36.2
11. Short-term funders	29.6	27.7	24.1	17.3
12. Government	0.0	0.0	0.0	0.0

Source: Financial Accounts of the United States.

That short-term funders financed only fairly modest portions of securities issued by the GSEs and by the issuers of private-label ABS is an important result of this chapter. It is fairly common to consider the GSEs and private-label securitizers—in their entirety—as part of the shadow banking system (e.g., see Pozsar et al. 2010; Bakk-Simon et al. 2012). These entities are clearly enormous nonbank intermediaries that deserve enormous scrutiny. Pricing of GSE securities and private-label ABS was in many cases prompted by unjustifiably high confidence about the securities' safety or by regulatory arbitrage, and, in any event, these securities certainly had dramatic implications for financial stability. However, a significant portion of securities issued by these sectors do not appear to have been used as inputs in the creation of runnable private money claims and therefore do not contribute significantly to my measure of shadow banking. According to this approach, securitization and shadow banking are not synonymous.

Figure 4.5 shows the results of the estimation method applied to all nonfinancial-sector debt. Short-term funders have been, and remain, a quite modest source of financing for the nonfinancial sector. As suggested by the results in tables 4.3 and 4.4, much more of the funding of the nonfinancial sectors has been provided by traditional banks, foreign entities, and long-term funders. In particular, at their peak in the fourth quarter of 2008, short-term funders provided financing for $3.7 trillion of funding to the non-financial sector, while traditional banks provided $10.6 trillion, long-term funders provided $11.8 trillion, and foreign funders provided $6.2 trillion. Thus, despite the justified notoriety garnered by the shadow banking system, it is, by this measure of short-term funders, remarkably small.

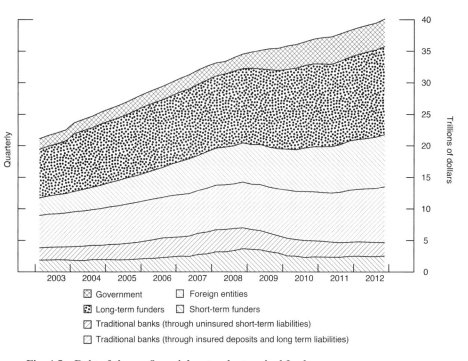

Fig. 4.5   Debt of the nonfinancial sector, by terminal funder
Source: Financial Accounts of the United States. The data are plotted through 2012:Q4.

As mentioned above, my measure of short-term funders does not include the portion of funding for traditional banks that comes from short-term and uninsured debt such as commercial paper and large time deposits. Such hot money is likely less sticky than traditional insured deposits (and long-term liabilities) and is potentially runnable. However, even if one were to consider this portion of traditional bank funding as part of the shadow banking system, shadow banks would still provide a quite modest portion of funding for the nonfinancial sectors.

Although short-term funders and hot-money funding at banks together were not major sources of funding for the nonfinancial sectors, they played outsized roles in the *changes* in the debt of the nonfinancial sector. Nonfinancial-sector debt increased a cumulative 15 percent from 2006:Q4 to 2008:Q4 (line 1 of table 4.5). Of this increase, short-term funders contributed about 4.25 percentage points (line 2), making them the largest single contributor.[19] Traditional banks, foreign entities, and long-term funders all contributed importantly to this increase.

In the two years following the onset of the financial crisis, the cumulative

19. Appendix table 4A.3 shows each terminal funder's cumulative growth rate.

Table 4.5   A decomposition of the growth rate of nonfinancial-sector debt

	2006:Q4–2008:Q4	2008:Q4–2010:Q4	Difference
	Percent change		
1. Total	14.9	6.9	–8.0
	Percentage point contributions		
2. Short-term funders	4.3	–3.7	–8.0
3. Traditional banks	3.0	–0.8	–3.8
Funded by uninsured, short-term liabilities	0.8	–2.2	–3.0
Funded by insured deposits and long-term liabilities	2.2	1.4	–0.7
4. Foreign entities	3.8	2.7	–1.1
5. Long-term funders	3.2	4.0	0.8
6. Government	0.6	4.7	4.1

Source: Financial Accounts of the United States.

growth rate of nonfinancial-sector debt was halved (to about 7 percent). The dramatic step-down in the growth rate of nonfinancial-sector debt was driven, at least in an arithmetic sense, by the sharp turnaround in financing from short-term funders: short-term funders subtracted 3.7 percentage points from the cumulative growth rate over this period. Indeed, the "swing" in the contribution of short-term funders from a strong positive to a strong negative accounts for the entire 8 percentage point decline in the growth rate of nonfinancial-sector debt (the column labeled "difference"). In contrast, the swing for traditional banks (–3.8 percentage points) was much more modest, and was itself almost entirely driven by the swing in funding provided by uninsured short-term liabilities. The swings in the contributions of foreign entities and long-term funders (lines 4 and 5) were essentially offsetting.

Financing provided by the government skyrocketed after 2008 as the US Treasury Department and the Federal Reserve System instituted a wide variety of programs in response to the financial crisis and the recession. These programs greatly boosted government funding of nonfinancial-sector debt, which had been minimal prior to the crisis (line 6).

Thus, a key feature of the provision of credit to the nonfinancial sector in the run-up to the 2008 financial crisis and in its aftermath was the rise and decline of financing from the shadow banking system. A second key feature was that government entities stepped in to provide a significant portion of the credit that had been, at least in an adding-up sense, supplied by short-term funders.

Table 4.6 summarizes changes in the funding of nonfinancial-sector debt from 2008 to the end of 2012. Debt growth has picked up somewhat over that period (line 1). Note that short-term funders contributed about 4 percentage points to the acceleration of nonfinancial-sector debt. Meanwhile, the

Table 4.6   **A decomposition of the growth rate of nonfinancial-sector debt**

	2008:Q4– 2010:Q4	2010:Q4– 2012:Q4	Difference
	Percent change		
1. Total	6.9	8.6	1.7
	Percentage point contributions		
2. Short-term funders	–3.7	0.4	4.1
3. Traditional banks	–0.8	1.8	2.6
Funded by uninsured, short-term liabilities	–2.2	–1.2	1.0
Funded by insured deposits and long-term liabilities	1.4	3.0	1.6
4. Foreign entities	2.7	3.0	0.3
5. Long-term funders	4.0	2.3	–1.6
6. Government	4.7	1.1	–3.6

Source: Financial Accounts of the United States.

contribution of long-term and government funders dropped (lines 5 and 6). Domestic shadow-bank funding of the nonfinancial sector increased from 2010 to 2012, but remained well below the level seen in late 2008.

4.3.1   Comparison to Other Measures of Shadow Banking

This is the first attempt of which I am aware to estimate the share of nonfinancial-sector debt that is funded by the shadow banking system. However, others have used proxies to measure the growth of the importance of the shadow banking system. For example, Gorton and Metrick (2010) used measures such as the size of broker-dealer balance sheets and the amount of repo outstanding at primary dealers to provide a rough sense of the size of the shadow banking system.

The measure of Pozsar et al. (2010) is more closely related to mine. Pozsar and colleagues use FA data to estimate the total liabilities of the shadow banking system, defined as the sum of outstanding levels of commercial paper, repurchase agreements, GSE liabilities, GSE pool securities, liabilities of private-label ABS issuers, and shares of money market mutual funds (netted to avoid counting both sides of commercial paper (CP) and repo transactions, resecuritizations of GSE securities, and other sources of double counting).

Figure 4.6 shows their measure of shadow-banking liabilities (the thin line) along with the liabilities of the traditional banking system (the thick line). That their measure of shadow-bank liabilities is above the liabilities of the traditional banking system is commonly cited evidence that the shadow banking system was as big or even bigger than the traditional banking system. The dotted line in the figure, which depicts my estimate of funding provided by short-term funders, suggests that the shadow banking system

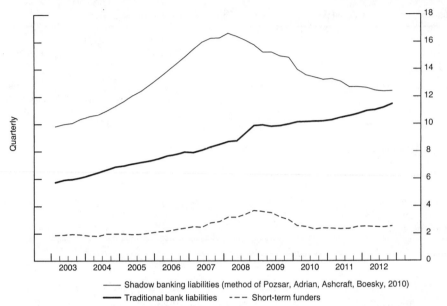

Fig. 4.6   Measures of shadow banking
Source: Financial Accounts of the United States. The data are plotted through 2012:Q4.

was (and is) not nearly as large as traditional banking in terms of credit extended to the nonfinancial sector.

The vast numerical difference between the two measures stems mainly from two significant conceptual differences. First, the method of Pozsar et al. (2010) counts one dollar of funding multiple times if there are multiple observable links in an intermediation chain. For example, imagine a long intermediation chain for a $100,000 home mortgage: suppose the mortgage is packaged into a GSE-backed mortgage pool security, which is then repackaged into a private-label ABS, which is then held on the balance sheet of a broker-dealer and funded through repo with a money fund. Using the method of Pozsar and colleagues, the funding of the underlying mortgage would be counted three times—as a GSE-backed security, as a private-label ABS, and as repo—and one would therefore find $300,000 in shadow-banking liabilities. My method—which is focused on understanding how the $100,000 is funded—would allocate only the $100,000 to the short-term funder and the funding from intermediate institutions would not be counted.

Second, the method of Pozsar et al. includes in shadow banking a significant portion of liabilities that I allocate to other terminal funders. In particular, by including *all* the liabilities of the GSEs and of private-label ABS issuers in their measure of shadow banking, Pozsar et al. attribute to the shadow banking system a significant amount of financing that is actually provided by the banks, insurance companies, pension funds, and mutual funds that purchase these securities.

The conceptual differences are not a matter of a clear and absolute "right" and "wrong" way to measure shadow banking. Rather, they stem from different views about what one is trying to measure. Consider the first conceptual difference, in which Pozsar et al. "gross up" the funding that occurs via long intermediation chains. If one is interested in measuring the importance of such chains, such grossing up is required. If one is interested in end-use funding of the nonfinancial sectors, one should avoid such grossing up. Both approaches are needed.

The second conceptual difference between the two measures reflects the breadth of definitions for shadow banking. The term shadow banking is typically attributed to Paul McCulley (2007). He referred to the shadow banking system as "the whole alphabet soup of levered up non-bank investment conduits, vehicles, and structures" that "fund themselves with un-insured commercial paper" and as such are vulnerable to runs.

To McCulley and others such as Gibson (2010), Ricks (2011, 2012), and myself, the key feature of these entities and activities is that they create something akin to private money, and as such are runnable. Thus, the relevant feature shared by traditional and shadow banks is money creation. The relevant difference is that traditional banks have direct access to the Federal Reserve's Discount Window and can offer government-insured deposits. Shadow banks do not; that is why they are susceptible to runs.

Pozsar et al. and others have defined the shadow banking system more broadly to include many kinds of financial intermediation that occurs outside of banks. Some even define shadow banking as any "credit intermediation involving entities and activities outside the regular banking system." (FSB 2011). In this view, the relevant feature shared by traditional and shadow banks is financial intermediation and the key difference is in regulatory regimes.

If one favors a broad measure of shadow banking, the measures of Pozsar et al. (and others such as Bakk-Simon et al. [2012]) are more appropriate. If one prefers a narrower definition that focuses on the creation of private money and runability, the more narrow definition used in this chapter and Rick's (2011, 2012) approach to measuring private money claims is more appropriate.

Policymakers clearly need to focus on risk taking and regulatory arbitrage conducted by nonbank financial intermediaries. But that does not mean we must call all nonbanks shadow banks. To do so seems wasteful of a new term: Why use "shadow banking" as a synonym (or near synonym) for "nonbanking" when "nonbanking" is a perfectly serviceable term? An overly broad definition of shadow banking risks diffusing the attention of policymakers and economists from the key weakness of shadow banking:

its inherent susceptibilities to runs, the resulting collapse of privately issued money, and the implications for asset prices and real economic activity.

4.4   Data Limitations and Potential Remedies

The fundamental limitation of using aggregate data from the FA is that, as already mentioned, such data fall short of the ideal of comprehensive information about counterparties, security types, and contract terms for all forms of lending. Several specific and salient limitations follow from this fundamental issue. First, for some holders of corporate bonds, the FA do not separately identify holdings of private-label ABS from holdings of corporate bonds issued by the nonfinancial sectors or issued by foreign entities.[20] Private-label ABS holdings for traditional banks and foreign entities can be separately identified. However, estimates of private-label ABS holdings of long-term and short-term funders must be based on an assumption about the share of private-label ABS in their total holdings of corporate bonds.

Second, the FA do not have any direct data for unregistered domestic private investment pools such as hedge funds, private equity, and so-called "liquidity" funds.[21] Any actual assets or liabilities of such funds are assigned by my method to long-term funders because the household sector in the FA is the residual holder of most instruments.[22] To the extent that these private pools are funded by any of the other terminal funders, my method will misclassify this financing.

The remedies for these two limitations are, broadly speaking, more comprehensive and detailed data on balance sheets of financial firms. Various government agencies are already working toward this goal. The SEC recently began collecting more detailed data on the holdings of US money market mutual funds, which could help identify the extent to which foreign entities are themselves runnable. The SEC has also begun a new data collection of balance-sheet information for hedge funds and other private funds; these data should improve our ability to monitor the shadow banking system.[23] In addition, the Office of Financial Research (OFR) was created by Congress to, among other things, improve the quality of financial-market data so that policymakers and market participants will be better able to evaluate

---

20. This is actually true for all bonds issued by the financial sectors, but is particularly important for the private-label ABS sector because of its size and importance in financial intermediation.

21. Unregistered liquidity funds are similar to registered money market mutual funds but are not required to comply with rule 2a-7 and may only sell to qualified investors.

22. For example, suppose there are only two holders of United States Treasury bonds, households and banks. The methodology of the FA is to use reported bonds outstanding from the Treasury Department and bank holdings from the Call Report, and allocate the residual to the household sector. Holdings of any unmeasured sector will therefore be assigned to the household.

23. See SEC release: http://www.sec.gov/rules/final/2012/ia-3308-secg.htm.

firm-specific and market risks. In particular, the OFR intends to collect data on financial transactions and positions and create a "catalog of financial entities and instruments" (OFR 2012). These efforts are a promising start toward improving the quality of financial statistics.

A third limitation is that, from the perspective of the FA, the foreign sector is a black box: one cannot tell what *types* of foreign entities fund the domestic nonfinancial sectors. In particular, one cannot tell how much of that debt is held by foreign entities that are themselves runnable. To the extent that this is true, the measure of financing provided to the nonfinancial that is funded by the shadow banking system is too low.

Foreign banks, especially those in Europe, faced a short-term, dollar-funding squeeze during 2008 and 2009, in part because they relied heavily on US money market mutual funds (Fender and McGuire 2010; McGuire and von Peter 2009; Baba, McCauley, and Ramaswamy 2009). It is difficult to distinguish MMFs financing of entities domiciled abroad (which are included in my measure of foreign funding) from financing of domestic entities with foreign parents (which would be excluded from foreign funding). The SEC data on money market funds could potentially be combined with foreign flow-of-funds and banking data to better determine what portion of foreign funding is runnable. I leave this for future work.

Finally, it is worth mentioning that the data on repo in the FA have certain well-known flaws. Gorton and Metrick (2012), Krishnamurthy, Nagel, and Orlov (2014), and Krishnamurthy and Nagel (2013) point out that there is a large "statistical discrepancy" between the repo assets and liabilities reported in the FA. In particular, reported repo liabilities (cash borrowing) in the accounts is larger than reported assets (cash lending), sometimes dramatically so. For example, in 2007, repo liabilities were about $1 trillion more than were repo assets. The discrepancy likely reflects the fact that the source data for entities such as commercial banks, broker-dealers, and REITs that are large cash borrowers in repo markets are more comprehensive than that for entities that are large cash lenders (Gorton and Metrick 2012). Because the FA rely significantly on regulatory filings, it seems likely that the cash lenders are less-regulated private investment pools such as hedge funds and private cash pools.[24] As mentioned above, the SEC has recently required information on such funds that may help reduce the discrepancy between repo assets and liabilities. In addition, staff at the Federal Reserve Board are working to improve the estimation of the repo data reported in the FA.

Although the repo discrepancy represents an important issue in the Financial Accounts' coverage of a key part of the shadow banking system, the size of the discrepancy by itself does not affect the estimates presented in this chapter. Recall that steps (2) and (3) of the estimation method rely

---

24. This problem may not be relevant for foreign hedge funds, which may be captured in the rest-of-world sector. Domestic hedge funds, however, are not captured.

on the *liability* structure of the various sectors in the Financial Accounts. In other words, poor measurement of repo assets does not affect the method.[25]

4.5 Conclusion

In this chapter I describe a way to use data from the Financial Accounts of the United States and other readily available sources to provide a "top-down" measure of how much debt financing of the nonfinancial sectors of the US economy is dependent on financial intermediation chains that contain at least one runnable link. I find that in the lead-up to the financial crisis of 2008, such "shadow banking" was a significant, but not dominant supplier of funding to the nonfinancial sectors of the economy: Despite the well-deserved notoriety garnered by the shadow banking system, this portion of the financial system did not account for a particularly large portion of nonfinancial-sector funding when compared to traditional bank funding and other nonbank institutions. However, I do find that funding from the shadow banking system dropped significantly after 2008. This contraction was, at least in an arithmetic sense, the *entire* reason for the slowdown in the growth rate of nonfinancial-sector debt over this period. In other words, the sharp contraction of the shadow banking system had enormous effects on nonfinancial-sector debt, and thus presumably on real economic activity.

Of course, this contraction did not occur in isolation. Runs on short-term funding drove asset fire sales that damaged the ability and desire of all sorts of entities to lend. In addition, shadow banking entities such as asset-backed commercial conduits had recourse to traditional commercial banks and thus shadow banking losses became traditional banking losses; securitization and off-balance sheet funding had not resulted in the transfer of risk (Acharya, Schnabl, and Suarez 2011).

From a policy perspective, the approach presented in this chapter offers a way to use aggregate data to track the reliance of the nonfinancial sectors on inherently fragile short-term funding markets. A high or rapidly growing reliance on such markets is suggestive evidence of systemic fragility that should raise warning flags for market participants and policymakers. Using the metaphor of Eichner, Kohn, and Palumbo (2010), aggregate short-term funding of the nonfinancial sectors provides a "grainy satellite photo" of the shadow banking system that could be augmented with stepped-up monitoring of specific markets, entities, and instruments. Indeed, such an approach toward financial-market monitoring has already been proposed by the Financial Stability Board (FSB 2011).

The measures in this chapter will be improved by ongoing efforts to im-

---

25. The estimation method in this chapter will suffer to the extent that hedge funds and other lightly regulated investment funds engage in significant maturity transformation. But that is a result of the fact that the Financial Accounts are missing those sectors rather than something specific about the repo discrepancy.

prove the collection of financial market statistics. For example, the SEC has improved its collection of data for money market mutual funds and in the process of collecting balance sheet and other information from private investment pools such as hedge funds. In addition, the Office of Financial Research was created by Congress to, among other things, improve the quality of financial-market data so that policymakers and market participants will be better able to evaluate firm-specific and market risks. Such improved data collections are an important element in improving our understanding of the risks to financial markets and the real economy.

Appendix
Details on Measuring the Size of the Shadow Banking System

Background on the Financial Accounts of the United States

The FA depend on a variety of data sources, including regulatory filings, public reports from government agencies such as the Bureau of Economic Analysis, the Department of the Treasury, and private data vendors. The quality and detail of the balance-sheet data varies by sector. The best data are for the government sectors, including the monetary authority (the Federal Reserve). Generally speaking, balance-sheet data for commercial banks and insurance companies are also of high quality because these institutions are required to report to various government agencies in significant detail about the types of assets they hold. Banks and thrifts must file quarterly Call Reports that include fairly detailed information on assets, including loans and securities such as Treasuries, agencies, municipal debt, a wide variety of ABS categories, and structured financial products (including synthetics). Beyond this fairly detailed set of securities, banks need only report "other debt securities."[26] Insurance companies also must make fairly detailed regulatory filings.

Balance-sheet data for most other financial sectors is available, but more limited. Private pension funds are a good example. The main data source for the FA is schedule H of Form 5500.[27] This form has entries for assets such as interest-bearing cash, US government securities, and corporate debt instruments. However, a significant fraction of private pension fund assets are held in the form of trusts and pooled separate accounts, for which the pensions funds currently provide no additional detail. The FA assumes that the asset allocation in these accounts is identical to that held outside the

---

26. However, this catch-all category is split between foreign and domestic sectors.

27. These filings are made with the IRS, the Department of Labor, the Employee Benefit Security Administration, and the Pension Benefit Guaranty Corporation.

accounts. Source data for other financial sectors such as broker-dealers, mutual funds, and finance companies have similar shortcomings that prevent sufficiently detailed breakdowns of assets and liabilities. More information on the sources and methods used in the FA can be found at the Financial Accounts Online Guide (http://www.federalreserve.gov/apps/fof/).

An Example Using Home Mortgages

Estimate the Share of Funding by Each Instrument
to be Allocated Directly to Each Funder

For each of the nine instruments listed in table 4.2, the FA has a table that shows who holds the instrument. For example, table 4A.1 shows FA data on holders of home mortgages, which totaled almost $10 trillion in 2012:Q4. The bold lines in the table show direct holdings of the terminal funders (lines 2, 7, 10, 11, and 18) and the intermediate funders (line 19). Indented under each of these categories are the FA sectors that I have assigned to each funding category. Note that most mortgages are not held directly by the terminal funders. Indeed, line 19 shows that the intermediate funders held almost 70 percent of mortgages at the end of 2012. Of those, most are held by the GSEs (either at the actual GSE entity or in off-balance sheet pools) and to a lesser extent at private-label ABS issuers.

In some cases the total amount outstanding for an instrument will not equal the amount outstanding from the nonfinancial sector because financial and foreign sectors issue that security. For example, REITs can issue mortgage debt and foreign entities can issue dollar denominated corporate bonds. We do not always have estimates of who holds the security that had been issued by the nonfinancial sector, and in those cases I typically assume that all funders hold equal proportions of the financial, nonfinancial, and foreign issuance.

Estimate Funding of Intermediate Funders

Estimating the funding of the intermediate funders requires the most assumptions. I treat GSEs (including mortgage pools) separately from the other intermediate funders because the data for GSEs are of higher quality. Table 4A.2 shows the terminal and intermediate funders of GSEs, which is done through agency- and GSE-backed securities. Using these data, I treat GSEs almost the same as I treat the nonfinancial sectors. The one difference is that GSEs own some GSE debt, so I must gross up all the other categories to estimate the amount of funding for the GSE sector that comes from outside the sector. Thus I am implicitly assuming that all GSEs hold other GSE debt in equal proportions.

What remains is to estimate how the other five intermediate funders fund themselves. The data gaps are widest here because we do not have high-quality data on what instruments these intermediaries use to fund them-

Table 4A.1   Home mortgages outstanding (end of period, 2012:Q4)

	Billions of dollars	Percent
1. Total	9,924	—
2. **Traditional banks**	**2,836**	**28.6**
3. US chartered depository institutions	2,488	25.1
4. Foreign banking offices in United States	2	0.0
5. Banks in US-affiliated areas	20	0.2
6. Credit unions	326	3.3
7. **Government**	**104**	**1.0**
8. State and local governments	78	0.8
9. Federal government	26	0.3
10. **Foreign entities**	—	**0.0**
11. **Long-term funders**	**103**	**1.0**
12. Household sector	59	0.6
13. Nonfinancial corporate business	31	0.3
14. Property-casualty insurance companies	—	0.0
15. Life insurance companies	7	0.1
16. Private pension funds	2	0.0
17. State and local govt. retirement funds	4	0.0
18. **Short-term funders**	—	**0.0**
19. **Intermediate funders**	**6,880**	**69.3**
20. GSEs and agency- and GSE-backed mortgage pools	5,811	58.6
21. ABS issuers	924	9.3
22. Finance companies	133	1.3
23. REITs	12	0.1

Source: Financial Accounts of the United States.

selves and to the extent we do know the instruments, we do not have good data on who holds them. My assumptions are as follows:

Private-label ABS issuers. The FA identify only two sources of funding for this sector, commercial paper and bonds. Unfortunately, the FA generally do not identify holders of ABS separately from total corporate and foreign bonds. For depository institutions and credit unions the FA do identify holdings of private-label MBS. I supplement these data with data from the Call Report to calculate bank holdings of nonmortgage ABS. I estimate foreign funders' holdings of ABS using data from the Treasury International Capital System. I do not have a good estimate of holdings of private-label ABS by long-term funders. This is an area of ongoing research. One starting point is to assume that long-term funders hold private-label ABS in proportion to their holdings of all corporate bonds. Instead, I calculated the proportion of all corporate and foreign bonds held by long-term funders and scaled down by 40 percent. This likely creates an upward bias to my estimate of the share financed by the short-term funders, which is calculated as the residual. I made this scaling assumption to ensure that the short-term share was positive in all periods (figure 4A.4). Indeed, in the extreme

Table 4A.2   Agency- and GSE-backed securities (end of period, 2012:Q4)

	Billions of dollars	Percent
1. **Total**	**7,544**	—
2. **Traditional banks**	**1,926**	**25.5**
3. US-chartered depository institutions	1,668	22.1
4. Foreign banking offices in the United States	32	0.4
5. Banks in US-affiliated areas	3	0.0
6. Credit unions	198	2.6
7. Holding companies	25	0.3
8. **Government**	**1,329**	**17.6**
9. Federal government	0	0.0
10. Monetary authority	1,003	13.3
11. State and local governments	325	4.3
12. **Foreign entities**	**1,077**	**14.3**
13. **Long-term funders**	**2,031**	**26.9**
14. Household sector	73	1.0
15. Nonfinancial corporate business	20	0.3
16. Property-casualty insurance companies	124	1.6
17. Life insurance companies	348	4.6
18. Private pension funds	223	3.0
19. State and local government retirement funds	201	2.7
20. Federal government retirement funds	7	0.1
21. Mutual funds	1,035	13.7
22. **Short-term funders**	**344**	**4.6**
23. Money market mutual funds	344	4.6
24. **Intermediate funders**	**838**	**11.1**
25. Government-sponsored enterprises	315	4.2
26. ABS issuers	1	0.0
27. REITs	352	4.7
28. Brokers and dealers	170	2.2

Source: Financial Accounts of the United States.

I could assume that long-term funders hold no private-label ABS. Even in this extreme (and false) case, short-term funders would remain a fairly small terminal funder of nonfinancial debt.

REITs. The short-term funder share equals the share of REIT credit market debt that is in the form of either repurchase agreements or commercial paper, the traditional bank share equals the share of REIT credit market debt that is bank loans, the foreign entity share is set to zero, and the long-term funder share is the residual (figure 4A.5).

Finance companies. The short-term funder share equals the share of finance company credit market debt that is in the form of repurchase agreements, the traditional bank share equals the share of finance company credit market debt that is bank loans, the foreign entity share is set to zero, and the long-term funder share is the residual (figure 4A.6).

Table 4A.3   **A decomposition of the growth rate of nonfinancial-sector debt**

	2006:Q4– 2008:Q4	2008:Q4– 2010:Q4	Difference
	Percent change		
1. Total	14.9	6.9	–8.0
2. Short-term funders	53.6	–34.7	–88.3
3. Traditional banks	9.2	–2.6	–11.8
Funded by uninsured, short-term liabilities	7.9	–22.9	–30.8
Funded by insured deposits and long-term liabilities	9.8	6.8	–3.0
4. Foreign entities	22.9	15.2	–7.7
5. Long-term funders	8.9	11.6	2.7
6. Government	8.1	70.4	62.3
	2008:Q4– 2010:Q4	2010:Q4– 2012:Q4	Difference
	Percent change		
7. Total	6.9	8.6	1.7
8. Short-term funders	–34.7	5.5	40.2
9. Traditional banks	–2.6	6.5	9.1
Funded by uninsured, short-term liabilities	–22.9	–16.9	6.0
Funded by insured deposits and long-term liabilities	6.8	14.2	7.5
10. Foreign entites	15.2	15.5	0.2
11. Long-term funders	11.6	6.5	–5.1
12. Government	70.4	10.7	–59.6

Source: Financial Accounts of the United States.

Broker-dealers. The short-term funder share equals the share of broker-dealer credit market debt that is in the form of repurchase agreements or security credit, the traditional bank share and the foreign entity share are set to zero, and the long-term funder share is the residual (figure 4A.7).[28]

Funding corporations. The long-term funder share equals the share of funding corporation credit market debt that is in the form of corporate bonds or government funding facilities,[29] the traditional bank and foreign entity shares are set to zero, and the short-term funder share is the residual (figure 4A.8).

28. The government facilities include the Federal Reserve's Primary Dealer Credit Facility and Asset-Backed Commercial Paper Money Market Mutual Fund Liquidity Facility.
29. This includes loans extended by the Federal Reserve to Maiden Lane LLC, Maiden Lane II LLC, Maiden Lane III LLC, the Commercial Paper Funding Facility LLC, American International Group (AIG), and loans extended by the federal government to the Term Asset-Backed Securities Loan Facility and to funds associated with PPIP.

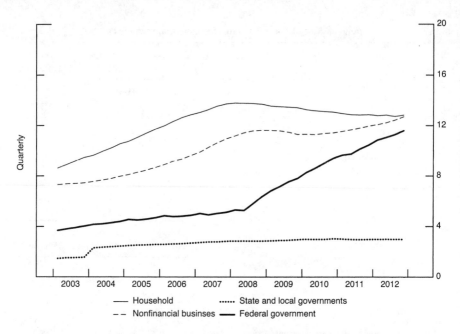

Fig. 4A.1   Credit market debt owed by nonfinancial sectors (by sector)
Source: Financial Accounts of the United States. The data are plotted through 2012:Q4.

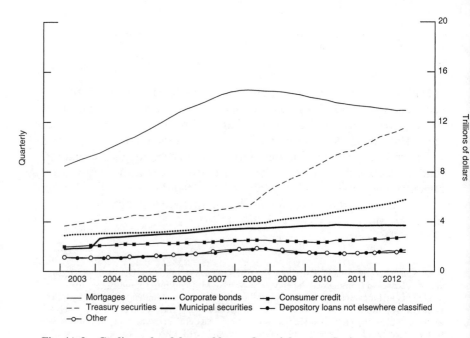

Fig. 4A.2   Credit market debt owed by nonfinancial sectors (by instrument)
Source: Financial Accounts of the United States. The data are plotted through 2012:Q4.

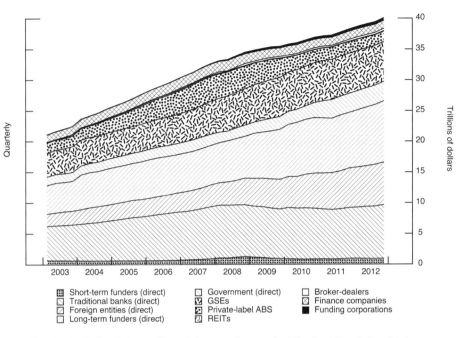

Fig. 4A.3   Debt of the nonfinancial sector, by terminal funder (directly) and intermediate funder

Source: Financial Accounts of the United States. The data are plotted through 2012:Q4.

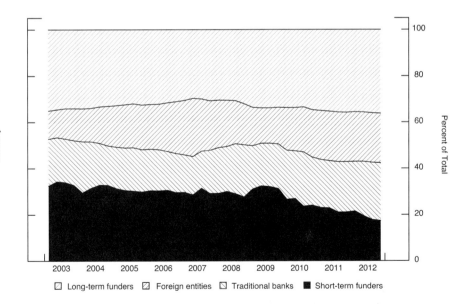

Fig. 4A.4   Estimated allocation shares: Private ABS

Source: Financial Accounts of the United States. The data are plotted through 2012:Q4.

119

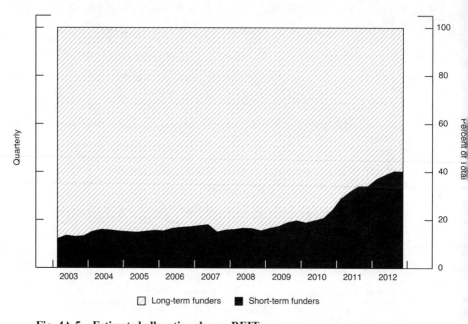

Fig. 4A.5   Estimated allocation shares: REIT

Source: Financial Accounts of the United States. The data are plotted through 2012:Q4.

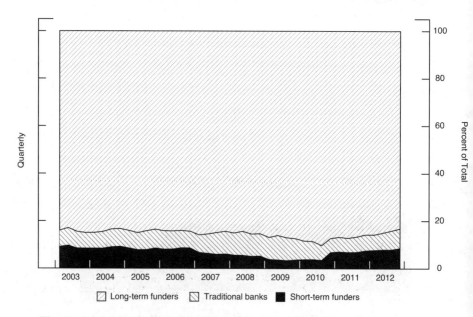

Fig. 4A.6   Estimated allocation shares: Finance companies

Source: Financial Accounts of the United States. The data are plotted through 2012:Q4.

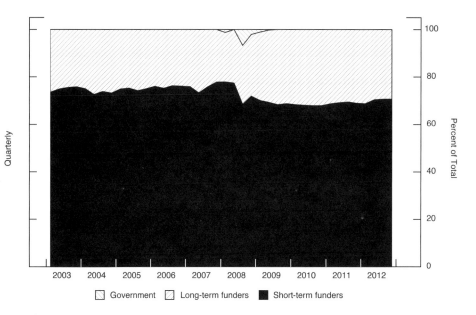

Fig. 4A.7   Estimated allocation shares: Brokers and dealers

Source: Financial Accounts of the United States. The data are plotted through 2012:Q4.

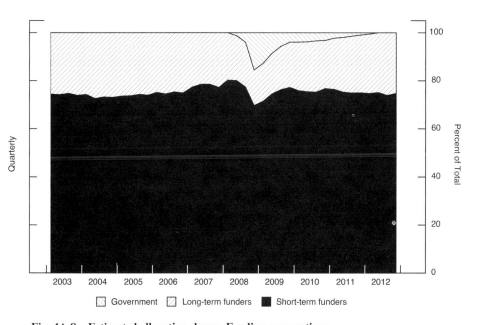

Fig. 4A.8   Estimated allocation shares: Funding corporations

Source: Financial Accounts of the United States. Data are plotted through 2012:Q4.

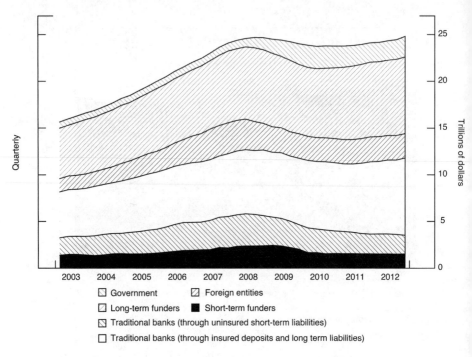

Fig. 4A.9   Debt of the private nonfinancial sector, by terminal funder
Source: Financial Accounts of the United States. Data are plotted through 2012:Q4.

References

Acharya, V. V., P. Schnabl, and G. Suarez. 2011. "Securitization without Risk Transfer." *Journal of Financial Economics* 107 (3): 515–36.
Baba, Naohiko, Robert McCauley, and Srichander Ramaswamy. 2009. "US Dollar Money Market Funds and Non-US Banks." *BIS Quarterly Review* March:65–81.
Bakk-Simon, Klára, Stefano Borgioli, Celestino Girón, Hannah Hempell, Angela Maddaloni, Fabio Recine, and Simonetta Rosati. 2012. "Shadow Banking in the Euro Area: An Overview." European Central Bank Occasional Paper no. 133, April.
Covitz, Daniel M., Nellie Liang, and Gustavo A. Suarez. 2009. "The Evolution of a Financial Crisis: Panic in the Asset-Backed Commercial Paper Market." Finance and Economics Discussion Series no. 2009–36. Washington, DC, Board of Governors of the Federal Reserve System.
Eichner, Matthew J., Donald L. Kohn, and Michael G. Palumbo. 2010. "Financial Statistics for the United States and the Crisis: What Did They Get Right, What Did They Miss, and How Should They Change?" Finance and Economics Discussion Series no. 2010–20 Washington, DC, Board of Governors of the Federal Reserve System.
Fender, Ingo, and Patrick McGuire. 2010. "European Banks' US Dollar Funding Pressures." *BIS Quarterly Review* June:57–64.

Financial Stability Board. 2011. "Shadow Banking: Scoping the Issues." www.finan
cialstabilityboard.org/publications/r_110412a.pdf.

Gibson, Michael. 2010. "How the Shadow Banking System Helped Cause the Financial Crisis and How to Avoid Suffering the Same Crisis Again." Unpublished
manuscript.

Gorton, Gary, and Andrew Metrick. 2010. "Regulating the Shadow Banking System." *Brookings Papers on Economic Activity* Fall:261–97.

———. 2012. "Who Ran on Repo?" NBER Working Paper no. 18455, Cambridge,
MA.

Han, Song, and Dan Li. 2010. "The Fragility of Discretionary Liquidity Provision:
Lessons from the Collapse of the Auction Rate Securities Market." Finance and
Economics Discussion Series no. 2010–50, Washington, DC, Board of Governors
of the Federal Reserve System.

Krishnamurthy, Arvind, and Stefan Nagel. 2013. "Interpreting Repo Statistics in the
Flow of Funds Accounts." NBER Working Paper no. 19389, Cambridge, MA.

Krishnamurthy, Arvind, Stefan Nagel, and Dmitry Orlov. 2014. "Sizing up Repo."
Journal of Finance doi: 10.1111/jofi.12168.

McCabe, Patrick. 2010. "The Cross Section of Money Market Fund Risks and
Financial Crises." Finance and Economics Discussion Series no. 2010–51, Washington, DC, Board of Governors of the Federal Reserve System.

McCulley, Paul. 2007. "Teton Reflections." PIMCO. http://www.pimco.com/EN
/Insights/Pages/GCBF%20August-%20September%202007.aspx.

McGuire, Patrick, and Goetz von Peter. 2009. "The US Dollar Shortage in Global
Banking." *BIS Quarterly Review* March:47–63.

Office of Financial Research. 2012. "Strategic Framework, FY2012–FY2014."
March. http://www.treasury.gov/initiatives/wsr/ofr/Documents/OFRStrategic
Framework.pdf.

Pozsar, Zoltan. 2011. "Institutional Cash Pools and the Triffin Dilemma of the US
Banking System." IMF Working Paper no. WP/11/190, Washington, DC, International Monetary Fund.

Pozsar, Zoltan, Tobias Adrian, Adam Ashcraft, and Hayley Boesky. 2010. "Shadow
Banking." Staff Report no. 458, Federal Reserve Bank of New York.

Ricks, Morgan. 2011. "A Regulatory Design for Monetary Stability." Harvard
John M. Olin Discussion Paper no. 706, Harvard John M. Olin Center for Law,
Economics, and Business, Cambridge, MA.

———. 2012. "The Case for Regulating the Shadow Banking System." In *Too Big
to Fail? Resolving Large Troubled Financial Institutions in the Future*. Washington,
DC: Brookings Institution Press.

Financial Intermediation in the National Accounts
Asset Valuation, Intermediation, and Tobin's *q*

Carol A. Corrado and Charles R. Hulten

5.1 Introduction

The collapse of the housing price bubble starting in mid-2006 has had far reaching consequences. It led to a crisis in the subprime mortgage market, a relatively small part of the overall debt market, but this soon propagated to the financial markets as a whole and then to the real economy. The financial crisis also altered the landscape of the financial sector, with many of the largest firms forced into buyouts or failure. The effects of the Great Recession are still felt as of this writing, six years later. The depth and duration of the crisis and its aftermath, invite the question: Why wasn't the approaching crisis more apparent in the macroeconomic data and models that inform economic policy?

This is a complex issue, involving the types and frequency of the data collected (or not collected), the way they are organized, and how they are interpreted and implemented. We focus in this chapter on one aspect of the problem: the underlying conceptual adequacy of the national income and wealth accounting practice. We ask the following question: Where in the conventional macroaccounts would one look to see a financial crisis approaching, or to track its progress as it unfolds? Because the epicenter of the recent crisis was located in the financial intermediation sector—the mortgage subsector and investment banks, among others—that would seem the natural place to look first. This raises the further question of where this

Carol A. Corrado is senior advisor and research director at The Conference Board and a senior policy scholar at the Georgetown University Center for Business and Public Policy. Charles R. Hulten is professor of economics at the University of Maryland and a research associate of the National Bureau of Economic Research.

For acknowledgments, sources of research support, and disclosure of the authors' material financial relationships, if any, please see http://www.nber.org/chapters/c12533.ack.

sector is actually located in the current accounting system and how well it is connected to the rest of the economy. This is the central focus of this chapter.

Our starting point in addressing this question is Knight's circular flow model (CFM), which describes the flow of inputs and output through factor and product markets, and the reverse flow of payments. It records the flows of gross domestic product (GDP) and gross domestic income (GDI), as well as their components. These accounts are primarily flow accounts, but the Bureau of Economic Analysis (BEA), which compiles the National Income and Product Account (NIPA) version of the CFM, also provides supplementary data on capital stocks. Data on financial flows and balance sheets are complied by the Federal Reserve Board (FRB) and published in the Financial Accounts of the United States, formerly called the Flow of Funds Accounts. Since 2007, these databases have been combined into the integrated macroeconomic accounts (IMAs), which were made quarterly in 2010. One goal of this chapter is to explore the theoretical underpinnings of the IMAs by expanding the conventional CFM to allow for a capital account like the one in the IMAs.

As part of this overall goal, we focus on the role played by financial intermediation in connecting saving to investment and wealth to the capital stock. The conventional accounting structure views the financial sector as one of many industries competing for scarce resources and providing value added to the economy. In our modified view of the wealth-augmented CFM, we accord the financial sector a separate and central role in connecting the goods-producing sectors of the economy to households, where consumption of these goods takes place. Financial intermediation in this model serves to "lubricate the wheels of industry and commerce," and we argue that the failure to provide adequate lubrication (liquidity) is one factor that enabled a crisis in a relatively small segment of the financial market to propagate so rapidly to the market as a whole, and then to the real economy. A data system designed to spot emerging crises must be able to spot "holes" in a labyrinth of interconnected financial tubes, and reveal how the tubes are connected (i.e., the counterparties to the transactions and the allocation of risk among the parties).

This connectivity perspective on intermediation also helps to understand the role played by the growth in complexity and nontransparency of the intermediation process following the introduction of increasingly complicated financial instruments (derivatives, options), organizations (shadow banking), and practices (computerized trading and hedging). As complexity increased, the difficulty in spotting "local" problems increased, as did systemic risk. Traditional banks report detailed condition data and undergo regular examination, and many financial instruments are traded on exchanges. But such scrutiny generally did not extend to the intermediaries and securities at the epicenter of the crisis.

We do not attempt a full data reconciliation of our wealth-augmented

CFM and the current IMAs. This would be a major undertaking far beyond the scope of this chapter. Moreover, the risk-map analysis of Cecchetti, Fender, and McGuire (2010) (essentially a map of the system tubing) suggests that it may even be beyond the capacity of large statistical agencies, given the multidimensional characteristics of the financial information required and the way the data are currently collected. What we do, instead, is modify the IMA treatment of the housing finance sector, so as to distinguish between capital stock and the associated wealth, an important step in any attempt to understand a crisis originating in the mortgage market. We then examine the behavior of the Tobin's average q statistic before and during the financial crisis. We also estimate the degree of leverage in these sectors, as an indicator of risk and potential illiquidity. One lesson that emerges from this analysis is the importance of the Modigliani-Miller Theorem in interpreting the results. Another lesson is that alternative ways of measuring the productive capital stock also play an import role in interpreting the observed pattern of the q statistic.

5.2   Accounting for Capital and Wealth

National income and growth accounting would be a relatively simple exercise if there were no capital to worry about. In this case, output would comprise only consumption goods and these goods would be produced by labor input alone. If all the output of consumption goods and labor inputs flowed through product and factor markets, the main job of income accounting would be to record the current flows. The aggregate expenditure for consumption would equal aggregate labor income.

The economic world becomes considerably more complicated when capital, in any of its various manifestations, is introduced. Indeed, Hicks (1981, 204) observed that "the measurement of capital is one of the nastiest jobs that economists have set to statisticians." One form of capital is implicit even in a simple all-consumption framework. Some workers may want to shift current consumption to later years, while others may want (or need) to consume more in the current year by borrowing against future consumption. If they can be brought together, the former may lend their current saving to the latter in the form of a consumption loan to be repaid in later years out of the future consumption of the borrowers. The loan of current consumption goods creates an asset (wealth) for the saver/lender and a liability for the dissaver/borrower.

The problem gets messier when capital goods are introduced. In this situation, some of the current capacity used to produce consumption goods is diverted to the production of capital goods. This investment provides an alternative way that current consumption can be shifted to future years, since, while the capital itself cannot be consumed directly, it can be employed in production to produce the desired future consumption. This reveals a key feature of capital: it is both a current output of the economic system, as investment, and a future input as part of the accumulated stock of past investments.

Another key feature of capital is that it is both a productive asset and a source of wealth. Whereas the capital stock is the net accumulation of past investments, wealth is the net accumulation of past saving (which is to say, past forgone consumption). As productive capital, its value reflects a balance between the discounted present net value of the output it produces over its useful life and the cost of acquiring units of fixed assets. From the standpoint of wealth, the value of the accumulated wealth is a balance between consumption forgone and the discounted present value of the future consumption made possible by the return to wealth. The acquisition cost reflects the opportunity cost in terms of consumption forgone.

When the capital stock is owned directly by the person whose own saving enables the acquisition of the capital, the distinction between the value of capital and wealth is somewhat artificial. Direct and unleveraged ownership means that the return to the stock of capital is equally the return to wealth, and capital stock equals wealth. However, owner utilization tends to obscure the fact that the decision to invest is separate and apart from the decision to save. The investment decision is based on the productivity of capital in production, while the saving decision is based upon the benefits of shifting consumption from one time period to another.

The arrangement in which capital is wholly owned by a sole user was more common in the past and important examples remain (e.g., owner-occupied housing without mortgages, unleveraged sole proprietorships). However, the decoupling of individual investments from individual savings was one of the most important innovations that enabled the evolution of modern economic organizations. Decoupling was made possible by the rise of financial intermediaries that, in effect, connected the supply of saving indirectly to the demand for investment. Financial intermediaries aggregate the savings of individual investors and transfer them through a variety of financial instruments to entrepreneurs and businesses, who then use the funds to acquire the capital necessary for their operations. Investment was no longer limited to the opportunities available to individual savers, leading to an increase in capital and a reallocation of assets that greatly increased the efficiency of investment and the return to savers.

This is where the measurement of capital really turns "nasty." With financial intermediation, the link between saving and investment runs through a chain of financial instruments that channel to return to investment back to the owners of the claims against the stock, the owners of the wealth. The households hold claims against the productive stock in the form of instruments like stocks or bonds that channel the income from the productive stock directly to the wealth holder. If the financial instruments connecting the sectors consisted exclusively of basic stocks and bonds issued by businesses and sold directly to the wealth holders, the degree of complexity would be limited. However, financial intermediaries have developed a variety of instruments that package and securitize the debt and equity issued by businesses for passage on to other financial intermediaries or to the ultimate wealth holder. These include more or less straightforward instruments like mutual funds, annuities, exchange-traded funds, and less straightforward ones like derivatives, structured investment vehicles, and private equity arrangements. The degree of complexity of these instruments has grown greatly in recent years with the result that the link between the source of capital income in the business sector and its destination in the household sector has become ever more indirect and opaque.

As noted in the introduction, this complexity and lack of transparency was seen by many observers as a contributing factor in the crisis. As the degree of complexity increased so did the degree of indirection and, therefore, the more steps in the valuation of assets and liabilities. The mortgage market at the center of the financial crisis is an important case in point. Individual mortgages that were, in the past, held by the originating banks, were increasingly pooled to form mortgage-backed securities (MBS), which, as the market evolved, were then pooled again and repackaged into tranches of collateralized debt obligations (CDO). The link back to the individual mortgages became progressively more tenuous, to the point that it became hard to value the complex derivatives or to prove or establish legal ownership of some properties in foreclosure proceedings. High degrees of leverage (with short-term borrowing) and use of credit default swaps (CDS) further complicated asset valuation.

Increasing complexity does not, however, necessarily imply that a valuation problem exists. Under the conditions of the Modigliani-Miller Theorem, an efficient market should see through the complexity and arbitrage away any valuation disconnects. The hold-to-maturity (H2M) value of assets would equal the mark-to-market (M2M) value at each stage of the intermediation process. A valuation crisis must therefore come from an unanticipated shock to the economy or financial markets. The bursting of the housing market bubble in 2006 was certainly a development that seems to have been largely unanticipated by the broader market, but once housing prices starting trending down, the growing understanding that mortgage underwriting standards had been lax and private-label MBS were overpriced seems to have been an even more severe shock. The M2M valuations fell more rapidly than valuation based on H2M, a point noted by Federal Reserve Board Chairman Ben Bernanke.[1] Combined with high degrees of leverage

---

1. An April 10, 2008, article in Reuters (http://www.reuters.com/article/2008/04/10/usa-economy-bernanke-accounting-idUSWBT00874820080410), "Bernanke: Mark-to-Market Accounting Challenging," reported that "Federal Reserve Chairman Ben Bernanke said on Thursday mark-to-market accounting has helped to destabilize markets for illiquid assets, but regulators need to be careful about any changes to the system. 'It's also true in the current

at investment banks and short-term borrowing to finance the longer-term asset positions, confidence in the solvency of counterparties declined and liquidity began to dry up, propagating the crisis in an unanticipated way. When financial markets have a hard time valuing the underlying worth of an asset class, the job of the statistician is very nasty indeed.

5.3   The Circular Flow Model

5.3.1   Basic Structure

Knight's circular flow model of an economy (CFM) is the conventional framework for organizing the economic flows in the economy as a whole, and is the conceptual underpinning of general equilibrium theory.[2] The CFM distinguishes two essential economic functions: production and consumption. Consumption takes place in the household sector, and, in a closed economy, they are the recipients of the flow of goods and services; they are also the source of the labor and capital used in the production sector. Production takes place in the business sector, which is divided into industries that deliver intermediate goods to each other, and final demand outside the sector. This sector uses labor and capital provided by the household sector.

A simplified version of the CFM is shown in figure 5.1. Resources flow into the factor markets from the household sector, where they are priced and sent on to producers. There, the resources are transformed into outputs via each industry's production function. The outputs are priced in the product markets and sent on to consumers, whose demand is determined by their utility function and incomes, which reflect their utility-maximizing supply decisions. The flow outputs though product markets creates a dollar value that is in principle equal to gross domestic product, and the value of the flow of inputs through factor markets equals gross domestic income. These flows are linked via the standard national income accounting identity, where output is the value of deliveries to final demand and income is split between labor and capital. The counterclockwise flows shown in figure 5.1 are denominated in current prices. The clockwise flows refer to the quantity flows of inputs and outputs between consumers and producers.

The CFM is helpful in laying out the logical structure of the economy and tracking the sources and uses of resources. It covers, in principle, all

---

context, that mark-to-market accounting has been sometimes destabilizing in that sales of assets into very illiquid markets had led to reductions in prices, which have caused write downs which have sometimes caused fire sales, and you get into an adverse dynamic which has caused problems in some of our markets,' Bernanke said in a question-and-answer session before a business group."

2. Patinkin (1973) traces the circular flow model, in its modern form, to the work of Frank Knight in the 1920s and 1930s, although earlier incomplete forms of the model can be found.

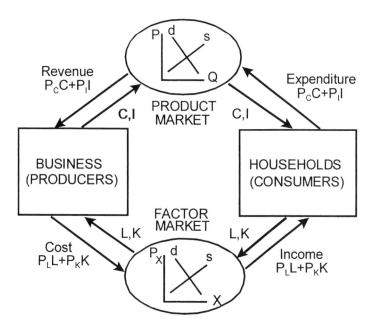

Fig. 5.1   Product market/factor market

sources and uses but, in practice, measured GDP records (with some exceptions) only goods and services that flow through markets. The use of market transactions provides a more-or-less objective, and largely available, metric with which to value the flows, but it is subject to the practical drawback that the market economy is only a fraction of total economic activity. Household production is omitted, and problems also arise from the omission of own-account intangible capital in the business sector.[3]

At a conceptual level, issues arise in the treatment of the government and owner-occupied housing sectors. From the structural standpoint of the CFM, the production of owner-occupied housing services is conceptually no different from the production of rental housing services. Therefore, both are appropriately located on the producer side of figure 5.1, and if the owners of housing assets chooses to rent to themselves, there is no substantive economic difference from the market rental option. A rent is paid to the

3. According to Landefeld and McCulla (2000), the nonmarket production of consumption goods by households amounted to 24 percent of measured GDP in 1946. More recent estimates of the value of investments in human capital alone are 23 percent of GDP in 2005 (Christian 2010). Estimates by Corrado, Hulten, and Sichel (2005, 2009) suggest that the omission of own-account intangible investment may understate the GDP by as much as 14 percent (though this will change in the United States with the capitalization of R&D expenditures in 2013).

landlord, who distributes the payment (less expenses and any interest payments) to the owners of the equity in the assets.[4]

5.3.2   A Wealth-Augmented Circular Flow Model

In the System of National Accounts (SNA) and conventional CFM, finance is treated as just another industry, as we have already noted, drawing from the pool of available resources to produce a flow of deliveries to final demand and deliveries to intermediate demand in other industries. This accounting convention is by no means wrong—it does keep track of the uses of resources—but neither does it illuminate one of the most important functions of financial intermediation, the connection of saving and investment.

The expanded circular flow model of figure 5.2 is designed to make this connection explicit, which is based on Hulten (2006). This formalizes the intent behind the integrated macroeconomic accounts, which combine the GDP flow accounts of the BEA with FRB balance sheets and financial capital flow data. In figure 5.2, a balance sheet is attached to each of the sectors in the diagram (the two circular areas adjacent to each box). The balance sheet associated with the production sector contains the net stock of productive capital in the sector as an asset, and debt and residual equity on the liability side. While businesses are treated as the legal owner of these assets, the household sector is the owner of the claims against the income generated by those assets. These claims form the basis for the net worth of the household sector, shown on the balance sheet on the right-hand side of figure 5.2. The two balance sheets are connected by the flow of saving and investment. Household saving is channeled into financial instruments, which are then held in the household balance sheets as increments to wealth, and the proceeds are channeled into the business sector in order to finance the purchase of investment goods.[5] The new capital goods are added to the existing stock, less reductions in the stock due to wear, tear, and obsolescence. In the process, the deferred consumption of households is matched by the shift in the current production of consumption goods to the production of capital goods that enable additional consumption in the future.

The flow of capital income moves in the opposite direction from saving

4. Similar remarks apply to the public sector. The government is a producer of services and can be located on the left-hand side of figure 5.1, along with other productive entities that draw on a common pool of labor and capital. The fact that government distributes much of its product outside market channels does not change the basic nature of these flows. Problems do arise from the collective nature of much of the consumption and from the collective nature of the "ownership" of public capital. Should these assets be treated as being held in common by the household sector, with the government a separate consumer within the household sector with its own utility function?

5. In practice, large companies can fund part of their investment program via retained earnings and the depreciation reserve. In the framework of figure 5.2, retained earnings are treated as an increment to the firm's capital assets that result in an increase in the value of household equity claims.

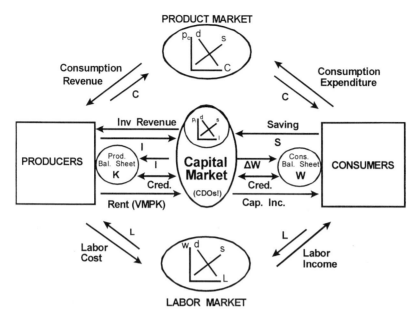

Fig. 5.2   Product market/capital market/labor market

and investment in figure 5.2. The income from the productive stock flows from its origin in the business sector (mostly) through financial intermediaries to households, along the pathways determined by the ownership structure of assets and liabilities. It provides the basis for the income accruing to the instruments held by households (the dividends, capital gains, interest, rents, and other payments associated with the various types of instrument). The channels may be more or less direct, depending on the degree of complexity of the ownership linkages.[6]

5.3.3   Adding Financial Intermediation to the Circular Flow Model

Financial intermediation is represented in figure 5.2 in the oval area in the middle of the diagram, which connects the real and financial markets. It is presented only in a summary way, without the complex channels (the inter-

6. There are, of course, many closely held firms, including family-held firms that control a lot of assets. According to the BEA/Federal Reserve's Integrated Macroeconomic Accounts, noncorporate business holds about 40 percent of the value of total nonfinancial business productive assets, and against this, about 65 percent is direct-owner equity (2001 to 2007). Thus, the equity income generated by about one-fourth of the stock of nonfinancial business productive assets in the United States is not intermediated but rather flows directly to owner-operators (and then back to financial business, to the extent assets are debt financed). Further, 90 percent of noncorporate income-generating assets are real estate assets, about two-thirds of which is residential housing.

connecting "financial tubes" of our introduction are not shown explicitly). This treatment is analogous to the treatment of intermediate input flows within the business sector, an input-output table connecting industry of origin to deliveries to final demand. The financial "input-output" array is more complex, connecting the income from productive business-sector capital to the holder of wealth claims against this capital via financial intermediaries. The risk-map paper by Cecchetti, Fender, and McGuire (2010) describes the multidimensional nature of the intermediation process, as assets are packaged, "sliced and diced," repackaged, leveraged, and hedged. Valuation depends on counterparty risk, currency risk, and local taxation and regulation. An attempt to construct this requires confidential data at the firm level of detail, collected at the global level. This is probably the kind of data needed to spot financial crises before they emerge, but also the kind of data that firms and even governments may be loathe to divulge (although there are new reporting requirements under the Dodd-Frank legislation that may help in this regard). Figure 5.2 indicates where such data are logically located, but not the details of the microintermediation flows.

The treatment of homeownership and mortgage in the balance sheets of figure 5.2 deserves special mention, since the homeowner is both a producer and a direct consumer of the housing services associated with a given home. As producer, the value of the home is recorded as an asset of the "business" balance sheet on the left-hand side of figure 5.2, and the mortgage used to finance the house is recorded as a balance sheet liability. The difference in value is recorded as a shadow net equity. The corresponding consumer balance sheet of the homeowner records the shadow net equity as an asset, and this net equity is also consumer net worth on the liability side of the account. The households that hold the mortgage, directly or through indirect equity (through intermediary securities like banks shares, mutual funds, or exchange-traded funds [ETFs]), record the value of the mortgage as an asset and as net worth on the liability side of their account. When individual household-sector balance sheets are consolidated into a single sheet, the total value of assets is the shadow equity plus the direct or indirect value of the mortgage components, leaving the value of the house as both an asset and an offsetting net worth entry.

This treatment of owner-occupied housing is symmetric with the accounting treatment of rental housing. If the homeowner decides to convert the home into a rental property, it becomes part of the business sector and would be counted as such on the business-sector balance sheet. Thus, there is no economic reason to treat owner-occupancy differently, and the framework of the preceding paragraph preserves this symmetry. This is an important issue when attempting to link the value of the capital stock to household wealth, in both the aggregate economy of figure 5.2 and in the housing subsector.

5.4   Accounting Equations and the Modigliani-Miller Theorem

5.4.1   Valuation of the Productive Capital Stock

The conventional approach to estimating the value of the stock of productive capital at any point in time, V_t, is the sum of the values of current and past vintages of investment goods, $P_{t,s}^I I_{t-s}$.

(1)
$$V_t = P_{t,0}^I I_{t-0} + P_{t,1}^I I_{t-1} + \cdots + P_{t,s}^I I_{t-s} + \cdots.$$

One procedure for measuring the stock is to estimate the book value of the asset carried on financial balance sheets. Another is to use the perpetual inventory method (PIM), an approach widely used in national income accounting.

The analytical difference in the two approaches becomes clearer when the deprecation process proceeds at a constant annual rate δ.[7] Because the value of older (used) capital shrinks at a rate δ (other things equal), owning one unit of a vintage of age s is equivalent to owning $(1 - \delta)^s$ units of a new asset, implying that $P_{t,s}^I = (1 - \delta)^s P_{t,0}^I$. In this case the value of capital, as shown in equation (1), becomes

(1′)
$$V_t = P_{t,0}^I I_{t-0} + (1-\delta) P_{t,0}^I I_{t-1} + \cdots + (1-\delta)^s P_{t,0}^I I_{t-s} + \cdots.$$

In the book value case, the accounting rate of depreciation is generally used, typically the straight-line form, and the prices reflect the historical cost of the new asset in each vintage when it was put in place, $P_{t-s,0}^I$ (generally leading to an underestimate). In contrast, under the PIM valuation approach, the rate of depreciation is based on estimates of economic (actual) depreciation, and the price of a new asset, $P_{t,0}^I$, is used in each year. In this, the contribution of each vintage to overall value can be interpreted as the effective quantity of vintage s investment surviving to the current year, $(1 - \delta)^s$, times the price of a new investment good, $P_{t,0}^I$.

The valuation form of the PIM, (1′), has a parallel quantity interpretation. The terms $(1 - \delta)^s P_{t,0}^I I_{t-s}$ can be rewritten as $[(1 - \delta)^s I_{t-s}] P_{t,0}^I$, and interpreted as the amount of vintage s investment surviving to the present years, measured in units of productive efficiency. The price terms can then be combined to give

(1″)
$$V_t = P_{t,0}^I \left[I_{t-0} + (1-\delta) I_{t-1} + \ldots + (1-\delta)^s I_{t-s} + \ldots \right].$$

---

7. The productive efficiency is assumed, in equation (1), to decline at a constant (geometric) rate, though a more general form can be adopted. A survey of the literature on capital measurement and depreciation is available in Hulten (1990).

The term in square brackets on the right-hand side of this equation is an index of the quantity of the capital stock, implicitly measured in constant prices,

(2) $K_t = I_{t-0} + (1-\delta)I_{t-1} + \ldots + (1-\delta)^s I_{t-s} + \ldots = I_{t-0} + (1-\delta)K_{t-1}$.

In this formulation, the stock K_t is the total amount of effective capital *denominated in units of new capital*; that is, the equivalent amount of new capital needed to replace the capacity of the actual stock with its various layers of vintage capital. This is the *replacement cost* approach to valuing the capital stock. The annual change in the capital stock is the quantity of new capital units put in place less the units that must be replaced, δK_{t-1}. The resulting value of the capital stock in (1') is therefore equivalent to $P^I_{t,0}K_t$.

We will revisit this replacement cost interpretation in our discussion of Tobin's *q*. The key point to note here is that the estimated value of the stock of capital, $P^I_{t,0}K_t$ is based on the price of new assets, and an externally imposed time-invariant estimate of the parameter δ. A negative shock would reduce the mark-to-market price of a vintage asset, that is, the spot price $P^I_{t,s}$ in equation (1), but the decline would not be apparent if this price is measured by the proxy $(1-\delta)^s P^I_{t,0}$ as per equation (1').

5.4.2   Asset Prices and User Costs

The value of the capital stock in any year is determined by the interaction of the supply price of producing investment goods and the demand of these goods. To complete the description of the demand side, it is necessary to connect the price of the investment good to the future returns generated by the asset. In an efficient-market model, this price of acquiring a unit of capital, $P^I_{t,s}$ in equation (1) is assumed to be equal to the discounted present value of the expected stream of future income, adjusted for depreciation. With a discount rate r_t the equilibrium price $P^I_{t,s}$ for an asset of age *s* is:

(3) $$P^I_{t,s} = \sum_{\tau=0}^{\infty} \frac{(1-\delta)^{s+\tau}E(P^K_{t,s+\tau})}{(1+r)^{\tau+1}} .$$

This formulation assumes that the present value on the right-hand side is fully arbitraged against the cost of acquiring the capital good. In many accounting applications, this formulation assumes perfect foresight on the part of the investor.

The term $E(P^K_{t,s})$ is the expected annual user cost of capital. Under profit maximization, the user cost is equal to the value of the marginal product of capital (*VMPK*), connecting the return to capital in the business sector to the flow of capital income. Following Jorgenson (1963), equation (3) can be used to derive an explicit form for the user cost in terms of its logical components: the opportunity cost of capital r_t, expected holding gains (or revaluation) π_t, which is equal to expected asset price change $dE(P^I_{t+1})/P^I_t$, and depreciation δ:

(4) $$P_{t,0}^{K} = \left(r_t - \pi_t + \delta \right) P_{t,0}^{I}$$

(we abstract, here, from within-year timing issues and taxes).[8] The $P_{t,0}^{K}$ is a cost to the user, but at the same time, a return to the owner whose components are part of the capital income flows in figure 5.2.

The total gross income generated by the capital stock in any year is the sum of the income from each of the individual vintages:

(5) $$P_{t,0}^{K} I_{t-0} + P_{t,1}^{K} I_{t-1} + \ldots + P_{t,s}^{K} I_{t-s} + \ldots = P_{t,0}^{K} K_t .$$

This is the gross capital income originating in the production sector of the circular flow model. It is the source of the income transferred to the household sector as part of gross domestic income. In view of equation (4), gross capital income from the production of output is the sum of the opportunity cost of capital less holding gains, plus depreciation: $P_{t,0}^{K} K_t + (r_t - \pi_t) P_{t,0}^{I} K_t + \delta P_{t,0}^{I} K_t$. The total return to holding a unit of K_t is equal to the $VMPK$ on the left-hand side net of depreciation plus any holding gain of the asset, that is, $r_t = VMPK_t - \delta + \pi_t = \rho_t + \pi_t$.

5.4.3   Household Saving and Wealth with Financial Intermediation

The asset value of the firm as a business, V_t in the formulation of equation (1), is the value of its productive capital, $P_{t,0}^{I} K_t$. To obtain a richer picture of a firm's balance sheet, its financial assets, F_t^{B}, must be added, along with the firm's liabilities, D_t^{B} plus net worth NW_t^{B}, in order to more accurately reflect a firm's true financial position (this is particularly important for financial firms where financial assets [loans] and liabilities [deposits] loom large).[9] The firm's "T" account is then

(6) $$V_t = P_{t,0}^{I} K_t + F_t^{B} = D_t^{B} + NW_t^{B} .$$

The items on the liability side of the business balance sheet are assets of households, which hold the legal claims to the income from these assets, $\rho_t P_t^{I} K_t$, in the form of financial instruments, equities E_t and debt D_t, or other instruments of direct ownership that establish legal control over assets and the income they generate and responsibility for the associated liabilities (for simplicity of exposition, we ignore the latter as a separate equity category). In our simplified model, the holders of the value of the equity have a residual claim to the net worth of businesses NW_t^{B} and are also the holders of the debt D_t^{B}.

The households' claims on business net worth come in the form of equity certificates E_t that are valued at a price P_t^{E} per unit (this is a market-

---

8. For a more complete description of the complexity involved in the user cost model, see Hall and Jorgenson (1967) and the survey by Hulten (1990).

9. The theory of user cost still applies (e.g., see Barnett [1978] and Fixler, Reinsdorf, and Smith [2003]).

determined value when such markets exist and a shadow price when they do not).

$$(7) \qquad P_t^E = \sum_{\tau=0}^{\infty} \frac{E(Div_{t+\tau}^K)}{(1+r)^{\tau+1}} .$$

The value of total household equity claims in any point in time is thus $P_t^E E_t$.

The value of debt is more complicated because it is typically issued in different vintages, each with its own price (a situation similar to the vintages of productive capital in equation [1]). Borrowers (firms in this case) typically carry debt at par value on their books, whereas value of the debt to the (household) lenders depends on market price at each point in time P_t^D. In a model with perfect information, this is not a problem and the aggregate value of the debt instruments carried on the household balance sheet is thus D_t^B. (With imperfect information, the "mark-to-market" disconnect, discussed above, can arise.) Net household assets (with just one type of debt, issued by business) are thus

$$(8) \qquad P_t^E E_t + P_t^D D_t = W_t ,$$

where W_t is household net worth, and intrahousehold lending nets out.

Ignoring sector distinctions and financial assets held by business (or treating them as just another form of K), the net capital income originating in the business sector is transferred to households via interest, dividends, capital gains, or additions to equity. Thus,

$$(9) \qquad \rho_t P_t^I K_t = \sum_n i_{t,n}^D P_t^D D_{t,n} + i_t^E P_t^E E_t,$$

where

i_N^D = interest rate paid on loan/debt security type n;
$P^D D_n$ = net value of liability in loan/debt security type n;
i^E = return on equity (ROE); and
$P^E E$ = value of equity.

The return to financial instruments held by households is derived from the return to the underlying income-generating assets K_t. This is true even when the intermediation process has multiple stages. Each stage involves a transaction in which an intermediate instrument is transferred from seller to buyer. For example, a pension plan may hold the assets of different managed funds, which may themselves hold the pooled assets of other funds, as well as options and other derivatives. The financial instruments held by households are the last stage in the chain, whatever its length and complexity, but the connection between saving to investment still occurs.

A great deal of simplification is achieved under the conditions of the Modigliani-Miller Theorem, which states that the value of the firm in equation (6) is independent of the debt-equity ratio under certain assumptions.

By implication, net worth is independent of the degree of leverage. In the M&M world, the degree of complexity of the financial instruments connecting the source of income to its distribution to wealth holders is not a problem *per se*, as long as arbitrage works to correct valuation "mistakes" at each point in the chain of intermediation.

5.5   Tobin's Average q Statistic

5.5.1   The "q" Theory

Tobin's average q is a statistic that links the real and financial sides of asset valuation. It thus has a potentially useful role in any discussion of the adequacy of macroeconomic data systems both before and after large-scale financial crises. Tobin's average q is defined in the CFM context as the ratio of the value of households' wealth (as ultimate owners of businesses) to the value of the income-generating capital held by businesses, or, in the notation of the preceding section:

$$(10) \qquad q = \frac{P_t^E E_t + P_t^D D_t}{P_{t,0}^I K_t + F_t^B} = \frac{W_t}{V_t} .$$

Under the Modigliani-Miller Theorem and the strong Efficient Market Hypothesis, Tobin's marginal q should equal one in a closed economy, given the following conditions: zero-rents and constant returns to scale, no adjustment costs, all capital is measured, and the value of the capital stock is constantly revalued. In this situation, Hayashi (1982) shows that average q is also equal to one under these conditions, implying that wealth W_t equals the value of capital stock, V_t, regardless of the degree of financial intermediation or the degree of leverage in the system.

Financial intermediation is present even in the model where q always equals one. The q in equation (8) is based on capital and wealth values at the end points of the intermediation chain. A more general formulation would go beyond the formulation $W_t = q_t V_t$ and allow for a separate q_i ratio for each transaction stage in the intermediation process, defined as the ratio of the value perceived by the owner of the asset and the value as perceived by the buyer. The stages are not independent, in the sense that the separate q_i ratios in any year refer back to the value of the same income-generating asset:

$$(11) \qquad P^E = \left(q_N \times q_{N-1} \ldots q_1\right) P^I = q P^I .$$

In the efficient market M&M world, this detail is superfluous, since the individual q_i are all equal to one. In variants of the q model in which this condition does not always hold, equation (11) could be used to identify the points of "failure" in the intermediation process. However, while this formulation may work as an expository device, it fails at a practical level. In the modern financial world of complex financial intermediation, there may be no single chain of q_i emanating from an initial dollar of V_t. Instead, there are multiple chains, just as there are usually multiple chains feeding into each dollar of W_t from different productive assets. This is the "risk map" problem.

5.5.2   Nonunitary Values of q

Violation of some of the assumptions may cause the level of average q to deviate from one. Hayashi shows that the existence of adjustment costs may cause this to happen, even though markets are efficient and profit is maximized. Moreover, the systematic omission of certain types of capital assets from the accounts, like the intangible capital studied by Corrado, Hulten, and Sichel (2005, 2009) will cause an upward bias in average q, since the unreported capital lowers measured V_t while it is included in W_t in an efficient market.[10]

The cyclical mismeasurement of capital can also lead to a nonunitary value of q. We have already noted that the perpetual inventory method of measuring V_t is not robust against an unexpected shock to the economic system. Capital is measured at replacement cost of an equivalent amount of new assets, as per equations (1″) and (2), and uses the vintage value $(1 - \delta)^s P_{t,0}^I I_{t,0}$ as a proxy for the value $P_{t,s}^I I_{t,s}$ in equation (1). The latter may decline in face of a shock because the remaining present value $P_{t,s}^I$ in equation (3), because effective $I_{t,s}$ declines as a result of bankruptcy or retirements from service, or because the rate at which capital is utilized falls. These declines will generally not be measured when $(1 - \delta)^s P_{t,0}^I I_{t,0}$ is used in the PIM. The result is that the replacement value of q based on using equation (1″) in the denominator will show a procyclical pattern, even if the true value of q^e measured as per equation (1) remained equal to one.

Asset-market disequilibrium can also lead q to deviate from one. The increase in complexity of the intermediation process and associated lack of transparency may have put pressure on the arbitrage processes of financial markets and created concerns about the reliability of the counterparties involved in certain transactions. In such cases, valuations based on equations like (3) and (7) may diverge, even though they are based on the same income-generating asset. The mark-to-market versus hold-to-maturity value of some assets (e.g., CDOs) seems to have diverged during the financial crisis because of a lack of transparency and the liquidity problems faced by some lenders who engaged in short-maturity borrowing to fund longer-maturity investments. If the wealth term in the numerator of the q ratio were valued

---

10. Hulten and Hao (2008) illustrate the importance of including intangible capital in estimates of the q ratio in their study of the price-to-book ratios of a sample of more than 600 R&D-oriented US corporations in 2006. The price-to-book ratio is the ratio of market capitalization to balance sheet net worth and is thus a variant of the q ratio. When intangible capital is added to the denominator of the price-to-book ratio, and tangible capital stock is adjusted to reflect current rather than historical prices, balance-sheet net worth explains 86 percent of the market capitalization of the firms. Without intangible capital, only 42 percent is explained.

on a M2M basis, while the valuation of capital held by business continued on a H2M basis, the disconnect would cause the ratio to fall during the financial crisis and return to its previous value in the aftermath. On the other hand, if both the numerator and denominator were M2M, the ratio would remain relatively stable, although not necessarily equal to one.

The numerator of the q ratio is much more prone to financial speculation than the value of underlying productive assets, and is another potential factor in the volatility of q. Here the mechanism is the wave of technology starting in the mid-1980s that made trading very cheap and more-or-less instantaneous, and not primarily the complexity/nontransparency mechanism. Computerized momentum trading, hedging strategies, and winners-curse are plausible factors causing more volatility in W_t than in V_t, leading to cyclical fluctuation in the q ratio.

The overall conclusion of this analysis is that Tobin's average q may be a weak statistic to use a priori to detect conditions that could lead to a financial crisis and to track a financial crisis should it occur. A crisis could occur with a cyclically varying value of q or with one that is relatively stable. Nor is a high q evidence about the cause of the crisis, given that its value may reflect mismeasurement of capital stocks. Still, the evidence presented in the following section suggests that variations in q over the last two decades have corresponded to real fluctuations in the economy and financial markets.

5.5.3   The Empirics of Tobin's q

The actual value of Tobin's q in any year is an empirical matter. We have therefore calculated the ratio for the years from 1960 to 2012 for the consolidated total US domestic private sector; that is, a sector that includes assets held by households and nonprofit institutions as well as businesses. Our estimates are based on data from the Flow of Funds Accounts (as they were known until recently) and integrated macroeconomic accounts, transformed to reflect the two-sector framework of the CFM and the q (equation [10]). These transformations are not typical, given the five-sector organization of the data, and the equilibrium orientation of each of these sectoral accounts, but all told they are straightforward and described in detail in the notes to charts.

The resulting q ratios are shown in figure 5.3. Consider first the solid line. Its numerator is essentially the value of household net worth (the sector's direct holdings of nonfinancial assets plus its net financial holdings), and its denominator is the value of all private nonfinancial assets at replacement cost. Debt holdings are almost completely consolidated in the numerator of this q ratio. The q ratio shows a steady rise starting in the late 1980s, and an acceleration in the mid-1990s leading to a peak in 2000, some 20 percent above the baseline value of one. This was followed by a sharp decline associated with the "tech wreck," with q falling back to the latter after a few years.

The value of q then began to rise again, retracing its 20 percent rise to

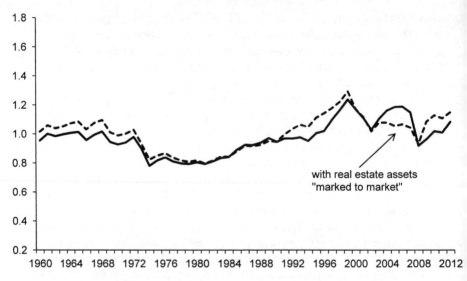

Fig. 5.3   Private sector Q: Value of financial claims relative to the replacement cost of privately held assets, 1960 to 2012

Source: Authors' elaboration of data from the Federal Reserve's Financial Accounts as of March 7, 2013, on the Federal Reserve website. Data for business intangible assets are from an unpublished update to Corrado and Hulten (2010) and Corrado, Hulten, and Sichel (2009).

Note: Financial claims are calculated as household net worth adjusted for (1) foreign holdings of domestic equity and debt issues, (2) household holdings of foreign equity issues, and (3) the net foreign investment position of the United States. The replacement cost of privately held productive assets includes assets held by (1) the IMA business sectors (financial business, nonfinancial corporations, and nonfinancial, noncorporate business); (2) its households and nonprofit institutions sector; and (3) business intangible assets not capitalized in the national accounts as of March 2013. The value of land is not included in replacement-cost measures. To account for this on the level of the Q ratio, the ratio in 1990 is indexed to a ratio calculated using real estate assets at market value in that year. The actual series for the ratio using real estate assets at market value is plotted as the dashed line, that is, where actual land values are used throughout.

its peak in 2007, followed again by a crash as the housing bubble burst and the financial crisis took hold. It has risen from its trough of around 0.90 to its 2012 value of around 1.10. The volatile pattern of the q ratio over these twenty years tracks fairly closely the volatility of the assets markets over the same period.

These results (the solid line) are based on the replacement version of q in which the value of capital in the denominator is based on the PIM, and they are therefore prone to the procyclical behavior noted above. The dashed line in figure 5.3 attempts to correct for this potential bias in the one class of business capital for which an adjustment can be made, real estate. The correction, reflected in the difference between the modified q ratio of the dashed line and the conventional solid line, makes an M2M adjustment for housing in the denominator of the ratio. The increase in the modified q^e ratio in the period preceding the financial crisis (2003 to 2007) now appears muted, rising to a value less than 1.10 before falling to the trough value of around 0.9. This pattern invites the question: What would the dashed line look like if we could measure all types of capital in the denominator on a M2M basis?

These patterns correlate well with the observed facts on the ground: the rise and fall of the stock market over the period of the tech boom and bust, and the collapse and recovery of household net worth. This correlation adds verisimilitude to the use of the Tobin's q, in either form, as an indicator of economic problems. This statistic is not, however, dispositive as to the mechanisms causing the observed patterns. Or, more precisely, as to the relative importance of the various factors that were potentially at work, or the points in the financial intermediation chain where these factors were operative.

5.5.4   Debt and Leverage

The Modigliani-Miller Theorem implies that leverage is not a determinant of asset valuation and should not affect the equilibrium value of q. However, many observers have pointed to a high degree of leverage in many systemically important financial institutions as a factor that greatly deepened the financial crisis. Curiously, the balance sheet data that are available from integrated macroeconomic accounts did not reveal the risks that were building on financial business balance sheets during the period leading up to the financial crisis (Palumbo and Parker 2009). Part of the difficulty owes to the aggregate nature of instruments and institution types in these accounts; another lies in their lack of information on the market values of debt. Although not all assets of financial businesses that were held in the form of debt securities were illiquid, the much-discussed maturity mismatch and build-up of short-term debt at systemically important institutions is not very evident in these data.

The upper panel of figure 5.4 depicts simple leverage ratios based on the balance sheet information for two of the three major business sectors in the IMAs (nonfinancial corporations and financial business). For each major sector, total assets/liabilities as a multiple of the value of equity is shown; that is, the following ratio is calculated:

$$(12) \qquad LVr = \left(\sum_n P^D D_n + P^E E \right) / P^E E.$$

The value of LVr for financial intermediaries as a whole (financial business) is shown on the right scale, and exhibits no evidence of overleverage, consistent with Palumbo-Parker. It should be noted that leverage ratios for individual banks calculated using total assets as a multiple of tangible common equity are one of the most basic measures of capital adequacy used in the regulatory analysis of banks and are similar to the ratio we calculate.

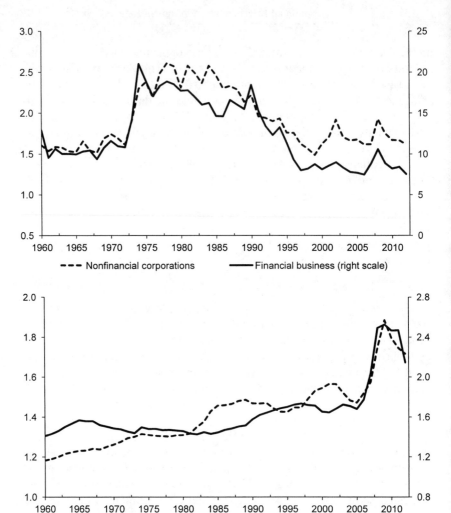

Fig. 5.4   Sector financial claims as a multiple of sector equity, 1960 to 2012

Source: Authors' elaboration of data from the Federal Reserve's Financial Accounts, as of March 7, 2013, on the Federal Reserve website.

Notes: Upper panel: For nonfinancial corporations, sector financial claims are total liabilities as shown in the sector's IMA balance sheet (table S.5.a, line 129) divided by equity and investment shares (line 139). For financial business, sector financial claims are total liabilities (table S.6.a, line 131) divided by the sum of corporate equity issues (line 142), foreign direct investment in the United States (line 145), noncorporate equity (line 146), and net investment by nonfinancial parents in finance company subsidiaries (line 147). Bottom panel: For nonfinancial, noncorporate business equity, a "shadow" value of equity is used, namely, net worth calculated such that total liabilities equal total assets (table S.4.a, line 116) plus the liability shown as equity and investment shares (line 111), which consists of real estate owned by foreigners. Equity and sector financial claims for homeowner "business" are from the FA balance sheet table (B100). Equity in homeowner business is shown on line 51 (itself calculated as line 4, the market value of owner-occupied real estate less home mortgages), and total claims are then the market value of owner-occupied real estate, which includes vacant land and mobile homes.

The bottom panel shows ratios for households as homeowners (and labeled homeowner "business") and for the nonfinancial, noncorporate business sector. As may be seen, both ratios spike after 2005, and both show a steady building of leverage beginning in the 1980s. The finding for households as homeowers is consistent with Palumbo-Parker, who concluded that households could be seen to be overleveraged in the data—but note this ratio implicitly assumes homeowner "business" q equals one because, as per our earlier discussion, if we wished to build a q for homeowner "business," we would need a market valuation for the precise financial assets held as claims against homeowner real estate. This is nowhere to be found in the IMAs. The same can be said for its counterpart in the noncorporate business sector, which as noted earlier, has large real estate holdings against which marketed debt securities are held.

5.6   Conclusion

Macroeconomic models and forecasts have not had much success in anticipating past economic downturns, even before the Great Recession. Diagnosing why this is so is a complicated (and controversial) undertaking that will hopefully occupy the economics profession in the years to come. We have looked at only a piece of the puzzle in this chapter; the way macroeconomic data on income and wealth are organized, and where problems may exist. We have focused on the treatment of financial intermediation in the accounts and argued that the centrality of financial intermediation for the functioning of the economy needs to be recognized more clearly in accounting practice. We have addressed this problem by placing the financial intermediation process at the center of a modified Knightian circular flow model (our figure 5.2). In this modified framework, nonfinancial businesses and households are linked by financial intermediaries, rather than treating these intermediaries as just another resource-using industry. Recognition of this link helps explain how shocks that affect even small parts of the economy can propagate rapidly and widely.

We have also pointed to the fact that the current framework for the macroaccounts is essentially based on a model that assumes the data are generated in a world in which economic equilibrium prevails. This is the subtext of the equations set out in our section 5.4, which can be traced back to the accounting work of Christensen and Jorgenson (1969, 1970). This approach is a highly useful way of organizing and interpreting macroeconomic data, because it uses theory as a guide to accounting practice and vice versa. This symbiosis is useful for many purposes: measuring productivity, studying the determinants of economic growth, and tracking structural changes in the composition of GDP and GDI. Advances by the BEA in recent years—the IMAs, the development of a full production account, and the capitalization of R&D expenditures and artistic originals—have made the accounts even more relevant for understanding a changing economy.

This said, if the objective is to spot, or at least track, emerging asset bubbles, the assumption of asset-market equilibrium is not helpful. To the extent that asset bubbles and their consequences are disequilibrium phenomena, the a priori imposition of equilibrium on the collection and organization of macrodata may conceal the very problems that the accounts were intended to inform, or lead analysts to misinterpret the data that are available.

Accounting frameworks need to be robust against this problem. We have attempted a start in this direction by suggesting an alternative treatment of financial intermediation in the conventional circular flow framework. This alternative is hard to implement, but we have at least suggested how and where the macroaccounts might be changed to be linked to the microfinancial data needed for a full "risk map" of the intermediation process.

Beyond this, major problems loom. Assembling a sufficiently detailed micromap involves data capabilities that are underdeveloped. Moreover, the dynamic economic theory needed to extend the equations of equilibrium-based accounts to a disequilibrium world commands no consensus, even if it can be said to exist in a general form. How is imperfect information to be treated? Risk? Shifting expectations about future states of the world? Unemployed resources? It is not enough for accounting purposes to set out general theories about these phenomena, statisticians must have precise instructions about what new data are needed, which old data must be transformed or discarded, and how the results are to be fitted together to provide estimates of GDP and GDI and their components. Hicks was certainly right: a nasty job indeed.

References

Barnett, William A. 1978. "The User Cost of Money." *Economic Letters* 1:145–49.
Cecchetti, Stephen G., Ingo Fender, and Patrick McGuire. 2010. "Toward a Global Risk Map." In *Central Bank Statistics: What Did the Financial Crisis Change?* Proceedings of the European Central Bank Conference, 2010.
Christensen, Laurits R., and Dale W. Jorgenson. 1969. "The Measurement of US Real Capital Input, 1929–1967." *Review of Income and Wealth* 15 (December): 293–320.
———. 1970. "US Real Product and Real Factor Input, 1929–1969." *Review of Income and Wealth* 16 (March): 19–50.
Christian, Michael S. 2010. "Human Capital Accounting in the Unites States, 1994 to 2006." *Survey of Current Business* June:31–36.
Corrado, Carol, and Charles Hulten. 2010. "How Do You Measure a 'Technological Revolution'?" *American Economic Review* May:99–104.
Corrado, Carol, Charles Hulten, and Daniel Sichel. 2005. "Measuring Capital and Technology: An Expanded Framework." In *Measuring Capital in the New Economy*, Studies in Income and Wealth, vol. 65, edited by C. Corrado, J. Haltiwanger, and D. Sichel, 11–41. Chicago: University of Chicago Press.

————. 2009. "Intangible Capital and US Economic Growth." *Review of Income and Wealth* 55 (3): 661–85.

Fixler, Dennis J., Marshall B. Reinsdorf, and George M. Smith. 2003. "Measuring the Services of Commercial Banks in the NIPAs: Changes in Concepts and Methods." *Survey of Current Business* 83:33–44.

Hall, Robert E., and Dale W. Jorgenson. 1967. "A Tax Policy and Investment Behavior." *American Economic Review* 57:391–414.

Hayashi, Fumio. 1982. "Tobin's Marginal q and Average q: A Neoclassical Interpretation." *Econometrica* 50:213–24.

Hicks, John. 1981. *Wealth and Welfare: Collected Essays in Economic Theory.* Cambridge, MA: Harvard University Press.

Hulten, Charles R. 1990. "The Measurement of Capital." In *Fifty Years of Economic Measurement: The Jubilee of the Conference on Research in Income and Wealth,* Studies in Income and Wealth, vol. 54, edited by Ernst R. Berndt and Jack E. Triplett, 119–52. Chicago: University of Chicago Press.

————. 2006. "The 'Architecture' of Capital Accounting: Basic Design Principles." In *A New Architecture for the US National Accounts,* Studies in Income and Wealth, vol. 66, edited by Dale Jorgenson, J. Steven Landefeld, and William Nordhaus, 193–214. Chicago: University of Chicago Press.

Hulten, Charles R., and Janet X. Hao. 2008. "What is a Company Really Worth? Intangible Capital and the 'Market to Book Value' Puzzle." NBER Working Paper no. 14548, Cambridge, MA.

Jorgenson, Dale W. 1963. "Capital Theory and Investment Behavior." *American Economic Review* 53 (2): 247–59.

Landefeld, J. S., and S. H. McCulla. 2000. "Accounting for Nonmarket Household Production Within a National Accounts Framework." *Review of Income and Wealth* 46 (3): 289–307.

Palumbo, Michael G., and Jonathan A. Parker. 2009. "The Integrated Financial and Real System of National Accounts for the United States: Does It Presage the Financial Crisis?" *American Economic Review* 99 (2): 80–86.

Patinkin, Don. 1973. "In Search of the 'Wheel of Wealth': On the Origins of Frank Knight's Circular Flow Diagram." *American Economic Review* 63 (5): 1037–46.

II

Advances in Measuring Wealth and Financial Flows

6

Adding Actuarial Estimates of Defined-Benefit Pension Plans to National Accounts

Dominique Durant, David Lenze, and Marshall B. Reinsdorf

The paucity of data on the growing risks to financial stability during the run-up to the financial crisis of 2007–2008 has highlighted the need for better data on the entities classified in the financial corporations sector in the System of National Accounts (SNA). For countries with high levels of participation in employer-sponsored defined-benefit (DB) plans, national accounts will take an important step toward this objective with the introduction of the new actuarial measures of DB pension plans that are recommended in the 2008 SNA (United Nations Statistical Division 2009). The 2008 SNA (17.191–17.206) also calls for a supplementary table showing actuarial measures of government-sponsored plans that will allow comparisons between countries where employer-sponsored DB pension plans have a major role in providing retirement income and countries where government-sponsored plans predominate. For both kinds of countries the new measures will provide a more complete picture of saving and wealth of households, and of pension expenses and pension liabilities of employers.

In many countries, including the United States and France, social security provides a base level of retirement income, with an overlay of a supplementary system of government-sponsored or employer-sponsored pen-

Dominique Durant, Banque de France, is deputy head of the research directorate at the Autorité de contrôle prudentiel et de résolution. David Lenze is an economist at the Bureau of Economic Analysis. Marshall B. Reinsdorf was chief of the National Economic Accounts research group at the Bureau of Economic Analysis when this chapter was written. He is now a senior economist at the International Monetary Fund.

Views expressed in the chapter are those of the authors and do not necessarily reflect the positions of the Autorité de contrôle prudentiel et de résolution, the International Monetary Fund, or the Bureau of Economic Analysis. For acknowledgments, sources of research support, and disclosure of the authors' material financial relationships, if any, please see http://www.nber.org/chapters/c12523.ack.

sion plans. Social security plans generally differ from other government-sponsored plans in the main features of their benefit formulas (the social security formula may have a benefit ceiling and may consider earnings over virtually the entire working-age portion of the life cycle, for example), but the two types of plans have some critical similarities that allow us to treat government-sponsored pension plans as a form of social security. Three noteworthy features of social security and government-sponsored pension plans separate them from employer-sponsored DB pension plans:

1. Payment of benefits that have been accrued under existing plan rules is not a contractual obligation, so retroactive reductions in the generosity of the benefit formula are possible.[1]
2. Mandatory participation for broad segments of the population and the negligible chances of a plan freeze or plan termination allow the plan to rely on contributions from future participants to help fund accrued benefits.
3. Contribution rates are usually fixed by law rather than adjusted as needed to maintain plan funding levels.

Because of the second and third features, analyses of the sustainability of government-sponsored plans must be based on open group projections, where an open group includes future participants in the plan. In particular, the ability to rely on contributions from future participants to pay accrued benefits allows government-sponsored plans covering a growing population of participants to operate on a pay-as-you-go (PAYGO) funding basis, so many of these plans are, or at least once were, PAYGO plans.

The measures of households' actuarial pension wealth used in national accounts will, however, be based on projections for the *closed group* comprising only the current participants in the plan (which include persons currently in covered employment or who are entitled to receive benefits). These measures will allow international comparisons of income, wealth, and saving, and for countries with well-developed systems of employer-sponsored DB pension plans, they will also be useful as sustainability indicators. Open group projections are rarely used to measure the sustainability of employer-sponsored DB pension plans because expected contributions from future cohorts of participants are too uncertain to count as an implicit asset. Also, the case of projected benefits that exceeded projected contributions linked to future participants would be handled by raising the assumed future con-

---

1. Based on this criterion, pension plans for general government employees will be treated as government-sponsored plans when member countries of the European Union start to include supplementary actuarial measures of social security and other government-sponsored plans in their national accounts (Eurostat-ECB 2011, 27).
2. An exception might be made for a pension plan that uses flawed actuarial methods or assumptions that can be projected to result in inadequate contributions for future participants. For example, state and local government plans often use a high interest rate to discount benefit payments, which leads to underestimation of service costs.

tribution rate.[2] Because transactions with future cohorts of participants are out of scope, to be considered fully funded an employer-sponsored DB plan needs to have assets equal to the actuarial value of the benefit claims of the current plan participants.

A challenge in developing a single set of international standards for actuarial measurement in national accounts was the diversity of pension institutions that exist in different parts of the world. To explore the implications of institutional diversity, in this chapter we develop actuarial measures of pension and social security plans for national accounts for countries that represent the two poles of this institutional diversity, the United States and France. In the United States, benefit entitlements from employer-sponsored pension plans are a major source of retirement wealth for households and only one industry has a government-sponsored pension plan, but in France DB pension benefits come almost entirely from government-sponsored plans. We therefore develop comparable measures of actuarial values of benefits from social security and government-sponsored pension plans for the United States and for France, and for the United States we also estimate actuarial values of household's income and wealth from employer-sponsored DB plans. Using these measures, we consider the kinds of international comparisons that are made possible by the new actuarial measures called for in the 2008 SNA.

A warning to bear in mind in using actuarial estimates of DB pension and social security plans, including ours, is that actuarial measures depend on assumptions about interest rates, mortality rates, separation rates, and future rates of increase in wages and prices. Also, the pension actuary must choose between an approach that seeks to smooth over the career the accretion of the projected pension wealth at retirement, or an approach that measures the present value of accrued-to-date benefits, which are sometimes defined as the benefits that would be due to plan participants if the plan were to be frozen or replaced with a different plan. In contrast, cash-accounting measures, such as the value of the assets in the trust fund or the employer's contribution to the plan, require no assumptions. The objective nature of cash measures is an attractive feature for national accounts purposes. Nevertheless, the ambiguities and uncertainties entailed in actuarial measurement are unavoidable if we want a full picture of the operations of social security plans and pension plans.

6.1   The Retirement Income Systems of the United States and France

6.1.1   The United States

Defined-benefit pension and social security are important elements of the retirement income system of the United States, but they are not the only important elements. The US retirement income system has four components:

- tax-advantaged accounts not sponsored by an employer, such as Individual Retirement Accounts (IRAs) and annuities purchased from life insurers;
- employer-sponsored defined-contribution (DC) pension plans, which provide resources in retirement based on the value of the assets in plan;
- employer-sponsored DB pension plans; and
- government social insurance plans, which include a social security plan for the general population, a government-sponsored pension plan for the employees of the railroad industry, and the Pension Benefit Guarantee Corporation (PBGC), which insures the receipt of benefits that have been accrued in private DB pension plans up to a ceiling.

The pension plan components of the system are needed because earnings replacement rates from social security are low for middle and higher earners. Social security has a highly progressive benefit formula and an earnings ceiling ($8,900 per month in 2010) above which earnings are not replaced at all, and it also reduces benefits for retiring before the full retirement age (presently sixty-six but scheduled to rise to sixty-seven). For example, the projected replacement rates in the 2009 Social Security Trustees' Report for prototypical low, middle, and high earners retiring at age sixty-five in 2010 are 54, 40, and 33 percent of averaged indexed monthly earnings, respectively. Nevertheless, pension plan coverage is far from universal. About half the jobs in the private sector and virtually all government jobs come with a pension plan. In the 2007 Survey of Consumer Finances, 57.7 percent of households had either a DB or a DC pension plan from a current or former employer (Bucks et al. 2009, A24).

Looking at assets held by retirement plans in the United States (table 6.1) in the government sector, DB pension plans predominate, with 4.321 trillion dollars in assets in 2007, compared with just 1.137 trillion dollars in DC plans. For the economy as a whole, DB plans are also more important, with about $7 trillion in assets, compared to about $5 trillion for DC plans. Over the past two decades, however, in the private sector newly established pension plans have been predominantly structured as DC plans, and many DB plans have also been frozen or terminated and replaced with DC plans. As a result, in the private sector, DC plans are now more important than private DB plans. Combining Simplified Employee Pension (SEP) plans and Savings Incentive Match Plan for Employees (SIMPLE) IRAs (which should be classified as DC pension plans because they are employer sponsored) with ordinary DC plans gives a total of 3.866 trillion dollars in assets for private DC plans in 2007, compared with 2.646 trillion dollars in private DB plans.[3]

---

3. Railroad retirement includes a component (tier 2) that functions like a DB plan even though it is a government social insurance program. If we add this part of railroad retirement to private DB pension plans, the total assets in private DB plans or plans that substitute for them is $2.747 trillion.

Table 6.1   Retirement assets of households in the United States by type of plan, 2007 (billions of dollars)

Type of plan	Assets
Defined-benefit pension or functional equivalent	**7,067.8**
Defined-benefit pension	**6,966.9**
Private[a]	2,646.3
Government sector	4,320.6
State and local government	3,368.9
Federal government employees	945.1
Federal Reserve system	6.6
Government social insurance that replaces DB plans	**100.9**
Pension Benefit Guarantee Corporation (single employer)	68.4
Railroad retirement, tier 2	32.5
Defined contribution	**5,003.0**
Private	3,866.0
Private plans[a]	3,537.0
SEP and SIMPLE IRAs	329.0
Government sector	1,137.0
State and local government[b] (403[b] and 457 plans)	904.0
Federal government (Thrift Savings Plan and FDIC plan)	233.0
Self-funded and rollover funded	**6,047.0**
Traditional and Roth IRAs	4,455.0
Annuities from life insurance companies	1,592.0
Total pension and self-funded	**18,177.8**
Social Security Old Age and Survivors Trust Fund and railroad retirement social security equivalent benefit account	**2,024.3**
TOTAL	**20,202.1**
Memo: Disposable personal income	**10,423.6**

Sources: Private DB and DC plans: EBSA Private Pension Plan Bulletin 2007, table A1; state and local government DB plans: 2007 Census of Governments; federal government: Sept. 2007 Treasury monthly statement; PBGC: PBGC 2008 Annual Report; Federal Reserve System: Federal Reserve System Thrift & Retirement Plans, 2007 Annual Report; Social Security: Social Security 2009 statistical supplement, table 4A1; IRAs, state and local government DC plans and annuities: Investment Company Institute *Research Fundamentals* (Brady, Holden, and Short 2010); Federal TSP: ICI *Research Fundamentals*, July 2008, fn 21.

[a] Filers of IRS Form 5500. Excludes plans with only one participant, and funds held by life insurance companies under allocated group insurance contracts for payment of retirement benefits, which amount to 10 to 15 percent of total private pension fund assets.

[b] Includes plans sponsored by nonprofit educational institutions serving households.

Furthermore, IRAs and annuities not held in IRAs rank ahead of DC plans in importance as measured by assets. However, much of the money in these vehicles comes from rollovers of amounts that were originally saved in DB or DC pension plans. For example, from 1990 to 2009 there were about 66,000 standard terminations of private DB plans.[4] In these terminations, the plan sponsor purchased group annuities to provide the benefits that were

4. See PBGC Pension Insurance Data Book 2009, table S-3.

accrued prior to the termination date or gave the plan participant a lump sum that could be rolled over into an IRA.

In 2007 Social Security had 162.3 million participants with covered earnings, compared with almost 42 million participants in private DB plans and about 70 million active participants in DC plans (US Dept. of Labor 2010, table A1).[5] Despite its much larger number of participants than private pension plans, the trust fund for the old age and survivors insurance (OASI) component had only about $2 trillion in assets in 2007, compared with about $2.6 trillion for private DB plans, and $3.6 trillion for private DC pension plans. The relative paucity of assets in the Social Security Trust Fund can be attributed to its late start on asset accumulation, which only began after the reforms of 1983, and to gaps between the present values of lifetime benefits and lifetime contributions for past participants. Had Social Security operated on a fully funded basis from its inception in 1935, the balance of the OASI fund alone would probably have been about $15 trillion (Board of Trustees 2008, 62). This figure is much larger than the $5.7 trillion trust fund balance in 2007 that was projected to be sufficient to maintain solvency of the OASI trust fund for the next seventy-five years, in part because of excesses of contributions over benefits (measured in present-value terms) for future participants. Benefits paid by Social Security (including the disability insurance component) are $575.6 billion in the national accounts for 2007, not much smaller than the $773.7 billion paid by private DB and DC pension plans put together. Allowing for the fact that the figure for private pension plan benefits includes some rollovers into annuities, early withdrawals by persons who are not retired, and benefits received by retirees below sixty-two (the youngest age of eligibility for Social Security), aged retirees probably receive more benefits from Social Security than from DB and DC pension plans.

6.1.2   France

The retirement income system of France consists of a general social security plan known as "Caisse nationale d'assurance vieillesse des travailleurs salariés" (CNAVTS), or now just as CNAV, and a network of thirty-five compulsory industry-specific "complementary" pension plans. Like tier 2 of railroad retirement in the United States, these complementary plans are government-sponsored plans. Despite some diversity in retiree and survivor benefit formulas, they are almost all converging to the same set of legal requirements for their main parameters, such as the required length of a full career and the minimum retirement age.[6] They are recorded in the social security sector in the national accounts of France with the exception of

---

5. Note that some employees have both a DB plan and a DC plan, so adding together the number of participants in each type of plan overstates the total number of employees who have a private pension plan.

6. The military and some other types of workers are still allowed to retire at earlier ages.

the state civil servant plan. That plan is included in the central government sector, but in the future this may change, as the 2010 pension law requires a report on the creation of an explicit plan for state civil servants.

The complexity of the French pension system derives from its history. The CNAVTS plan was created just after the end of World War II as a PAYGO social security plan, and a 1946 law was supposed to extend its coverage to the whole population. This plan provided wage earners a basic pension equal to 50 percent of the reference salary up to a ceiling, adjusted by the ratio of the actual length of the career to the required length of a full career.[7] The ceiling in CNAVTS was low, however, so there was a need for complementary pension plans. Managers started the first of these (AGIRC) in 1947 with an interprofessional agreement, and a plan for nonsupervisors (ARRCO) followed in 1961. Participants in these pension plans accrue points as they and their employer make contributions during their working years, and benefits during retirement equal the number of points accrued during the career times an annually published value of a point. Independent social security plans were also created in 1948 and 1952 for own-account workers with their own complementary pension plans.

Finally, even though CNAVTS was supposed to cover the whole employed population, some previously existing pension plans (e.g., state civil servants, miners, sailors, railway, public utilities, central bank, national opera and theater) never joined the system. These plans, which are known as the "special regimes," offered benefits that were generally high enough so that an additional benefit from CNAVTS was unnecessary. For example, the state civil servant plan, which many of the special plans resemble, provides a pension equal to 75 percent of the final salary excluding bonuses times a ratio equal to the actual length of the career divided by the required length of a full career. The relative size in terms of numbers of contributors and amounts of benefits paid of the various types of retirement plans in France is shown in table 6.2. The benefits row of the table also includes assistance provided by the general government and privately purchased supplementary annuities from life insurance companies.

All of the basic and complementary pension plans are classifiable as government social insurance. A 1972 law mandated participation of all wage earners in a complementary pension plan and established the principle of interprofessional solidarity. As a result, the plans are interconnected by financial interchanges in which "younger" plans with relatively high numbers of contributors help the older ones. Furthermore, integration of the special regimes into the CNAV is always a possibility if their finances become too out of balance; for example, the public utilities plan, the clergymen plan,

---

7. Before 1971, the reference salary was defined as the final salary and the required number of years was thirty. After this date, the reference salary was the average of the ten best years and the required number of years was 37.5.

Table 6.2   Relative size of the French retirement regimes as measured by contributors and benefits paid, 2009 (percentages of national total)

	Private wage earners		State civil servant	Other "special regimes"	Self-employed	Assistance	Supplementary annuities from life Insurers
	Basic	Complementary					
Contributors	71.7	71.7	9.3	9.3	9.7	n/a	n/a
Benefits	33.9	24.1	14.9	12.4	9.7	4.6	2.3

and some smaller plans were absorbed into the CNAV in 2005 or 2006. Furthermore, despite the diversity of the plans, the solidarity principles of social security are respected, thanks to rules that specify a uniform set of policies regarding minimum benefits, the supplements for children, and the noncontributive periods included in pension calculation. Contributions to the plans during periods of unemployment, maternity leave, illness, and disability are financed by general tax revenue channeled through the "Fonds de solidarité vieillesse" (FSV). Changes in laws applying to social security are also applied to all the compulsory plans. (Though, with such a large number of them, achieving universal compliance is not necessarily easy!)

The compulsory pension plans have little or no income from assets and receive only a limited amount of external funding from general tax revenue via the FSV, so their finances can be approximated by the equation that links the outlays of a PAYGO plan to its income:

$$\text{average contribution} \times \text{no. of contributors}$$
$$= \text{average benefit} \times \text{no. of beneficiaries.}$$

The three "internal" parameters of the above equation are: the contributor-beneficiary ratio, the contribution rate, and the replacement rate (i.e., average pension/average salary). Unfortunately, declines in birth rates (and, to a lesser extent, rising longevity) have resulted in a downward trend in the contributor-beneficiary ratio. It was 4 in 1960, 1.8 in 2008, and it would have fallen to around 1.2 in 2040 if not for the increase in the retirement age in the 2010 reform of the retirement system.

To cope with the imbalances created by the downward trend in the contributor-beneficiary ratio, a series of pension reforms have been undertaken. Because the plans are not organized as American-style, employer-sponsored pension plans, cuts to existing benefit entitlements are possible, and indeed, only those who were already retired at the time of the reform have been spared from sacrifice. A 1993 reform of private sector pensions changed indexation from wage growth to prices and increased the minimum length of career for a full pension from 37.5 to 40 years for people reaching 60 in 2008, or to 41 years for people reaching 60 in 2012. The 1993 reform also increased the number of years for calculation of the reference salary for social security from ten to twenty-five. In 2003, the extension of the required length of career was also applied to the special regimes, and additional benefit reductions were imposed on early retirees in all types of plans. The 2003 reform also provided for regular reviews of the plans' finances (the next of which will occur in 2018), with measures taken as necessary to correct imbalances. There was also a reform of AGIRC and ARRCO in 1994 that increased the cost of a point and changed the indexation of the value of a point. Another step to cope with future declines in contributors was the creation in 1999 of a buffer fund (the "Fond de réserve des retraites"[FRR]) to close the financing gap of the CNAV after 2020. At the end of 2009, its assets amounted to 1.75 percent of the gross domestic product (GDP).

Unfortunately, the financial crisis of 2007–2008 deepened the structural imbalances of the French retirement system. The combined deficits of the CNAVTS and FSV grew to 13.8 billion euros in 2010. With the system's annual deficits projected to reach about 2 percent of GDP by 2020, the government decided to undertake another reform. The minimum retirement age was raised for most people, including the government's own employees, from sixty to sixty-two starting in 2018, and the full retirement age was also raised from sixty-five to sixty-seven.[8] Also, the required length of career was extended to 41.25 years in 2013. However, this last reform is projected to have a limited impact on the financing gap. This is confirmed by the authors' estimates with PROST, a social security modeling program of the World Bank (see appendix B).

The past rounds of pension reforms have highlighted for French households the lack of certainty of the benefits that they are currently scheduled to receive when they retire. In response, many households have begun to invest in privately funded retirement accounts. A popular vehicle for this is investments with the life insurance industry, whose technical reserves have grown at the average pace of 12 percent a year since 1993, double the growth rate of total financial assets in general. (Life insurance represents 36 percent of households' financial assets in 2009 but only 12 percent of total assets, as real estate plays a major role in households' wealth in France.) Yet pension plans sponsored by employers still have a very limited place in France. Apart from book reserve plans, which are difficult to estimate, they consist of DB plans managed exclusively by insurance corporations and, since 2003, defined-contribution plans known as PERCO (*plan d'épargne pour la retraite collectif*) plans, which resemble the 401(k) plans of the United States. Providing for only 2.3 percent of retiree benefits in 2008, the employer-sponsored plans comprise between 64 billion euros of entitlements in defined-contribution plans (of which 2 billion euros are in PERCO) and 43 billion euros of benefit entitlements in defined-benefit plans (table 6.3).[9] All together, they amount to 12 percent of technical provisions in life insurance, but just 1.3 percent of

---

8. The minimum age for claiming benefits had been reduced from sixty-five to sixty in 1982.
9. Personal retirement accounts have an additional 28 € billion.

Table 6.3   Private pension plans in France by type of plan (amounts in € billion)

Nature		Sources	Type	Status in fin. accounts	Reserves	Contributions	Pensions
	Collective insurance contracts with employer contribution						
Social insurance in life insurance	Defined contribution (art 82 CGI)	DREES	dc	Life insurance reserves	2.9	0.3	0.2
	Defined contribution (art 83 CGI)	DREES	dc		42.0	2.9	1.2
	Individual workers (Madelin)	DREES	dc		16.2	2.2	0.4
	Farm workers	DREES	dc		2.7	0.2	
	Defined benefit (art 39 CGI)	DREES	db	Life insurance reserves	31.5	3.6	2.8
	Retirement lump sum	FFSA	db		9.7	0.9	1.1
	Collective employment related schemes						
Social insurance in pension funds	PERCO	AFG	dc	Mutual funds shares	1.9	0.9	
	Individual pension plans						
Life insurance	PERP	DREES	dc	Life insurance reserves	4.1	1.0	
	Other individual plans	DREES	dc		24.5	1.0	0.5
	Book reserves						
Employer sector	companies net liabilities	Mercer	?	Not yet recorded	27.0	?	?

total household sector assets. The total pension wealth held in these plans is about 5.5 percent of GDP, compared with DB and DC plan pension wealth of about 90 percent of GDP in the United States.

6.2   Measurement of Social Security Plans in National Accounts

Like tier 2 of railroad retirement in the United States, the thirty-five government-sponsored pension plans of France meet the SNA criteria to be classified as social security (United Nations Statistical Division 2008, 4.124). Even though all the plans, including the CNAVTS, are managed by representatives of the employers and the employees, they are subject to detailed regulation and to oversight by state auditors, they receive government subsidies, and the state has the ability to reduce the value of benefits that have already been earned and bears ultimate responsibility for shortfalls in plan funding. They are all recorded in the social security sector in the national accounts of France, except for the state civil servant plan. At present this plan is included in the central government sector because of its lack of existence as a distinct institutional unit, but in the future this may change as the 2010 pension reform law requires a report on the creation of an explicit plan for state civil servants in the interest of financial transparency.

Accounting for social security plans (and other government social insurance programs) in the core national accounts is very straightforward. Neither the social security trust fund nor the actuarial value of scheduled future benefits is treated as part of households' net worth. Household income from social security is therefore recorded when benefits are paid, and contributions to social security are excluded from household income.

A new supplementary table that shows benefit entitlements for all pension and social security plans is recommended in the 2008 SNA (17.191–17.206). The measures of social security plans in this table will be similar to the measures that are used for employer-sponsored DB pension plans, but with some differences in nomenclature. In particular, the gap between the actuarial value of benefits accrued during the year and actual contributions during the year will be labeled "employer-imputed social contributions" in the case of DB employer-sponsored pension plans, whereas for social security plans this gap will be labeled "other (actuarial) accumulation of pension entitlements."

6.3   Measurement of Employer-Sponsored
Pension Plans in National Accounts

The French national accounts do not, as yet, include a pension plan sector. The PERCO plans are included in the mutual fund sector and pension plans managed by insurance corporations are in the insurance sector. According to SNA 2008 (4.116) "The pension fund subsector consists of only those social insurance pension funds that are institutional units separate from the units that create them." The status of these plans as social insurance is clear, but it is less obvious that they qualify as independent institutional units. The PERCO are collective agreements and not institutional units. Funds are managed by investment fund managers and kept with a custodian, but they are owned by the beneficiaries. As defined-contribution schemes, returns net of the management fees go entirely to beneficiaries. In addition, the plans that are managed by insurance companies are not isolated from other life insurance contracts unless the insurance company decides to ring-fence such collective contracts and the corresponding assets under the 2008 law on supplementary pension institutions. At the end of 2009, none of the life insurance plans had such a ring fencing. Nevertheless, even if it is decided that a separate pension fund sector is unnecessary for these employment-related pension plans, a change in the treatment of employer contributions to be part of the compensation of employees will still be appropriate.

In contrast to France, the United States has a well-developed system of employer-sponsored pension plans. These plans are currently accounted for in the US National Accounts in accordance with the recommendations of the 1993 SNA (United Nations Statistical Division 1993). In the comprehensive revision of the US National Accounts that is scheduled for 2013 the treatment of DB pension plans will change, however. The new treatment will be consistent with the measurement goals of the new recommended method for measuring DB pension plans in the 2008 SNA. However, it will depart from the detailed guidelines of the 2008 SNA in some notable ways.

6.3.1   The Approach of the 1993 SNA

In the 1993 SNA, funded DB pension plans are accounted for in the same way as DC pension plans in measuring household saving. In a DC pension plan, the participants' pension wealth consists of the assets held in the plan, so employer contributions to DC plans represent compensation income to the plan participants. Benefit payments from those plans do not represent income flows, because they merely move participants' wealth from one location to another.

Similarly, treating the assets of funded DB pension plans as the property of the plan participants means that compensation income for households should be recorded when employers make contributions to these plans, and that the investment income from the plan assets should be included in the property income of households. In addition, under this approach payments of benefits to retirees, along with contributions made by employees to DB plans, are purely financial transactions. Finally, the plans' administrative expenses are included in household consumption expenditures.

In the US National Accounts, the same approach is used both to measure household saving and to measure household income. In this chapter, we will also measure employer-sponsored pensions in just one way, using the kind of approach that the SNA recommends for measuring household saving for purposes of measuring both household income and household saving. However, to avoid confusion, we acknowledge that the SNA (in both its 1993 and 2008 versions) treats pension plans differently when measuring household income from the approach that we take in this chapter. In particular, the SNA places employer-sponsored pension plans outside the boundary of the household sector when measuring household income, and inside that boundary when measuring household saving. With the plans outside the boundary of the household sector, payments of benefits represent flows of income to households, so in measuring household saving, the original measure of household income in the SNA is adjusted by adding saving by pension plans, or, in the language of the SNA, "adjustment for the change in pension entitlements." This has the effect of removing benefit payments from household income and replacing them with pension contributions plus investment income earned by the pension plan's assets because saving by a funded DB plan equals the plans' income from employer contributions, employee contributions and investment returns less the plans' expenses for benefit payments and administration.[10]

6.3.2   The Approach of the 2008 SNA for Purposes of Measuring Household Saving

A key innovation in the 2008 SNA is actuarial measurement of employer-sponsored DB pension plans, including ones that are unfunded. This will allow the national accounts to move from a cash approach to an accrual approach to measuring DB pension plans. The most straightforward way to implement the actuarial approach for a DB plan is to treat the actuarial value of the benefit entitlement as the sole pension asset of the plan participants, and this is the approach that the 2008 SNA (17.151–17.176) recommends. Also, the new measure of compensation income is to be the present value of the claims to benefits earned by active participants through service to the employer. The new accrual approach therefore avoids the arbitrariness in the timing of the recording of compensation income that occurs under the cash accounting approach when employers defer their actual contributions and then later make extra contributions to catch up with funding targets.[11]

---

10. The NIPA tables published by the BEA do not report saving by defined-benefit pension plans, but estimates of saving by DB pension plans are occasionally published as part of a set of alternative measures of personal saving. See Perozek and Reinsdorf (2002), Reinsdorf (2004), and Reinsdorf (2005).

11. Under an idealized set of assumptions, cash accounting would provide a complete picture of the operations of a defined-benefit plan. In particular, the assets in a defined-benefit plan will measure the wealth of the plan's participants in the form of accrued benefit entitlements and the employer's contribution to the plan will measure the income of the participants in the form of benefit accruals if there are no deviations of: (a) realized investment returns from the assumed interest rate; (b) employer contributions from benefit accruals net of any required employee contributions; (c) outcomes for salary increases, separations, and mortality from previous assumptions; and (d) plan features from those in effect at the time of plan inception. These assumptions may not be even approximately true in practice.

In the new table on the transactions of DB pension plans that is recommended in the 2008 SNA, the cash measure of employee compensation from participation in DB pension plans will still be shown, but it will be labeled as "employer actual contributions." The difference between the actuarial value of benefits earned through service to the employer plus the administrative expenses of the plan minus employee contributions to the plan will be also shown with the label "employer-imputed contributions." Total employer contributions then equal the amount that employers need to contribute to cover the cost of claims to benefits arising from covered employment and the administrative cost of running the plans. Employer contributions represent the compensation income that employees receive in the form of rights to pension benefits and the administrative services of the pension plan manager.

In addition, rather than measuring property income of the households participating in DB plans by the income generated by plan assets, the 2008 SNA measures household property income by the interest accruing on households' benefit entitlements. This has the important advantage that the sum over the lifetime of a participant in a DB plan of the actuarial value of the benefit entitlements earned through service to the employer and the interest on accumulated benefit entitlements equals the sum of the benefits paid if the assumptions used in the actuarial calculations are all realized. The accrual measure of household income of the 2008 SNA from actual and imputed employer contributions and from interest on the benefit entitlement thus corresponds to the future cash flows of benefits to households. It is also consistent with the growth in household wealth from participation in DB plans.

Nevertheless, despite these important advantages, the measure of household income from DB pension plans in the 2008 SNA has an implication that users of the national accounts may find paradoxical: the saving of the DB plans themselves will generally be nonzero. Nonzero saving by DB plans means that income resources and income uses of DB pension plans are not in balance. For example, negative saving by DB plans, which is much more likely than positive saving, implies that households are accruing claims on the plans that exceed the amounts that the plans will be able to pay if they have no other resources besides those counted in plan income.

In the recording scheme of the SNA, the income received by DB plans consists of property income on plan assets, actual contributions of employers and employees, and imputed employer contributions. The imputed contributions are defined as having the value that is necessary to bring total contributions (actual plus imputed) into balance with the value of the benefit entitlements being accrued via service to employers (plus the value of the pension plan administrative services). Imputing analogous payments of interest income from employers to plans (or from plans to employers if the plans have more property income than is needed to satisfy the claims of households) would bring the plans' receipts and payments of property income into balance as well. Yet the SNA has no imputed receipts of property income by plans, so in the recording scheme of the SNA, saving by DB plans equals the difference between the property income that the plans receive on their assets and the imputed interest that households receive on their benefit entitlements. This difference is likely to be negative for plans that are underfunded, or for plans that invest in assets that are expected to generate holding gains even if they are fully funded.

Investors in equities treat holding gains as a substitute for dividends, and over the long run investment returns on equities often come more from holding gains than from dividends. Holding gains on plan assets are commonly relied upon by DB pension plans as a source of funding for their benefit obligations. Yet they are excluded from the definition of income in national accounts because holding gains and losses arise from changes in the price of assets that already exist, not economic production. In the full sequence of accounts that is recommended by the SNA, holding gains and other changes in assets are shown in accounts that appear below those showing income and saving.[12]

If the SNA measure of saving by DB plans is negative because the plans have invested in assets that are expected to provide investment returns in the form of holding gains, an argument can be made that the negative saving by DB plans has a reasonable economic interpretation. The argument is that to use holding gains to fund benefit payments, cash must be raised by selling the appreciated assets. But using sales of assets to cover expenses that exceed current income means that saving is negative. Thus, depicting fully funded DB pension plans that hold assets that are supposed to generate holding gains as having negative saving is justifiable even though the plans' finances are expected to be sustainable.

In contrast, no rationale exists for allowing DB pension plans to have negative saving if the shortfalls in their property income are attributable to shortfalls in plan assets and in past contributions. Delays in making the contributions needed to cover the cost of newly accrued benefit entitlements result in a funding gap for the DB pension plan because they deprive the plan of the opportunity to earn property income. For the plan to have the means to pay the benefits when they fall due, the property income that the plan would have earned had the contributions been made on time will eventually have to be replaced by someone.

If the lack of property income is caused by plan underfunding, a flow

12. In France, the INSEE publishes the current account showing saving and investment and the Banque de France publishes the financial accounts. In the latter, the change in the balance sheet from one period to the next is decomposed through three sets of accounts: the transaction accounts (where new issues, redemptions, acquisitions and sales are traced and balanced with net lending/borrowing); the valuation accounts for holding gains and losses; and the other changes in assets accounts for reclassifications. In the US statistical system, the BEA publishes estimates of saving and capital transfers in the NIPAs and the Federal Reserve Board publishes estimates for the personal sector of net acquisitions of assets, holding gains and losses, and change in wealth in the Flow of Funds Accounts (FFAs). The BEA brings together information from the NIPAs and the FFAs in its integrated macroeconomic accounts.

of imputed interest income to the DB plan from the party responsible for replacing the plans' missing property income should be recorded. This will prevent the accounts from showing negative saving by DB pension plans. In the institutional setting of the United States, the responsible party is the employer; indeed, in its treatment of employer-imputed contributions, the SNA seems to assume that the responsible party is always the employer. Nevertheless, it is possible that in some institutions' settings the plan participants or the government may have to bear at least some of the burden of adjustment. If no one can predict whether the cost of filling pension plan funding gaps will ultimately be borne by employers, employees and retirees, or the government, the best recourse may be to allow underfunded pension plans to be shown as having negative saving.

6.3.3   Measuring the DB Plans of the United States in a Way That Makes Their Saving Zero

In the institutional setting of the United States, employers are generally legally or contractually responsible for ensuring the payment of the benefits due to the participants in the DB plans that they sponsor. The measurement framework that is recommended in the 2008 SNA is not well suited for handling underfunded pension plans in this kind of institutional setting.[13] In particular, to reflect the growth in employers' obligations to make additional pension fund contributions when plans lack property income as a result of lack of assets, interest charges on the claim of the DB plan on the employer for the contributions needed to cover the unfunded actuarial liability (UAL) must be imputed. In effect, failure to make actuarially required contributions when they are due is treated as borrowing from the pension plan, with an associated interest expense for the borrower.

Counting imputed interest on the UAL as an income source for DB plans may, however, not be enough to prevent a negative estimate of saving by these plans if the interest accruing on the total benefit entitlement is used to measure the property income that households receive from the plans. Suppose that we measure households' property income in this way for a plan that has a positive UAL. Then the imputed interest received by the plan from the employer in connection with the UAL cancels the imputed interest paid by the plan on the unfunded portion of benefit entitlement, so saving by the

---

13. The 2008 SNA (paragraph 17.165) does provide for a special treatment of DB plans when employers are contractually liable to a third party for the funding gaps of their plans, recommending that in this case a claim of the plans on the employers should be recorded such that the plans have a net worth of zero at all times. The implications of doing this closely resemble the approach that we recommend here, so the main difference between our approach and the 2008 SNA is that we treat employers as liable for plan-funding shortfalls under a broader range of circumstances. Indeed, it could be argued that these circumstances are overly broad because state and local government employers do sometimes respond to pension-funding gaps by shifting some of the burden of closing those gaps to their employees via increases in contribution rates. Adjusting our estimates to allow for this would, however, be practical.

plan equals the plan's property income from interest, dividends, and rental income earned by its assets less its interest expense calculated by multiplying the rate of interest assumed in the actuarial calculations by the value of the plan assets. Multiplying the interest rate assumed in the actuarial calculations by the value of the plan assets implies a predicted value for the returns on the plan investments. If the plan invests in equities and other assets are expected to provide some of their returns in the form of holding gains, the interest, dividends, and rental income generated by the plan assets are likely to be lower than this predicted value. The holding gains needed to make up for this shortfall in property income can then be treated as a measure of the value of the holding gains implied by the interest rate assumption, as shown in the following set of equations:

Saving by DB pension plans = property income from plan assets + imputed
    interest on claim on the employer for the UAL – interest payable on benefit
    entitlements
    = property income from plan assets – (interest rate × plan assets)
    = –(implied holding gains on plan assets).

Using holding gains to help fund benefit payments that retirees use for spending does lower national saving, so showing the DB plans that do this as having negative saving is a reasonable way to portray the economic effect of their funding model. Furthermore, if the assumption that the plan assets will generate holding gains is reasonable, then the only way to estimate correctly both the expense to employers of sponsoring pension plans and the income that the plans provide to households is to allow the DB plans to have negative saving.

Nevertheless, accounting for DB pension plans in a way that allows them to have nonzero saving also has disadvantages. First, allowing projecting holding gains on assets held in DB pension plans to enter household income the treatment of holding gains different for assets in DB plans than for assets in DC plans or held directly by households; holding gains on DC plan assets or other assets do not add to household income in any way. Second, because negative saving of DB pension plans results in household interest income that is not paid by business or government, the decomposition of national income by sector will no longer add up to the correct total unless an adjustment for saving by DB pension plans is somehow incorporated. To be consistent with the framework recommended by the 2008 SNA this could be done by adding the negative saving of DB pension plans to the profits of a financial corporation sector, but this decomposition would be hard to follow for most users of the US National Accounts.

To avoid these disadvantages, we will account for the DB pension funds of the United States in a way that makes their saving identically zero. We define the property income received by the households that participate in DB pension plans as equal to the sum of the property income that the plans obtain from their assets and the imputed interest that the plans receive on their claims on employers for the funding of their UAL. If the plan assets include equities, the property income from the plan assets will usually be less than the income that the assets would earn if they paid the rate of interest assumed in the actuarial calculations by an amount that can be viewed as the holding gains implied by the interest rate assumption. In effect, we exclude expected holding gains used to fund benefit payments from the measure of household income and treat these instead as an implied holding gains component of the change in households' DB pension wealth. This reduces the measure of household saving compared to the one that would result from treating the implied holding gains as the negative saving by DB pension plans.

6.4   Choice of Actuarial Method for Measuring the DB Plans of the United States

6.4.1   Alternative Treatments of Effects of Salary Growth

Two general approaches are possible for estimating the actuarial value of benefit entitlements. Unfortunately, no consensus exists concerning which approach should generally be used in practice, though there is some agreement among national income accountants about the principles that can guide the choice between these approaches. To understand the practical implications of these approaches, it is helpful to consider a typical traditional DB plan benefit formula that makes the benefit equal to final pay (or average pay in the last few years of the career) times the length of the career times a fixed percentage replacement rate. With this kind of formula, salary increases raise the value of the pension, and we can either account for this salary growth effect on an ex post basis, or attempt to incorporate the effect of projected future salary increases into the value of the benefits being earned today.

The ex post approach focuses on the accrued benefit obligation (ABO), which equals the present discounted value of the benefits that would be due to participants if the plan were to be frozen on the valuation date. This approach adheres strictly to the definition of an accrued liability because it excludes benefits that are contingent on future actions by the employer. Under the ABO approach, the value of the benefits earned in a given year ("service cost" or "normal cost") is measured as the increment to the value of benefit entitlements that results from working that year, including both the effect of credit for an additional year of service and the effect of pay raises received during the year. Assuming that the benefit level depends on final pay, the effect of a pay raise on the value of the benefit entitlement will be large for participants who have accumulated credit for many years of service. As a result, the ABO approach tends to produce relatively high estimates of normal cost in the last years of the career and relatively low estimates of accumulated pension wealth in the early and middle stages of the career. The *average level* of normal costs over the course of the career must be higher if their profile is tilted so that estimates of normal costs are high in the last years of the career because the back loading of normal costs implies that less time is available to accumulate property income. In other words, the ABO approach will tend to produce relatively high estimates of compensation income and relatively low estimates of imputed property income for households.

An alternative to focusing on the accrued-to-date benefit entitlement (as defined by the present value of the benefits that would be due if the plan were to be frozen) is to focus on the benefits that are expected to have been accrued at the time of retirement. To do this, a participant's ultimate level of benefits is projected on the assumptions that the plan will continue in its present form and that the participant will receive future salary increases.

The projected unit credit (PUC) method applies an expected salary growth rate to the benefits earned to date, so in effect its main difference from the ABO method is that it discounts projected benefits by a real rate of interest equal to the assumed nominal rate minus the assumed salary growth rate, not by the nominal interest rate itself. In financial accounting used by private business, this method is often known as the projected benefit obligation (PBO) approach. Allowing for projected future pay increases produces higher estimates of normal cost for employees in the early part of their career than under the ABO approach, and it also produces higher estimates of the value of the benefit entitlement for employees not at the end of the career. (At the end of the career, all the methods agree.) This means that over the career as a whole, more household income from participation in DB plans is attributed to interest and less is attributed to compensation than under the ABO approach.

On the other hand, government-sector employers often want a method that yields an evenly smooth profile of normal costs over the career than occurs with the PUC method. Most government plans in the United States use the entry age normal (EAN) method, which solves for the constant percent of pay that must be contributed to the plan over the course of an employee's career to accumulate the necessary assets at the time of retirement. The EAN method generally implies higher values of pension wealth for participants early in their career than the PUC method, so it is viewed as a conservative funding standard. Yet for national accounts purposes, a key implication of higher measures of pension wealth is that more of the income of the plan participants is attributed to imputed interest income, leaving less to be attributed compensation. Indeed, if employers actually follow the EAN funding schedule, with plan assets earning the assumed rate of return, their contributions can have a lower average over the course of the career than if they use a more delayed schedule for making contributions.

The ABO, PUC, and EAN methods for measuring benefit entitlements are illustrated in box 6.1 at the end of the following section. A number of elaborations of these methods also exist, along with methods that use a different kind of approach that effectively counts projected future increases in contributions as current assets.

6.4.2   Possible Decision Criterion

A criterion for determining whether an ABO approach or a forward-looking approach is more appropriate is whether employees effectively have a secure right to accrue benefits under the plan formula in future years. Models of the option value of pensions developed by Lazear and Moore (1988) and Stock and Wise (1990) imply that besides the benefits that have already been accrued, the right to accrue future benefits is also a valuable asset if the probability of a plan freeze or plan termination is low. This option value is part of the buy-out that would be necessary to induce an employee covered by a defined-benefit pension plan to take early retirement. To agree to retire early, the employee would have to be compensated both for the loss of projected future wages net of the opportunity cost of the employee's time and for the forfeited option to accrue additional benefit rights. (If the employee has reached the point in the life cycle where the value of leisure exceeds the wage, the minimum buy-out necessary to induce the employee to retire early would just be the value of the employee's option to accrue additional benefits.) Because the option value is part of the pension wealth of participants that have the right to accrue future benefits under the existing plan rules, the ABO understates their pension wealth. Smoothing the profile of their wealth accumulation over the career, as is done by forward-looking methods, is therefore reasonable.

In the United States, many private sector sponsors of DB plans have frozen or terminated their plans, depriving participants of the opportunity to accrue additional benefit entitlements. Because neither law nor custom obligates the plan sponsor to give participants future opportunities to accrue benefits, the ABO approach is appropriate for measuring the current pension wealth of private plan participants in the United States. Current government employees in the United States were, on the other hand, traditionally treated as having the right to continue in the same plan until retirement, under the so-called "California rule" (Monahan 2012). Yet in recent years, the taboo against stripping current employees of future opportunities to earn benefits has begun to disappear. In particular, many state and local governments have raised employee contribution rates, and some have announced plans to force their employees into less generous pension plans. In other cases, state and local governments have significantly cut their workforce, so loss of employment has become an additional threat to the opportunity to accrue additional benefit rights for some employees. The facts that once favored a forward-looking approach for state and local government plans have therefore become more ambiguous. Nevertheless, a forward-looking approach using either the EAN or PUC method remains justifiable for plans for federal government employees. In addition, the PBO approach is recommended for government employees plans in Europe by the Eurostat-ECB technical compilation guide (2011, 85).

Box 6.1 Example of ABO approach and two PBO methods

In this box a simple hypothetical pension plan illustrates some of the differences between the possible ways of calculating pension benefit liabilities. Three methods are considered: the accrued benefit obligation (ABO) approach, the projected unit credit (PUC) version of the projected benefit obligation (PBO) approach, and the constant percent of pay variant of the entry age normal (EAN) version of the PBO approach. Participants in this pension plan work for three years, retire in the fourth year, and die in the fifth year. Their salary grows 5 percent per period from a starting level of $25,000. Vesting is immediate, there are no breaks in service, and there is no early retirement. The accrued retirement benefit equals 10 percent of salary times the number of periods worked times final salary. The interest rate is 15 percent.

Table 6.4 follows a single participant through the career and retirement. For simplicity, we assume that service cost is measured as of the beginning of the year, so that year one service cost equals the year two opening liability discounted back by one year. The table shows that the PUC and EAN measures of the future benefit liability are higher than the ABO liability except at retirement, when they equal the ABO measure. The PUC and EAN service cost measures are higher than the ABO at first, but are much lower in the last year of the career.

Table 6.5 follows a plan that starts with ten newly hired participants and adds ten new hires in each of the next two years. Hiring then ceases. As the workforce ages, the ABO measure of service cost rises faster than the PUC measure. The EAN measure using the level percent of pay version of the entry age normal method does not rise at all. If the distribution of ages in the workforce is uniform, the ABO measure of service cost is higher than the PUC and EAN, so on the whole the ABO approach tends to attribute the growth of pension wealth more to compensation in the form of imputed contributions (and the other methods tend to it attribute it more to property income in the form of imputed interest earned on the plan's benefit liability).

Table 6.4 Plan's benefit liability and service cost for a single employee using the ABO approach and two PBO methods

Age	Assumptions			Liability for future benefits			Service cost			Service cost percent of salary		
	Salary	Benefits paid	Accrued benefits	ABO	Projected unit credit	Entry age normal	ABO	Projected unit credit	Entry age normal	ABO	Projected unit credit	Entry age normal
1	25,000	0	0	0	0	—	1,644	1,812	1,979	6.58	7.25	7.92
2	26,250	0	2,500	1,890	2,084	2,276	2,079	2,084	2,078	7.92	7.94	7.92
3	27,563	0	5,250	4,565	4,793	5,008	2,625	2,397	2,182	9.52	8.70	7.92
4	0	8,269	8,269	8,269	8,269	8,269	0	0	0	n/a	n/a	n/a
5	0	0	0	0	0	0	n/a	n/a	n/a	n/a	n/a	n/a

Table 6.5   Plan's benefit liability and service cost from plan inception to termination using the ABO approach and two PBO methods (dollar amounts in thousands)

	Assumptions			Future benefit liability			Service costs			Service costs percent of payroll			No. of participants	
Year	Payroll	Benefits paid	Accrued benefits	ABO	Projected unit credit	Entry age normal	ABO	Projected unit credit	Entry age normal	ABO	Projected unit credit	Entry age normal	Active	Retired
1	250	0	0	0	0	—	16.4	18.1	19.8	6.6	7.3	7.9	10	0
2	513	0	25	18.9	20.8	22.8	37.2	39.0	40.6	7.3	7.6	7.9	20	0
3	788	0	78	64.6	68.8	72.8	63.5	62.9	62.4	8.1	8.0	7.9	30	0
4	788	83	160	147.2	151.5	155.5	63.5	62.9	62.4	8.1	8.0	7.9	30	10
5	788	83	160	147.2	151.5	155.5	63.5	62.9	62.4	8.1	8.0	7.9	30	10
6	538	83	160	147.2	151.5	155.5	47.0	44.8	42.6	8.7	8.3	7.9	20	10
7	276	83	135	128.3	130.6	132.8	26.3	24.0	21.8	9.5	8.7	7.9	10	10
8	0	83	83	82.7	82.7	82.7	0	0	0	n/a	n/a	n/a	0	10

6.5   Estimates of Income and Saving from
DB Pension Plans in the United States

6.5.1   Private Plans

Our measures of US household income and saving from participation in private DB plans are calculated from a database of pension plan tax returns (IRS Form 5500). In this database missing values are common for some variables (particularly dividend and interest income on plan assets), and comparisons of the population of filers in successive years imply that significant numbers of plans are missing in 2000–2002, even though the data are supposed to be a census of all private plans in the United States. We therefore include imputations for missing values of key variables and for missing plans in 2000–2002 in our estimates of national totals, as described in Reinsdorf and Lenze (2009, 55).

Under the cash approach, households' compensation income from participation in DB plans is measured by employer contributions, and their property income is measured by the interest, dividends, and rental income earned by plan assets. On average over the years 2000–2007, employer contributions are almost $80 billion per year and property income is almost $58 billion per year, so the cash measure of household income is $137.6 billion. After subtracting administrative expenses of around $8 billion, the cash measure household saving averages almost $130 billion per year (table 6.6). The accrual measure of household saving from participation in these plans averages just $8 billion more, with employer-imputed contributions averaging about $2 billion and employer-imputed interest payments on the UAL averaging about $6 billion. Using actuarial measures, therefore, has a trivial effect on the average level of household income and saving in the case of private plans.

On the other hand, using the actuarial approach greatly reduces the volatility of household income from employer contributions and also from all sources combined. For example, after including employer-imputed contributions, the accrual measure of compensation income from participation in private DB plans rises from $73.1 billion in 2000 to $81.9 billion in 2002. Yet in 2000 a nearly unprecedented streak of five good years of stock market returns had left many plans overfunded, so employer contributions to private DB plans were only $32.8 billion.[14] Two years later, after the dot-com stock market crash and bear market, beginning-of-year assets were down by over 250 billion dollars and contributions rebounded to 100.2 billion dollars.

---

14. Reinsdorf (2007, 9) finds that before the bull market of 1995–2000, cash saving by private and government DB pension plans was adding about 1.6 percentage points to the personal saving rate, compared with zero in 2000.

Table 6.6   Household income, saving and wealth from private defined-benefit pension plans: ABO actuarial approach (billions of US dollars except as noted; years defined by plan year-ending date)

	2000	2001	2002	2003	2004	2005	2006	2007
Household income	**122.1**	**130.6**	**143.0**	**156.5**	**143.8**	**150.6**	**152.7**	**165.7**
Employer contributions to DB plans	73.1	77.0	81.9	82.8	78.8	82.9	85.6	89.3
Actual contributions	32.8	52.2	100.2	100.8	95.4	92.7	89.2	74.8
Imputed contributions	40.3	24.8	-18.3	-18.0	-16.6	-9.8	-3.6	14.5
Imputed employer payment of interest on UAL	-14.3	-4.4	12.0	24.8	11.2	10.6	3.4	7.4
Property income from plan assets	63.3	58.0	49.1	48.9	53.8	57.1	63.7	69.0
LESS: Plan administrative expenses	7.3	7.2	6.9	7.4	8.3	8.6	9.2	9.9
Household saving	**114.8**	**123.4**	**136.1**	**149.1**	**135.5**	**142.0**	**143.5**	**155.8**
Implied holding gains on plan assets	**57.4**	**57.1**	**56.2**	**50.6**	**62.9**	**69.2**	**71.4**	**71.9**
Current change in household wealth	**172.2**	**180.5**	**192.3**	**199.7**	**198.4**	**211.2**	**214.9**	**227.7**
Benefits and withdrawals	118.2	124.5	134.8	135.7	141.9	139.8	152.7	161.5
Change in benefit entitlements	54.8	56.7	58.6	64.9	57.3	72.4	63.2	67.2
Less: Employee contributions	0.8	0.7	1.1	0.9	0.8	1.0	1.0	1.0
Employer expenses	**58.8**	**72.6**	**93.9**	**107.6**	**90.0**	**93.5**	**89.0**	**96.7**
Of which, imputed expenses	26.0	20.4	-6.3	6.8	-5.4	0.8	-0.2	21.9
ABO, BOY	**1,773.9**	**1,844.6**	**1,954.4**	**2,071.3**	**2,130.9**	**2,282.0**	**2,309.1**	**2,472.4**
Plan net assets, BOY	**2,011.7**	**1,918.4**	**1,755.0**	**1,657.6**	**1,944.7**	**2,105.8**	**2,249.7**	**2,474.3**
Unfunded actuarial liability	**-237.8**	**-73.8**	**199.4**	**413.7**	**186.2**	**176.2**	**59.4**	**-1.9**
Change in ABO at 6% rate	**70.7**	**109.8**	**116.9**	**59.5**	**151.1**	**27.1**	**163.3**	**NA**
Of which, changes in assumptions and plan rules	15.9	53.1	58.3	-5.4	93.8	-45.3	100.1	NA
Change in plan net assets	**-93.3**	**-163.4**	**-97.4**	**287.1**	**161.1**	**143.9**	**224.6**	**178.5**
Of which, holding gains, capital transfers, and other changes in volume of assets	-64.7	-142.6	-106.1	279.6	161.3	141.5	232.6	205.1
Change in unfunded actuarial liability	**164.0**	**273.2**	**214.3**	**-227.6**	**-10.0**	**-116.8**	**-61.3**	**NA**

Source: Authors' estimates from IRS form 5500 data, except change in plan assets in 2007, which comes from Private Pension Plan Bulletin Historical Tables and Graphs, Employee Benefits Security Administration, March 2012.

176 Dominique Durant, David Lenze, and Marshall B. Reinsdorf

The current change in household wealth equals employer contributions plus the interest on the benefit entitlement minus plan administrative expenses. As was explained in section 6.3.3, the difference between the interest on the benefit entitlement and the property income received by the plans (both imputed and actual) represents implied holding gains on plan assets. These implied holding gains average about $62 billion, about the same as the change in benefit entitlements. Because the private DB plans tend be offered by established businesses with stagnant or shrinking workforces, a large fraction of their participants are retired. Benefit payments are thus so high that virtually all of the plans' accrued property and contribution income is used for benefits or administrative expenses. Indeed, on a cash basis, saving of the pension plans themselves averages –9 billion dollars per year.

On the other hand, holding gains, which range from –142.6 billion dollars in 2001 to 279.6 billion dollars in 2004, are sufficiently positive to bring the average growth in plan assets up to about 80 billion dollars per year, or 66 billion dollars in 2007, which was estimated based on EBSA Bulletins, is excluded. Although average holding gains would have been lower had 2008 been included, at least for the years covered by table 6.6, holding gains contributed even more to asset growth than the holding gains implied by the calculation of the change in the benefit entitlement.

Households are often found to have low marginal propensities to consume out of holding gains (3 percent is a typical estimate), but in the case of private DB plans, holding gains are a close substitute for ordinary income as a source of funding for benefits. Indeed, government regulations against both deliberate overfunding and underfunding of DB pension plans tend to cause employer contributions to vary inversely with holding gains. Thus, holding gains on assets are used more frequently to fund consumption expenditures of US households when the assets are held by a DB pension plan than when the assets are held by households directly.

6.5.2   State and Local Government Plans

The DB plans for employees of state and local governments cover fewer active participants than private plans (14.3 million in 2007, compared with 18.5 million in nonfrozen private DB plans), but they generate about the same amount of income for households as the private DB plans if income is measured on a cash basis. The cash measure of household income (employer actual contributions plus property income from plan assets) averages $139 billion for state and local government plans (table 6.7). One reason for this seeming generosity of the state and local plans is that several million of the participants in these plans are not covered by Social Security, so their benefits have to be high enough to make up for the lack of Social Security benefits. Another is that retirement eligibility occurs at younger ages (often in the late fifties) for many state and local government employees in jobs such

Table 6.7   Household income, saving and wealth from state and local government DB pension plans using the ABO approach.[a] (Billions of dollars, or as noted)

	2000	2001	2002	2003	2004	2005	2006	2007	2008
Household income	**183.3**	**188.1**	**209.1**	**244.2**	**246.2**	**265.0**	**287.2**	**297.0**	**294.0**
Employer contributions to DB plans	136.2	143.9	147.9	148.4	161.9	171.2	179.3	193.7	202.2
Actual contributions	39.6	39.2	42.1	56.4	55.8	61.9	67.2	75.2	82.5
Imputed contributions	96.5	104.8	105.9	91.9	106.1	109.3	112.2	118.5	119.7
Imputed employer payment of interest or UAL	-37.9	-26.8	-9.0	17.9	1.7	10.2	17.8	10.3	14.5
Property income from plan assets	85.1	71.0	70.2	77.9	82.6	83.6	90.1	93.0	77.4
LESS: Plan administrative expenses	**4.8**	**7.2**	**7.8**	**7.7**	**7.9**	**10.3**	**10.2**	**15.3**	**13.8**
Household saving	**178.6**	**180.9**	**201.3**	**236.6**	**238.3**	**254.7**	**277.0**	**281.8**	**280.3**
Implied holding gains on plan assets	**56.5**	**69.5**	**64.9**	**40.5**	**49.2**	**60.6**	**61.9**	**80.6**	**104.0**
Current change in household wealth	**235.1**	**250.3**	**266.2**	**277.0**	**287.4**	**315.3**	**338.9**	**362.3**	**384.2**
Benefits and withdrawals	100.3	110.0	121.3	132.6	141.7	151.0	162.1	174.0	186.1
Change in benefit entitlements	160.5	167.4	173.4	174.5	176.7	196.2	210.2	223.8	236.2
Less: Employee contributions	25.7	27.1	28.5	30.1	30.9	31.8	33.4	35.5	38.1
Employer expenses	**98.3**	**117.1**	**139.0**	**166.3**	**163.6**	**181.4**	**197.1**	**204.0**	**216.6**
Of which, imputed expenses	58.6	77.9	96.9	109.9	107.8	119.6	129.9	128.8	134.2
ABO, BOY	**1,728.4**	**1,892.8**	**2,100.7**	**2,272.6**	**2,426.3**	**2,607.5**	**3,086.6**	**3,344.5**	**3,560.8**
Plan net assets, BOY	2,360.2	2,340.3	2,250.3	1,973.5	2,396.0	2,621.3	2,763.4	3,156.6	3,297.9
Unfunded actuarial liability	-631.8	-447.4	-149.5	299.0	30.3	186.2	323.2	187.9	262.8
Change in ABO	**164.5**	**207.9**	**171.8**	**153.7**	**381.2**	**279.1**	**257.9**	**216.3**	**226.6**
of which, changes in assumptions and plan rules	4.0	40.5	-1.6	-20.8	204.6	82.9	47.7	-7.5	-9.6
Change in plan net assets	**-20.0**	**-90.0**	**-276.7**	**422.4**	**225.3**	**142.2**	**393.1**	**141.4**	**-883.3**
of which, holding gains, capital transfers, and OCVA	-65.3	-110.0	-288.4	398.2	205.6	126.1	374.8	127.0	-881.3
Change in unfunded actuarial liability	**184.4**	**297.9**	**448.6**	**-268.7**	**155.9**	**136.9**	**-135.2**	**74.9**	**1,109.9**

Note: Flows are measured for years ending on December 31; stocks are measured as of December 31.

[a] Assumed interest rate in actuarial calculations is 6 percent from 2000 to 2004 and 5.5 percent thereafter.

as police, firefighter, or teacher. However, the effects of high benefits and early retirement ages on employer pension expenses are partly offset by relatively large employee contributions, which average over $30 billion per year.

On the whole, employer actual contributions to state and local government do not respond as dramatically to changes in plan funding status as is the case for private plans, though when the plans became underfunded in 2003, actual employer contributions increased. Thus, in this instance, imputed contributions had a more modest effect on the volatility of household income. Another noteworthy effect of the 2003 drop in plan assets is a $26.9 billion rise in imputed interest on the UAL that is offset by a $24.4 billion dip in implied holding gains. Household income was actually more volatile in 2003 under the actuarial approach than under the cash approach because imputed interest on the UAL was included in household income, but not implied holding gains. (This source of volatility is avoided by the SNA 2008 approach, which includes in interest income of households the amounts that we treat as implied holding gains.)

Yet the most important finding in table 6.7 is that imputed employer contributions have a large effect on the level of household income. Imputed contributions average over $107 billion in 2000–2008 and account for nearly half of the average level of household saving from participation in these plans, which is $236.6 billion. The weak response of employer contributions to plan-funding shortfalls and the low level of these contributions compared to the actuarial estimates of employer service costs is possible because the plans are not subject to the same tax and regulatory constraints as private plans. Another factor that helps to keep the level of actual contributions low is that state and local government plan actuaries tend to assume a high rate of interest, often 8 percent. For example, Moody's (2012, 6) estimates that lowering the discount rate assumption from 8 percent to its preferred assumption of 5.5 percent would increase a representative plan's accrued actuarial liability by 35.6 percent.

The financial soundness of DB pension plans sponsored by state and local governments has recently become a topic of controversy, with arguments that these plans are assuming rates of interest that are too high featuring prominently in this debate. The state and local government plans justify their high interest rate assumptions as the expected rate of return on the stocks that they hold, but Brown and Wilcox (2009) argue that using expected rate of return of risky assets to discount plan liabilities is inappropriate and prefer to use Treasury bond interest rates. Treasury bond rates are too low for actuarial purposes, however, as these bonds are sometimes held for liquidity or collateral requirement reasons rather than for their yield. Also, the actuarial liabilities of state and local government plans no longer seem as risk free as they seemed to be when Brown and Wilcox wrote their paper. One alternative is to use the interest rate assumptions that the PBGC uses to value its benefit obligation, which are based on surveys of rates offered on annuities purchased from life insurers. Those rates allow the PBGC to calculate market values of annuities equivalent to the benefits due to DB plan participants, and are typically slightly higher than Treasury bond rates. However, for US National Accounts purposes, adoption of the mean interest rate that the private plans are required to use for tax and regulatory purposes on Schedule B of Form 5500 has the advantage of a unified approach to state and local government and private DB plans. This interest rate is based on high-grade corporate bonds. Our interest assumption for actuarial estimates of the state and local government plans is therefore 6 percent in 2000–2004 and 5.5 percent thereafter.[15]

Using these rate assumptions, employer expense for imputed interest on the UAL averages about zero, but that is because the plans were overfunded on an ABO basis (though not using the EAN method) in 2000–2002. The financial crisis caused an extremely large holding loss in 2008, and property income from assets also declined in that year. At the same time, the ABO grew by $226.6 billion, and the gap between the change in assets and the change in the ABO resulted in an increase in the UAL of $1.1 trillion. Thus, employer interest on the UAL will likely be positive and substantial going forward. The large capital loss of 2008 also changed the average level of holding gains over a period starting in 2000 from +96 billion dollars per year to –12.6 billion dollars per year. In contrast, the change in the value of the benefit entitlement attributed to implied holding gains averages $60 billion per year over 2000–2007 and $65 billion per year over 2000–2008. In most years, virtually all of the change in plan assets comes from holding gains and losses, as the cash inflows to the state and local government plans from contributions and property income on assets barely exceed the cash outflows for benefits and administrative expenses.

6.5.3   Federal Government Employee Plans

Except for some inflation-indexed TIPS (Treasury Inflation-Protected Security) bonds bought by the military plan, the main DB plans for federal government employees do not invest in assets that generate holding gains. We therefore exclude implied holding gains from our treatment of these plans. In addition, our estimates cover only the two main federal DB plans (Civil Service Retirement System [CSRS] and Federal Employee Retirement System [FERS]) and the main military plan. The excluded smaller federal

---

15. On July 2, 2012, Moody's Investors Service also announced a plan to use interest rates on high-grade corporate bonds to value actuarial liabilities of state and local government plans. Novy-Marx and Rauh (2010) find in a study of state government plans that replacing the plans' interest rate assumptions with tax-adjusted interest rates on state general obligation municipal bonds raises the estimate of the aggregate ABO in 2009 from $2.76 trillion to $3.20 trillion. Using Treasury bond rates raises the estimate to $4.43 trillion. The EAN method estimate using the interest rate assumption of 8 percent is $3.15 trillion, so in this particular case, the effect of adopting the ABO approach instead of the EAN method used by the plans is about the same as the effect of using the states' tax-adjusted borrowing rate.

plans account for less than 5 percent of the total DB pension benefit payments of the federal government. We account for the federal plans using the EAN method for actuarial calculations because the available actuarial reports for these plans use the EAN method. The nominal interest assumptions used by the federal plan actuaries are high compared with our assumptions in tables 6.6 and 6.7 of 6 percent in 2000–2004 and 5.5 percent thereafter (bottom panel of table 6.8). The federal actuaries' salary growth and inflation assumptions are also high, however, and it is the real interest assumption (generally around 2.5 percent) that drives the federal actuarial estimates.

For the main federal plans, employer contributions per active participant are quite high, with a range from 16,000 to 28,000 dollars per year, or roughly 33 percent of covered payroll. Higher benefit levels to compensate for the lack of social security in the older civilian retirement plan and the military plan and the early retirement ages of the military plan explain some of the difference between these employer contributions and those for private DB plans (which are typically around or below 5,000 dollars). Yet the large employer contributions per active employee for the federal plans are primarily an example of what happens when an underfunded DB plan reaches maturity. Federal employee plans have high numbers of retired participants, so their benefit payments, which average $91.4 billion over the years covered by table 6.8, are much higher than employer normal cost for benefits earned by active participants, which average only $34.7 billion. Returns on assets would fund most of the benefit expenses of a fully funded, mature plan with a high ratio of retired to active participants, but the federal plans are only about 40 percent funded because they have never been able to close the funding gap inherited from their historical operation as pay-as-you-go plans. As a result, only 45 percent of employer actual contributions are used to cover normal cost for active employees. This means that the cash approach to measuring DB pension plans overstates current employee compensation by an average of $44.8 billion over the period covered by table 6.8, as shown by averaging the imputed employer contributions and reversing the sign.

The largest component of the actual federal contributions is the amount paid toward the cost of interest on the UAL. Paying a large fraction of the interest accruing on the UAL keeps it from growing rapidly. However, the interest cost of the UAL exceeds imputed employer contributions by an average of about $36 billion. Household income from participation in federal DB plans is therefore higher under the actuarial approach than under the cash approach, even though compensation income is lower.

6.5.4   Combined Actuarial Estimates for All DB Plans

Expressing the combined figures for private, state, and local government and federal government plans as a percent of disposable personal income (DPI) from the NIPAs shows that participation in DB plans provides income

Table 6.8 Household wealth and income from the main federal government DB pension plans. PBO approach using interest, inflation, and salary growth rates assumed in plans' actuarial reports (billions of dollars, except as noted)

	2000	2001	2002	2003	2004	2005	2006	2007	2008
Household income	**143.9**	**149.0**	**151.1**	**157.1**	**162.9**	**171.3**	**173.7**	**180.1**	**185.2**
Employer contributions to DB plans	28.2	28.8	31.5	33.0	34.1	37.7	37.7	39.3	42.3
Actual contributions	64.2	65.8	69.7	68.1	74.4	81.1	85.8	91.4	114.9
Imputed contributions	−36.0	−37.0	−38.2	−35.1	−40.3	−43.4	−48.1	−52.1	−72.6
Imputed employer payment of interest on UAL	69.2	71.7	71.2	77.1	82.9	86.5	87.2	93.1	90.0
Property income from plan assets	46.5	48.5	48.5	47.0	45.9	47.1	48.9	47.6	52.9
LESS: Plan administrative expenses	0.1	0.1	0.1	0.1	0.1	0.1	0.1	0.2	0.2
Household saving	**143.8**	**148.9**	**151.0**	**157.0**	**162.8**	**171.2**	**173.6**	**179.9**	**185.0**
Benefits and withdrawals	78.0	81.2	83.7	85.5	88.8	93.2	98.6	104.4	109.0
Change in benefit entitlements	70.6	72.1	71.5	75.8	78.2	82.1	78.9	79.3	79.8
Less: Employee contributions	4.7	4.3	4.2	4.3	4.2	4.1	3.9	3.8	3.7
Employer expenses	**97.4**	**100.5**	**102.6**	**110.1**	**117.0**	**124.2**	**124.8**	**132.5**	**132.3**
Of which, imputed expenses	33.2	34.7	32.9	42.0	42.6	43.1	39.0	41.1	17.4
PBO, BOY	1,800.8	1,871.4	1,943.5	2,015.0	2,090.9	2,169.1	2,251.2	2,330.1	2,409.4
Plan net assets, BOY	642.8	684.2	717.4	756.0	789.7	825.1	863.8	903.3	924.6
Unfunded actuarial liability	1,158.0	1,187.2	1,226.1	1,259.0	1,301.2	1,344.0	1,387.4	1,426.8	1,484.8
Change in PBO	**70.6**	**72.1**	**71.5**	**75.9**	**78.2**	**82.1**	**78.9**	**79.3**	**79.8**
of which, assumption changes or other changes in plans	0	0	0	0	0	0	0	0	0
Change in plan net assets	**41.4**	**33.2**	**38.6**	**33.7**	**35.4**	**38.7**	**39.5**	**21.3**	**62.2**
of which, capital transfers and timing differences	4.1	−4.1	0.0	−0.1	−0.2	−0.3	−0.4	−16.9	−0.1
Change in unfunded actuarial liability	**29.2**	**38.9**	**32.9**	**42.2**	**42.8**	**43.4**	**39.4**	**58.0**	**17.6**
Assumptions (%):									
Interest rate assumption, civilian plans	7.00	6.75	6.75	6.25	6.25	6.25	6.25	6.25	6.25
Inflation assumption, civilian plans	4.00	3.75	3.75	3.25	3.25	3.25	3.50	3.50	3.50
Rate of salary growth, civilian plans	4.25	4.25	4.25	4.00	4.00	4.00	4.25	4.25	4.25
Interest rate assumption, military plans	6.25	6.25	6.25	6.25	6.25	6.25	6.00	6.00	5.75
Inflation assumption, military plans	3.00	3.50	3.00	3.00	3.00	3.00	3.00	3.00	3.00
Rate of salary growth, military plans	3.50	3.50	3.50	3.75	3.75	3.75	3.75	3.75	3.75

Note: Estimates exclude smaller federal plans and the plan for employees of the Board of Governors of the Federal Reserve.

to households falling between 6.1 and 6.3 percent of DPI in most years (table 6.9). From an accounting point of view, these plans therefore add 6.1 percentage points to the personal saving rate on average. However, subtracting benefits payments net of employee contributions shows that personal saving in the form of growth in pension-plan equity amounts to only 2.3 percent of DPI on average. In addition, the imputed portion of employer pension expenses averages 1.7 percent of DPI, so the cash measure of personal saving from participation in DB plans averages just 4.4 percent of DPI and the cash measure of growth in pension plan equity averages just 0.6 percent of DPI. Finally, the SNA 2008 measure of household saving would count the amount that we treat as imputed holding gains as part of household-imputed interest income, which would raise the measure of household saving from participation in DB plans to an average of 7.5 percent of DPI, and raise the measure of growth in DB plan equity including household saving to an average of 3.7 percent of DPI.

Imputed employer expenses for contributions and interest subtract the same amount from saving by employers as the 1.7 percent of DPI that they add to household saving. Most of the subtraction comes from imputed employer contributions for state and local government plans, and the total average subtraction from saving by state and local governments (which have average saving of about zero in the present version of the national accounts) amounts to 1.2 percent of DPI. Imputed interest paid by the federal government to its DB plans averages 0.9 percent of DPI, which is partially by imputed employer contributions averaging –0.5 percent of DPI. Finally, imputed pension plan expenses for private employers are a relatively trivial 0.1 percent of DPI.

6.5.5   Social Security in the United States

Sections 6.5.1 to 6.5.4 have illustrated the changes that the United States may make in its presentation of employer-sponsored DB plans. The United States has not yet developed a plan to publish supplementary actuarial information on Social Security, but US Social Security Administration actuaries calculate three kinds of actuarial measures of Social Security's benefit obligation. The "open group" unfunded liability is a measure of the plan's long-run solvency. The "closed group" liability is useful for analyzing intergenerational burden sharing. The "maximum transition cost" is useful for analyzing the cost of proposals to replace Social Security with some other system, such as individual accounts, while letting participants keep the Social Security benefits that they have already earned (Schultz and Nickerson 2010). It is therefore an ABO-type measure of benefit entitlements.

Even though ABO measures are well suited to measuring employer-sponsored pension plans for national accounts purposes, their meaningfulness is less clear when it comes to social security. In sharp contrast to most traditional DB pension plans, for Social Security the ABO measure

Table 6.9 Household income from DB pension plans: US totals using the actuarial approach[a] (percentages of disposable personal income)

	2000	2001	2002	2003	2004	2005	2006	2007
Household income	**6.1**	**6.1**	**6.3**	**6.7**	**6.2**	**6.3**	**6.2**	**6.2**
Employer contributions to DB plans	3.2	3.3	3.3	3.2	3.1	3.1	3.1	3.1
Actual contributions	1.9	2.1	2.6	2.7	2.5	2.5	2.4	2.3
Imputed contributions	1.4	1.2	0.6	0.5	0.6	0.6	0.6	0.8
Imputed employer payments of interest on UAL	0.2	0.5	0.9	1.4	1.1	1.2	1.1	1.1
Property income from plan assets	2.7	2.3	2.1	2.1	2.1	2.0	2.0	2.0
LESS: **Plan administrative expenses**	**0.2**	**0.2**	**0.2**	**0.2**	**0.2**	**0.2**	**0.2**	**0.2**
Household saving	**6.0**	**5.9**	**6.1**	**6.5**	**6.0**	**6.1**	**6.0**	**5.9**
Implied holding gains on plan assets	**1.6**	**1.7**	**1.5**	**1.1**	**1.3**	**1.4**	**1.3**	**1.5**
Current change in household wealth	**7.5**	**7.6**	**7.6**	**7.6**	**7.3**	**7.5**	**7.3**	**7.4**
Benefits and withdrawals	4.0	4.1	4.2	4.2	4.2	4.1	4.2	4.2
Less: Employee contributions	0.4	0.4	0.4	0.4	0.4	0.4	0.4	0.4
Change in benefit entitlements	3.9	3.9	3.8	3.8	3.5	3.8	3.6	3.6
Employer expenses	**3.5**	**3.8**	**4.2**	**4.6**	**4.2**	**4.3**	**4.1**	**4.2**
Of which, imputed	1.61	1.74	1.54	1.89	1.63	1.76	1.70	1.84
Private plans	0.35	0.27	-0.08	0.08	-0.06	0.01	0.00	0.21
State and local government plans	0.80	1.02	1.21	1.31	1.21	1.29	1.31	1.24
Federal plans	0.45	0.45	0.41	0.50	0.48	0.46	0.39	0.39
Addendum:								
Household income, cash approach	**4.5**	**4.4**	**4.7**	**4.8**	**4.6**	**4.6**	**4.5**	**4.3**
Household benefit entitlement, BOY	**72.4**	**73.3**	**74.9**	**75.9**	**74.8**	**78.2**	**77.1**	**78.2**
of which, changes in assumptions or plan rules and OCVA	**0.3**	**1.2**	**0.7**	**-0.3**	**3.4**	**0.4**	**1.5**	**0.0**
Plan net assets, BOY	**68.4**	**64.6**	**59.0**	**52.4**	**57.7**	**59.8**	**59.3**	**62.7**
of which, holding gains/losses, capital transfers and OCVA	**-1.7**	**-3.4**	**-4.9**	**8.1**	**4.1**	**2.9**	**6.1**	**0.0**
Unfunded actuarial liability	**2.2**	**7.1**	**14.3**	**21.5**	**15.1**	**17.2**	**16.9**	**15.2**
Change in benefit entitlement	**4.2**	**5.1**	**4.5**	**3.5**	**6.9**	**4.2**	**5.0**	**2.8**
Change in plan net assets	**-1.0**	**-2.9**	**-4.2**	**8.9**	**4.8**	**3.5**	**6.6**	**1.6**
Change in unfunded actuarial liability	**5.2**	**7.8**	**8.3**	**-5.5**	**2.8**	**0.9**	**-0.9**	**1.5**
Memo: Disposable personal income	**7,327**	**7,649**	**8,010**	**8,378**	**8,889**	**9,277**	**9,916**	**10,424**

[a]Smaller federal government plans and terminated private DB plans are excluded.

of benefit entitlements tends to rise quickly in the early part of the career because Social Security's benefit formula is highly progressive and uses career average pay instead of final pay. Thus, even if lifetime contributions equal lifetime benefits in present-value terms for every participant, Social Security would look underfunded using an ABO approach. Furthermore, active participants cannot easily escape from future obligations to contribute, so an evaluation of their position that includes projected future benefits but not projected future contributions is of limited usefulness. This suggests that the closed group liability would be better suited for national accounts purposes than the other measures produced by the Social Security actuaries.

6.6   Alternative Measures of Household Saving in France based on the SNA Treatment of Pensions and Social Security

The particular changes that a country will need to make in its national accounts to implement the SNA 2008 recommendations depend on its economic institutions. France has some private retirement plans that are managed by life insurance companies as social insurance. To comply with the 2008 SNA, these plans may be treated as employer-sponsored DC pension plans. We show the current treatment of these plans and the possible new treatment of these plans in appendix A (table 6A.1). In the new treatment, employer contributions to these plans are recorded as compensation rather than as purely financial transactions, which raises the measure of household saving in 2007 by 10.3 billion euros.

By far the largest component of the French retirement system is, however, social security and the web of government-sponsored plans that are linked to social security. For these plans, the new actuarial measures of the 2008 SNA will be shown as part of a supplementary table that shows benefit entitlements in all pension and social security plans, not in the core accounts. In table 6A.2 in appendix A, we illustrate the differences between the core accounts and the supplementary table using data for France and estimates of benefit entitlements from social security and government-sponsored pension plans that we calculated using PROST, a social security modeling program of the World Bank that calculates accrued-to-date liabilities. Because the treatment of social security in the supplementary table is supposed to parallel the treatment of DB pension plans in the core accounts, in this table we call the difference between the actuarial value of benefits accrued through service and actual contributions "employer-imputed social contributions." In addition, we record the interest accruing on the social security benefit entitlement as household contribution supplements and as negative saving by the plan. Recording negative saving by the plan is appropriate because a social security plan with a funding gap does not have a claim on employers to cover this gap.

In the core accounts, saving by households equals the benefits received net of employee contributions, or 159 billion euros, but in the supplementary table, household saving equals the sum of employer contributions (€126 billion), imputed contributions (€31 billion) and imputed interest on the benefit entitlement (€287 billion), or €444 billion. This amount can also be decomposed into net benefits and the change in the benefit entitlement (household reserves in pension funds) of €285 billion.

6.6.1   International Comparison of France and the United States

The supplementary table on DB pension plans and social security that was introduced in the 2008 SNA will make it possible to calculate comprehensive measures of household income and saving that can be compared across countries with different retirement systems. Yet before accounting for differences in retirement systems, an international comparison must first account for other differences in the role of government in the economy (Durant and Frey 2009). To do this, we adjust household disposable income to include the value of social transfers in kind of government services for individual consumption, which consist mainly of education and health care. The unadjusted measure of disposable income is lower when these services are financed by income taxes than when they are purchased directly by households (Audenis, Grégoir, and Louvot 2002; Harvey 2004), but an international comparison should be invariant to how these services are financed. In the United States, the value of individual consumption items furnished by government is about 8.5 percent of disposable household income, whereas in France their value is 27 percent of disposable household income.[16] Thus, the use of a lower denominator is one reason why the headline household saving rate of France tends to be much higher than that of the United States. In addition, the headline saving rate is gross of consumption of fixed capital (CFC) in France but net of CFC in the United States. Our starting point for comparing saving rates of the United States and France is therefore adjusted disposable household income net of CFC, shown for 2007 at the top of table 6.10.

The next part of table 6.10 corrects the initial measures of adjusted disposable household income to implement the recommendations of the 2008 SNA on employer-sponsored pensions in the core account. In the case of the United States, the correction consists of adding imputed employer contributions to DB pension plans and the difference between the interest accruing on the benefit entitlement and actual property income from plan assets. This difference equals the sum of imputed interest on the claim of the plans on the employer for unfunded benefit entitlements and the implied holding gains of plan assets shown in tables 6.6, 6.7, and 6.8. Including imputed employer contributions to DB plans and the SNA measures of imputed

---

16. See table 102 of the accounts for international comparisons at http://www.bea.gov /national/sna.htm.

Table 6.10   Household saving and wealth including the measures from the supplementary table on pensions and social security of the 2008 SNA: Comparison of the United States and France in 2007[a] (billions of local currency unless otherwise stated)

	United States	France
Household disposable income and saving		
Adjusted household disposable income[b]	**11,313**	**1,491**
Household saving as percent of adjusted disposable income	**2.2**	**9.6**
"Correction" of treatment of pension plans	**344**	**10**
Imputed employer contributions to DB pension plans	81	
Imputed property income and implied holding gains, DB plans	263	
Actual employer contributions to DC pension plans	10	
Corrected household income	**11,657**	**1,501**
Corrected household saving as percent of corrected income	**5.1**	**10.2**
Effect of actuarial treatment of social securityc	**1,732**	**285**
Actual employer contributions	310	126
Actual contributions from employees and self-employed persons	360	72
Imputed contributions from government	−148	31
Actual and imputed property income	1,731	287
LESS: Benefits	521	231
Harmonized household disposable income	**13,390**	**1,786**
Household saving as percent of harmonized disposable income	**17.4**	**24.5**
Balance sheet, in years of harmonized disposable income		
Core accounts, current methods:		
Assets	**5.9**	**6.0**
Nonfinancial assets	1.9	3.9
of which, real estate	1.6	3.5
Financial assets	4.0	2.1
of which, from life insurers and pension funds	1.1	0.7
Liabilities	**1.0**	**0.6**
Adjustments including in harmonized balance sheet	**1.7**	**3.2**
Unfunded benefit entitlements in DB pension plans	0.1	
Benefit entitlements in social security plans	1.7	4.1
LESS: Financing gap of social security	0.1	0.9
Total harmonized assetsd	**7.5**	**9.2**
Total harmonized net worth	**6.5**	**8.6**

[a]Baseline income and saving estimates reflect national accounts data as published in 2010.
[b]Net of consumption of fixed capital (CFC). Nonprofit institutions serving households are included with households in estimates for the United States.
[c]Social security includes civil servant pension plans in the case of France.
[d]Totals.

property income raises the measure of the US household saving rate from 2.2 percent of adjusted disposable income to 5.2 percent of corrected disposable income. In the case of France, the "correction" consists of adding actual employer contributions to DC pension plans administered by life insurance companies. For France, the impact of the reclassification as social insurance of pensions currently recorded in life insurance is modest, at only 0.6 percentage points, because the value of these pensions is small (1.3 percent of households' total assets). Thus, correcting the measurement of household saving arising from participation in employer-sponsored pension plans helps to close the large gap between household saving rates of the United States and France.

We next convert the corrected measures of household income and saving into "harmonized" measures by changing the treatment of social security and similar government-employee pension plans from the standard treatment used in the core accounts to one based on the actuarial measures of the supplementary table. Household disposable income from social security in the core accounts equals benefits received less employee contributions, while in the supplementary table it comprises actual and imputed employer contributions and interest on the benefit entitlement. The difference between the two income concepts therefore equals total contributions plus interest on the benefit entitlement minus benefits received.

To make comparable estimates of benefit entitlements from social security for the United States and France we used PROST, a social security modeling program of the World Bank that calculates accrued-to-date liabilities. For comparison purposes, we used the same nominal discount rate, 4 percent, for both countries (see appendix B for more details). We did not include railroad retirement in the adjustment for Social Security in the United States because the effect of substituting an actuarial measure of railroad retirement for a cash measure is tiny in recent years.

The harmonized saving rates are much higher than the corrected saving rates in both the United States and France because the imputed interest on benefit entitlements is very large. In the United States, the "harmonized" saving rate with an actuarial treatment of Social Security is 17.4 percent. The amounts of social security benefit entitlements (including those of civil servants) in France are even larger than in the United States; indeed, the property income accruing to households at our assumed 4 percent rate amounts to 16 percent of their "harmonized" disposable income. This helps to bring the harmonized household saving rate for France up to 24.5 percent. Nevertheless, the gap between harmonized saving rates of 7.1 percentage points is smaller than the original gap between the adjusted saving rates.

Despite their higher saving rate, French households had about the same ratio of assets to harmonized disposable income as US households on the eve of the financial crisis of 2008. The total assets of US households recorded in the Flow of Funds Accounts amounted to around 5.9 years' worth of harmonized disposable income, compared with assets worth six years of disposable income for French households (bottom panel of table 6.10). In the United States, the financial assets are larger, while French households rely more on real estate, which in France has tended to be relatively stable. Strong holding gains in many of the years from 1995 to 2006 are one factor that enabled US households to build assets while having comparatively low saving. Households in the United States also seem to have made more use of leverage to finance asset purchases, as their liabilities are relatively high. Subtracting liabilities implies a lower net worth figure for US households before benefit entitlements of 4.9 years of income, compared to 5.4 years of income in France.

To arrive at corrected and harmonized measures of household wealth, we add the value of unfunded benefit entitlements from the DB pension plans of the United States and total benefit entitlements from social security. We also deduct an allowance for the financing gap of the social security plan because we do not want to count benefits that might not be paid as part of social security wealth. For France, our estimates of the benefit entitlement and the funding gap include the effect of the 2010 reform increasing the minimum retirement age to sixty-two, which brought the present discounted value of the financing gap down from 29 percent of benefit entitlements to 26 percent.[17] The social security funding gap reflects the reductions in benefits or increases in contribution rates that are projected, based on the information available at the time of the projection, to be necessary to keep the system solvent. In assigning all of the funding gap liability to households that are currently alive we are making a conservative assumption: future generations could shoulder a significant part of the burden if this gap is closed just by increasing contribution rates.

In the United States, unfunded DB benefit entitlements amount to 0.1 years' worth of harmonized disposable income in 2007 and the value of benefit entitlements in Social Security is equivalent to 1.5 years of income. In France, benefit entitlements in social security are worth 3.2 years of harmonized disposable income. After subtracting liabilities and the social security financing gap, we find that households in France have a comprehensive wealth-to-income ratio of 8.6, compared to 6.5 years' worth of income for US households.

The higher harmonized saving rate and wealth-to-income ratio of France partly reflects the fact that French people need to save more because they retire at younger ages and have slightly longer life expectancies. (In 2010, the average retirement age in France was 61.5 compared with an average age for claiming Social Security benefits in the United States of 63.6.) The saving rate of US households may also be lower because US households rely more on holding gains as a means of building wealth (documented in Durant and Reinsdorf [2008], though, of course, in the years after the financial crisis that strategy did not work so well). Accessibility of credit may also play a

17. In 2012 the new administration announced a partial reversal of these reforms to allow certain employees with careers of more than forty years to retire at age sixty. We have not taken these reform reversals into account. See appendix B, figure 6.B2 for estimates of the future net cash flows of social security in France as percentages of GDP.

role in the lower saving rate of the United States: easy access to credit for US households can substitute for precautionary balances and reduce the precautionary motive for saving.

In addition, the need for saving is greater when risks are higher, and French households probably perceive their retirement wealth as riskier than American households do. Participants in the DB pension plans of the United States generally have property rights to the benefits that they have accrued, and in the private sector benefits are insured by the PBGC. Furthermore, almost thirty years have passed since the only time that Social Security was reformed in the United States, and in that reform the benefit cuts only affected those who were more than twenty years away from the normal retirement age. In contrast, France has had three major retirement reforms since 1993, with more to come, as the funding gap of French social security remains large. In the past reforms, the benefit cuts have included employees nearing retirement and encompassed both pension plans and social security.

In France, in the years after World War II, the generations who reached retirement age had lost most of their savings in war. A delay in the start of benefit payments while the social security system built up the reserves required to operate as a funded plan was therefore impossible. Rather than building up a trust fund, the contributions of the active participants had to be used to fund current benefit payments. The system continued on in this way, based on a kind of intergenerational lending where people hope to obtain from the younger what they gave to the older. Yet the "rate of return" of such a pay-as-you-go system depends on the ratio of contributors to beneficiaries adjusted for increases in labor productivity. When the demographic return from population growth decreases, as nowadays with the so-called "pappy boom," the implicit rate of return of social security must fall, necessitating reforms. It is thus rational for French households to save more because their main asset, consisting of social security benefit entitlements, is risky. To be sure, reforms will also be needed to keep the US Social Security solvent over the long run, but the relative size of the social security financing gap is smaller in the case of the United States, and the importance of social security wealth in households' comprehensive net worth is also smaller.[18]

18. Romig (2008) projected that if no reforms of US Social Security are enacted, currently scheduled benefits will automatically be cut by 22 percent in 2041, rising to a cut of 25 percent in 2082. She was unsure whether monthly benefits will be reduced or whether payments will be delayed until enough funds are available to pay the full amount of a scheduled monthly benefit, resulting in fewer payments per year. Recently, the projections have worsened. According to the 2012 Social Security Trustee's Report, funds will only be available to pay 75 percent of scheduled benefits beginning in 2033.

6.7   Conclusion

A full picture of the operations of pension and social security plans has become a critical part of understanding the economic situation of most countries because populations are aging and DB pension plans have rising numbers of retired participants. For employer-sponsored pension plans, national accounts will be able to provide this full picture by changing from an approach based on cash accounting to the approach based on actuarial estimates of accrued benefit entitlements that is recommended in the 2008 SNA. For Social Security and similar government-sponsored pension plans, the new actuarial measures will not provide complete information for purposes of gauging sustainability, but they will permit international comparisons of countries that have different systems for providing retirement income.

Employer-sponsored DB pension plans play a major role in the US retirement income system. This chapter shows how the new actuarial approach provides the information needed to understand the economics of the operations of these plans. For private DB plans, we find that the actuarial approach provides a more meaningful measure of pension-related compensation by avoiding the excessive volatility that the cash approach suffers when employers alternate between taking a contribution holiday and making large catch-up contributions to fill funding gaps. For plans for employees of state and local governments in the United States (whose funding gaps have recently become a topic of debate—see Novy-Marx and Rauh [2009], [2010], [2011]; Rauh [2010]), we find that the value of claims-to-benefits accrued through service to the employer exceeds cash contributions by more than $100 billion in every year starting in 2004, so the cash approach substantially underestimates saving by households and overestimates saving by state and local governments. For federal government plans in recent years, large amounts of interest accruing on unfunded benefit entitlements of retired participants are included in actual employer contributions, so they are mischaracterized by the cash approach as compensation income for employed participants. Furthermore, additional amounts of interest on unfunded benefit entitlements that are not covered by actual contributions are ignored by the cash approach. Because the cash approach understates compensation income of participants in state and local government plans and understates interest income of participants in federal plans, using the actuarial approach raises the overall estimate of the household saving rate from 2.9 percent to 4.6 percent in 2002–2007, an increase of 1.7 percentage points.

This chapter also demonstrates the usefulness of the actuarial measures of social security and government-sponsored pension plans that are included in a supplementary table in the 2008 SNA for international comparisons of saving rates and wealth of countries with different kinds of retirement systems. The large gap between the high saving rate of households in France and the low saving rate of households in the United States implied by the cash treatment of pensions and social security in the national accounts of the two countries narrows when actuarial measures are used. However, if only employer-sponsored pension plans were included in the actuarial measures, the gap between the French and US saving rates would be substantially understated, because in France government-sponsored pensions, which are included with social security in the supplemental table called for in the 2008 SNA, substitute for the employer-sponsored pension plans of the United States.

Finally, this chapter suggests three modifications to the actuarial measures introduced in the 2008 SNA to depict the operations of DB pension plans more accurately or to communicate additional details about the operations of pension and social security plans. First, we argue that in institutional settings where employers are responsible for ensuring the solvency of the DB plans that they sponsor, underfunded pension plans should be recorded as receiving imputed interest on their claim on the employer. When employers delay making actuarially required contributions the pension plan is deprived of opportunities to earn property income, so this imputed interest reflects amounts that must be paid to the plan if it is to have sufficient funds to pay the benefits that it owes to the plan participants. Second, when a DB pension plan uses holding gains to help fund benefit expenses, the property income component of its return on investments is likely to be smaller than the interest accruing on the funded portion of its actuarial liability. In the framework of the 2008 SNA, this gap is recorded as negative saving by the DB plan because the plan pays more property income to households than it receives. In the institutional setting of the United States, we prefer to show the saving of the DB pension plan as zero, and to identify the implied funding of pension benefits from holding gains on pension plan assets as implied holding gains received by households.

Third, the supplementary table on social security called for in the 2008 SNA is intended to be comparable with the measures provided in the core accounts for employer-sponsored DB plans, so the actuarial measures of social security exclude future participants. This limits their relevance for questions about sustainability, because for social security sustainability analysis requires "open group" measures that take into account the projected contributions of future participants. We resolve the conflict between comparability with measures of employer-sponsored pension plans and providing information on sustainability by including in our balance sheet measures an allowance for the social security funding gap. This funding gap is deducted in the calculation of households' social security wealth. Besides permitting a more accurate valuation of risky claims to future payments of social security benefits, this allowance enables the accounts to include a kind of sustainability indicator for social security assuming that the plan parameters remain unchanged.

Appendix A

Treatment of Pensions and Social Security in the 2008 SNA Compared with Current Treatment: The Case of France

Table 6A.1 SNA 2008 treatment of employer-sponsored pensions compared with current treatment in the national accounts of France, 2007 (billions of euros)

		SNA 2008						Current accounting					
		Uses			Resources			Uses			Resources		
		Pension scheme	Households	Employer	Pension scheme	Households	Employer	Pension scheme	Household	Employer	Pension scheme	Household	Employer
P1	Output				0.5								
D121	Employer actual social contributions			10.3		10.3							
D122	Employer-imputed social contributions												
D44	Investment income	4.2				4.2		4.2				4.2	
D611	Employer actual social contributions		10.3		10.3								
D612	Employer-imputed social contributions												
D613	Households actual social contributions												
D614	Households pension contribution supplement		3.8		3.8								
D62	Social benefit	4.3				4.3							
P3	Consumption		0.5						0.5				
D8	Adjust. for change in household reserves in pension funds	9.8				9.8							
B8	Saving	-3.8				14.1	-10.3				-3.8	3.8	

		Assets	Liabilities	Assets	Liabilities
	Beginning of the year balance sheet				
F2	Deposits	6.5		85.9	
F611	Life insurance technical reserves	85.9	85.9		85.9
F612	Household reserves in pension funds	9.8			9.8
F79	Other accounts payable/receivable				
B90	Net worth	−85.9	85.9	−85.9	85.9
					10.3
	Financial account				
F2	Deposits	6.5		3.8	
F611	Life insurance technical reserves	9.8	10.3	9.8	
F612	Household reserves in pension funds	9.8			9.8
F79	Other accounts payable/receivable			0.6	0.6
B9	Net lending/borrowing	−3.3	13.6	−3.9	3.8
			−10.3		−10.3
	Revaluation account				
F2	Deposits				
F611	Life insurance technical reserves	−1.2	−1.2	−1.2	−1.2
F612	Household reserves in pension funds				
F79	Other accounts payable/receivable				
B10.3	Change in net worth due to revaluation	1.2	−1.2	1.2	−1.2
	End-of-the-year balance sheet				
F2	Deposits	6.5		3.8	
F611	Life insurance technical reserves	94.5	10.3	95.7	95.7
F612	Household reserves in pension funds	94.5			9.8
F79	Other accounts payable/receivable			0.6	0.6
B90	Net worth	−88.0	98.3	−88.6	88.5
			−10.3		−10.3

Table 6A.2 Social security treated as a pension plan in the supplementary table of the 2008 SNA, France, in 2007 (billions of euros; estimated by the authors from PROST)

	Supplementary table SNA 2008						Core accounts SNA 2008					
	Uses			Resources			Uses			Resources		
	Pension scheme	Households	Employer	Pension scheme	Households	Employer	Households	Pension scheme	Employer	Households	Pension scheme	Employer
Output												
Employer actual social contributions			126		126				126	126		
Employer-imputed social contributions			31		31							
Investment income	287				287							
Employer actual social contributions		126		126			126				126	
Employer imputed social contributions		31		31								
Households' actual social contributions		72		72			72				72	
Households' pension contribution supplement		287		287								
Social benefit	231				231			231		231		
Consumption												
Adjust. for change in household reserves in pension funds	285				285							
Saving	−287				444	−157		−33		159		−126

	Assets	Liabilities	Assets	Liabilities
Beginning of the year balance sheet				
Deposits	7,035	7,035		
Life insurance technical reserves	231	105	231	126
Household reserves in pension funds	285	285		
Other accounts payable/receivable		−7,035		−126
Net worth		7,035		
Financial account				
Deposits				
Life insurance technical reserves	231	105	231	126
Household reserves in pension funds	285	285		
Other accounts payable/receivable				
Net lending/borrowing	−389	516		−126
Revaluation account				
Life insurance technical reserves	74	74		
Change in net worth due to revaluation	−74	74		
End-of-the-year balance sheet				
Deposits	7,394	7,394		
Life insurance technical reserves	231	105	231	126
Household reserves in pension funds	7,394	285		
Other accounts payable/receivable				−126
Net worth	−7,498	7,625		

Appendix B
Using PROST to Estimate Accrued-to-Date Pension Entitlements on Social Security

PROST is a generational model developed by the World Bank (Holzmann, Palacios, and Zviniene 2001). We use it to calculate accrued-to-date benefit entitlements for social security, which are not available from official data sources for France. In order to assess the quality of the estimates, the financing gap produced by PROST have been compared to official estimates (OASDI report in the United States, and the "Conseil d'Orientation des retraites" 2010 report in France). For the sake of comparison between the two countries, the nominal discount rate has been fixed to 4 percent, which with effective inflation, makes a variable real discount rate.

PROST calculates the accrued-to-date entitlements with the projected benefit obligation method that is taking into account the future increase in salary until retirement date. The exact formula adds accrued-to-date entitlements of present retirees in equation (1) to accrued-to-date entitlements of future ones in equation (2).

(1) $= \sum_{t=1}^{T}$ *(number of new retirees by age, gender, salary cluster)*
    × *(present value of futute pension paid by age, gender, salary c luster conditional to being in life)*

(2) = (1) for current contributors by age, gender, salary cluster ×
    number of years already worked/total career

Data needed are the following:

- population, number of contributors and beneficiaries by gender and age;
- salaries and pensions (amount) by age and decile of revenue;
- contribution rate, under ceiling and without ceiling, with indexation rule for ceiling;
- legal retirement age, with possible discount for early retirement;
- maximum replacement rate and number of years needed to attain it;
- indexation on pension on inflation or wage growth;
- invalidity and widows' pensions; and
- GDP growth, real wage growth, inflation rate, discount rate.

For France, the model was applied to all contributors and retirees, except the state civil servants. The model was originated in 1993, in order to capture the evolution entailed by the reforms of required length of career and number of years used to calculate the reference salary depending on the age of the retiree. The data were benchmarked on the "Conseil d'orientation des retraites" (COR), a board of experts and social partners that was created in 2000 in order to provide analysis on the evolution of the pension system. These analyses are the basis for the discussions organized at the "meeting points," where decisions and laws are to be taken to restore the long-term balance of the pension system.

Data sources were the following:

- Population: INSEE projection;
- Contributors = active population less state civil servants × activity rate by age from the INSEE;
- Unemployment rate by age from INSEE and decrease of 2 percent from 2015 onward for people under age fifty and from 1 percent onward for people over age fifty, due to the increase in retirement age;
- Combined contributions to CNAVTS and AGIRC-ARRCO with a distinction between contribution under social security ceiling (2.3 percent from 2006 onward) and contribution above ceiling (21.7 percent);
- Legal retirement age: sixty and sixty-two after 2010 after reform;
- Maximum replacement rate of 95 percent attainable in 37.5 years in 1993 up to 41.75 years in 2020. This lead to an incremental replacement rate of 2.53 in 1993 going down to 2.28 in 2020;
- Number of years used to calculate the reference salary form 10 in 1993 to 25 in 2008 onward;
- Inflation, GDP growth, labor productivity growth are updated up to 2009. Afterward, inflation rate is set at 2 percent and other variables are aligned on COR C scenario.

Table 6B.1   **Macroeconomic parameters used by the COR and in PRST estimates**

	2009–2013	2014–2020	2021–2050
	Scenario B		
Unemployment rate	8.4	7.7	4.5
GDP real growth	1.3	2.2	1.6
Labor productivity growth	1.4	1.8	1.6
	Scenario C		
Unemployment rate	8.4	7.7	7
GDP real growth	1.3	2	1.6
Labor productivity growth	1.4	1.8	1.6

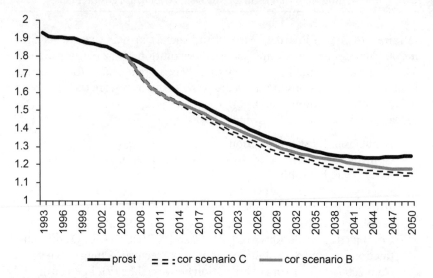

Fig. 6B.1   Ratio of contributors to retirees in France (based on PROST using benchmarks from the COR)

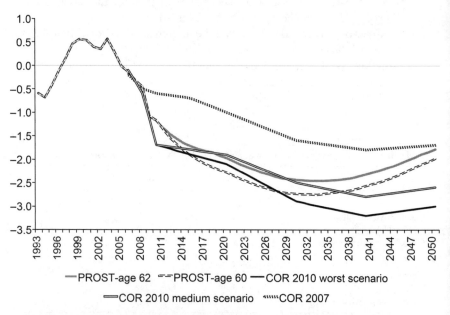

Fig. 6B.2   Projected net cash flow for social security in France, as a percent of GDP (based on the authors' simulations using PROST and the COR)

Notes: For the United States, the model was applied to the entire population. The model was started in 2003. Data sources were the following: the Census bureau regarding population, the Bureau of Labor regarding wages, and the OASDI trustee report regarding Social Security. The contribution rate was fixed to 6.2 percent under ceiling and 6.2 percent above ceiling. The maximum replacement rate was fixed to 64 percent after forty-five years of contribution, which lead to an incremental replacement rate of 1.43 percent a year. The minimum retirement age is 65 in 2002, 66 in 2006, and 67 in 2027.

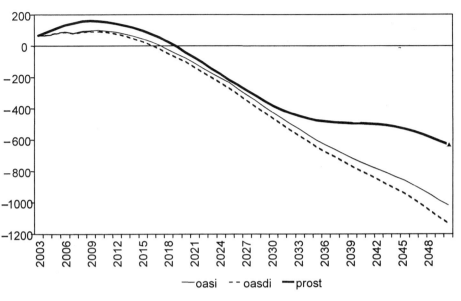

Fig. 6B.3 Projected net cash flow for Social Security in the United States (billions of dollars)

Appendix C

Harmonized Saving Rates and Wealth-to-Income Ratios for the United States and France

Table 6C.1   United States (billions of dollars, unless otherwise marked)

	2003	2004	2005	2006	2007	2008
GDP (billions of dollars)	11,417	12,145	12,916	13,612	14,291	14,191
Adjusted disposable income	**9,097**	**9,638**	**10,072**	**10,756**	**11,313**	**11,966**
Current measure of saving, as percent of adjusted disposable income	3.2	3.3	1.4	2.4	2.2	4.9
Correction for actuarial treatment of pension plans						
Actual employer contributions	225	226	236	242	241	301
Imputed employer contributions	39	49	56	61	81	38
Actual property income	174	182	188	203	210	205
Imputed property income[a]	211	208	237	242	263.3	278
Benefits	354	372	384	413	440	461
Corrected disposable income	**9,347**	**9,895**	**10,365**	**11,058**	**11,657**	**12,281**
Corrected saving rate	5.8	5.8	4.2	5.1	5.1	7.4
Social security						
Actual employer contributions	254	267	281	296	310	327
Imputed employer contributions	−175	−164	−131	−65	−148	−146
Actual employee contribution	292	308	325	343	360	377
Imputed property income at 4% interest rate	1,429	1,494	1,565	1,645	1,731	1,819
Benefits	479	488	495	505	521	541
Harmonized disposable income	**10,668**	**11,313**	**11,910**	**12,772**	**13,390**	**14,116**
Harmonized saving rate	17.4	17.6	16.6	17.8	17.4	19.4
Household sector balance sheet, in years of harmonized disposable income						
Current recording						
Nonfinancial assets	1.9	2.0	2.2	2.1	1.9	1.6
Of which, real estate	*1.5*	*1.7*	*1.8*	*1.8*	*1.6*	*1.2*
Financial assets	3.5	3.6	3.8	4.0	4.0	3.1
Of which, life insurance	*0.1*	*0.1*	*0.1*	*0.1*	*0.1*	*0.1*
Pension funds	*0.9*	*0.9*	*1.0*	*1.0*	*1.0*	*0.7*
Total assets	**5.3**	**5.6**	**6.0**	**6.1**	**5.9**	**4.7**
Liabilities	**0.9**	**0.9**	**1.0**	**1.0**	**1.0**	**1.0**
Harmonized recording						
Correction to DB pension plans	0.18	0.13	0.14	0.14	0.12	0.12
Benefit entitlements from social security	1.71	1.69	1.68	1.65	1.66	1.65
Less: Financing gap	−0.10	−0.10	−0.10	−0.10	−0.10	−0.10
Railroad retirement and PBGC	0.01	0.01	0.01	0.01	0.01	0.01
Total corrected assets	**7.2**	**7.4**	**7.7**	**7.8**	**7.5**	**6.3**

[a]SNA 2008 measure of imputed property income includes amounts treated as implied holding gains in tables 6.4 and 6.5.

Table 6C.2   **France (billions of euros, unless otherwise marked)**

As % of corrected disposable income (unless otherwise indicated)	2003	2004	2005	2006	2007	2008
GDP	1,588	1,656	1,718	1,798	1,887	1,933
Adjusted disposable income	1,267	1,320	1,363	1,422	1,491	1,539
Current saving rate as % of adj. DI	9.6	9.9	9.0	9.1	9.6	9.5
Pension entitlements						
Actual contributions	7	7	8	9	10	11
Actuarial contributions	0	0	0	0	0	0
Actual property income	3	3	3	3	4	4
Imputed property income up to 4% rate	0	0	0	0	0	0
Benefits	3	3	4	4	4	6
Corrected disposable income	1,274	1,327	1,371	1,431	1,501	1,550
Corrected saving rate	10.1	10.4	9.5	9.7	10.2	10.0
Social security (incl. civil servant)						
Employer actual contributions	104	110	116	122	126	124
Employer actuarial contributions	39	36	30	26	31	45
Employee actual contributions	60	63	67	70	72	68
Property income at 4.0% rate	244	254	268	279	287	301
Benefits	188	197	207	219	231	243
Harmonized disposable income	1,533	1,592	1,645	1,710	1,786	1,845
Corrected saving rate	25.3	25.3	24.6	24.4	24.5	24.4

Balance sheet, in year of corrected disposable income

Current recording						
Nonfinancial assets	2.8	3.2	3.6	3.8	3.9	3.8
Of which, real estate	2.5	2.8	3.2	3.4	3.5	3.4
Financial assets	1.7	1.8	1.9	2.0	2.0	1.9
Of which, pension entitlements in insurance corp.	0.0	0.0	0.0	0.1	0.1	0.1
Of which, other life insurance	0.5	0.5	0.6	0.6	0.6	0.6
Total asset	4.6	5.0	5.5	5.8	6.0	5.6
Liabilities	0.5	0.5	0.6	0.6	0.7	0.7
Harmonized recording						
Pension entitlements on social security	4.1	4.1	4.1	4.1	4.1	4.2
Less cumulated financing gap	–0.9	–0.9	–0.9	–0.9	–0.9	–0.9
Total corrected assets	7.7	8.1	8.7	9.0	9.2	8.8

References

Audenis, Cédric, Stéphane Grégoir, and Claudie Louvot. 2002. "The Various Measures of the Saving Rate and their Interpretation." Presented at OECD Meeting of National Accounts Experts, Paris, October 8.

Board of Trustees, Federal Old-Age and Survivors Insurance and Federal Disability Insurance Trust Funds. 2008. The 2008 Annual Report of the Board of Trustees, Federal Old-Age and Survivors Insurance and Federal Disability Insurance Trust Funds. Washington, DC: US Government Printing Office.

Brady, Peter, Sarah Holden, and Erin Short. 2010. "The US Retirement Market, 2009." *Investment Company Institute Research Fundamentals* 19 (3). http://www.ici.org/pdf/fm-v19n3.pdf.

Brown, Jeffrey R., and David W. Wilcox. 2009. "Discounting State and Local Pension Liabilities." *American Economic Review* 99 (2): 538–42.

Bucks, Brian K., Arthur B. Kennickell, Traci L. Mach, and Kevin B. Moore. 2009. "Changes in US Family Finances from 2004 to 2007: Evidence from the Survey of Consumer Finances." *Federal Reserve Bulletin* (February):A1–A56.

Conseil d'Orientation des Retraites. 2010. *Retraites: Perspectives Actualisées à Moyen et Long Terme en Vue du Rendez-vous de 2010.* 8th report. April.

Durant, Dominique, and Laure Frey. 2009. "Une Première Comparaison des Droits à Pension des Ménages Français et Américains." Document de travail n°280. Paris: Banque de France.

Durant, Dominique, and Marshall Reinsdorf. 2008. "Implicit Social Security and Pension Wealth in Households' Assets in the US and France." Paper prepared for the 30th General Conference of the International Association for Research in Income and Wealth, Portoroz, Slovenia, August.

European Central Bank. 2010. "Entitlements of Households under Government Pension Schemes in the Euro Area—Results on the Basis of the New System of National Accounts." *ECB Monthly Bulletin* January:85–101.

Eurostat-European Central Bank. 2011. "Technical Compilation Guide for Pension Data in National Accounts." Eurostat Methodologies and Working Papers. http://www.ecb.europa.eu/pub/pubbydate/2012/html/index.en.html.

Harvey, Ross. 2004. "Comparison of Household Saving Ratios: Euro Area, United States, Japan." *OECD Statistics Brief* June:1–7.

Holzmann, Robert, Robert Palacios, and Asta Zviniene. 2001. "Implicit Pension Debt: Issues, Measurement and Scope in International Perspective." Pension Reform Primer Collection, World Bank, August.

Lazear, Edward P., and Robert L. Moore. 1988. "Pensions and Turnover." In *Pensions in the US Economy*, edited by Z. Bodie, J. Shoven, and D. Wise, 163–88. Chicago: University of Chicago Press.

Monahan, Amy B. 2012. "Statutes as Contracts? The 'California Rule' and its Impact on Public Pension Reform." *Iowa Law Review* 97:1031–83.

Moody's Investors Service. 2012. "Adjustments to US State and Local Government Reported Pension Data." http://www.moodys.com/research/Moodys-proposes-adjustments-to-US-public-sector-pension-data—PR_249988.

Novy-Marx, Robert, and Joshua Rauh. 2009. "The Liabilities and Risks of State-Sponsored Pension Plans." *Journal of Economic Perspectives* 23 (4): 191–210.

———. 2010. "Policy Options for State Pensions Systems and Their Impact on Plan Liabilities." Prepared for NBER Conference on State and Local Pensions, August 19–20, Jackson Hole, Wyoming.

———. 2011. "The Revenue Demands of Public Employee Pension Promises." www.kellogg.northwestern.edu/faculty/rauh/research/RDPEPP.pdf.

Perozek, Maria, and Marshall B. Reinsdorf. 2002. "Alternative Measures of Personal Saving." Survey of Current Business 82 (4): 13–24.

Rauh, Joshua. 2010. "Are State Public Pensions Sustainable? Why the Federal Government Should Worry about State Pension Liabilities." *National Tax Journal* 63 (3): 585–602.

Reinsdorf, Marshall B. 2004. "Alternative Measures of Personal Saving." *Survey of Current Business* 84 (September): 17–27.

———. 2005. "Saving, Wealth, Investment, and the Current-Account Deficit." *Survey of Current Business* 85 (April): 3.

———. 2007. "Alternative Measures of Personal Saving." *Survey of Current Business* 87 (February): 7–13.

Reinsdorf, Marshall B., and David G. Lenze. 2009. "Defined Benefit Pensions and Household Income and Wealth." *Survey of Current Business* 89 (August): 50–62.

Romig, Kathleen. 2008. *Social Security: What Would Happen if the Trust Funds Ran Out?* Washington, DC: Congressional Research Service.

Schultz, Jason, and Daniel Nickerson. 2010. "Unfunded Obligation and Transition Cost for the OASDI Program." Office of the Chief Actuary, Actuarial Note no. 2010–1, September. Washington, DC, Social Security Administration.

Stock, James H., and David A. Wise. 1990. "Pensions, the Option Value of Work, and Retirement." *Econometrica* 58 (September): 1151–80.

United Nations Statistical Division. 1993. "System of National Accounts, 1993." Commission of the European Communities, International Monetary Fund, OECD, United Nations, and World Bank. https://unstats.un.org/unsd/national account/sna1993.asp.

———. 2009. "System of National Accounts, 2008." Commission of the European Communities, International Monetary Fund, OECD, United Nations, and World Bank. https://unstats.un.org/unsd/nationalaccount/sna2008.asp.

US Department of Labor. 2010. *Private Pension Plan Bulletin: Abstract of 2007 Form 5500 Annual Reports*, version 1.4, Washington, DC, June.

The Return on US Direct
Investment at Home and Abroad

Stephanie E. Curcuru and Charles P. Thomas

7.1 Introduction

A longstanding puzzle is that the United States is a net borrower from the rest of the world and yet somehow manages to, on net, receive income on its external position. Net investment income receipts reported in the US balance of payments (BOP), the top line in figure 7.1, have continued to grow even while the net liabilities position, the bottom line, has also grown. This situation has mystified economists for almost a quarter-century:

> Clearly, if our investments abroad are yielding a positive return, their capital value must be positive not negative. Is this a defect of the figures on current flows, or is it a defect of the balance-sheet figures? (Milton Friedman 1987)[1]

The income received on the US external position plays an important role in one of the biggest issues confronting international macroeconomists—the sustainability (or lack thereof) of the US current account deficit. Net income receipts, which equaled 33 percent of the goods and services balance

Stephanie E. Curcuru is a senior economist in the Division of International Finance at the Board of Governors of the Federal Reserve System. Charles P. Thomas is an associate director in the Division of International Finance at the Board of Governors of the Federal Reserve System.

The authors thank Ralph Kozlow and participants at the International Finance Seminar at the Federal Reserve Board, the CRIW/NBER Joint Conference on Wealth, Income and Financial Intermediation, and an anonymous referee for comments and suggestions. We thank Corinne Land for excellent research assistance. The views in this chapter are solely the responsibility of the authors and should not be interpreted as reflecting the views of the Board of Governors of the Federal Reserve System or of any other person associated with the Federal Reserve System. For acknowledgments, sources of research support, and disclosure of the authors' material financial relationships, if any, please see http://www.nber.org/chapters/c12538.ack.

1. Personal correspondence with Charles Thomas, June 1987.

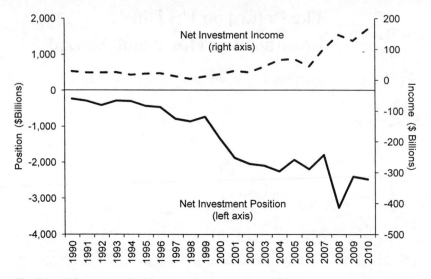

Fig. 7.1   US cross-border investment income and position

Source: Net investment income is from the US balance of payments and the net investment position from the US international investment position, both published by the Bureau of Economic Analysis.

in 2010, provide a significant stabilizing force for the current account. Future sustainability will depend, in part, on the persistence of these net income receipts. So an understanding of what is generating this income will help economists assess how the US imbalance might evolve.

One asset class is responsible for the puzzle. Net income receipts in the BOP owe entirely to a difference between the yields (income divided by the position) on direct investment claims and liabilities (Hung and Mascaro 2004; Bosworth, Collins, and Chodorow-Reich 2008; Bridgeman 2008; Curcuru, Dvorak, and Warnock 2008). The aggregate yield on US cross-border claims averaged 140 basis points per year higher than that paid on US cross-border liabilities from 1990–2010, shown in the first columns of figure 7.2. The next columns show that the main driver of this difference was foreign direct investment (FDI); the average yield received on US FDI claims was an impressive 620 basis points per year higher than that paid on liabilities. In contrast, for portfolio equity and debt, the average yields on claims and liabilities were nearly identical. The overall yield advantage was enough to move the income balance in favor of US claims despite the large net liability position.[2]

Why is there such a large difference between the yield received on US direct

2. Although there is a difference between the asset compositions of claims and liabilities, it contributes very little to the yield differential.

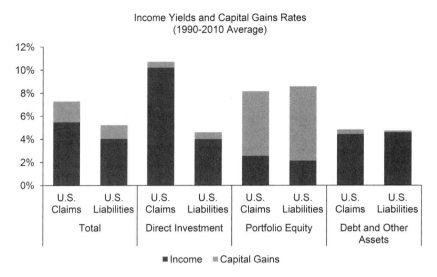

Fig. 7.2   Income yields and capital gains on US cross-border positions
Source: Income and capital gains are from Gohrband and Howell (chapter 8, this volume) for 1990–2009 and from the US balance of payments and international investment position published by the Bureau of Economic Analysis for 2010.
Note: Yields are computed by scaling income and capital gains with positions. Direct investment positions valued at current cost.

investment abroad (USDIA) and that paid on foreign direct investment in the United States (FDIUS)? Several studies suggest that the large difference between these yields is the result of USDIA earnings that are unusually high, FDIUS earnings that are unusually low, or a combination of the two. These conclusions are drawn from comparisons between US FDI yields and yields which, at least on the surface, appear to be similar. However, a closer look at the comparator yields used in these studies reveals some important differences. Some studies compare pretax with posttax yields. Other studies use comparator yields that are only valid in certain situations, such as when the affiliate borrows only from the parent firm. Our approach in this chapter is to first closely examine direct investment (DI) earnings and position data to find the most comparable measures before constructing yields. We then identify any remaining differences between the investments and quantify how these differences might affect yields.

We identify several reasons for the large differential between USDIA and FDIUS yields. In foreign countries, US multinational enterprises (MNEs) earn about the same on their USDIA as do investors from other countries, but the yield on USDIA is above that of firms operating in the United States. For USDIA we focus on the return from the parent firm's perspective and calculate the return net of all tax liabilities and estimate the amount of compensation for the risks specific to investing abroad. We find that taxes and risk account for all but about 50 basis points of the average difference between USDIA yields and those earned by US firms on their domestic operations (USIUS) since 2004, and all but about 100 basis points over the entire sample. Compensation for the sunk costs of investing abroad can account for the rest. Years in which FDIUS significantly underperformed domestic investments followed significant increases in US investments by foreign parents—in other words, FDIUS performed relatively poorly when it was relatively young. In recent years, however, FDIUS has performed about as well as other investments in the United States.

Taken together, compensation for taxes, risk, sunk costs, and age account for virtually all of the difference between USDIA and FDIUS yields. Favorable transfer prices associated with trade between related firms further narrows the gap. Therefore we agree with Bosworth, Collins, and Chodorow-Reich (2008) that the difference between USDIA and FDIUS yields is not "an illusion of bad data" as suggested in the quotation in the opening paragraph; rather, data quirks and investment differences create a divergence between these returns, the effect of which has decreased in recent years. Looking ahead, we expect this differential will narrow further if the FDIUS capital stock continues to age or the relative perceived risk of investing abroad decreases.

This chapter contributes to the literature on sustainability, returns differentials, and FDI in several ways. Work by Cavallo and Tille (2006) and Kitchen (2007) shows that the positive income yield differential limits pressure on the exchange rate in the event of a trade balance adjustment. Our results, which suggest the yield differential is likely to persist, tend to lower the probability of a rapid decline of the US exchange rate predicted by these models. Several papers have noted the large yield and capital gains differential between US claims and liabilities (Lane and Milesi-Ferretti 2005; Obstfeld and Rogoff 2005; Meissner and Taylor 2006; Gourinchas and Rey 2007; Forbes 2010; Habib 2010; Gourinchas, Rey, and Govillot 2010), although some of the difference in capital gains may be overstated because of inconsistent data (Curcuru, Dvorak, and Warnock 2008, 2009; Lane and Milesi-Ferretti 2009). This work is also the first to fully account for all the components of the DI differential. Throughout this chapter we discuss implications for the yield differentials of the extensive work done by Desai, Foley, and Hines on the factors influencing FDI decisions.

The chapter proceeds as follows: section 7.2 summarizes existing literature; section 7.3 compares USDIA yields with those on direct investment liabilities reported by other countries; section 7.4 compares USDIA and FDIUS yields with yields on the domestic operations of US firms; section 7.5 summarizes what the results suggest for future differences between USDIA and FDIUS yields; and section 7.6 concludes.

7.2   Existing Literature

Existing literature suggests that USDIA yields are abnormally high, FDIUS yields are abnormally low, or a combination of the two. The focus of most studies has been the role of firm characteristics (firm age, industry, intangibles, productivity), transfer costs, and taxes.

7.2.1   Firm Characteristics

Several papers link low FDIUS yields to the relative youth of FDIUS affiliates (Lupo, Gilbert, and Liliestedt 1978; Landefeld, Lawson, and Weinberg 1992; Grubert, Goodspeed, and Swenson 1993; Laster and McCauley 1994; Grubert 1997; Mataloni 2000; McGrattan and Prescott 2010). Many new firms have relatively high expenses associated with depreciation of newly purchased assets or interest on debt used to finance acquisitions. Inexperience can also lead to relatively poor performance for younger firms.

The industry mix of FDIUS is dramatically different than USDIA and US investment more generally, with a large share of USDIA classified as holding companies and a large share of FDIUS classified as manufacturing firms. However, Mataloni (2000), the only study examining the role of industry composition, finds that the return on FDIUS assets was below that of US operations for most industries.

Other work suggests that differing amounts of investment in intangible capital (defined in Bridgeman [2008] as patents, trademarks, trade secrets, and organizational knowledge) is responsible for the large difference between FDIUS and USDIA yields. The value of intangible capital is excluded from the valuation method for DI that the Bureau of Economic Analysis (BEA) features, the current-cost method, because of measurement difficulties.[3] Bridgeman (2008) estimates the stocks of intangible assets and finds that including them in the USDIA and FDIUS positions reduces the gap between USDIA and FDIUS yields by three-fourths. McGrattan and Prescott (2010) finds the FDIUS yield is held down by the large amount of research and development investment these firms engage in, which is accounted for as an expense. However, they find that the USDIA yield is higher than can be explained by intangible capital and other factors in their model.[4]

Studies in the trade literature find that more productive US firms are more likely to engage in FDI, which leads to higher USDIA yields relative to

3. Investments in intangible capital are generally excluded from the US National Accounts because of difficulties in measuring its production and depreciation. The BEA plans to start including some intangible assets related to research and development in the accounts in 2013.
4. In related work, Hausmann and Sturznegger (2006) infer from the large net income receipts that USDIA intangible investment is much larger than FDIUS intangible investment, although Buiter (2006) challenges their methodology.

domestic-only firms (Helpman, Meliz, and Yeaple 2004; Fillat and Garetto 2010). These models also suggest the high return of USDIA relative to USIUS is compensation for the higher sunk costs and risks associated with FDI.

7.2.2   Transfer Pricing

Early studies find little evidence that the low FDIUS yield arises from favorable intrafirm transfer pricing. Laster and McCauley (1994) and Mataloni (2000) find no difference in the earnings of firms with a significant share of imports from the foreign parent and those with a smaller share. Similarly, Grubert (1997) finds no difference in the earnings of FDIUS affiliates, which are wholly owned by the parent, and those with a smaller share of foreign ownership. In more recent work Bernard, Jensen, and Schott (2006) examines detailed price and transaction data on US exports and imports and finds that the prices of exports to related firms are systematically lower than exports to unrelated firms, while the prices of imports from related firms are systematically higher. These pricing anomalies should have some effect on USDIA or FDIUS yields. Although reliable estimates of the size of the effects cannot be constructed because firm nationality is not tracked in the trade data, we provide some sense of their magnitude in section 7.5.

7.2.3   Tax Issues

A series of papers by Desai, Foley, and Hines (hence DFH) shows that affiliate funding, dividend repatriations, and the location of MNE subsidiaries are heavily influenced by tax considerations. Because US tax laws generally allow US MNEs to defer US taxes on foreign income until that income is repatriated, foreign operations in low-tax jurisdictions are disproportionately funded using reinvested earnings rather than new equity capital. In contrast, affiliates in relatively high-tax jurisdictions are funded using debt finance (Feldstein 1994; DFH 2001, 2003, 2004). DFH (2001) finds that USDIA affiliates in countries with 1 percent lower tax rates on foreign income have 1 percent lower dividend payout rates. Looking across affiliate countries, DFH (2004) finds that USDIA affiliates located in countries with relatively high tax rates had a higher debt-to-asset ratio in order to take advantage of the tax deductibility of interest payments, and that internal borrowing was particularly sensitive to tax rates. Complementary work by Grubert (1998) finds that interest payments to USDIA parents are higher for affiliates in countries with higher statutory tax rates. DFH (2006) finds that large US MNEs with heavy research and development spending and relatively large amounts of intrafirm trade are most likely to have affiliates located in tax havens. Bosworth, Collins, and Chodorow-Reich (2008) estimate that the diversion of income to low-tax jurisdictions accounts for one-third of the difference in USDIA and USIUS yields.

7.2.4   Other Areas of Research

Other explanations for the low FDIUS yield include a relatively low cost of capital in the home country (Grubert, Goodspeed, and Swenson 1993), price concessions to gain access to the US market or scarce raw materials (Landefeld, Lawson, and Weinberg 1992), and several high profile US. investments by foreigners in the 1980s that had particularly poor results (Laster and McCauley 1994; Jorion 1996). Other explanations for the large gap between USDIA and FDIUS yields include compensation for the additional risk of investing in countries with low sovereign credit ratings (Hung and Mascaro 2004), the venture capitalist nature of the US external position, which issues safe assets while investing in risky assets (Gourinchas and Rey 2007), and the "erroneous" inclusion of reinvested earnings in income that artificially boosts USDIA earnings (Gros 2006).

7.3   USDIA and Direct Investment by Other Countries

The USDIA yields are double those earned by other cross-border claims and liabilities (figure 7.2), which has led some to conclude that the data are misreported (Gros 2006; Hausmann and Sturzenegger 2006). In our first analysis we take a different approach than earlier papers that compared USDIA yields to those earned on other assets or in different locations. We focus our comparison on similar investments; at the country level we compare USDIA yields in a given country with the yield on all direct investment in that country (ACDIA). To the extent that USDIA investment in each country is similar to that undertaken by non-US investors, the yields should be similar. A finding of similar yields would suggest that the seemingly high USDIA yields are not unusual or temporary.

A close look at global direct investment earnings and positions data needed for a cross-country comparison of DI yields reveals that neither is reported on a consistent basis across countries. USDIA earnings are measured using the current operating performance concept (COPC) recommended by the International Monetary Fund (IMF), which includes reinvested earnings and intercompany debt payments in income and excludes capital gains and losses. In a survey conducted by the IMF only nineteen out of sixty-one countries (eight Organisation for Economic Co-operation and Development [OECD] countries) fully applied the COPC to inward DI earnings, and only sixteen out of sixty-one (seven OECD) to outward earnings.[5] These deviations from the COPC standard can have a large impact on reported DI earnings. For example, France excludes the reinvested earnings of indirectly held subsidiaries from income; a similar omission from

---

5. See http://www.imf.org/external/pubs/ft/fdis/2003/fdistat.pdf for a description of the COPC and the survey results.

USDIA earnings would lower yields by one-third or over 300 basis points per year.[6] In addition, it is difficult to estimate the market values of private companies, particularly in countries without liquid stock markets, so the DI positions published by most countries value firms using some combination of historical cost and market values. Because of these data variations we focus on the eight countries that fully apply the COPC method, and provide results for an expanded selection of countries in the appendix. The ACDIA yield for each country is the ratio of net income payments associated with DI liabilities to the amount of DI liabilities from the balance of payments statistics published by the IMF.[7]

In addition to different measures of earnings, accounting methods also vary. The BEA reports country-level earnings on a financial accounting (historical cost) basis, and computes current-cost adjustments needed to transform earnings to an economic accounting basis only at the aggregate level. We use historical-cost earnings to compute yields because this is how earnings are reported in the United Kingdom and many other countries. However, including current-cost adjustments in earnings does not change our conclusions.[8] Similarly, country-level positions are reported at historical cost value and the adjustments needed to transform the position to a current-cost or market-value basis are released by BEA only at the aggregate level. We adjust the country-level positions from a historical-cost to current-cost basis using the ratio of the aggregates when we compute USDIA country-level yields.[9]

We find that USDIA yields in most countries are similar to or below those earned by other foreign investors in those countries. For five out of eight countries in table 7.1 the USDIA yield is below the ACDIA yield, significantly so for three countries. In the United Kingdom, where 13 percent of USDIA is located, US investors earn 6.7 percent on their USDIA, while all foreign investors in the United Kingdom earn significantly more—8.5 per-

---

6. In 2009, reinvested earnings in USDIA holding company affiliates totaled $110 billion or one-third of total earnings. Most of this income was generated by indirectly held affiliates. Excluding these reinvested earnings lowers aggregate USDIA earnings in 2009 from 9.7 percent to 6.4 percent.

7. We also estimated the yield earned by only non-US investors in each country by subtracting the USDIA earnings and position in each country from IMF DI liabilities. The resulting yields for the eight countries in the main sample were similar to those reported, but these estimates could not be constructed for the expanded sample for several countries because inconsistent reporting resulted in US income receipts or positions reported by the BEA that were larger than total DI payments or liabilities reported by that country.

8. Current-cost adjustments increase USDIA earnings and lower FDIUS earnings and the differential between USDIA and FDIUS yields widens to 650 basis points.

9. The aggregate USDIA yield falls to 6.6 percent, and the aggregate differential drops to 125 basis points per year when yields are computed using the market value estimate of the position. Using aggregate income and positions to compute yields may mask significant heterogeneity in the underlying data. Unfortunately, those data are maintained by the BEA and access to them by individuals from other government agencies, including the authors of this paper, is prohibited.

Table 7.1   US direct investment abroad (USDIA) and all countries direct investment abroad (ACDIA) yields for selected countries

Country	USDIA	ACDIA	Difference	Share of position	Data available
United Kingdom	6.7	8.5	−1.9**	13.0	1983–2010
Canada	7.5	7.6	−0.1	7.6	1983–2010
Ireland	17.6	21.6	−4.0**	4.9	2002–2010
Australia	7.7	7.5	0.2	3.4	1987–2010
Hong Kong	12.4	8.8	3.7**	1.4	1998–2010
Sweden	6.4	8.3	−1.9	0.8	1983–2010
New Zealand	6.3	8.4	−2.1**	0.2	1990–2010
Finland	13.6	10.7	2.9**	0.1	1983–2010
Weighted average yields for 8 countries:	7.5	8.5	−1.1*	31.3	

Notes: All values are average percentages over the sample period; share is of 2010 USDIA position. Sample includes countries that fully apply the current operating performance concept (COPC) to direct investment income reporting. The USDIA yield in each country is computed using BEA income and position data. The BEA country-level positions are only available at historical cost; we use the ratio of the aggregate position at current cost to the aggregate position at historical cost for each year to adjust the position to a current-cost basis. The ACDIA is the ratio of DI income payments reported in the IMF balance of payments for each country to the DI liabilities position for that country. The last line of the table presents yields weighted by the historical cost share of USDIA investment in each country each year.
**Significant at the 5 percent level.
*Significant at the 10 percent level.

cent, on average. In Canada, home to almost 8 percent of USDIA, the average yields of US and foreign investors on their DI are nearly identical. The yield on USDIA investments in Ireland is surprisingly high—almost 18 percent per year—but not as high as that earned on all DI in Ireland, which earns almost 22 percent per year.[10]

The last line of table 7.1 presents average USDIA and ACDIA yields, where the average is weighted by the USDIA position share in the sample each year. The average yield is *lower* for USDIA—7.5 percent for USDIA versus 8.5 percent for ACDIA —and the difference is statistically significant at the 10 percent level. Figure 7.3 shows these yields track each other very closely over the sample period. The weighted average USDIA yield for this sample is noticeably lower than the aggregate USDIA yield because the sample excludes many tax havens that do not report the data needed to calculate ACDIA yield. For an expanded selection that includes countries that do not fully apply the COPC method (see appendix table 7A.1), the weighted USDIA yield averages 30 basis points per year higher than ACDIA, and the

10. The yield on all DI liabilities in Ireland calculated from IMF data slightly overstates the yield on those liabilities because recorded DI income payments are not net of interest income associated with lending from Irish affiliates to foreign parents.

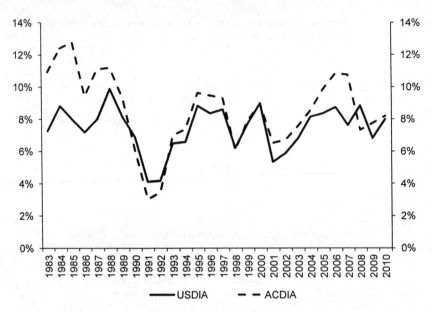

Fig. 7.3   US direct investment abroad (USDIA) and all countries direct investment abroad (ACDIA) yields

Note: The USIDA and ACDIA series are those shown in the last line of table 7.1; see notes to table 7.1 for a description.

difference between the two weighted yields is not significant. At least by this measure, there is no evidence that USDIA earnings are unusual or is there any indication that they should not persist. Next, we examine how USDIA and FDUIS yields compare with yields on other US investments.

7.4   Domestic Operations of US Firms

Several studies find that USDIA yields are significantly higher than those of US domestic operations (USIUS), while FDIUS yields are significantly lower (Bosworth, Collins, and Chodorow-Reich 2008; MacGrattan and Prescott 2010). We begin this section with a discussion of alternative measures of USIUS yields, and then move to comparisons of USIUS yields with USDIA and FDIUS yields.

7.4.1   USIUS Yields

Many studies use the yield on tangible assets (YTA) for all US firms as a benchmark for evaluating USDIA and FDIUS yields (Howenstine and Lawson 1991; Bosworth, Collins, and Chodorow-Reich 2008, among others). This measure excludes financial assets and liabilities and their associated interest expenses from the position and income. Compared with YTA,

USDIA yields appear unusually high, while FDIUS yields appear unusually low.

Despite its frequent use, YTA is a weak benchmark for US DI yields because YTA cannot be constructed from the available DI data. The DI income reported in the BOP includes earnings on all assets, including net interest income associated with financial assets, and includes interest payments on intercompany debt paid to the United States (for USDIA) or foreign (for FDIUS) parent. The BEA does not separately report net financial assets and interest expenses of the affiliates—it only reports those associated with intercompany debt—so YTA cannot be constructed for USDIA and FDIUS affiliates. The YTA may differ markedly from a yield measure that includes net financial assets if affiliates have significant borrowing from entities other than the parent firm, which US FDI surveys suggest is indeed the case.[11]

Given this weakness of YTA as a DI yield benchmark, we instead construct a yield that includes net interest payments in earnings and financial assets in the position, and is much closer in spirit to the yield that can be constructed for USDIA and FDIUS affiliates from BEA data. We label this net yield measure USIUS_min. (To maintain comparability with earlier literature we also show YTA, which we label USIUS_max.) The USDIA, FDIUS, and USIUS yields are shown in figure 7.4, and details on the data series used to construct these yields are given in appendix table 7A.2. Consistent with earlier literature, USDIA yields are significantly higher than both FDIUS and USIUS yields, and for much of the sample FDIUS is below USIUS. We reconcile the differences between these yields in the next sections.

7.4.2   USDIA versus USIUS

As we did with ACDIA, our first step is to make sure we are making an apples-to-apples comparison between USDIA and USIUS yields. We then compute the USDIA return from the parent firms' perspective, and estimate the magnitude of other systematic factors that might account for differences between the two yields including tax accounting and compensation for risk and the sunk costs of investing abroad.

After-Tax USDIA Yield

The USDIA earnings reported in the BOP and USIUS earnings reported in the National Income and Product Accounts (NIPA) have different tax treatments. The USDIA earnings in the BOP are net of foreign taxes, but the US taxes paid by US parents on those earnings are not deducted. This

---

11. The BEA (2006), table III.C.1, reports that current liabilities and long-term debt owed by majority-owned nonbank FDIUS affiliates totaled $2.7 trillion in 2002, of which $719 billion (or 27 percent) was owed to the foreign parent. In contrast, BEA (2008), table III.C.1, reports that current liabilities and long-term debt owed by majority-owned nonbank USDIA affiliates totaled $4.2 trillion in 2004, of which $523 billion (or 12 percent) was owed to the US parent.

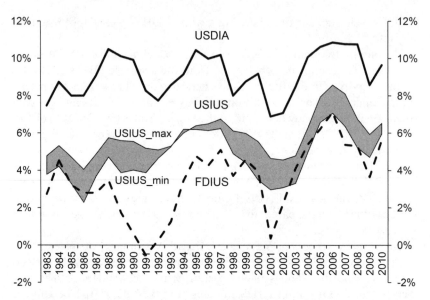

Fig. 7.4   Yields on US direct investment abroad (USDIA), foreign direct investment in the United States (FDIUS), and US investment in the United States (USIUS)

Notes: The USDIA series is the ratio of aggregate DI income receipts to the USDIA position reported by the BEA. The FDIUS series is the ratio of aggregate DI income payments to the FDIUS position reported by the BEA. The USIUS_max yield is the return (excluding interest payments) on tangible US nonfinancial corporate assets excluding USDIA and FDIUS, with tangible assets valued at replacement cost. The USIUS_min yield is the return on all US nonfinancial corporate assets excluding USDIA and FDIUS, with assets valued at replacement cost. The data series used to construct these yields are listed in appendix table 7A.2. Direct investment income does not include current-cost adjustments and positions are valued at current cost.

is because US taxes due on USDIA earnings are paid by the US parent firm, so they are not cross-border transactions. While US parents receive a credit for foreign income taxes paid against their US tax liability, because the US tax rate is generally higher, most US parents still owe some US tax on repatriated earnings even after this credit (Hines 1996). So, as implied in Bridgeman (2008), the USDIA yield computed using unadjusted BOP data generally overstates the after-tax earnings of the US parent firm. In contrast, USIUS and FDIUS earnings are already net of all taxes.[12]

We estimate the US taxes owed on USDIA earnings in two steps. First, we construct an estimate of the USDIA yield net of US taxes associated with earnings repatriated to the US parent firm. We estimate the yearly tax liability on repatriated income using the US tax rates from KPMG (2010),

12. The United States has a "worldwide taxation" policy that taxes income generated by US MNEs regardless of where it is earned. In contrast, most other countries have a policy of "territorial taxation" and only tax income generated by domestic activities. See the section "International Taxation for Beginners" in Hines (1999) for an overview of tax issues.

Table 7.2   **Summary statistics for yields, 1983–2010**

	Mean (%)	Standard deviation (%)	Sharpe ratio	Chi-squared test: Equal Sharpe ratios	
				USIUS_max	USIUS_min
USDIA, before US taxes	9.1	1.2	3.3	26.9** [0.00]	34.2** [0.00]
USDIA, after US taxes on repatriated earnings	8.3	1.2	2.8	31.5** [0.00]	34.0** [0.00]
USDIA, after US taxes on all earnings	7.3	1.1	2.7	22.4** [0.00]	24.0** [0.00]
USDIA, after US taxes on all earnings and risk	6.4	1.3	1.9	5.6** [0.02]	13.3** [0.00]
USIUS_max	5.8	1.1	1.4	—	—
USIUS_min	4.7	1.3	0.8	—	—
FDIUS	3.5	1.9	0.2	19.0** [0.00]	9.3** [0.00]

Notes: Details of how the yield series were constructed are in appendix table 7A.2. Direct investment income does not include current-cost adjustments and positions are valued at current cost. The Sharpe ratio is the ratio of average returns in excess of the risk-free (Tbill) rate to standard deviation. The last column is chi-squared test statistic for the null hypothesis that the Sharpe ratio is equal to the USIUS Sharpe ratio indicated by the column heading; probability that the null is rejected is shown. Asymptotic *p*-values computed from Newey and West (1987) standard errors are in brackets.

**Significant at the 5 percent level.
*Significant at the 10 percent level.

less a credit for foreign taxes paid if the US tax rate is higher than the foreign tax rate.[13] If the foreign tax rate is higher than the US tax rate, there is no additional US tax liability. Deducting estimated US tax payments from affiliate earnings reduces the USDIA yield by about 80 basis points, shown in table 7.2, from an average of 9.1 percent to 8.3 percent per year. We view this as a lower-bound for the compensation required by US parent firms for the US tax liability associated with USDIA earnings.

In the second step, we adjust the yield for all taxes that will eventually be paid, including taxes on reinvested earnings that are not immediately due. The US parents pay US taxes on foreign affiliate earnings only when

13. Foreign tax rates are inferred from a 2004 benchmark survey (BEA 2008) and earlier surveys. An increasing number of multinational corporations include holding companies as intermediate firms between the parent company and foreign subsidiaries because several jurisdictions offer attractive tax treatment (DFH 2003; Ibarra-Caton 2010, chart A). See figure 1 in DFH (2003) for common ownership structures used by firms located in tax havens. The aggregate foreign tax rate is a relatively low 14 percent because of the large share of intermediate holding companies that almost entirely avoid foreign taxes. In practice, the foreign tax credit may be smaller than our estimate because credits against US taxes are given for only certain types of tax payments (DFH 2004).

those earnings are repatriated, which allows firms to defer a portion of their US tax liability by reinvesting earnings in a foreign affiliate. US MNEs use intricate corporate structures to aggressively funnel earnings to low income tax jurisdictions and defer US taxes on those earnings by reinvesting them abroad.

Although US taxes on reinvested earnings are not paid immediately, the potential US tax liability associated with those earnings is likely an important factor when firms decide whether the earnings potential of a DI investment offers a high enough return. This is because the firm might not be certain, ex ante, of how much they will need to repatriate to support domestic operations. While US firms might obviously prefer to never repatriate affiliate earnings in order to forever delay the additional US tax liability, there is evidence that many firms choose repatriation strategies that are not optimal from a tax perspective.[14] So as an upper bound for the tax-related compensation required by US parent firms, we calculate and subtract from earnings US taxes that would be due had the affiliate repatriated all of its earnings.[15] This reduces the USDIA yield by an additional 100 basis points per year to 7.3 percent (table 7.2), bringing the average adjustment for US taxes to 180 basis points per year. The tax-adjusted yields, plotted in figure 7.5, are much closer to the USIUS yields, particularly during the last decade.

The remaining difference between USDIA and USIUS yields—150 to 260 basis points depending on the USIUS measure—is greater than can be explained solely by earnings volatility. Table 7.2 also reports that the Sharpe (1966) ratio of the after-tax USDIA yield is significantly higher than that of even our upper-bound estimate for USIUS.[16] Some of this remaining difference could be compensation for other risks associated with investing abroad, discussed next.

Risk-Adjusted USDIA Yield

Some of the risks faced by MNEs beyond those faced by domestic-only firms include foreign regulations, foreign tax policy, fluctuations in foreign demand, US tax policy for foreign investments, and dependence on the for-

---

14. For example, Hines and Hubbard (1990) find that many firms repatriate earnings during the same period in which they inject equity, and that some firms with excess tax credits reinvest earnings. Similarly, DFH (2007) finds that the amount firms repatriate depends on domestic funds available to meet dividend payments to external shareholders and domestic investment needs.

15. US MNEs reinvest a substantial fraction of USDIA earnings—60 percent on average from 1999 to 2009—most of which is reinvested by holding company affiliates (Ibarra-Caton 2010). While 60 percent is the average, Hines and Hubbard (1990) find significant heterogeneity between firms. The 60 percent average excludes reinvested earnings in 2005 because reinvested earnings were large and negative in that year because firms took advantage of temporary reduction in the US tax liability on repatriated earnings contained in the American Jobs Creation Act of 2004.

16. Hung and Mascaro (2004) report a similar result using the USDIA (pretax) and FDIUS yields.

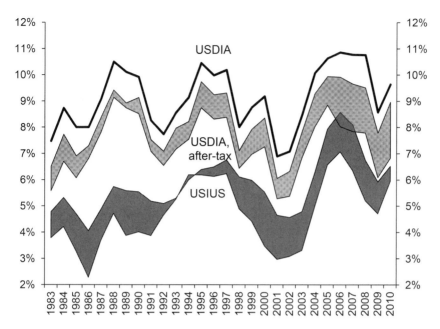

Fig. 7.5   Tax-adjusted USDIA yields

Notes. The USDIA series is the ratio of aggregate DI income receipts to the USDIA position reported by the BEA. The top boundary of the range of after-tax USDIA yields subtracts from income estimated US taxes on repatriated income (reported in the second line of table 7.2), the bottom boundary subtracts from income US taxes on all income (reported in the third line of table 7.2). Direct investment income does not include current-cost adjustments and positions are valued at current cost. The USIUS yields are from figure 7.4.

eign labor and goods markets. So the relatively high yields earned by MNEs likely represent compensation for these additional risks relative to domestic-only firms. Otherwise, as pointed out in Fillat and Garetto (2010), investors would not bother holding the equities of domestic-only firms in equilibrium.

To estimate how much might be required to compensate investors for the additional risks associated with investing abroad we use credit-default swaps (CDS) spreads on sovereign debt when they are available, and corporate debt spreads in earlier years. The CDS are a form of insurance that compensates the holder when the issuer of the underlying bond defaults (i.e., fails to make an interest or principal payment), and are commonly used as a proxy for the amount of compensation required for investors to invest in a country. We calculate the average difference between foreign country and US CDS spreads on sovereign debt, weighted by the share of the USDIA position in each country each year. Because of the extensive use of intermediate firms in low-income-tax and low-sovereign risk jurisdictions—about 36 percent of USDIA in 2010—recent USDIA positions have been shown to be a poor representation of where the activity of foreign affiliates actually occurs

Table 7.3   Sovereign CDS spreads

Country	Average sovereign CDS spread over United States	Share of USDIA position
United Kingdom	12.1	17.8
Netherlands	2.8	10.0
Canada	5.3	9.8
Japan	9.2	4.5
Germany	–0.7	4.4
France	4.7	3.5
Brazil	216.5	3.1
Mexico	104.2	3.1
Australia	7.8	2.9
Panama	162.6	2.8
Ireland	65.1	2.1
Hong Kong	17.7	1.9
Belgium	15.9	1.8
Singapore	4.7	1.7
Spain	35.9	1.6
Other	288.4	13.4
Total:		84.4
Weighted avg. of 49 countries:	70.4	

Note: Each value is the average difference between the CDS spreads on five-year sovereign debt and the CDS spread on five-year US Treasuries in basis points from 2004–2010. The CDS spreads are from Markit. Share is of 1999 USDIA position calculated from BEA data.

(Borga and Mataloni 2001). So we construct weights based on the positions in 1999, when the use of intermediate holding companies was more limited (about 7 percent of USDIA).

The average difference between US and foreign sovereign CDS spreads, our proxy for compensation for sovereign risk, averaged 70.4 basis points per year between 2004 and 2010 (table 7.3).[17] For earlier years when US and other CDS spreads are unavailable, we follow Hung and Mascaro (2004) and use the spread between the yields on Aaa- and Baa-rated corporate debt published by Moody's as a proxy for risk compensation.[18] For these earlier years, the weighted risk adjustment averages 98 basis points. Putting the two risk adjustments together, the estimated compensation for risk over the entire sample averages 91 basis points per year.

After adjustments for taxes and risk, the estimated yield on USDIA falls

17. The weighted spread is about 45 basis points using 2003 or 2009 weights.
18. Hung and Mascaro (2004) estimated that 11 percent of USIDA was invested in AAA-rated Canada, 17 percent in BB-rated Latin American countries, 50 percent in AA-rated European countries, and the weighted-average rating estimate for all countries was BBB, using Standard & Poor's ratings and the 2003 positions. We follow Hung and Mascaro and use the difference between Aaa and Baa corporate debt yields as an estimate of the additional risk of USDIA.

to 6.4 percent per year (table 7.2). The total compensation for taxes and risk averages 270 basis points per year, which is the bulk of the 330–440 basis point difference per year between unadjusted USDIA and USIUS yields. The remaining difference might represent compensation for the sunk costs of investing abroad, discussed next.

Sunk Costs of USDIA

The remaining difference between USDIA (after-tax) and USUIS yields averages between 60 and 170 basis points per year over the entire sample (table 7.2), and all but 50 basis points of the difference since 2004. Other literature suggests that foreign investments should also include compensation for sunk costs specific to investing in a foreign country. For example, in the models of Helpman, Melitz, and Yeaple (2004) and Fillat and Garretto (2010), FDI investments are subject to sunk costs beyond those encountered domestically. Fillat and Garetto (2010) estimate that compensation for these sunk costs adds 25 percent to MNE yields relative to the yields of domestic-only exporters. This translates to 120–145 basis points based on our USIUS estimates, roughly equal to the difference that remains between USDIA and USIUS yields after we adjust for taxes and risk. In sum, we estimate that compensation for taxes, risk, and sunk costs accounts for around 400 basis points of the 9.1 percent yield on USDIA. Now that we have reconciled the difference between USDIA and USIUS yields, we turn to FDIUS yields.

7.4.3   FDIUS versus USIUS

Existing literature reports that the yield on FDIUS has been low relative to YTA (USIUS_max in figure 7.4), and for much of the sample FDIUS also underperformed the net US yield (USIUS_min). This underperformance was striking in the early 1990s and early in the twenty-first century—totaling almost 600 basis points in 1991 and averaging over 300 basis points per year between 1988 and 2002. However, figure 7.4 shows that since 2002 the gap has closed considerably, suggesting a permanent change has affected the relative profitability of FDIUS.

One potential explanation for the comparatively low yield earned by FDIUS affiliates is their age. Several studies suggest that the relative youth of FDIUS affiliates has played a role in their low profitability relative to other US firms (Lupo, Gilbert, and Liliestedt 1978; Landefeld, Lawson, and Weinberg 1992; Grubert, Goodspeed, and Swenson 1993; Laster and McCauley 1994; Grubert 1997; Mataloni 2000). Younger firms may underperform more experienced firms because of inexperience, startup costs, or interest expenses on debt used to fund acquisitions.

To see how age affects FDIUS yields we construct several proxies for affiliate age using the equation:

(1) $$AGE_t = \frac{\sum_{i=1}^{T} \omega^{i-1} \times AGEVAR_{t-i}}{FDIUS\_Position_t},$$

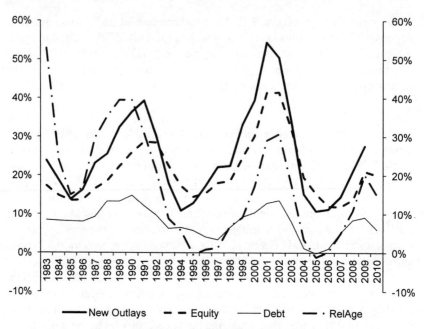

Fig. 7.6   Age of FDIUS affiliates

Notes: The chart shows several alternative proxies for the age of FDIUS given by:

$$AGE_t = \frac{\sum_{i=1}^{T} \omega^{i-1} \times AGEVAR_{t-i}}{FDIUS\_Position_t},$$

for $\omega = 1.0$, $T = 3$; $AGEVAR$ is new outlays (http://www.bea.gov/international/xls/io_ind_0508 .xls), gross debt flows (BOP table 7a line 96 or 7b line 61), equity flows (BOP table 7a line 92 or 7b line 57), or relative age (the difference between the annual growth rate of the FDIUS and USIUS_min. positions; see table 7A.2 for definitions). RelAge is not scaled by the FDIUS position when AGE_t is constructed.

where AGE represents the "newness" of the FDIUS investment; specifically, the share of FDIUS that has occurred in the last T years. We use several types of investment in $AGEVAR$, including outlays to acquire or establish new FDIUS, increases in US affiliates' intercompany debt payables, and increases in parent equity. We also construct a measure of the relative age of FDIUS and USIUS using the differential between the growth rates of the respective positions. The weight variable ω (≤ 1) represents effects such as learning, which decay the importance of new investment over time. We sum weighted investment over T prior years and scale by the FDIUS position. Estimates for AGE, shown in figure 7.6, suggest that there have been three waves of new FDIUS investment during the last thirty years; 1987–1990, 1998–2001, and to a lesser extent 2008–2010. Glancing back at figure 7.4, it is apparent that FDIUS underperformed USIUS during these three investment waves, suggesting that affiliate age does depress the FDIUS yield.

To more precisely measure the relationship between AGE and FDIUS yields we regress FDIUS yields on USIUS yields and AGE from equation (1):

(2) $FDIUS_t = \alpha + \beta \times AGE_t + \gamma \times USIUS_t.$

A significant and negative β will confirm results from earlier studies that the underperformance is linked to firm age. The regressions results, presented in table 7.4, suggest that FDIUS performance is indeed related to new investment by foreign parents as β is negative and significant in every specification. The adjusted-R^2 values are quite high, ranging between 41 percent and 74 percent. New intercompany debt has the most explanatory power, suggesting that debt service costs play a large role, likely in the form of higher outside borrowing costs. The age effect subtracts 150 basis points on average from FDIUS (based on the first specification in table 7.4), and in the absence of age effects the FDIUS yield increases to 5 percent—higher than USIUS_min, which averages 4.7 percent (table 7.2). An FDIUS esti-

Table 7.4   **FDIUS age regressions**

USIUS	AGEVAR	ω	T	α	β	γ	Adj. R^2
USIUS_min.	Outlay	1.0	3	2.61**	−6.47**	0.52**	0.41
				(0.88)	(2.76)	(0.18)	
USIUS_min.	Debt	1.0	3	4.69***	−30.73***	0.27	0.54
				(1.23)	(7.13)	(0.21)	
USIUS_min.	Equity	1.0	3	2.33**	−8.71*	0.64**	0.43
				(1.15)	(4.83)	(0.19)	
USIUS_max.	Debt	1.0	3	1.18	−23.37**	0.72**	0.62
				(1.75)	(6.08)	(0.22)	
USIUS_min.	Debt	1.0	5	7.27**	−34.84**	0.09	0.74
				(1.37)	(6.14)	(0.16)	
USIUS_min.	Debt	0.7	5	5.75**	−44.98**	0.20	0.61
				(1.55)	(11.57)	(0.21)	
USIUS_min.	RelAge	1.0	3	2.07**	−5.73**	0.52**	0.44
				(0.98)	(2.48)	(0.19)	

Notes: This table shows coefficient estimates from the regression:

$$FDIUS_t = \alpha + \beta \times AGE_t + \gamma \times USIUS_t$$

where:

$$AGE_t = \frac{\sum_{i=1}^{T} \omega^{i-1} \times AGEVAR_{t-i}}{FDIUS\_Position_t}$$

The USIUS variable is either USIUS_max or USIUS_min from table 7A.2. The AGEVAR is either new outlays (http://www.bea.gov/international/xls/io_ind_0508.xls), gross debt flows (BOP table 7a line 96 or 7b line 61), equity flows (BOP table 7a line 92 or 7b line 57), or the difference between the annual growth rate of the FDIUS and USIUS_min. positions (table 7A.2). RelAge is not scaled by the FDIUS position when AGE_t is constructed. Newey and West (1987) standard errors are in parentheses. Estimation period is 1983–2009 for regressions that include the outlay variable; 1983–2010 for all other regressions.
**Significant at the 5 percent level.
*Significant at the 10 percent level.

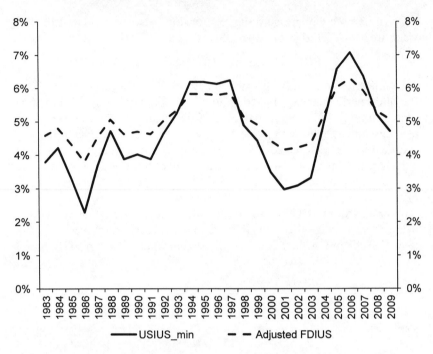

Fig. 7.7   US domestic yields (USIUS) and foreign direct investment in the United States (FDIUS) adjusted for age effects

Note: The dashed line is the FDIUS yield predicted by the regression in the first line of table 7.4, with the contribution of age removed. The USIUS_min yield is the return on all US non-financial corporate assets excluding USDIA and FDIUS with assets valued at replacement cost.

mate where the effects of age have been removed, plotted in figure 7.7, closely tracks USIUS_min, even during new investment waves.

This evidence confirms the results of previous studies that concluded that age was an important factor in the comparatively poor performance of FDIUS. However, since 2002 FDIUS affiliates have matured and there is little underperformance. So far we have accounted for most of the difference between FDIUS and USIUS, in addition to accounting for most of the difference between USDIA and USIUS. We end this section with a discussion of the difference between USDIA and FDIUS.

7.5   USDIA versus FDIUS

To recap, we estimate that compensation for taxes, risk, and sunk costs can account for as much as 400 basis points of the 9.1 percent average USDIA yield (table 7.2), and that age subtracts 150 basis points from the FDIUS yield, which averages 3.5 percent (tables 7.2 and 7.4). Taken together, these adjustments account for just about all of the 560 basis point difference between USDIA and FDIUS.

Although evidence on the existence of transfer-pricing effects is mixed, the results of one paper suggest transfer pricing might add further to the wedge between USDIA and FDIUS yields. Bernard, Jensen, and Schott (2006) find that the prices of US exports to related firms in 2004 were systematically lower than those to unrelated firms, while the prices of US imports from related firms were systematically higher. This mispricing will have a downward effect on the earnings of firms located in the United States and an upward effect on the earnings of related firms located abroad. Unfortunately, firm nationality is not reported in the customs data used in that study so a direct link to USDIA or FDIUS earnings cannot be made. However, if half the $15.7 billion mispricing identified by the authors is attributed to USDIA and the other half to FDIUS, that would account for 80 basis points of the 480 basis point difference between USDIA and FDIUS yields in 2004.[19] So while transfer pricing effects play a role in the DI yield differential, their effect is less than that of taxes or sunk costs.

Looking ahead, we can say a few things about how much of the difference between USDIA and FDIUS we expect to persist. The performance of FDIUS affiliates has caught up to other US firms in recent years, probably because the capital stock has reached a comparable maturity level. So we suspect that FDIUS affiliates will continue to earn about the same yields as USIUS firms, or even outperform because of the tendency of only the most productive firms to engage in FDI. Further, we do not have a reason to expect the yield of USDIA affiliates to decline—absent a change in US tax laws or the perception of the relative risk of investing in the United States versus abroad. Taken together, this suggests that the difference between USDIA and FDIUS yields might remain near or slightly below the 2010 difference of 400 basis points. How this yield difference will translate into net income will depend on the relative amount of capital flows into USDIA and FDIUS affiliates and other changes in the values of the positions.

7.6 Conclusion

In this chapter we showed that compensation for taxes, risk, sunk costs, and age account for just about all of the difference between USDIA and FDIUS yields, which is behind the puzzling behavior of the US net income. Unless there is a change in the underlying factors driving the difference—the perception of investment in the United States as relatively safe and the relatively high US tax rate—we expect the difference to remain near or slightly

---

19. Bernard, Jensen, and Schott (2006) estimate that US exports to related parties in 2004 were underreported by $1.9 billion, while US imports to related parties were overreported by $13.8 billion, for a total of $15.7 billion.

below the 400 basis points recorded in 2010. Therefore the United States will continue to, on net, earn income on the net liability position, which, in turn, will continue to provide a stabilizing force for the US current-account deficit.

Our results provide evidence against misreporting of USDIA earnings (Gros 2006), or that the United States is earning abnormally high returns because of the role of the dollar as an international reserve currency (Gourinchas and Rey 2007). In sum, we agree with Bosworth, Collins, and Chodorow-Reich (2008) that the large difference between USDIA and FDIUS yields is not "an illusion of bad data."

This study suggests several areas of future research. One obvious extension is to verify all of our results using the firm-level data available on-site at the BEA, as the existence of significant heterogeneity in the underlying firm data might result in different conclusions. Our results have implications for the sustainability of the US current-account deficit, so it would be interesting to see how they change the predictions of sustainability models such as those presented in Kitchen (2007) or Gourinchas and Rey (2007). Finally, our results can also inform policy discussions on the potential effect of changes in the taxation of MNEs.

Appendix
ACDIA for an Expanded Selection of Countries

In table 7A.1 we extend our comparison of USDIA and ACDIA yields to include countries that do not fully apply the COPC to earnings. These countries either include capital gains and losses in direct investment income, which could either overstate or understate the ACDIA yield, or exclude some reinvested earnings or interest on intercompany debt, which would tend to understate the ACDIA yield. The USDIA yield for these countries averages 8.3 percent per year, lower than the 9.1 percent per year reported in table 7.2. This is because yields in countries for which IMF BOP data are not available, such as Bermuda or the Cayman Islands, have a higher yield than the reported countries.

For this less comparable sample the USDIA yield averages only 0.3 higher per year than the ACDIA yield and the difference is not statistically significant. Therefore our conclusion remains unchanged—US investors earn about the same yields on their USDIA as investors from other countries earn on their FDI.

Table 7A.1   **US direct investment abroad (USDIA) and all countries direct investment abroad (ACDIA) yields for selected countries**

Country	USDIA	ACDIA	Difference	Share of position	Data available
A. ACDIA income includes capital gains and losses					
Austria	11.7	8.4	3.3**	0.4	1983–2010
Belgium	5.3	4.5	0.8	1.9	2002–2010
Chile	11.6	12.4	–0.8	0.7	1998–2010
Norway	26.0	12.7	13.3**	0.9	1999–2009
Russia	12.6	10.8	1.8	0.3	2000–2010
Switzerland	11.2	5.8	5.4**	3.7	1984–2010
B. ACDIA is missing intercompany debt payments and/or reinvested earnings					
France	5.7	5.0	0.8	2.4	2000–2009
Germany	7.3	7.1	0.1	2.7	1983–2010
Japan	8.1	9.2	–1.1	2.9	1991–2010
Mexico	9.3	3.6	5.7**	2.3	2002–2010
Netherlands	12.0	8.0	4.0**	13.3	1983–2010
Spain	9.7	5.2	4.5**	1.5	1983–2010
Weighted average yields for 20 countries in table 7.1 and panels A and B above:					
	8.3	7.9	0.3	64.1	

Notes: All values are average percentages over the sample period; share is of 2010 USDIA position. Sample includes countries that do not fully apply the current operating performance concept to direct investment income reporting. See notes to table 7.1 for a description of the USDIA yields. The ACDIA yield is the ratio of total direct investment income payments reported by the IMF's BOP statistics to the liabilities position with two exceptions: DeNederlandsche Bank data that includes special financial institutions are used for the Netherlands starting in 2000, and returns for France are from Banque de France report (http://www .banque-france.fr/gb/stat_conjoncture/telechar/bdp/FDI-overview-1999–2009.pdf). The last line of the table presents returns weighted by the historical cost share of USDIA investment in each country each year.

**Significant at the 5 percent level.
*Significant at the 10 percent level.

Table 7A.2   Yield definitions

Variable name	Description	Source
1 USDIA	Yield on US direct investment abroad	[BOP table 7a, 7b line 10]/[IIP table line 18]
2 FDIUS	Yield on foreign direct investment in the United States	–[BOP table 7a line 75 or 7b line 51]/[IIP table line 35]
3 USIUS_max	Yield on tangible assets	[NIPA 1.14 line 38 + NIPA 1.14 line 25 – (FOF F.7 line 14 – FOF F.7 line 19)]/[FOF B.102 line 2 – FOF B.102 line 3 + FOF B.102 line 33 + FOF B.102 line 34]
4 USIUS_min	Yield on net assets	[NIPA 1.14 line 38 + (BOP table 7a line 80 – BOP Table 7a line 83) – (FOF F.7 line 14 – FOF F.7 line 19)]/ [FOF B.102 line 32 – FOF B.102 line 3 + FOF B.102 line 33 + FOF B.102 line 34 –FOF L.102 line 17]

Notes: FOF = flow of funds; BOP = balance of payments; NIPA = National Income and Product Accounts.

References

Bernard, Andrew B., J. Bradford Jensen, and Peter K. Schott. 2006. "Transfer Pricing by US-Based Multinational Firms." NBER Working Paper no. 12493, Cambridge, MA.

Borga, Maria, and Raymond J. Mataloni Jr. 2001. "Direct Investment Positions for 2000: Country and Industry Detail." *Survey of Current Business* 81:16–25.

Bosworth, Barry, Susan M. Collins, and Gabriel Chodorow-Reich. 2008. "Returns on FDI: Does the US Really Do Better?" In *Brookings Trade Forum 2007: Foreign Direct Investment*, edited by Susan M. Collins, 177–210. Washington, DC: Brookings Institution Press.

Bridgeman, Benjamin. 2008. "Do Intangible Assets Explain High US Foreign Direct Investment Returns?" Bureau of Economic Analysis Working Paper no. 2008–06, Washington, DC.

Buiter, Willem. 2006. "Dark Matter or Cold Fusion?" Global Economics Paper no. 136, Goldman Sachs, London.

Bureau of Economic Analysis. 2006. "Foreign Direct Investment in the United States: 2002 Benchmark Survey, Final Results." http://www.bea.gov/international/exe/fdius02bmrkpdf.exe.

———. 2008. "US Direct Investment Abroad: 2004 Final Benchmark Data." http://www.bea.gov/international/usdia2004f.html.

Cavallo, Michele, and Cedric Tille. 2006. "Could Capital Gains Smooth a Current Account Rebalancing?" Federal Reserve Bank of New York Staff Report no. 237. http://www.newyorkfed.org/research/staff_reports/sr237.pdf.

Curcuru, Stephanie E., Tomas Dvorak, and Francis E. Warnock. 2008. "Cross-Border Returns Differentials." *Quarterly Journal of Economics* 123:1495–530.

Curcuru, Stephanie E., Charles P. Thomas, and Francis E. Warnock. 2009. "Current Account Sustainability and Relative Reliability." In *NBER International Seminar on Macroeconomics 2008*, edited by J. Frankel and C. Pissarides, 67–109. Chicago: University of Chicago Press.

Desai, Mihir A., C. Fritz Foley, and James R. Hines Jr. 2001. "Repatriation Taxes and Dividend Distortions." *National Tax Journal* 54 (4): 829–51.

———. 2003. "Chains of Ownership, Regional Tax Competition, and Foreign Direct Investment." In *Foreign Direct Investment in the Real and Financial Sector of Industrial Countries*, edited by Heinz Herrmann and Robert Lindsay, 61–98. Heidelberg, Germany: Springer Verlag.

———. 2004. "A Multinational Perspective on Capital Structure Choice and Internal Capital Markets." *Journal of Finance* 59 (6): 2451–88.

———. 2006. "The Demand for Tax Haven Operations." *Journal of Public Economics* 90 (3): 513–31.

———. 2007. "Dividend Policy inside the Multinational Firm." *Financial Management* 36 (1): 5–26.

Feldstein, Martin. 1994. "Taxes, Leverage and the National Return on Outbound Foreign Direct Investment." NBER Working Paper no. 4689, Cambridge, MA.

Fillat, Jose L., and Stefania Garetto. 2010. "Risk, Returns and Multinational Production." Working Paper, Boston University.

Forbes, Kristin. 2010. "Why Do Foreigners Invest in the United States?" *Journal of International Economics* 80 (1): 3–21.

Gourinchas, Pierre-Olivier, and Hélène Rey. 2007. "From World Banker to World Venture Capitalist: The US External Adjustment and the Exorbitant Privilege." In *G7 Current Account Imbalances: Sustainability and Adjustment*, edited by R. Clarida, 11–55. Chicago: University of Chicago Press.

Gourinchas, Pierre-Olivier, Hélène Rey, and Nicolas Govillot. 2010. "Exorbitant Privilege and Exorbitant Duty." Bank of Japan IMES Discussion Paper no. 2010-E-20, Institute for Monetary and Economic Studies.

Gros, Daniel. 2006. "Foreign Investment in the US, II: Being Taken to the Cleaners?" CEPS Working Document no. 243, Brussels, Centre for European Policy Studies, April.

Grubert, Harry. 1997. "Another Look at the Low Taxable Income of Foreign-Controlled Companies in the United States." Office of Tax Analysis Paper no.74, Washington, DC, US Treasury Department.

———. 1998. "Taxes and the Division of Foreign Operating Income among Royalties, Interest, Dividends and Retained Earnings." *Journal of Public Economics* 68 (2): 269–90.

Grubert, Harry, Timothy Goodspeed, and Deborah Swenson. 1993. "Explaining the Low Taxable Income of Foreign-Controlled Companies in the United States." In *Studies in International Taxation*, edited by Alberto Giovannini, R. Glenn Hubbard, and Joel Slemrod, 237–75. Chicago: University of Chicago Press.

Habib, Maurizio M., 2010. "Excess Returns on Net Foreign Assets: The Exorbitant Privilege from a Global Perspective." European Central Bank Working Paper Series no. 1158, Frankfurt, Germany.

Hausmann, Ricardo, and Federico Sturzenegger. 2006. "Global Imbalances or Bad Accounting? The Missing Dark Matter in the Wealth of Nations." Center for International Development Working Paper no. 124, Cambridge, MA, Harvard University.

Helpman, Elhanan, Marc J. Melitz, and Stephen R. Yeaple. 2004. "Exports versus FDI with Heterogeneous Firms." *American Economic Review* 94 (1): 300–16.

Hines Jr., James R. 1996. "Dividends and Profits: Some Unsubtle Foreign Influences." *Journal of Finance* 51 (2): 661–89.

———. 1999. "Lessons from Behavioral Responses to International Taxation." *National Tax Journal* 52 (2): 305–22.

Hines Jr., James R., and R. Glenn Hubbard. 1990. "Coming Home To America: Dividend Repatriations by US Multinationals." In *Taxation in the Global Economy*, edited by A. Razin and J. Slemrod, 161–200. Chicago: University of Chicago Press.

Howenstine, Ned G., and Ann M. Lawson. 1991. "Alternative Measures of the Rate of Return on Direct Investment." *Survey of Current Business* 71 (8): 44–45.

Hung, Juann H., and Angelo Mascaro. 2004. "Return on Cross-Border Investment: Why Does US Investment Abroad Do Better?" Technical Paper no. 2004–17, Washington, DC, Congressional Budget Office, December.

Ibarra-Caton, Marilyn. 2010. "Direct Investment Positions for 2009: Country and Industry Detail." *Survey of Current Business* 90 (7): 20–35.

Jorion, Philippe. 1996. "Returns to Japanese investors from US investments." *Japan and the World Economy* 8:229–41.

Kitchen, John. 2007. "Sharecroppers or Shrewd Capitalists? Projections of the US Current Account, International Income Flows, and Net International Debt." *Review of International Economics* 15 (5): 1036–61.

KPMG. 2010. KPMG's Corporate and Indirect Tax Rate Survey, 2010. http://www.kpmg.com/Global/en/IssuesAndInsights/ArticlesPublications/Documents/Corp-and-Indirect-Tax-Oct12-2010.pdf.

Landefeld, J. Steven, Ann M. Lawson, and Douglas B. Weinberg. 1992. "Rates of Return on Direct Investment." *Survey of Current Business* 72:79–86.

Lane, Philip R., and Gian Maria Milesi-Ferretti. 2005. "A Global Perspective on External Positions." NBER Working Paper no. 11589, Cambridge, MA.

———. 2009. "Where Did All the Borrowing Go? A Forensic Analysis of the US External Position." *Journal of the Japanese and International Economies* 23 (2): 177–99.

Laster, David S., and Robert N. McCauley. 1994. "Making Sense of the Profits of Foreign Firms in the United States." *Federal Reserve Bank of New York Quarterly Review* Summer-Fall:44–75.

Lupo, L. A., Arnold Gilbert, and Michael Liliestedt. 1978. "The Relationship between Age and Rate of Return of Foreign Manufacturing Affiliates of US Manufacturing Parent Companies." *Survey of Current Business* 58 (August): 60–6.

Mataloni Jr., Raymond. 2000. "An Examination of the Low Rates of Return of Foreign-Owned US Companies." *Survey of Current Business* 80 (March): 55–73.

McGrattan, Ellen R., and Edward C. Prescott. 2010. "Technology Capital and the US Current Account." *American Economic Review* 100:1493–522.

Meissner, Christopher M., and Alan M. Taylor. 2006. "Losing Our Marbles in the New Century? The Great Rebalancing in Historical Perspective." NBER Working Paper no. 12580, Cambridge, MA.

Newey, W. K., and K. D. West. 1987. "A Simple, Positive Semi-Definite, Heteroskedasticity and Autocorrelation Consistent Covariance Matrix." *Econometrica* 55:703–8.

Obstfeld, Maurice, and Kenneth S. Rogoff. 2005. "Global Current Account Imbalances and Exchange Rate Adjustments." *Brookings Papers on Economic Activity* 1:67–123.

Sharpe, William F. 1966. "Mutual Fund Performance." *Journal of Business* 39: 119–38.

8

US International Financial Flows and the US Net Investment Position
New Perspectives Arising from New International Standards

Christopher A. Gohrband and Kristy L. Howell

8.1 Introduction

The recent global financial crisis was precipitated in part by an inadequate understanding by regulators and policymakers of the size and scope of risks undertaken by financial market participants around the world. These events have drawn attention to gaps and limitations in aggregate statistics for financial flows and positions, particularly for the purpose of international comparisons. Although data gaps are, as the International Monetary Fund (IMF) points out, "an inevitable consequence of the ongoing development of markets and institutions," they become more apparent when the "lack of timely, accurate information hinders the ability of policymakers and market participants to develop effective responses" (IMF 2009, 4). In addition, some economists believe that policy responses might have been better informed if macroeconomic aggregate statistics that were fully integrated with more detailed data on the composition of financial asset and liability flows had been available.[1] With this in mind, several inter-

Christopher A. Gohrband is chief of the financial accounts branch at the US Bureau of Economic Analysis. Kristy L. Howell is assistant chief of the balance of payments division for goods and services at the US Bureau of Economic Analysis.

The views expressed in this chapter are solely those of the authors and not necessarily those of the US Bureau of Economic Analysis or the US Department of Commerce. The authors wish to thank their colleagues at the US Bureau of Economic Analysis, the organizers and participants of the NBER-CRIW Conference on Wealth, Financial Intermediation and the Real Economy, and two anonymous referees for their valuable comments. They also wish to thank Kyle Westmoreland for his assistance in preparing the estimates presented in the chapter as well as Barbara Berman, Elena Nguyen, Dena Holland, and Helen Bai for their contributions. For acknowledgments, sources of research support, and disclosure of the authors' material financial relationships, if any, please see http://www.nber.org/chapters/c12539.ack.

1. See, for example, Eichner, Kohn, and Palumbo (chapter 2, this volume), Bosworth (chapter 1, this volume), and Palumbo and Parker (2009).

national organizations, including the IMF and the Organisation for Economic Co-operation and Development (OECD), have undertaken efforts to address data gaps in financial information and to improve the comparability of external account statistics across countries.

One step that will help to close some of the information gaps is the timely implementation of recently updated international standards for the compilation of international economic accounts, in particular, the sixth edition of the IMF's *Balance of Payments and International Investment Position Manual* (BPM6) released in 2009.[2] This revision of the BPM was undertaken partly in response to the product innovation and rapid growth in financial markets since the standards were last updated in 1993. Extensive recommendations for the presentation of financial transactions and the greater prominence placed on the international investment position in BPM6 will result in more informative international accounts that meet international recommendations made in the aftermath of the financial crisis.

The US Bureau of Economic Analysis (BEA) produces the US balance of payments (BOP) and the US international investment position (IIP), as well as related statistics on direct investment and the operations of multinational companies.[3] The US BOP accounts summarize the economic transactions between the United States and the rest of the world during a specific time period, while the US IIP shows the value of US claims on nonresidents and US liabilities to nonresidents at a given point in time. The BOP consists of a current account, which reports flows of goods, services, and income; a capital account, which reports capital transfers and other nonfinancial transactions; and a financial account, which reports transactions in financial assets and liabilities. International accounts statistics are important for understanding the role of an economy in the international financial markets, for evaluating the impact of globalization on the domestic economy, and for examining the changing nature of international investment over time. However, the usefulness of the US international accounts is limited by the current presentation of the statistics.

In this chapter, we describe a planned restructuring of the financial account in the US BOP and the US IIP to align their presentation and underlying concepts more closely with the international standards recommended in BPM6.[4] The BEA's new presentation will place greater emphasis on the composition of financial flows and positions in terms of functional cate-

---

2. IMF (2009).
3. The US balance of payments accounts are also known as the US international transactions accounts.
4. The BEA is also using the fourth edition of the OECD *Benchmark Definition of Foreign Direct Investment* (BD4) (OECD 2008) as a source of guidance for the international accounts. The BPM6 and BD4 are consistent in their approach to direct investment statistics. The BEA first introduced its plans and strategy for implementing BPM6 and BD4 and making other improvements to the international economic accounts in Howell and Yuskavage (2010). Updates were provided in Howell and Howenstine (2011), Howell (2012), and Howell and Westmoreland (2013).

gories such as direct investment and portfolio investment, on the types of instruments and maturities comprised by investment within these categories, and on the broad sectors of both US creditors and debtors. We also provide experimental statistics that are reorganized according to the new international guidelines.

We then explain some of the benefits of the transformed US BOP and IIP statistics in a section on cross-border rates of return on investment. We show that the restructured BOP and IIP statistics can also provide better information on analytical issues addressed in the international economics literature. Because only limited information on time series for capital gains and losses have been available in the IIP, researchers have found it challenging to estimate rates of return on detailed cross-border investment positions using BEA statistics. Differences in assumptions have led to different conclusions by researchers using these statistics. To fill this information gap, we present rates of return measures based on previously unpublished time series for capital gains for major types of investment including: direct investment, long-term portfolio debt, and portfolio equity. Results demonstrate that there are considerable benefits to data users from adopting the new presentation and providing more detailed data. The chapter concludes with a progress report on recent initiatives to make the international accounts more detailed and more timely.

8.2   A New Presentation of the Balance of Payments and International Investment Position

The reorganized presentation of the financial account of the BOP and of the IIP provides a uniform classification of international transactions and positions, with greater comparability between the US accounts and those of other countries that follow the international guidelines.

Tables 8.1 and 8.2 present experimental statistics for the new presentation of the U.S. BOP and the IIP based on a reorganization of currently published statistics according to the new international guidelines.[5] Tables 8.3 and 8.4 present the new presentations for the financial account of the BOP and for the IIP alongside the existing presentations to give a preliminary indication of how the structure of the accounts will be changed in the new presentation.

8.2.1   Balance of Payments

The proposed new presentation of the financial account of the BOP is presented in table 8.3 (right panel), alongside the existing financial account presentation (left panel). In the new presentation, transactions are arranged

---

5. The BOP tables also reflect planned changes to the current and capital accounts. With the exception of changes to the primary income account (within the current account), which correspond to changes to the financial account, the changes to the current and capital accounts are outside the scope of this chapter and will not be discussed here.

Table 8.1   US international transactions (billions of dollars)[a]

Line		2006	2007	2008	2009	2010	2011
	Current account						
	Credits:						
1	**Exports of goods and services and income receipts**	**2,221.7**	**2,570.5**	**2,752.2**	**2,276.1**	**2,614.1**	**2,953.9**
2	Exports of goods and services	1,460.8	1,656.4	1,845.2	1,581.7	1,844.1	2,104.9
3	Goods, balance of payments basis	1,042.2	1,167.9	1,312.5	1,072.9	1,292.4	1,499.7
4	General merchandise	1,030.6	1,150.3	1,288.6	1,055.5	1,271.1	1,461.9
5	Foods, feeds, and beverages	66.0	84.3	108.3	93.9	107.7	126.2
6	Industrial supplies and materials	279.1	316.3	386.9	293.5	388.5	484.4
7	Capital goods	404.0	433.0	457.7	391.5	447.8	493.2
8	Automotive vehicles, parts, and engines	107.3	121.3	121.5	81.7	112.0	133.1
9	Consumer goods	129.1	146.0	161.3	149.5	165.2	175.0
10	Other goods	45.2	49.5	53.0	45.4	50.0	50.0
11	Net exports of goods under merchanting	2.8	4.2	5.2	3.4	3.7	3.5
12	Nonmonetary gold	8.8	13.3	18.7	13.9	17.6	34.3
13	Services	418.5	488.5	532.7	508.8	551.8	605.2
14	Manufacturing services on physical inputs owned by others	n/a	n/a	n/a	n/a	n/a	n/a
15	Maintenance and repair services, n.i.e.	8.2	10.0	10.6	12.9	14.6	16.1
16	Transport	57.8	66.2	75.5	62.7	72.3	80.4
17	Travel	111.3	123.3	139.1	123.4	134.2	149.3
18	Construction	1.9	2.7	3.9	4.0	2.6	3.1
19	Insurance and pension services[b]	9.4	10.8	13.4	14.6	14.5	15.5
20	Financial services[c]	47.9	61.4	63.0	64.4	70.3	74.1
21	Charges for the use of intellectual property[d]	83.6	97.8	102.1	98.4	107.2	120.8
22	Telecommunications, computer, and information services	17.2	20.2	23.1	23.8	25.1	28.2
23	Other business services	61.2	74.3	82.1	82.9	89.7	94.5
24	Personal, cultural, and recreational services[e]	1.7	1.8	2.2	2.4	3.0	2.9
25	Government goods and services, n.i.e.	18.4	19.9	17.7	19.2	18.3	20.5
26	Primary income receipts	693.0	843.9	823.5	609.2	683.4	751.3
27	Investment income	688.0	838.8	818.3	603.7	677.8	745.5
28	Direct investment	333.2	380.8	423.4	365.4	451.2	486.9
29	Portfolio investment	166.2	221.6	241.3	184.4	190.3	219.6

30	Other investment	187.5	235.0	152.1	53.2	35.6	38.1
31	Reserve assets	1.2	1.4	1.5	0.8	0.7	0.8
32	Compensation of employees	5.0	5.1	5.2	5.5	5.6	5.8
33	Other primary income	n/a	n/a	n/a	n/a	n/a	n/a
34	Secondary income (current transfer) receipts	67.9	70.3	83.5	85.3	86.5	97.7
	Debits:						
35	**Imports of goods and services and income payments**	**3,023.6**	**3,282.5**	**3,431.2**	**2,660.4**	**3,058.5**	**3,422.2**
36	Imports of goods and services	2,215.3	2,354.7	2,545.5	1,963.2	2,341.3	2,667.1
37	Goods, balance of payments basis	1,878.5	1,986.6	2,141.6	1,580.0	1,938.4	2,239.9
38	General merchandise	1,872.9	1,977.7	2,129.2	1,571.2	1,925.8	2,223.5
39	Foods, feeds, and beverages	76.1	83.0	90.4	82.9	92.5	108.2
40	Industrial supplies and materials	613.6	648.6	799.1	469.6	610.4	765.7
41	Capital goods	422.6	449.1	458.7	374.1	450.3	513.4
42	Automotive vehicles, parts, and engines	256.0	258.5	233.2	159.2	225.6	255.2
43	Consumer goods	447.9	480.0	486.7	431.4	486.5	517.4
44	Other goods	56.8	58.5	61.0	54.0	60.5	63.6
45	Nonmonetary gold	5.6	8.8	12.5	8.8	12.6	16.4
46	Services	336.8	368.2	403.8	383.2	402.9	427.2
47	Manufacturing services on physical inputs owned by others	n/a	n/a	n/a	n/a	n/a	n/a
48	Maintenance and repair services, n.i.e.	4.6	5.2	5.7	5.9	6.6	8.1
49	Transport	82.0	83.5	88.5	67.7	78.5	85.8
50	Travel	78.5	83.0	86.9	80.6	82.5	86.2
51	Construction	1.7	2.5	3.5	3.6	2.4	2.4
52	Insurance and pension services[b]	39.4	47.5	58.9	63.8	61.0	56.6
53	Financial services[c]	14.7	19.2	17.2	14.4	14.8	16.2
54	Charges for the use of intellectual property[d]	25.0	26.5	29.6	31.3	33.4	36.6
55	Telecommunications, computer, and information services	19.8	22.4	24.7	25.8	29.1	32.2
56	Other business services	41.6	47.9	57.6	56.0	59.7	68.8
57	Personal, cultural, and recreational services[e]	1.0	1.0	1.1	1.3	1.5	1.6
58	Government goods and services, n.i.e.	28.6	29.5	30.1	32.8	33.3	32.6
59	Primary income payments	648.9	742.4	676.4	489.5	499.5	524.3
60	Investment income	633.3	727.7	660.5	476.1	486.7	510.5
61	Direct investment	159.2	136.3	139.1	112.4	153.3	165.2
62	Portfolio investment	304.9	381.8	400.0	332.5	313.6	324.5

(continued)

Table 8.1   (continued)

Line		2006	2007	2008	2009	2010	2011
63	Other investment	169.2	209.7	121.4	31.3	20.0	20.8
64	Compensation of employees	15.5	14.7	15.9	13.3	12.8	13.8
65	Other primary income	n/a	n/a	n/a	n/a	n/a	n/a
66	Secondary income (current transfer) payments	159.5	185.4	209.3	207.7	217.6	230.8
	Capital account						
67	**Credits**	**0.0**	**0.5**	**6.2**	**0.0**	**0.0**	**0.0**
68	Gross disposals of nonproduced nonfinancial assets	0.0	0.5	0.0	0.0	0.0	0.0
69	Capital transfer receipts	0.0	0.0	6.2	0.0	0.0	0.0
70	**Debits**	**1.8**	**0.1**	**0.2**	**0.1**	**0.2**	**1.2**
71	Gross acquisitions of nonproduced nonfinancial assets	0.1	0.0	0.0	0.0	0.0	0.1
72	Capital transfer payments	1.7	0.1	0.2	0.1	0.2	1.2
	Financial account						
73	**Net acquisition of financial assets, excluding financial derivatives**	**1,336.9**	**1,572.5**	**-309.5**	**108.7**	**1,004.6**	**507.2**
74	Direct investment	296.1	532.9	351.7	278.6	393.0	442.9
75	Equity and investment fund shares	266.3	431.4	360.1	247.5	356.4	401.0
76	Equity other than reinvestment of earnings	49.0	200.9	127.0	18.2	41.1	52.4
77	Reinvestment of earnings	217.3	230.5	233.1	229.3	315.3	348.6
78	Debt instruments	29.7	101.6	-8.4	31.1	36.6	41.8
79	US parents' claims on their foreign affiliates	11.7	22.7	-29.0	32.0	28.2	51.9
80	US affiliates' claims on their foreign parent groups	18.0	78.9	20.6	-0.9	8.4	-10.1
81	Portfolio investment	493.7	379.7	-285.7	375.1	174.9	83.0
82	Equity and investment fund shares	137.3	147.8	-38.5	63.7	79.1	89.0
83	Debt securities	356.4	231.9	-247.2	311.4	95.8	-6.1
84	Short term[f]	116.1	14.6	-84.0	135.5	44.4	-60.4
85	Long term[f]	240.3	217.3	-163.2	175.9	51.4	54.3
86	Other investment	549.5	659.8	-380.3	-597.3	434.9	-34.5
87	Other equity	n/a	n/a	n/a	n/a	n/a	n/a
88	Currency and deposits	298.6	358.9	265.8	-413.6	178.7	-80.7
89	Loans	247.3	290.2	-642.4	-184.2	250.1	43.6

#		col1	col2	col3	col4	col5	col6
90	Insurance, pension, and standardized guarantee schemes	n/a	n/a	n/a	n/a	n/a	n/a
91	Trade credits and advances	3.5	10.7	-3.7	0.5	6.0	2.6
92	Other accounts receivable	n/a	n/a	n/a	n/a	n/a	n/a
93	Reserve assets	-2.4	0.1	4.8	52.3	1.8	15.9
94	Monetary gold	0.0	0.0	0.0	0.0	0.0	0.0
95	Special drawing rights	0.2	0.2	0.1	48.2	0.0	-1.8
96	Reserve position in the International Monetary Fund	-3.3	-1.0	3.5	3.4	1.3	18.1
97	Other reserve assets	0.7	1.0	1.3	0.7	0.5	-0.5
98	Currency and deposits	0.3	0.5	0.6	0.1	0.1	-0.9
99	Securities	0.3	0.3	0.4	0.5	0.4	0.4
100	Financial derivatives	0.0	0.0	0.0	0.0	0.0	0.0
101	Other claims	0.1	0.2	0.2	0.1	0.0	0.0
102	**Net incurrence of liabilities, excluding financial derivatives**	**2,116.3**	**2,183.5**	**454.0**	**303.5**	**1,373.4**	**1,024.5**
103	Direct investment	294.3	340.1	332.7	139.6	271.0	257.5
104	Equity and investment fund shares	184.1	190.4	294.9	148.5	199.2	180.6
105	Equity other than reinvestment of earnings	115.0	142.3	255.7	126.8	131.6	93.2
106	Reinvestment of earnings	69.1	48.2	39.1	21.7	67.5	87.4
107	Debt instruments	110.1	149.6	37.9	-8.9	71.8	76.9
108	US affiliates' liabilities to their foreign parent groups	77.1	109.6	35.9	1.1	15.1	43.3
109	US parents' liabilities to their foreign affiliates	33.1	40.0	2.0	-10.0	56.7	33.6
110	Portfolio investment	1,126.7	1,156.6	523.7	357.4	808.9	336.6
111	Equity and investment fund shares	145.5	275.6	126.8	219.3	177.6	27.4
112	Debt securities	981.3	881.0	396.9	138.1	631.3	309.3
113	Short term[f]	25.4	166.6	297.3	-122.5	-60.3	-81.6
114	Long term[f]	955.9	714.4	99.6	260.5	691.6	390.9
115	Other investment	695.3	686.9	-402.4	-193.4	293.6	430.4
116	Other equity	n/a	n/a	n/a	n/a	n/a	n/a
117	Currency and deposits	301.3	240.7	111.8	-98.5	93.5	457.3
118	Loans	388.4	425.6	-520.9	-148.9	180.5	-43.6
119	Insurance, pension, and standardized guarantee schemes	n/a	n/a	n/a	n/a	n/a	n/a
120	Trade credits and advances	5.7	20.6	6.7	6.4	19.6	16.7
121	Other accounts payable	n/a	n/a	n/a	n/a	n/a	n/a
122	Special drawing rights	0.0	0.0	0.0	47.6	0.0	0.0

(continued)

Table 8.1 (continued)

Line		2006	2007	2008	2009	2010	2011
123	**Financial derivatives and employee stock options, net transactions (credit [+] or debit [-])**[g]	-29.7	-6.2	32.9	-44.8	-14.1	-39.0
	Balances (surplus [+] or deficit [-])						
124	Current account (line 1 less line 35)	-801.9	-712.0	-679.1	-384.3	-444.4	-468.3
125	Goods and services (line 2 less line 36)	-754.5	-698.4	-700.3	-381.6	-497.2	-562.2
126	Goods (line 3 less line 37)	-836.3	-818.7	-829.1	-507.1	-646.0	-740.2
127	Services (line 13 less line 46)	81.8	120.3	128.9	125.6	148.8	178.0
128	Primary income (line 26 less line 59)	44.2	101.5	147.1	119.7	183.9	227.0
129	Secondary income (line 34 less line 66)	-91.5	-115.1	-125.9	-122.5	-131.1	-133.1
130	Capital account (line 67 less line 70)	-1.8	0.4	6.0	-0.1	-0.2	-1.2
	Net lending or net borrowing and statistical discrepancy						
	Net lending (+) or net borrowing (–) derived from:						
131	Current account and capital account (line 124 plus line 130)	-803.6	-711.6	-673.1	-384.5	-444.6	-469.5
132	Financial account (line 73 less line 102 plus line 123)	-809.1	-617.3	-730.6	-239.7	-382.9	-556.3
133	Statistical discrepancy (line 132 less line 131)	-5.5	94.4	-57.5	144.8	61.7	-86.8

Note: n/a = data are not currently available for these transactions; n.i.e. = not included elsewhere.

[a] This is a prototype of a new table that will replace "Table 1. US International Transactions" published regularly by BEA when BEA introduces the new presentation of the international accounts in June 2014. The prototype table is indicative of the categories that will be presented in the new table. This table may not be identical to the table that is ultimately published in June 2014 because the new presentation is still under review.

[b] Statistics currently cover only insurance services.

[c] Statistics currently cover only explicit charges for financial services.

[d] Statistics currently include transactions for the outright sale, rights to use, and rights to distribute intellectual property.

[e] Statistics currently cover only sports, performing arts, and training services.

[f] Short-term debt securities are those with an original maturity of one year or less. Long-term debt securities are those with an original maturity of greater than one year.

[g] Statistics currently cover only financial derivatives transactions.

Table 8.2   US International investment position at year end (billions of dollars)[a]

Line		2006	2007	2008	2009	2010	2011
1	**Net international investment position (lines 2 + 3)**	**-2,191.6**	**-1,796.0**	**-3,260.2**	**-2,321.8**	**-2,473.6**	**-4,030.2**
2	Financial derivatives, net (line 5 less line 30)	59.8	71.5	159.6	126.3	110.4	126.3
3	Net international investment position, excluding financial derivatives (line 6 less line 31)	-2,251.5	-1,867.5	-3,419.8	-2,448.1	-2,584.0	-4,156.5
4	**US-owned assets abroad (lines 5 + 6)**	**14,887.7**	**18,982.6**	**20,069.5**	**19,114.0**	**20,976.4**	**21,831.0**
5	Financial derivatives (gross positive fair value)	1,239.0	2,559.3	6,127.5	3,489.8	3,652.3	4,704.7
6	US-owned assets abroad, excluding financial derivatives (lines 7 + 12 + 17 + 22)	13,648.7	16,423.3	13,942.1	15,624.2	17,324.1	17,126.3
7	Reserve assets	219.9	277.2	293.7	403.8	488.7	536.0
8	Gold	165.3	218.0	227.4	284.4	367.5	400 4
9	Special drawing rights	8.9	9.5	9.3	57.8	56.8	55.0
10	Reserve position in the International Monetary Fund	5.0	4.2	7.7	11.4	12.5	30.1
11	Other reserve assets	40.7	45.5	49.3	50.2	51.8	50.6
12	Direct investment at current cost	3,407.7	4,136.0	4,353.3	4,631.7	4,984.9	5,380.2
13	Equity and investment fund shares	2,772.1	3,369.1	3,574.2	3,818.5	4,118.9	4,468.3
14	Debt instruments	635.6	767.0	779.1	813.2	865.9	911.9
15	US parents' claims on foreign affiliates	463.0	510.1	504.2	537.1	586.6	649.0
16	US affiliates' claims on foreign parent groups	172.6	256.9	274.9	276.1	279.4	262.9
17	Portfolio investment	6,017.1	7,262.0	4,320.8	6,058.6	6,865.2	6,375.6
18	Equity and investment fund shares	4,329.0	5,248.0	2,748.4	3,995.3	4,646.9	4,158.2
19	Debt securities	1,688.1	2,014.1	1,572.4	2,063.3	2,218.3	2,217.3
20	Short term[b]	388.8	383.9	314.1	437.5	472.8	440.5
21	Long term[b]	1,299.3	1,630.2	1,258.3	1,625.8	1,745.5	1,776.9
22	Other investment	4,004.0	4,748.0	4,974.2	4,530.1	4,985.4	4,834.5
23	Other equity	n/a	n/a	n/a	n/a	n/a	n/a
24	Currency and deposits	1,960.7	2,316.9	2,813.1	2,539.6	2,771.3	2,590.4
25	Loans	2,010.5	2,389.3	2,126.4	1,958.0	2,175.8	2,201.2
26	Insurance, pension, and standardized guarantee schemes	n/a	n/a	n/a	n/a	n/a	n/a
27	Trade credits and advances	32.8	41.8	34.8	32.5	38.4	42.9
28	Other accounts receivable	0.0	0.0	0.0	0.0	0.0	0.0

(continued)

Table 8.2 (continued)

Line		2006	2007	2008	2009	2010	2011
29	**Foreign-owned assets in the United States (lines 30 + 31)**	**17,079.3**	**20,778.6**	**23,329.7**	**21,435.8**	**23,450.0**	**25,861.2**
30	Financial derivatives (gross negative fair value)	1,179.2	2,487.9	5,967.8	3,363.4	3,541.9	4,578.4
31	Foreign-owned assets in the Unites States, excluding financial derivatives (lines 32 + 37 + 42)	15,900.2	18,290.8	17,361.9	18,072.3	19,908.1	21,282.8
32	Direct investment at current cost	2,613.6	2,928.9	3,002.2	3,000.5	3,275.7	3,607.4
33	Equity and investment fund shares	1,756.5	1,892.1	1,911.5	1,916.7	2,110.7	2,365.8
34	Debt instruments	857.1	1,036.7	1,090.7	1,083.8	1,165.0	1,241.6
35	US affiliates' liabilities to foreign parent groups	570.1	710.6	760.8	757.7	766.3	805.9
36	US parents' liabilities to foreign affiliates	287.0	326.1	329.9	326.2	398.7	435.7
37	Portfolio investment	8,843.5	10,327.0	9,475.9	10,463.2	11,876.1	12,505.1
38	Equity and investment fund shares	2,791.9	3,231.7	2,132.4	2,917.7	3,545.6	3,597.9
39	Debt securities	6,051.6	7,095.3	7,343.4	7,545.6	8,330.5	8,907.2
40	Short term[b]	621.1	789.8	1,099.6	976.1	919.3	837.5
41	Long term[b]	5,430.5	6,305.6	6,243.8	6,569.5	7,411.2	8,069.7
42	Other investment	4,443.0	5,034.9	4,883.8	4,608.6	4,756.3	5,170.3
43	Other equity	n/a	n/a	n/a	n/a	n/a	n/a
44	Currency and deposits	1,764.5	2,020.8	2,331.7	2,248.5	2,349.3	2,788.4
45	Loans	2,626.8	2,954.4	2,491.3	2,238.7	2,267.5	2,230.7
46	Insurance, pension, and standardized guarantee schemes	n/a	n/a	n/a	n/a	n/a	n/a
47	Trade credits and advances	44.4	52.0	53.3	66.1	85.1	97.0
48	Other accounts payable	0.0	0.0	0.0	0.0	0.0	0.0
49	Special drawing rights	7.4	7.7	7.5	55.4	54.4	54.2
	Memoranda:						
50	Direct investment assets at market value	4,929.9	5,857.9	3,707.2	4,889.5	5,444.7	5,198.6
51	Equity and investment fund shares	4,294.3	5,091.0	2,928.1	4,076.3	4,578.8	4,286.7
52	Debt instruments	635.6	767.0	779.1	813.2	865.9	911.9
53	Direct investment liabilities at market value	3,752.6	4,134.2	3,091.2	3,597.7	4,075.4	4,208.0
54	Equity and investment fund shares	2,895.5	3,097.5	2,000.5	2,513.9	2,910.4	2,966.3
55	Debt instruments	857.1	1,036.7	1,090.7	1,083.8	1,165.0	1,241.6

Note: n/a = transactions are possible, but data are not available.

[a]This is a prototype of a new table that will replace "Table 2. International Investment Position of the United States at Year end" published annually by BEA with the US international investment position press release and in the July issue of the *Survey of Current Business* when BEA introduces the new presentation of the international accounts in June 2014. The prototype table is indicative of the categories that will be presented in the new table. This table may not be identical to the table that is ultimately published in June 2014 because the new presentation is still under review.

Table 8.3   Current and BPM6-based structures for the financial account, 2011

Current structure by US sector	Billions of dollars	Line[a]	BPM6-based structure by functional category	Billions of dollars
US-owned assets, excluding financial derivatives	**483.7**	73	**Net acquisition of assets, excluding financial derivatives**	**507.2**
US official reserve assets	15.9	93	Reserve assets	15.9
Gold	0.0	94	Monetary gold	0.0
Special drawing rights	−1.8	95	Special drawing rights	−1.8
Reserve position in the International Monetary Fund	18.1	96	Reserve position in the International Monetary Fund	18.1
Foreign currencies	−0.5	97	Other reserve assets	−0.5
		98	Currency and deposits	−0.9
		99	Securities	0.4
		100	Financial derivatives	0.0
		101	Other claims	0.0
US government assets, other than official reserve assets	103.7	74	Direct investment[b]	442.9
US credits and other long-term assets	7.3	75	Equity and investment fund shares	401.0
Repayments of US credits and other long-term assets	−3.3	76	Equity other than reinvestment of earnings	52.4
US foreign currency holdings and other short-term assets	99.7	77	Reinvestment of earnings	348.6
		78	Debt instruments	41.8
US private assets	364.1	79	US parents' claims on foreign affiliates	51.9
Direct investment (outward)[2]	419.3	80	US affiliates' claims on foreign parent groups	−10.1
Foreign securities	146.8			
US claims on unaffiliated foreigners reported by US nonbanking concerns	11.6	81	Portfolio investment	83.0
US claims reported by US banks and securities brokers	−213.6	82	Equity and investment fund shares	89.0
		83	Debt securities	−6.1
		84	Short term	−60.4
		85	Long term	54.3
		86	Other investment	−34.5
		87	Other equity	n/a
		88	Currency and deposits	−80.7
		89	Loans	43.6
		90	Insurance, pension, and standardized guarantee schemes	n/a
		91	Trade credit and advances	2.6
		92	Other accounts receivable	n/a

(continued)

Table 8.3   (continued)

Current structure by foreign counterpart	Billions of dollars	Line[a]	BPM6-based structure by functional category	Billions of dollars
Foreign-owned assets in the United States, excluding financial derivatives	**1,001.0**		**Net incurrence of liabilities, excluding financial derivatives**	**1,024.5**
Foreign official assets in the United States	211.8	102	Direct investment[b]	257.5
US government securities	158.7	103	Equity and investment fund shares	180.6
US Treasury securities	171.2	104	Equity other than reinvestment of earnings	93.2
Other	-12.4	105	Reinvestment of earnings	87.4
Other US government liabilities	9.1	106	Debt instruments	76.9
US liabilities reported by banks and securities brokers	30.0	107	US affiliates' liabilities to foreign parent groups	43.3
Other foreign official assets	14.0	108	US parents' liabilities to foreign affiliates	33.6
Other foreign assets in the United States	789.2	109	Portfolio investment	336.6
Direct investment (inward)[b]	234.0	110	Equity and investment fund shares	27.4
US Treasury securities	240.9	111	Debt securities	309.3
US securities other than US Treasury securities	-56.4	112	Short term	-81.6
US currency	55.0	113	Long term	390.9
US liabilities to unaffiliated foreigners reported by US nonbanking concerns	6.6	114		
US liabilities reported by US banks and securities brokers	309.2	115	Other investment	430.4
		116	Other equity	n/a
		117	Currency and deposits	457.3
		118	Loans	-43.6
		119	Insurance, pension, and standardized guarantee schemes	n/a
		120	Trade credits and advances	16.7
		121	Other accounts payable	n/a
		122	Special drawing rights	0.0
Financial derivatives, net	**-39.0**	123	**Financial derivatives, net**	**-39.0**

Note: n/a = transactions are possible, but data are not available. BPM6 = International Monetary Fund (2009).

[a]The line numbers are from table 8.1.

[b]Direct investment flows on the BPM6 basis are on the asset/liability basis. The current basis flows are on the directional basis, where the changes in the US entity's liabilities are netted against the changes in its assets. The difference between the current basis and the BPM6 basis is due to the grossing up of these asset and liability transactions.

Table 8.4   Current and BPM6-based structures for the international investment position, 2011

Current structure	Billions of dollars	Line[a]	BPM6-based structure by functional category	Billions of dollars
Net international investment position of the United States	**-4,030.2**	**1**	**Net international investment position (lines 2 + 3)**	**-4,030.2**
Financial derivatives, net	126.3	2	Financial derivatives, net (line 5 less line 30)	126.3
Net international investment position, excluding financial derivatives	-4,156.5	3	Net international investment position, excluding financial derivatives (line 6 less line 31)	-4,156.5
US-owned assets abroad	**21,132.4**	**4**	**US-owned assets abroad (lines 5 + 6)**	**21,831.0**
Financial derivatives (gross positive fair value)	4,704.7	5	Financial derivatives (gross positive fair value)	4,704.7
US-owned assets abroad, excluding financial derivatives	16,427.7	6	US-owned assets abroad, excluding financial derivatives (lines 7 + 12 + 17 + 22)	17,126.3
US official reserve assets	536.0	7	Reserve assets	536.0
Gold	400.4	8	Gold	400.4
Special drawing rights	55.0	9	Special drawing rights	55.0
Reserve position in the International Monetary Fund	30.1	10	Reserve position in the International Monetary Fund	30.1
Foreign currencies	50.6	11	Other reserve assets	50.6
US government assets, other than official reserve assets	178.9	12	Direct investment at current cost[2]	5,380.2
US credits and other long-term assets	78.4	13	Equity and investment fund shares	4,468.3
Repayable in dollars	78.1	14	Debt instruments	911.9
Other	0.3	15	US parents' claims on foreign affiliates	649.0
US foreign currency holdings and US short-term assets	100.5	16	US affiliates' claims on foreign parent groups	262.9
US private assets	15,712.8	17	Portfolio investment	6,375.6
Direct investment at current cost[2]	4,681.6	18	Equity and investment fund shares	4,158.2
Foreign securities	5,922.0	19	Debt securities	2,217.3
Bonds	1,763.8	20	Short term	440.5
Corporate stocks	4,158.2	21	Long term	1,776.9
US claims on unaffiliated foreigners reported by US nonbanking concerns	796.8			

(*continued*)

Table 8.4 (continued)

Current structure	Billions of dollars	Line[a]	BPM6-based structure by functional category	Billions of dollars
US claims reported by US banks and securities brokers, n.i.e.	4,312.4	22	Other investment	4,834.5
		23	Other equity	n/a
		24	Currency and deposits	2,590.4
		25	Loans	2,201.2
		26	Insurance, pension, and standardized guarantee schemes	n/a
		27	Trade credits and advances	42.9
		28	Other accounts receivable	0.0
Foreign-owned assets in the United States	**25,162.6**	**29**	**Foreign-owned assets in the United States (lines 30 + 31)**	**25,861.2**
Financial derivatives (gross negative fair value)	4,578.4	30	Financial derivatives (gross negative fair value)	4,578.4
Foreign-owned assets in the Unites States, excluding financial derivatives	20,584.2	31	Foreign-owned assets in the Unites States, excluding financial derivatives (lines 32 + 37 + 42)	21,282.8
Foreign official assets in the United States	5,250.8	32	Direct investment at current cost[b]	3,607.4
US government securities	4,277.3	33	Equity and investment fund shares	2,365.8
US Treasury securities	3,653.1	34	Debt instruments	1,241.6
Other	624.3	35	US affiliates' liabilities to foreign parent groups	805.9
Other US government liabilities	119.4	36	US parents' liabilities to foreign affiliates	435.7
US liabilities reported by US banks and securities brokers, n.i.e.	209.6			
Other foreign official assets	644.5	37	Portfolio investment	12,505.1
		38	Equity and investment fund shares	3,597.9
Other foreign assets	15,333.4	39	Debt securities	8,907.2
Direct investment at current cost[2]	2,908.8	40	Short term	837.5
US Treasury securities	1,418.1	41	Long term	8,069.7
US securities other than US Treasury securities	5,968.2			
Corporate and other bonds	2,910.0	42	Other investment	5,170.3
Corporate stocks	3,058.2	43	Other equity	n/a

		Line	
US currency	397.1	44	Currency and deposits	2,788.4
US liabilities to unaffiliated foreigners reported by US nonbanking concerns	629.7	45	Loans	2,230.7
US liabilities reported by US banks and securities brokers, n.i.e.	4,011.6	46	Insurance, pension, and standardized guarantee schemes	n/a
		47	Trade credits and advances	97.0
		48	Other accounts payable	0.0
		49	Special drawing rights	54.2
Memoranda:			**Memoranda:**	
Direct investment abroad at market value[b]	4,500.0	50	Direct investment assets at market value[b]	5,198.6
		51	Equity and investment fund shares	4,286.7
		52	Debt instruments	911.9
Direct investment in the United States at market value[b]	3,509.4	53	Direct investment liabilities at market value[b]	4,208.0
		54	Equity and investment fund shares	2,966.3
		55	Debt instruments	1,241.6

Note: n/a = transactions are possible, but data are not available. n.i.e. = not included elsewhere. BPM6 = International Monetary Fund (2009).

[a] The line numbers are from table 8.2.

[b] Direct investment positions on the BPM6 basis are on the asset/liability basis. The current basis positions are on the directional basis, where the US entity's liabilities are netted against its assets. The difference between the current basis and the BPM6 basis is due to the grossing up of these asset and liability positions.

first according to whether they represent a change in an asset or a liability position, and then according to four major functional categories: direct investment, portfolio investment, other investment, and reserve assets. Transactions in a fifth major functional category, financial derivatives, are shown on a net basis because the source data on the gross flows are not available.

These functional categories are intended to "facilitate analysis by distinguishing categories that exhibit different economic motivations and patterns of behavior" (IMF 2009, 99). They capture the diversity of situations, motivations, and behaviors at work in the financial world. Direct investment recognizes that enterprises seek profits through long-term influence or control of other enterprises. Portfolio investment captures the behavior of investors trading negotiable instruments and altering their portfolios to meet a variety of objectives ranging from capital preservation to aggressive growth. Other investment encompasses yet another distinct set of activities including the bank payments settlement system and financial intermediation through financial institutions that offer deposit and near-deposit investment instruments as well as credit via loans and similar instruments. Reserve assets are a unique category of assets controlled by monetary authorities and used to meet balance of payments financing needs and to implement exchange rate policies, and as such, are classified separately from assets held by other entities. Financial derivatives include a variety of instruments that are used to trade risk in financial markets.

Within each of the functional categories, transactions are further disaggregated according to instrument classification. For example, direct investment and portfolio investment transactions are separated into debt and equity components. Some information on transactions by sector and by original maturity is also provided within functional categories. This uniform presentation of changes in assets and liabilities is preferable to the existing structure of the US financial account because it allows users to more easily compare similar transactions for assets and for liabilities. For example, statistics on foreign investment in US portfolio securities can be easily compared with those on US investment in foreign portfolio securities to gain insight into the relative risk preferences of these investors. Under the existing structure of the financial account, which arranges transactions according to the US sector for assets, and the sector of the foreign counterparty for liabilities, and then by a mix of reporter types and instruments, these comparisons are much more difficult.

In the new presentation, more detail is presented in the primary BOP table. Additional breakdowns by instrument, sector, and maturity will be provided by BEA in underlying detail tables organized by the functional categories and standard components of BPM6. Users will be able to drill down into the greater detail and compare asset and liability transactions by functional category, by instrument, and other characteristics. Some detail in the current presentation that is not found in BPM6, such as a delineation of liabilities according to the sector of the foreign counterparty (i.e., whether the counterparty is a foreign official agency or a private foreign resident) will continue to be published in supplemental tables because this information still has value to users.

In addition to the reorganization of financial account transactions, a new definition and presentation of direct investment is also introduced in the new BOP presentation. Historically, direct investment has been presented according to the "directional," or net, basis—that is, according to the direction of the direct investment relationship; for example, US direct investment abroad and foreign direct investment in the United States—as recommended in previous international guidance. On a directional basis, transactions related to debt investments of foreign affiliates in their US parents (known as reverse investment because they represent financial obligations, or liabilities, of the parents) are subtracted from transactions related to debt investments of US parents in their foreign affiliates, which are financial claims, or assets, of the parents. The net transactions are included in the financial account as US direct investment abroad. A similar treatment is used to derive net transactions for foreign direct investment in the United States.

In contrast, in the new presentation direct investment is presented on an "asset/liability" basis, which is the basis recommended by the new standards.[6] In the asset/liability basis, debt claims and liabilities of related entities are not netted. Instead, all debt claims of US parents and US affiliates on their foreign affiliated counterparties are reported as gross amounts under direct investment assets. Likewise, all debt liabilities of US parents and US affiliates to their foreign affiliated counterparties are reported as gross amounts under direct investment liabilities (table 8.3, right panel, lines 78–80 and 107–109). Although direct investment statistics on a directional basis are useful for understanding changes in foreign ownership and control, the presentation of direct investment on an asset/liability basis facilitates comparability between the international accounts and domestic financial and balance sheet statistics.[7]

6. The directional principle has not been entirely displaced by the asset/liability basis. For presentations of direct investment vis-à-vis a single partner country (bilateral statistics) the fourth edition of the OECD *Benchmark Definition of Foreign Direct Investment* recommends using the directional principle.

7. In the new presentation, direct investment statistics are presented on an asset/liability basis to the extent possible given the available data. To achieve this, reverse intercompany debt transactions have been reclassified from a directional basis to an asset/liability basis. However, BEA's direct investment data collection system is not designed to fully capture reverse equity investment or investments between certain related enterprises ("fellow enterprises") that BPM6 defines as direct investment. Reverse equity investment transactions and some transactions among fellow enterprises are commingled in source data from the US Department of the Treasury and cannot be separately identified. Therefore, the asset/liability basis can only be approximated using currently available source data. For further discussion, see Howell and Yuskavage (2010) and Howell (2012).

8.2.2   International Investment Position

The proposed new presentation of the IIP, shown in table 8.4 (right panel) alongside the existing IIP presentation (left panel), uses the same functional categories introduced in the new BOP table and presents direct investment according to the asset/liability basis. The presentation of the IIP thus mirrors that of the financial account of the BOP.

Unlike the BOP the existing presentation of the US IIP does not include underlying detail tables, so much of the detail on instrument and maturity that is shown in the new table was not previously published. For example, details about short-term instruments, which are needed to construct portfolio investment according to international standards, are not currently published.[8] The new IIP presentation also represents a significant improvement in the accessibility of these statistics because they are now provided in a consistent time series in one table.

In the IIP, direct investment is presented with equity valued at both current cost and market value. The current-cost and market-value methods are two methods used by BEA to revalue direct investment equity positions from historical cost to current period prices. The current-cost method revalues parent companies' shares of their affiliates' investments in tangible assets—plant and equipment, land, and inventory—using a perpetual inventory model, general price indexes, and current replacement cost, respectively. The market-value method revalues historical cost direct investment equity positions to current period prices using the relationship between the book value and the current stock market price for portfolio investment securities.[9]

Debt is valued at the reported book value for both measures in the IIP. Unlike the current presentation, the new IIP presentation reports the equity and debt components of direct investment separately. Previously this split was shown only in direct investment tables published annually (in the September issue of the *Survey of Current Business*) and only at historical cost. The introduction of separate equity and debt components of direct investment at both current cost and market value is in response to frequent requests from customers.

8.2.3   Underlying Detail Tables

Underlying detail tables that provide additional analytical information, including detail on sector and maturity, on components of the balance of payments—such as portfolio investment, direct investment, and income—will also form part of the new presentation of the international accounts. As examples of detail tables, table 8.5 provides information on portfolio investment

8. Short-term securities are those with an original maturity of one year or less.
9. For more information, see Landefeld and Lawson (1991)

Table 8.5   Portfolio investment (billions of dollars)

Line		2006	2007	2008	2009	2010	2011
	Assets and liabilities by instrument						
A1	**Net acquisition of portfolio investment assets (table 1, line 81)**	**493.7**	**379.7**	**−285.7**	**375.1**	**174.9**	**83.0**
2	Equity and investment fund shares	137.3	147.8	−38.5	63.7	79.1	89.0
3	*Of which: Investment fund shares*	n/a	n/a	n/a	n/a	n/a	10.7
4	Debt securities	356.4	231.9	−247.2	311.4	95.8	−6.1
5	Short term[a]	116.1	14.6	−84.0	135.5	44.4	−60.4
6	Negotiable certificates of deposit	66.3	−3.1	−29.9	62.2	−20.7	−32.0
7	Commercial paper	18.9	−1.7	−12.9	64.8	17.1	−22.0
8	Other short-term securities	30.9	19.4	−41.3	8.6	48.0	−6.4
9	Long term[a]	240.3	217.3	−163.2	175.9	51.4	54.3
10	*Of which: Negotiable certificates of deposit*	12.5	−1.4	−4.4	12.6	−8.5	−3.4
11	**Net incurrence of portfolio investment liabilities (table 1, line 110)**	**1,126.7**	**1,156.6**	**523.7**	**357.4**	**808.9**	**336.6**
12	Equity and investment fund shares	145.5	275.6	126.8	219.3	177.6	27.4
13	*Of which: Investment fund shares*	n/a	n/a	n/a	n/a	n/a	5.5
14	Debt securities	981.3	881.0	396.9	138.1	631.3	309.3
15	Short term[a]	25.4	166.6	297.3	−122.5	−60.3	−81.6
16	Treasury securities	−11.4	49.4	455.3	−7.6	−40.2	−62.0
17	Federally sponsored agency securities	−22.9	87.4	−98.8	−49.2	−9.7	−11.7
18	Negotiable certificates of deposit	10.3	28.7	3.5	−17.3	−4.3	−7.6
19	Other securities, including commercial paper	49.3	1.1	−62.7	−48.4	−6.1	−0.2
20	Long term[a]	955.9	714.4	99.6	260.5	691.6	390.9
21	Treasury securities	161.7	115.9	256.3	562.0	780.0	474.1
22	Federally sponsored agency securities	245.6	162.7	−129.9	−176.8	−62.6	−12.4
23	Negotiable certificates of deposit	2.2	0.5	−10.9	−5.1	−1.9	−1.0
24	Corporate securities	546.3	435.3	−16.0	−119.6	−23.9	−68.4
25	State and local government securities	n/a	n/a	n/a	n/a	n/a	−1.4

(continued)

Table 8.5 (continued)

Line		2006	2007	2008	2009	2010	2011
	Assets by sector of US holder						
B1	**Net acquisition of portfolio investment assets (table 1, line 81)**	**493.7**	**379.7**	**−285.7**	**375.1**	**174.9**	**83.0**
2	**Deposit-taking institutions, except central bank**	**n/a**	**n/a**	**n/a**	**n/a**	**n/a**	**3.3**
3	Equity and investment fund shares	n/a	n/a	n/a	n/a	n/a	1.8
4	Debt securities	n/a	n/a	n/a	n/a	n/a	1.5
5	Short term[a]	3.2	30.0	−28.5	−1.5	4.2	−0.2
6	Long term[a]	n/a	n/a	n/a	n/a	n/a	1.8
7	**Other financial institutions**	**n/a**	**n/a**	**n/a**	**n/a.**	**n/a**	**60.9**
8	Equity and investment fund shares	n/a	n/a	n/a	n/a.	n/a	75.7
9	Debt securities	n/a	n/a	n/a	n/a	n/a	−14.8
10	Short term[a]	104.1	−13.9	−55.5	133.7	37.7	−57.0
11	Long term[a]	n/a	n/a	n/a	n/a	n/a	42.2
12	**Nonfinancial institutions, except general government**	**n/a**	**n/a**	**n/a**	**n/a**	**n/a**	**18.8**
13	Equity and investment fund shares	n/a	n/a	n/a	n/a	n/a	11.6
14	Debt securities	n/a	n/a	n/a	n/a	n/a	7.2
15	Short term[a]	n/a	n/a	n/a	n/a	n/a	−3.2
16	Long term[a]	n/a	n/a	n/a	n/a	n/a	10.4
	Liabilities by sector of US issuer						
17	**Net incurrence of portfolio investment liabilities (table 1, line 110)**	**1,126.7**	**1,156.6**	**523.7**	**357.4**	**808.9**	**336.6**
18	**Deposit-taking institutions, except central bank**	**n/a**	**n/a**	**n/a**	**n/a**	**n/a**	**−15.5**
19	Equity and investment fund shares	n/a	n/a	n/a	n/a	n/a	1.1
20	Debt securities	n/a	n/a	n/a	n/a	n/a	−16.6
21	Short term[a]	26.9	44.3	−19.8	−16.5	−21.2	−6.7
22	Long term[a]	n/a	n/a	n/a	n/a	n/a	−9.9

#							
23	**Other financial institutions**	n/a	n/a	n/a	n/a	n/a	**20.8**
24	Equity and investment fund shares	n/a	n/a	n/a	n/a	n/a	6.8
25	Debt securities	n/a	n/a	n/a	n/a	n/a	13.9
26	Federally sponsored agencies	222.7	250.1	-228.6	-226.0	-72.3	-24.2
27	Short term[a]	-22.9	87.4	-98.8	-49.2	-9.7	-11.7
28	Long term[a]	245.6	162.7	-129.9	-176.8	-62.6	-12.4
29	Other	n/a	n/a	n/a	n/a	n/a	38.1
30	Short term[a]	37.6	-11.6	-27.8	-21.5	7.8	60.0
31	Long term[a]	n/a	n/a	n/a	n/a	n/a	-21.9
32	**Nonfinancial institutions, except general government**	n/a	n/a	n/a	n/a	n/a	**-79.3**
33	Equity and investment fund shares	n/a	n/a	n/a	n/a	n/a	19.4
34	Debt securities	n/a	n/a	n/a	n/a	n/a	-98.7
35	Short term[a]	-4.9	-2.8	-11.7	-27.7	3.0	-61.1
36	Long term[a]	n/a	n/a	n/a	n/a	n/a	-37.6
37	**General government**	**150.3**	**165.3**	**711.6**	**554.4**	**739.8**	**410.7**
38	Debt securities	150.3	165.3	711.6	554.4	739.8	410.7
39	Short term[a]	-11.4	49.4	455.3	-7.6	-40.2	-62.0
40	Long term[a]	161.7	115.9	256.3	562.0	780.0	472.7

Note: n/a = data are not available for these transactions prior to 2011.

[a]Short-term debt securities are those with an original maturity of one year or less. Long-term debt securities are those with an original maturity of greater than one year.

transactions, and table 8.6 provides information on primary income transactions.

Table 8.5 provides a good illustration of the benefits of the new symmetrical presentation of assets and liabilities. Statistics on portfolio investment are presented by instrument in section A of the table, with total equity and short-term and long-term debt transactions and positions separately identified. The new presentation allows users to observe total foreign portfolio investment in US securities in a single table; transactions of foreign official and private foreign investors are combined. A comprehensive view of short-term debt, which was previously commingled with other banking instruments in the US international accounts, is important for understanding the investment activity leading up to and during the financial crisis.

Table 8.5 shows that foreign demand for long-term US securities, especially corporate debt, was very strong in 2006 and 2007, partly as a result of the sale of securitized US mortgages and other assets to foreigners. Residents of the United States also purchased significant amounts of long-term foreign debt and equity.

The intensification of the financial crisis in 2008 brought about significant changes in patterns of cross-border portfolio investment. Investors in the United States moved out of foreign securities as reflected in a shift from net purchases to net sales. Foreign investors moved out of most types of corporate and agency debt and purchased short- and long-term US Treasury debt in record amounts (table 8.5, lines A16 and A21).

In 2009 and 2010, US demand for foreign securities recovered, although it was tempered in 2010 by the rise of the debt crisis in Europe. The continuing concerns over European sovereign debt have kept foreign demand of US Treasury securities strong and net foreign sales of US corporate and agency debt have continued.

Table 8.6 provides additional information on primary income flows between US and foreign residents, including investment income and compensation of employees. Investment income is classified similarly to financial account transactions and positions; that is, according to the same functional categories (direct investment, portfolio investment, other investment, and reserve assets) and then by the type of income (income on equity and interest income). This parallel presentation of income in the BOP and positions in the IIP facilitates the calculation of rates of return by type of instrument.

8.3   Evaluating Rates of Return on Cross-Border Investment

To demonstrate the usefulness of the additional detail and the parallel presentations planned for income and positions in the BOP and IIP, we are introducing previously unpublished data in this chapter, providing a new perspective on the differentials in rates of return on US investment abroad and foreign investment in the United States from 1990 to 2005.

Table 8.6   Primary income (billions of dollars)

Line		2006	2007	2008	2009	2010	2011
1	**Primary income receipts (table 1, line 26)**	**693.0**	**843.9**	**823.5**	**609.2**	**683.4**	**751.3**
2	Investment income	688.0	838.8	818.3	603.7	677.8	745.5
3	Direct investment	333.2	380.8	423.4	365.4	451.2	486.9
4	Income on equity and investment fund shares	319.0	363.4	405.5	351.6	438.5	473.3
5	Dividends and withdrawals	101.7	132.8	172.4	122.3	123.2	124.6
6	Reinvested earnings	217.3	230.5	233.1	229.3	315.3	348.6
7	Interest	14.2	17.5	17.8	13.8	12.7	13.6
8	US parents' receipts from their foreign affiliates	9.6	11.3	12.2	9.3	8.4	9.3
9	US affiliates' receipts from their foreign parent groups	4.6	6.2	5.6	4.4	4.3	4.3
10	Portfolio investment	166.1	221.6	241.3	184.4	190.3	219.6
11	Income on equity and investment fund shares	84.3	116.1	143.9	108.6	111.8	137.3
12	Dividends on equity excluding investment funds shares	n/a	n/a	n/a	n/a	n/a	120.8
13	Income attributable to investment fund shareholders	n/a	n/a	n/a	n/a	n/a	16.5
14	Interest	81.8	105.5	97.4	75.8	78.4	82.3
15	Short term[a]	17.9	22.7	12.5	3.3	1.9	1.6
16	Long term[a]	63.9	82.8	85.0	72.6	76.5	80.7
17	Other investment	187.5	235.0	152.1	53.2	35.6	38.1
18	Interest[b]	180.5	226.7	141.8	42.8	27.0	29.5
19	Income attributable to policyholders in insurance, pension schemes, and standardized guarantee schemes[c]	6.9	8.3	10.4	10.3	8.6	8.6
20	Reserve assets	1.2	1.4	1.5	0.8	0.7	0.8
21	Income on equity and investment fund shares	0.0	0.0	0.0	0.0	0.0	0.0
22	Interest[b]	1.2	1.4	1.5	0.8	0.7	0.8
23	Compensation of employees	5.0	5.1	5.2	5.5	5.6	5.8
24	Other primary income	n/a	n/a	n/a	n/a	n/a	n/a

(continued)

Table 8.6 (continued)

Line		2006	2007	2008	2009	2010	2011
25	**Primary income payments (table 1, line 59)**	**648.9**	**742.4**	**676.4**	**489.5**	**499.5**	**524.3**
26	Investment income	633.3	727.7	660.5	476.1	486.7	510.5
27	Direct investment	159.2	136.3	139.1	112.4	153.3	165.2
28	Income on equity and investment fund shares	132.3	101.8	104.9	80.9	122.7	132.9
29	Dividends and withdrawals	63.2	53.6	65.7	59.3	55.1	45.5
30	Reinvested earnings	69.1	48.2	39.1	21.7	67.5	87.4
31	Interest	26.8	34.5	34.2	31.5	30.6	32.3
32	US affiliates' payments to their foreign parent groups	23.0	30.6	30.2	28.3	27.8	30.0
33	US parents' payments to their foreign affiliates	3.8	3.9	4.0	3.1	2.8	2.3
34	Portfolio investment	304.9	381.8	400.0	332.5	313.5	324.5
35	Income on equity and investment fund shares	44.9	54.9	70.1	59.7	60.0	73.3
36	Dividends on equity excluding investment funds shares	n/a	n/a	n/a	n/a	n/a	58.6
37	Income attributable to investment fund shareholders	n/a	n/a	n/a	n/a	n/a	14.7
38	Interest	260.1	326.9	329.9	272.8	253.5	251.2
39	Short term[a]	28.9	34.1	22.2	5.9	2.1	1.3
40	Long term[a]	231.2	292.7	307.7	266.9	251.3	249.9
41	Other investment	169.2	209.7	121.4	31.3	20.0	20.8
42	Interest[b]	167.1	207.7	119.2	29.1	18.0	18.6
43	Income attributable to policyholders in insurance, pension schemes, and standardized guarantee schemes[c]	2.1	2.0	2.2	2.2	2.0	2.2
44	Compensation of employees	15.5	14.7	15.9	13.3	12.8	13.8
45	Other primary income	n/a	n/a	n/a	n/a	n/a	n/a
46	**Balance on primary income (surplus [+] or deficit [−], table 1, line 128)**	**44.2**	**101.5**	**147.1**	**119.7**	**183.9**	**227.0**
	Memoranda:						
47	Other investment income receipts interest before FISIM	n/a	n/a	n/a	n/a	n/a	n/a
48	Other investment income payments interest before FISIM	n/a	n/a	n/a	n/a	n/a	n/a

Note: n/a = data are not currently available. FISIM = financial intermediation services indirectly measured.

[a] Short-term debt securities are those with an original maturity of one year or less. Long-term debt securities are those with an original maturity of greater than one year.

[b] Interest receipts and payments are not currently adjusted to exclude interest that represents charges for services. These charges are often referred to as implicit service fees or financial intermediation services indirectly measured. The BEA plans to develop estimates of the portion of interest that represents such charges and adjust the accounts to remove them from interest and include them in services.

[c] Statistics currently reflect only income attributable to insurance policyholders.

Research into differentials in rates of return between US investment abroad and foreign investment in the United States has led to a range of conclusions. Some researchers have found that the United States enjoys a significant advantage in investment returns. Based on an average of three earlier studies, Curcuru, Dvorak, and Warnock (2008) report a differential of around 3 percent more per year on US investment abroad compared to foreigners' investments in the United States. Based on their own estimates, Curcuru, Dvorak, and Warnock find that the differential for 1990–2005 for all types of investment was about 1.0 percent, mainly attributable to the differential in income yields on direct investment.[10] Curcuru and Thomas (chapter 7, this volume) find a slightly higher average differential of 1.4 percent for all types of investment over the period 1983–2010, which they attribute entirely to a 5.6 percentage point gap between returns on US direct investment abroad and foreign direct investment in the United States.

The calculation of rates of return for components of the US international investment position has been hindered by a lack of publicly available detail on revised valuation adjustments for the components. Although BEA publishes detailed time-series statistics of investment positions and related financial flows and investment income, BEA has not published detailed time-series statistics identifying changes in investment value (valuation changes) due to price changes, exchange rate changes, and other (statistical) changes for components of US-owned assets abroad or foreign-owned assets in the United States.[11] In this chapter, we draw on a previously unpublished series of revised valuation adjustments (table 8.7) to clarify the rates of return from capital gains implied by price and exchange rate changes for components of investment relative to annual investment positions.

Table 8.7 provides annual time series from 1989 to 2009 of investment positions, changes in investment positions due to price, exchange rate, and other changes, and income accrued on investment for inward and outward investment by four major components of investment. The major components are direct investment, portfolio investment in long-term debt securities, portfolio investment in equity securities, and all other investment in short-term securities, bank deposits, trade credits, and similar instruments.[12] Using these time series we compute estimates for the total rate of return, the rate of return from income accrued, and the rate of return from capital gains.

10. The BEA has addressed rates of return on direct investment in two articles in the *Survey of Current Business*: Landefeld, Lawson, and Weinberg (1992) and Mataloni (2000).

11. Since this chapter was first presented, the BEA has begun publishing revised time-series statistics disaggregating the year-over-year change in the IIP into financial flows, price changes, exchange-rate changes, and other changes beginning with the year 2003. Prior to the June 2012 release of the US IIP, this disaggregation was only published for the most recent year. See the link for "Changes in yearend positions" at http://www.bea.gov/international/index.htm#IIP.

12. In the new presentation, all income and IIP tables will be organized by common functional categories, providing a clearer and more precise relationship between income statistics and underlying position statistics.

Table 8.7   Cross-border investment and income, 1989–2009

A. US-owned assets abroad and total investment income receipts, positions exclude derivatives and include US direct investment abroad at market value (billions of dollars)

Year	Position beginning	Changes in position						Position ending	Total investment income receipts
		Attributable to							
			Valuation adjustments					
		Financial flows (a)	Price changes (b)	Exchange-rate changes (c)	Other changes (d)	Total (a + b + c + d)			
1988		—	—	—	—	—		2,008.4	160.3
1989	2,008.4	175.4	144.6	-16.3	38.2	341.9		2,350.2	170.6
1990	2,350.2	81.2	-221.1	67.3	16.4	-56.2		2,294.1	147.9
1991	2,294.1	64.4	82.9	2.1	27.1	176.5		2,470.6	132.0
1992	2,470.6	74.4	-29.0	-82.8	33.2	-4.1		2,466.5	134.2
1993	2,466.5	200.6	355.3	-29.1	98.2	624.9		3,091.4	164.6
1994	3,091.4	178.9	-86.5	85.5	45.8	223.7		3,315.1	208.1
1995	3,315.1	352.3	229.5	50.9	16.7	649.4		3,964.6	223.9
1996	3,964.6	413.4	315.8	-74.6	31.7	686.3		4,650.8	254.5
1997	4,650.8	485.5	456.2	-233.7	20.4	728.3		5,379.1	259.4
1998	5,379.1	353.8	368.9	79.2	-1.9	800.0		6,179.1	291.2
1999	6,179.1	504.1	802.1	-130.1	44.5	1,220.6		7,399.7	348.1
2000	7,399.7	560.5	-305.4	-298.3	44.6	1.5		7,401.2	287.9
2001	7,401.2	382.6	-714.1	-168.7	29.4	-470.7		6,930.5	278.1
2002	6,930.5	294.6	-848.8	266.0	162.4	-125.9		6,804.6	317.6
2003	6,804.6	325.4	767.5	483.6	-68.4	1,508.1		8,312.7	410.9
2004	8,312.7	1,000.9	468.7	309.0	113.6	1,892.2		10,204.9	532.4
2005	10,204.9	546.6	1,079.2	-441.7	368.7	1,552.9		11,757.8	679.3
2006	11,757.8	1,285.7	1,111.6	412.5	143.6	2,953.5		14,711.3	826.6
2007	14,711.3	1,475.7	559.4	719.6	36.6	2,791.3		17,502.6	793.5
2008	17,502.6	-156.1	-4,341.0	-788.6	261.4	-5,024.3		12,478.3	585.3
2009	12,478.3	140.5	1,815.4	473.1	211.5	2,640.4		15,118.7	

B. US direct investment abroad at market value and direct investment income receipts (billions of dollars)

				Changes in position					
				Attributable to					
				Valuation adjustments					
Year	Position beginning	Financial flows (a)	Price changes (b)	Exchange-rate changes (c)	Other changes (d)	Total (a + b + c + d)	Position ending	Direct investment income receipts
1988	—	—	—	—	—	—	692.5	62.0
1989	692.5	43.4	113.9	−14.6	−2.7	140.0	832.5	66.0
1990	832.5	37.2	−169.3	38.2	−6.7	−100.7	731.8	58.7
1991	731.8	37.9	63.3	−2.8	−2.7	95.8	827.5	57.5
1992	827.5	48.3	−26.3	−46.6	−4.3	−28.9	798.6	67.2
1993	798.6	84.0	205.3	−18.8	−7.8	262.7	1,061.3	77.3
1994	1,061.3	80.2	−46.6	40.4	−20.6	53.3	1,114.6	95.3
1995	1,114.6	98.8	131.1	28.7	−9.3	249.2	1,363.8	102.5
1996	1,363.8	91.9	186.6	−29.7	−4.2	244.5	1,608.3	115.3
1997	1,608.3	104.8	265.4	−97.5	−1.7	270.9	1,879.3	104.0
1998	1,879.3	142.6	225.8	39.1	−7.2	400.3	2,279.6	131.6
1999	2,279.6	224.9	452.3	−110.7	−6.5	560.0	2,839.6	151.8
2000	2,839.6	159.2	−203.9	−95.8	−5.1	−145.6	2,694.0	128.7
2001	2,694.0	142.3	−441.7	−57.0	−22.7	−379.1	2,314.9	145.6
2002	2,314.9	154.5	−525.6	107.9	−29.1	−292.3	2,022.6	186.4
2003	2,022.6	149.6	362.7	200.1	−5.8	706.5	2,729.1	250.6
2004	2,729.1	316.2	215.8	117.2	−15.6	633.7	3,362.8	294.5
2005	3,362.8	36.2	435.6	−203.7	7.1	275.2	3,638.0	324.8
2006	3,638.0	244.9	401.7	183.3	2.4	832.3	4,470.3	370.7
2007	4,470.3	414.0	112.6	267.6	10.5	804.6	5,275.0	403.2
2008	5,275.0	351.1	−2,265.1	−204.4	−53.0	−2,171.3	3,103.7	346.1
2009	3,103.7	268.7	737.1	194.2	−0.8	1,199.1	4,302.9	

(continued)

Table 8.7 (continued)

C. US portfolio investment in foreign long-term debt and associated interest receipts (billions of dollars)

Year	Position beginning	Financial flows (a)	Price changes (b)	Exchange-rate changes (c)	Other changes (d)	Total (a + b + c + d)	Position ending	Interest receipts
1988	—	—	—	—	—	—	104.2	10.3
1989	104.2	4.9	2.9	(*)	5.1	12.8	116.9	12.0
1990	116.9	21.4	-1.4	2.5	5.3	27.8	144.7	15.1
1991	144.7	15.0	7.3	-0.6	10.4	32.1	176.8	17.4
1992	176.8	16.8	4.2	-7.0	10.0	24.0	200.8	20.6
1993	200.8	82.9	8.5	-1.8	19.2	108.8	309.7	23.9
1994	309.7	14.9	-27.0	7.4	5.4	0.7	310.4	24.6
1995	310.4	56.9	34.3	3.1	8.6	102.9	413.3	28.2
1996	413.3	66.6	-3.0	-6.2	10.7	68.1	481.4	31.1
1997	481.4	59.6	8.1	-19.5	13.9	62.0	543.4	35.5
1998	543.4	28.8	17.3	4.3	0.6	51.0	594.4	37.5
1999	594.4	7.9	-53.4	-1.1	0.3	-46.2	548.2	37.9
2000	548.2	21.2	18.7	-15.8	0.4	24.5	572.7	34.5
2001	572.7	-18.5	11.6	-9.3	0.5	-15.6	557.1	40.9
2002	557.1	31.6	28.4	13.2	72.4	145.7	702.7	46.5
2003	702.7	28.7	5.4	35.8	96.3	166.2	868.9	50.5
2004	868.9	85.8	-1.0	20.9	10.3	116.0	985.0	55.4
2005	985.0	64.5	-22.5	-19.4	4.0	26.6	1,011.6	63.9
2006	1,011.6	227.8	-10.7	13.5	33.3	264.0	1,275.5	82.7
2007	1,275.5	218.7	8.1	27.9	56.8	311.6	1,587.1	84.9
2008	1,587.1	-158.9	-123.0	-51.0	-16.9	-349.8	1,237.3	75.4
2009	1,237.3	144.9	84.1	27.3	0.0	256.3	1,493.6	

D. US portfolio investment in foreign equity and associated dividend receipts (billions of dollars)

Year	Position beginning	Financial flows (a)	Price changes (b)	Exchange-rate changes (c)	Other changes (d)	Total (a + b + c + d)	Position ending	Dividend receipts
				Changes in position				
			Attributable to					
			Valuation adjustments					
1988	—	—	—	—	—	—	128.7	4.5
1989	128.7	17.2	30.1	-2.5	23.9	68.7	197.3	6.9
1990	197.3	7.4	-47.6	16.8	23.6	0.3	197.6	7.3
1991	197.6	30.7	22.1	4.1	24.5	81.4	279.0	10.1
1992	279.0	32.4	-1.6	-24.7	29.2	35.3	314.3	10.5
1993	314.3	63.4	126.1	-8.7	48.9	229.6	543.9	10.5
1994	543.9	48.3	-10.5	25.0	20.1	82.9	626.8	15.5
1995	626.8	65.5	62.9	15.7	19.8	163.9	790.6	19.5
1996	790.6	82.7	136.7	-29.6	25.6	215.5	1,006.1	23.3
1997	1,006.1	57.3	203.4	-100.5	41.5	201.7	1,207.8	24.6
1998	1,207.8	101.4	126.4	23.7	15.8	267.2	1,475.0	26.5
1999	1,475.0	114.3	402.5	-8.0	19.9	528.7	2,003.7	30.1
2000	2,003.7	106.7	-116.0	-172.3	30.7	-150.9	1,852.8	33.5
2001	1,852.8	109.1	-284.5	-88.9	24.2	-240.2	1,612.7	34.2
2002	1,612.7	17.0	-370.1	114.5	0.0	-238.7	1,374.0	38.2
2003	1,374.0	118.0	381.3	206.1	0.0	705.4	2,079.4	41.6
2004	2,079.4	84.8	248.9	147.4	0.0	481.0	2,560.4	54.1
2005	2,560.4	186.7	645.8	-177.4	102.2	757.3	3,317.7	64.6
2006	3,317.7	137.3	689.5	184.5	0.0	1,011.3	4,329.0	84.3
2007	4,329.0	147.8	386.0	385.3	0.0	919.0	5,248.0	116.1
2008	5,248.0	-39.0	-1,962.4	-498.2	0.0	-2,499.6	2,748.4	143.9
2009	2,748.4	63.3	937.3	228.4	0.0	1,229.0	3,977.4	107.4

(continued)

Table 8.7 (continued)

E. All other US investment abroad and associated interest receipts[a] (billions of dollars)

Year	Position beginning	Changes in position — Attributable to — Financial flows (a)	Valuation adjustments — Price changes (b)	Valuation adjustments — Exchange-rate changes (c)	Other changes (d)	Total (a + b + c + d)	Position ending	Interest receipts
1988	—	—	—	—	—	—	1,083.1	—
1989	1,083.1	109.9	-2.3	0.9	11.9	120.4	1,203.5	83.5
1990	1,203.5	15.3	-2.8	9.8	-5.8	16.5	1,220.0	85.6
1991	1,220.0	-19.2	-9.8	1.4	-5.0	-32.7	1,187.3	66.8
1992	1,187.3	-23.0	-5.4	-4.6	-1.6	-34.6	1,152.8	46.9
1993	1,152.8	-29.7	15.4	0.2	37.9	23.8	1,176.6	35.9
1994	1,176.6	35.6	-2.4	12.7	40.9	86.8	1,263.4	47.9
1995	1,263.4	131.1	1.2	3.5	-2.3	133.4	1,396.8	68.7
1996	1,396.8	172.2	-4.6	-9.1	-0.5	158.1	1,555.0	70.0
1997	1,555.0	263.8	-20.8	-16.1	-33.2	193.7	1,748.7	83.5
1998	1,748.7	81.0	-0.6	12.1	-11.0	81.5	1,830.1	93.4
1999	1,830.1	156.9	0.6	-10.3	30.8	177.9	2,008.1	92.0
2000	2,008.1	273.4	-4.1	-14.3	18.6	273.6	2,281.6	124.8
2001	2,281.6	149.6	0.5	-13.5	27.5	164.2	2,445.8	90.5
2002	2,445.8	91.6	18.5	30.4	119.0	259.5	2,705.3	53.4
2003	2,705.3	29.1	18.1	41.7	-158.9	-70.1	2,635.3	43.2
2004	2,635.3	514.1	5.1	23.5	118.8	661.5	3,296.7	55.8
2005	3,296.7	259.2	20.2	-41.1	255.5	493.8	3,790.5	117.8
2006	3,790.5	675.7	31.1	31.2	107.9	846.0	4,636.5	206.3
2007	4,636.5	695.2	52.8	38.7	-30.7	756.1	5,392.6	257.1
2008	5,392.6	-309.3	9.4	-35.0	331.3	-3.7	5,388.9	161.4
2009	5,388.9	-336.4	56.9	23.1	212.4	-44.0	5,344.9	56.4

F. Foreign-owned assets in the United States and total investment income payments. positions exclude derivatives and include foreign direct investment in the United States at market value (billions of dollars)

		Changes in position						
		Attributable to						
			Valuation adjustments					
Year	Position beginning	Financial flows (a)	Price changes (b)	Exchange- rate changes (c)	Other changes (d)	Total (a + b + c + d)	Position ending	Total investment income payments
1988	—	—	—	—	—	—	1,986.9	139.2
1989	1,986.9	222.8	137.4	-1.0	37.9	397.1	2,383.9	139.7
1990	2,383.9	139.4	-72.5	10.8	-18.0	59.7	2,443.6	121.1
1991	2,443.6	108.2	178.7	-2.5	-14.1	270.3	2,713.9	104.8
1992	2,713.9	168.3	46.6	-8.1	-22.2	184.7	2,898.6	105.6
1993	2,898.6	279.8	62.6	-7.2	-20.6	314.6	3,213.2	143.4
1994	3,213.2	303.2	-109.7	12.9	5.9	212.3	3,425.4	183.1
1995	3,425.4	435.1	382.0	12.1	-12.5	816.7	4,242.1	197.5
1996	4,242.1	547.9	231.6	-8.7	-33.7	737.0	4,979.1	237.5
1997	4,979.1	704.5	548.2	-26.5	-37.9	1,188.2	6,167.4	250.6
1998	6,167.4	420.8	656.7	11.3	-43.3	1,045.5	7,212.9	272.1
1999	7,212.9	742.2	472.4	-4.3	-21.3	1,189.0	8,401.9	322.3
2000	8,401.9	1,038.2	-439.1	-28.0	-35.0	536.1	8,938.0	251.0
2001	8,938.0	782.9	-489.9	-17.2	11.8	287.5	9,225.5	245.2
2002	9,225.5	795.2	-783.6	35.2	-56.8	-10.0	9,215.6	266.6
2003	9,215.6	858.3	775.4	68.8	-312.3	1,390.2	10,605.8	337.6
2004	10,605.8	1,533.2	278.5	39.5	111.4	1,962.6	12,568.3	453.6
2005	12,568.3	1,247.3	-66.8	-50.6	-24.7	1,105.3	13,673.6	624.6
2006	13,673.6	2,065.2	529.1	44.4	267.4	2,906.0	16,579.6	720.0
2007	16,579.6	2,107.7	243.2	81.0	-57.4	2,374.4	18,954.1	634.2
2008	18,954.1	454.7	-2,516.1	-91.8	1.3	-2,151.9	16,802.2	456.0
2009	16,802.2	305.7	971.6	77.7	23.5	1,378.5	18,180.7	

(continued)

Table 8.7   (continued)

G. Foreign direct investment in the United States at market value and direct investment income payments (billions of dollars)

Year	Position beginning	Changes in position Attributable to Financial flows (a)	Valuation adjustments Price changes (b)	Valuation adjustments Exchange-rate changes (c)	Other changes (d)	Total (a + b + c + d)	Position ending	Direct investment income payments
1988	—	—	—	—	—	—	391.5	7.0
1989	391.5	68.3	72.0	0.0	3.0	143.2	534.7	3.5
1990	534.7	48.5	-40.6	0.0	-3.0	4.9	539.6	-2.3
1991	539.6	23.2	108.4	0.0	-2.0	129.5	669.1	2.2
1992	669.1	19.8	15.8	0.0	-8.6	27.0	696.2	2.2
1993	696.2	51.4	28.6	0.0	-7.7	72.2	768.4	7.9
1994	768.4	46.1	-28.7	0.0	-28.0	-10.5	757.9	22.2
1995	757.9	57.8	187.8	0.0	2.3	247.9	1,005.7	30.3
1996	1,005.7	86.5	144.9	0.0	-8.0	223.4	1,229.1	33.1
1997	1,229.1	105.6	303.8	0.0	-1.1	408.3	1,637.4	43.0
1998	1,637.4	179.0	368.3	0.0	-5.7	541.6	2,179.0	38.4
1999	2,179.0	289.4	345.0	0.0	-15.3	619.2	2,798.2	53.4
2000	2,798.2	321.3	-328.7	0.0	-7.6	-15.0	2,783.2	56.9
2001	2,783.2	167.0	-338.7	0.0	-51.3	-222.9	2,560.3	12.8
2002	2,560.3	84.4	-527.6	0.0	-95.3	-538.5	2,021.8	43.2
2003	2,021.8	63.8	381.7	0.0	-12.4	433.1	2,454.9	73.8
2004	2,454.9	146.0	117.6	0.0	-1.1	262.5	2,717.4	99.8
2005	2,717.4	112.6	-22.8	0.0	10.7	100.6	2,818.0	121.3
2006	2,818.0	243.2	227.1	0.0	4.9	475.1	3,293.1	150.8
2007	3,293.1	271.2	22.7	0.0	10.0	303.8	3,596.9	129.1
2008	3,596.9	328.3	-1,207.2	0.0	-165.4	-1,044.3	2,552.6	115.5
2009	2,552.6	134.7	422.7	0.0	10.6	568.0	3,120.6	94.0

H. Foreign portfolio investment in US Long-term debt and associated interest payments (billions of dollars)

Year	Position beginning	Financial flows (a)	Price changes (b)	Exchange-rate changes (c)	Other changes (d)	Total (a + b + c + d)	Position ending	Interest payments
1988	—	—	—	—	—	—	439.6	—
1989	439.6	86.7	9.3	-1.4	37.8	132.5	572.1	54.8
1990	572.1	38.0	-15.5	9.0	-14.8	16.6	588.7	53.9
1991	588.7	47.1	25.5	-2.3	-10.9	59.5	648.1	54.7
1992	648.1	77.6	-4.9	-5.9	-12.9	53.9	702.0	52.9
1993	702.0	90.1	10.4	-6.6	-10.7	83.2	785.3	40.6
1994	785.3	138.5	-71.7	8.8	-8.0	67.6	852.9	59.7
1995	852.9	193.8	58.9	11.9	-15.7	249.0	1,101.9	66.9
1996	1,101.9	321.7	-25.1	-5.3	-18.3	273.0	1,374.9	79.5
1997	1,374.9	266.1	30.9	-17.2	-33.4	246.5	1,621.4	98.7
1998	1,621.4	145.6	32.9	3.0	-38.0	143.5	1,764.8	105.6
1999	1,764.8	173.3	-121.4	-1.5	-29.3	21.0	1,785.9	112.3
2000	1,785.9	243.0	62.4	-20.8	-28.8	255.7	2,041.6	126.0
2001	2,041.6	306.9	54.7	-9.5	1.4	353.5	2,395.0	125.7
2002	2,395.0	373.5	79.3	18.7	-140.8	330.8	2,725.8	126.1
2003	2,725.8	486.3	-13.0	45.6	-79.9	438.9	3,164.7	131.5
2004	3,164.7	705.0	-21.7	27.4	-40.1	670.7	3,835.4	150.4
2005	3,835.4	785.8	-112.0	-29.4	-58.0	586.4	4,421.8	181.5
2006	4,421.8	953.7	-28.7	25.4	32.7	983.1	5,404.9	230.0
2007	5,404.9	713.9	90.0	53.0	7.6	864.5	6,269.4	291.1
2008	6,269.4	110.0	-46.1	-67.0	-36.7	-40.0	6,229.4	307.2
2009	6,229.4	325.0	11.8	56.3	-8.5	384.6	6,614.0	266.3

(continued)

Table 8.7 (continued)

I. Foreign portfolio investment in US equity and associated dividend payments (billions of dollars)

Year	Position beginning	Changes in position						Position ending	Dividend payments
		Attributable to							
			Valuation adjustments						
		Financial flows (a)	Price changes (b)	Exchange-rate changes (c)	Other changes (d)		Total (a + b + c + d)		
1988	—	—	—	—	—		—	213.8	8.3
1989	213.8	9.0	56.2	0.0	−2.9		62.3	276.1	9.3
1990	276.1	−16.0	−16.4	0.0	0.0		−32.3	243.8	9.5
1991	243.8	10.4	44.8	0.0	0.0		55.2	299.0	9.6
1992	299.0	−5.6	35.6	0.0	0.0		30.0	329.0	10.0
1993	329.0	20.9	23.6	0.0	0.0		44.5	373.5	11.2
1994	373.5	0.9	−9.4	0.0	32.7		24.2	397.7	12.0
1995	397.7	16.5	135.3	0.0	0.0		151.8	549.5	13.2
1996	549.5	11.1	111.8	0.0	0.0		122.9	672.4	14.0
1997	672.4	67.0	213.5	0.0	0.0		280.5	952.9	15.8
1998	952.9	42.0	255.5	0.0	(*)		297.4	1,250.3	17.1
1999	1,250.3	112.3	248.9	0.0	0.0		361.2	1,611.5	19.6
2000	1,611.5	193.6	−172.8	0.0	10.9		31.7	1,643.2	21.1
2001	1,643.2	121.5	−205.8	0.0	13.9		−70.5	1,572.7	23.6
2002	1,572.7	54.1	−335.3	0.0	44.3		−236.9	1,335.8	25.7
2003	1,335.8	34.0	406.7	0.0	63.0		503.7	1,839.5	37.0
2004	1,839.5	61.8	182.6	0.0	39.4		283.7	2,123.3	38.1
2005	2,123.3	89.3	68.0	0.0	23.5		180.8	2,304.0	44.9
2006	2,304.0	145.5	330.7	0.0	11.7		487.9	2,791.9	54.9
2007	2,791.9	275.6	130.5	0.0	33.6		439.8	3,231.7	70.1
2008	3,231.7	126.4	−1,262.7	0.0	37.2		−1,099.1	2,132.6	59.3
2009	2,132.6	160.5	537.1	0.0	0.0		697.6	2,830.2	

J. All other foreign investment in the United States and associated interest payments[a] (billions of dollars)

				Changes in position				
				Attributable to				
				Valuation adjustments				
Year	Position beginning	Financial flows (a)	Price changes (b)	Exchange-rate changes (c)	Other changes (d)	Total (a + b + c + d)	Position ending	Interest payments
1988	—	—	—	—	—	—	941.9	—
1989	941.9	58.8	0.0	0.3	(*)	59.1	1,001.0	69.0
1990	1,001.0	68.8	0.0	1.8	-0.1	70.5	1,071.5	73.0
1991	1,071.5	27.5	0.0	-0.1	-1.2	26.2	1,097.7	59.1
1992	1,097.7	76.5	0.0	-2.2	-0.6	73.7	1,171.4	40.1
1993	1,171.4	117.4	0.0	-0.6	-2.3	114.6	1,286.0	47.1
1994	1,286.0	117.7	0.0	4.1	9.2	131.0	1,417.0	50.4
1995	1,417.0	167.0	0.0	0.1	0.9	168.0	1,585.0	73.9
1996	1,585.0	128.6	0.0	-3.5	-7.4	117.7	1,702.8	71.7
1997	1,702.8	265.7	0.0	-9.3	-3.5	253.0	1,955.7	81.9
1998	1,955.7	54.2	0.0	8.4	0.4	63.0	2,018.7	90.8
1999	2,018.7	167.2	0.0	-2.8	23.3	187.7	2,206.4	89.3
2000	2,206.4	280.4	0.0	-7.2	-9.5	263.6	2,470.0	119.8
2001	2,470.0	187.5	0.0	-7.8	47.8	227.5	2,697.5	91.3
2002	2,697.5	283.2	0.0	16.6	134.9	434.6	3,132.1	52.3
2003	3,132.1	274.2	0.0	23.2	-283.0	14.5	3,146.6	35.7
2004	3,146.6	620.4	0.0	12.1	113.1	745.6	3,892.3	50.3
2005	3,892.3	259.7	0.0	-21.2	-1.0	237.5	4,129.8	112.7
2006	4,129.8	722.8	0.0	19.0	218.2	960.0	5,089.8	199.0
2007	5,089.8	847.0	0.0	28.1	-108.6	766.4	5,856.2	244.8
2008	5,856.2	-110.0	0.0	-24.8	166.2	31.4	5,887.6	141.4
2009	5,887.6	-314.5	0.0	21.4	21.4	-271.7	5,615.9	36.4

[a]All other investment includes short-term portfolio investment, other investment, and (for US assets) US reserve assets; derivatives are not included.
*Transactions are less than + or – $500 million.

The calculation of capital gains explains much of the difference in results of different studies of rates of return. The computation methodology for computing rates of return (the total rate of return and its two components, income return and capital gains return) is summarized in the following equations:

(1) $RTOT_t = (INC_t + PRCHG_t + XRTCHG_t)/AVGPOS_t$,

(2) $RINC_t = (INC_t)/AVGPOS_t$,

(3) $RKG_t = (PRCHG_t + XRTCHG_t)/AVGPOS_t$,

where $RTOT_t$ is the total rate of return for year t; $RINC_t$ is the rate of return from income for year t; RKG_t is the rate of return from capital gains or losses for year t; INC_t is income for year t; $PRCHG_t$ is the change in the investment position caused by a change in price for year t; $XRTCHG_t$ is a change in the investment position caused by a change in exchange rates for year t; and $AVGPOS_t$ is the average investment position for year t, computed by taking the average of the investment position for year t and the investment position for year $t - 1$.

Price changes and exchange rate changes from table 8.7 are included in our measure of capital gains because these changes affect the value of assets held by investors in a given year. "Other changes" from table 8.7 are excluded because these changes in value do not accrue to investors over the year. They instead indicate that assets in a particular account were found to be larger or smaller at the end of the year for statistical reasons that do not reflect return to investors.

"Other changes" are changes in position that cannot be attributed to price changes, exchange rate changes, or financial flows. Often, "other changes" reflect changes in IIP positions from series breaks in the underlying data. For example, the introduction of new derivatives data caused "other changes" for US assets abroad and foreign assets in the United States to be very large in 2005. That "other changes" are statistical in nature and do not belong in measures of investment returns does not make them unimportant. "Other changes" have had a significant impact on the international investment position over time. Because any revision to positions automatically generate price and exchange rate changes in the methodologies used to compile the IIP, it is unlikely that significant price or exchange rate changes have been erroneously included in "other changes." It is far more likely that financial flows have been commingled with statistical changes in the "other changes" category. This has happened when surveys of positions caused revisions to position estimates, but surveys of transactions did not detect the transactions that caused the revisions to positions. The unexplained changes in positions could not be attributed to financial flows, price changes, or exchange rate changes and were classified as other changes.

Rates of return based on the table 8.7 time series are presented in table 8.8. The difference between total returns on US assets and total returns on US

Table 8.8   Rates of return on investment (1990–2005)

	Claims (%)	Liabilities (%)	Difference (%)
All asset classes			
Total return	7.6	6.1	1.5
Yield	5.0	3.8	1.2
Capital gains	2.6	2.3	0.3
Direct investment at market value			
Total return	10.2	6.8	3.4
Yield	6.9	2.1	4.8
Capital gains	3.2	4.7	−1.4
Long–term debt			
Total return	7.7	6.4	1.3
Yield	7.0	6.3	0.6
Capital gains	0.7	0.0	0.6
Equities			
Total return	8.5	10.3	−1.9
Yield	2.5	2.1	0.3
Capital gains	6.0	8.2	−2.2
Other assets			
Total return	4.3	3.9	0.4
Yield	4.2	3.9	0.3
Capital gains	0.1	0.0	0.1

liabilities is 1.5 percent as compared to 1.0 percent from Curcuru, Dvorak, and Warnock for the same time period (1990–2005). Most of the difference between our results and those of Curcuru, Dvorak, and Warnock is attributable to capital gains. This study's difference in capital gains is 0.3 percent, whereas Curcuru, Dvorak, and Warnock found a difference of zero. The total return differences reported in this chapter lie between those found by Curcuru, Dvorak, and Warnock and by those studies reported by Curcuru, Dvorak, and Warnock averaging 3 percent.

The largest of the total returns differentials between claims and liabilities is for direct investment at 3.4 percent, where the differential for income yields is partly offset by a negative differential for capital gains.[13] As noted also by

13. Direct investment at market value is used to derive the results in this chapter. The international standards for compiling the international investment position recommend the market value of direct investment as the preferred valuation. Positions for equity and debt securities are also presented at market value. The BEA publishes three valuations for direct investment (available at http://www.bea.gov/international/index.htm#iip). These three valuations are market value, current cost, and historic cost. Historic cost is also known as book value.

If the rates of return were recalculated using either current cost or historic cost, capital gains would be much lower because, unlike the market value, these valuations are not influenced much by equity prices, which tended to raise asset valuations from 1990 to 2005. Also, the differential for income yields on direct investment would still be large. A refinement of this study would utilize different measures of income from direct investment that would reflect different valuations of the direct investment positions when measuring income yields.

Curcuru and Thomas (chapter 7, this volume), total returns differentials for other investment categories show little evidence of a significant advantage for US investors. The differential for long-term debt is 1.3 percent, for equities it is –1.9 percent, and for other types of investment it is 0.4 percent.

8.4   Progress Report on Initiatives to Improve the International Accounts

Improved source data will be needed to make the new international accounts presentation as complete and accurate as possible. Some new source data have already become available and discussions are taking place to make changes to collection procedures for other source data. Several lines in the proposed tables discussed earlier are denoted "not available" (n/a) because the required source data are not currently available. In many cases, the transactions for those lines are included elsewhere in the accounts but we are not currently able to present the transactions separately. For instance, some financial flows related to insurance companies' liabilities to their customers are included indistinguishably with other changes in liabilities and cannot be reported under the new instrument category "insurance, pension, and standardized guarantee schemes." Howell and Westmoreland (2013) describe several of these improvements that are still under study.

The BEA has been working with the US Department of the Treasury to introduce revisions in monthly, quarterly, and annual data collected through the Treasury International Capital (TIC) reporting system, the primary source of data on financial transactions and positions for the US international accounts. These revisions will allow BEA to increase and improve sector and maturity breakdowns throughout the international accounts. Also, BEA has recently incorporated new data from the new TIC form SLT, "Report of US and Foreign Resident Aggregate Holdings of Long-term Securities," that collects cross-border holdings of US and foreign long-term securities.[14] As shown in table 8.5, these data allow BEA to provide sector breakdowns for US assets and US equity liabilities that were not previously available. In addition, the new data have improved the position estimates for long-term securities that BEA previously projected using transactions data and price changes. The new source data also provide new information that will allow BEA to improve its coverage of financial flows.

The financial crisis and subsequent events in global financial markets resulted in a call for more frequent and timely information on cross-border linkages and the exposure of economies to global market developments. As a result, in May 2010, the IMF executive board prescribed quarterly reporting of IIP statistics with a four-year transition period as a requirement of the Special Data Dissemination Standard, to which the United States is a

---

14. For more information on the TIC Form SLT, see http://www.treasury.gov/resource -center/data-chart-center/tic/Pages/forms-slt.aspx.

subscriber.[15] Consistent with this requirement, the BEA committed to intro-ducing quarterly IIP statistics by 2014 and the BEA published quarterly IIP statistics for the first time on March 26, 2013.[16] These statistics provide users with more frequent and more timely information on the US external position that can be compared with quarterly BOP statistics and other information on current market developments and trends. It will also improve the com-parability of the US IIP statistics with those of partner countries, many of which now publish IIP statistics on a quarterly basis.

8.5   Conclusion

The restructuring of the US financial account and IIP to align them with the new international statistical standards will present cross-border transac-tions statistics in relevant functional categories by instrument, sector, and maturity. The new presentations will enable further analyses of rates of return, addressing important questions raised by users of the data that could not be fully addressed using the existing presentation. By moving to the internationally accepted standards, the financial account and the IIP will be more comparable to foreign statistics that follow BPM6 and to related national accounts statistics that follow the SNA.

References

Curcuru, Stephanie E., Tomas Dvorak, and Francis E. Warnock. 2008. "Cross-Border Returns Differentials." NBER Working Paper no. 13768, Cambridge, MA.
Howell, Kristy L. 2012. "Modernizing and Enhancing BEA's International Eco-nomic Accounts: A Progress Report." *Survey of Current Business* 92 (May): 37–50.
Howell, Kristy L., and Ned G. Howenstine. 2011. "Modernizing and Enhancing BEA's International Economic Accounts: A Progress Report." *Survey of Current Business* 91 (May): 6–18.
Howell, Kristy L., and Kyle L. Westmoreland. 2013. "Modernizing and Enhancing BEA's International Economic Accounts: A Progress Report and Plans for Imple-mentation." *Survey of Current Business* 93 (May): 44–53.
Howell, Kristy L., and Robert E. Yuskavage. 2010. "Modernizing and Enhancing BEA's International Economic Accounts: Recent Progress and Future Direc-tions." *Survey of Current Business* 90 (May): 6–20.
International Monetary Fund. 2009. *Balance of Payments and International Invest-ment Position Manual*, 6th ed. Washington, DC: IMF.

15. Quarterly reporting of IIP statistics is one of a number of recommendations provided by the IMF and the Financial Stability Board at the request of the Group of Twenty (G-20) finance ministers and central bank governors that are aimed at closing information gaps that came to light during the financial crisis. For more information, see International Monetary Fund and Financial Stability Board (2009).
16. See http://www.bea.gov/newsreleases/international/intinv/intinvnewsrelease.htm for the latest IIP release.

International Monetary Fund and Financial Stability Board. 2009. "The Financial Crisis and Information Gaps." Report to the G-20 Finance Ministers and Central Bank Governors, Washington, DC, IMF. www.imf.org/external/np/g20/pdf /102909.pdf.

Landefeld, J. Steven, and Ann M. Lawson. 1991. "Valuation of the US Net International Investment Position." *Survey of Current Business* 71 (May): 40–49.

Landefeld, J. Steven, Ann M. Lawson, and Douglas B. Weinberg. 1992. "Rates of Return on Direct Investment." *Survey of Current Business* 72 (August): 79–86.

Mataloni Jr., Raymond J. 2000. "An Examination of the Low Rates of Return of Foreign Owned US Companies." *Survey of Current Business* 80 (March): 55–73.

Organisation for Economic Co-operation and Development. 2008. *Benchmark Definition of Foreign Direct Investment*, vol. 4. Paris: OECD.

Palumbo, Michael G., and Jonathan A. Parker. 2009. "The Integrated Financial and Real System of National Accounts for the United States: Does It Presage the Financial Crisis?" *American Economic Review: Papers and Proceedings* 99 (May): 80–6.

III

How Did the Financial Crisis Affect Households and Businesses?

9

Household Debt and Saving during the 2007 Recession

Rajashri Chakrabarti, Donghoon Lee,
Wilbert van der Klaauw, and Basit Zafar

9.1 Introduction

During the 2007 recession many households saw their wealth decline sharply and their income and employment opportunities deteriorate. In this chapter we use microeconomic data to analyze changes in household financial decisions during this period and, in particular, changes in household saving and debt. More specifically, we focus on the following three questions: What is the nature and prevalence of financial distress and how does it vary across households? How have households responded to these new economic conditions? What are consumers' expectations about future economic outcomes and their future financial behaviors?

Our analysis in this chapter is based on several unique data sources. First, the Federal Reserve Bank of New York (FRBNY) Consumer Credit Panel, which is based on credit report records, provides detailed insights into developments on the liability side of household balance sheets since 1999. Second, we use information on household financial decisions and expectations, such as on spending and saving, from several recent household surveys. We analyze survey evidence collected between November 2008 and February 2009

Rajashri Chakrabarti is a senior economist at the Federal Reserve Bank of New York. Donghoon Lee is a senior economist at the Federal Reserve Bank of New York. Wilbert van der Klaauw is a senior vice president at the Federal Reserve Bank of New York. Basit Zafar is a senior economist at the Federal Reserve Bank of New York.

The views expressed are those of the authors and do not necessarily reflect those of the Federal Reserve Bank of New York. We have benefitted from helpful comments from Andrew Haughwout, Meta Brown, and Joseph Tracy. Maricar Mabutas provided excellent research assistance. For acknowledgments, sources of research support, and disclosure of the authors' material financial relationships, if any, please see http://www.nber.org/chapters/c12525.ack.

by RAND to assess the impact of the financial crisis.[1] In addition, and of particular importance for this study, we analyze data we collected ourselves through a special survey on saving, administered between the end of October 2009 and January 2010 as part of the Household Inflation Expectations Project.[2] Both the RAND and NYFed surveys were administered as part of the RAND American Life Panel (ALP), an Internet-based survey. Brief descriptions of the ALP and the FRBNY Consumer Credit Panel are provided in the appendix. We also verified some of our findings using data from the Consumer Finance Monthly (CFM), a monthly telephone survey conducted by Ohio State University since 2005.

We begin in section 9.2 with an analysis of the extent and nature of the impact of the financial and economic crisis on households. We focus on four main channels, distinguishing between changes in the housing market, stock market, labor market, and credit market. In section 9.3 we evaluate the different ways in which households have responded to these changes in their economic environment. We then assess individuals' expectations regarding future conditions and behavior in section 9.4, and provide a brief summary in section 9.5.

9.2   The Nature and Prevalence of Financial Distress during the Recession

9.2.1   The Housing Market

Perhaps the most defining aspect of the 2007 recession, and considered by many to be the origin of the financial crisis, has been the decline in the housing market. As shown in figure 9.1, since reaching a peak in April 2007, by the end of 2009 US house prices as measured by the FHFA home price index had fallen 13 percent nationwide.[3] This overall decrease masks considerable variation across states and metropolitan areas. For example, average prices dropped by 39 percent and 38 percent, respectively, from their peaks in California and Florida, while average home prices fell by 4 percent in Colorado and increased by 1 percent in Texas.

The large increase in home prices until 2007 (an increase of 44 percent from 2002 levels) and the decline since then implies that home value losses experienced by consumers depend greatly on when a home was purchased. Overall, in nominal terms, only for those who bought their homes in 2005 or later is the average value of their home currently lower than what they paid

---

1. The RAND survey module was designed by Mike Hurd and Susann Rohwedder. Detailed discussions of related and additional findings from this survey, as well as a number of follow-up surveys, are provided in Hurd and Rohwedder (2010).

2. For further information about the Household Inflation Expectations Project, see Bruine de Bruin et al. (2010).

3. Other indices, such as the CoreLogic HPI and S&P/Case-Shiller HPIs showed even larger average declines of up to 30 percent during this period.

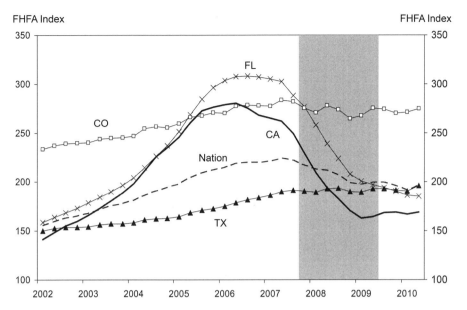

Fig. 9.1   FHFA home price trends
Source: FHFA.
Note: FHFA HPI-purchase only (NSA, quarterly).

for it. As shown in figure 9.2, those who experienced the greatest losses in nominal terms were those who bought their homes in 2007. The average loss by the beginning of 2010, as measured by the FHFA home price index, was a little over 10 percent for this group. Interestingly, the average self-reported change in house value for this group was only about 6 percent in the NY Fed survey. This is consistent with earlier findings in the literature suggesting that individual perceptions of home price changes generally are more optimistic than suggested by official numbers.[4]

An important consequence of the initial increase and subsequent fall in average house prices for households, not conveyed in figure 9.2, is the dramatic fall in home equity. As shown in figure 9.3, with the rise in home prices total equity of homeowners rose. However, it did so at a much lower rate with homeowners' equity share in their homes actually staying relatively constant until the end of 2006. On average, for each 1 percent increase in home prices, homeowners increased their mortgage debt by 1 percent (through higher balances on first mortgages, cash-out refinances, second mortgages, and home equity lines of credit), so that proportionally their equity share in their

---

4. Note that those individuals who bought their homes in 2009 perceived on average that their homes had increased in value by 6.5 percent at the end of 2009 (although the median reported change was 0 percent).

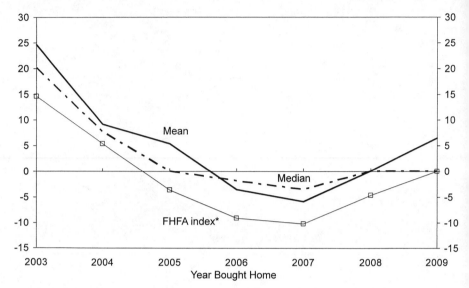

Total Home Price Change

Total Home Price Change

Fig. 9.2 Self-reported home value change since time bought
Source: NYFed survey.
*FHFA HPI-purchase only (NSA, annual).

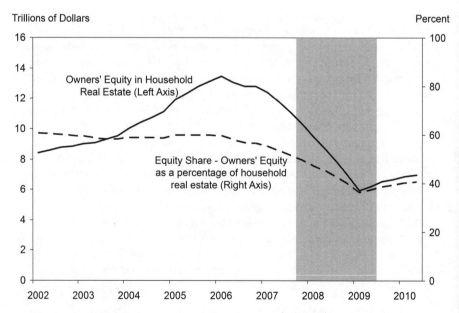

Fig. 9.3 Trends in owners' equity
Source: FHFA.

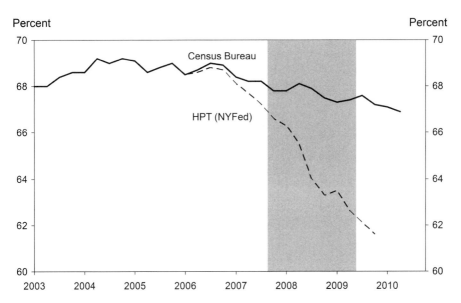

Fig. 9.4   Homeownership rates
Source: US homeownership rate (NSA), Census Bureau. Effective homeownership rate as in Haughwout, Peach, and Tracy (2010).

homes actually remained constant. When home prices began to fall in 2007, owners' equity in household real estate began to fall rapidly from almost $13.5 trillion in 1Q 2006 to a little under $5.3 trillion in 1Q 2009, a decline in total home equity of over 60 percent. At the end of 2009 owners' equity was estimated at $6.3 trillion, still more than 50 percent below its 2006 peak.

With the loss in home equity, a growing proportion of homeowners in fact lost all equity in their homes, finding the mortgage debt on their property to exceed its current market value. While the decline in house prices was accompanied by a small decline in the overall home ownership rate,[5] the "effective homeownership rate" as defined in Haughwout, Peach, and Tracy (2010) as the proportion of individuals with a positive amount of home equity, fell since 2007 by more than 7 percentage points (figure 9.4).[6]

Exposure to declines in housing values varied not only geographically, but also across different age and income groups. As shown in table 9.1, ownership rates during the survey period (November 2009–January 2010)

5. After reaching a peak in 2004, by early 2010 the homeownership rate in the United States had declined by almost 2 percentage points from around 69 percent to 67 percent. The decline was greatest among younger age groups, varying from 3 percent for those younger than 35, 4 percent for those age 35–45, 3 percent for those ages 45–55, and a little over 1 percent for those over 65 (Census Bureau, homeownership by age of householder, not seasonally adjusted [NSA]).
6. See Haughwout, Peach, and Tracy (2010).

Table 9.1   Exposure to the housing market decline

	All	Age			Income			College	Bubble states
		<40	40–55	>55	<30K	30–75	>75K		
Obs. (unweighted)	899	244	315	340	171	352	376	466	183
Percent (unweighted)	27	35	38	10	39	42	52	20	
Percent weighted	40	29	31	29	36	35	27	24	
Percent own home	72	58	78	84	50	71	91	80	68
HOMEOWNERS									
Aver. [median] price change past year	-5.3 [-2.4]	-5.2 [-4.0]	-5.6 [0.0]	-5.2 [-2.2]	-5.4 [-4.0]	-6.1 [-2.4]	-4.7 [-2.0]	-4.8 [-2.3]	-9.8 [-7.7]
Percent home worth less than when bought	24	37	19	17	27	24	23	23	35
Percent bought home after 2005	18	31	13	12	21	18	18	25	19
Percent has mortgage+	57	69	60	43	44	56	64	65	53
Percent underwater*	21	31	18	11	21	22	21	16	29
Percent underwater+	13	23	12	5	10	13	14	10	17
Percent underwater—all	9	13	9	4	5	9	13	8	12

Source: NYFed survey.

Notes: Homeownership is based on the question: Do you (or your spouse/partner) own a home? For the purposes of this survey a home is defined as a house, condo, apartment, mobile home, and so forth (with or without a mortgage). "Underwater" is based on the following question: "If you sold your home today, would the proceeds be sufficient to pay off all mortgage loans and any costs of completing the sale?" For those who own more than one home, data used were for the most recently purchased home.

* Among mortgage debt holders.

+ Among homeowners.

varied from 58 percent for those under 40, to 78 percent among those age 40–55, and 84 percent for those older than 55.[7] Homeownership rates also increased monotonically with household income, with 50 percent of those with incomes under $30,000 owning a home, while 91 percent did so among those earning more than $75,000. The homeownership rate among college graduates was 80 percent, while in what we refer to as the "bubble states," the five states that experienced the largest housing booms and/or busts, the rate was 68 percent, slightly below the overall sample mean of 72 percent.[8]

As shown in table 9.1, the average and median perceived price declines during the year preceding the interview date varied little by age, education, and income, but were considerably larger in the bubble states, in which prices during the past year were believed to have fallen on average by almost 10 percent. Similarly, the proportion of people who perceived the current value of their home to be lower than what they paid for it was 35 percent in the bubble states, whereas for the country as a whole it was 24 percent. The rate was also higher among homeowners under age forty and those with incomes under $30,000, of whom a much higher proportion bought their homes after 2005.

Reflecting a greater share of homeowners who have paid off their mortgages, the proportion of owners who have an outstanding balance on their mortgage is much lower among older individuals. Among homeowners with mortgages at the end of 2009, 21 percent reported to be "underwater" at the time of the survey, with the fraction being the highest among those under age forty (31 percent) and those living in the bubble states (29 percent).[9] As shown in table 9.2, these higher proportions of individuals who report to be underwater on their mortgages partly reflect a greater share of homeowners who bought their homes after 2005. However, it also reflects how much equity was taken out by owners during the housing boom, with the proportion with negative equity being much larger among those with higher mortgage debt. Finally, the share of mortgage holders underwater is much higher among investors, defined here as those with three or more first mortgages. This is consistent with ongoing research based on the FRBNY Consumer Credit Panel, showing that while historically lower, delinquency rates among this group has recently been much higher than that for noninvestors.

In summary, the direct impact of the housing crisis has been confined to homeowners, who are on average somewhat older and have higher incomes

---

7. All survey statistics (for NYFed and RAND samples) presented in this chapter are calculated using sample weights based on population statistics calculated from the 2009 CPS March Supplement survey (see appendix).

8. The "bubble states" include Arizona, California, Florida, Michigan, and Nevada.

9. A homeowner is defined to be underwater if they answered no to the question "If you sold your home today, would the proceeds be sufficient to pay off all mortgage loans and any costs of completing the sale?" The overall rate of 21 percent is comparable to that computed by First American CoreLogic, which reported that more than 11.3 million, or 24 percent, of all residential properties with mortgages were in negative equity at the end of the fourth quarter of 2009 (First American CoreLogic Q4 2009 Negative Equity Report, 2010).

Table 9.2   Characteristics of mortgage debt holders

	Percent of mortgage holders *above* water who	Percent of mortgage holders *underwater* who
Bought home after 2005	16	29
Have mortgage debt <100K	58	35
Have mortgage debt (100K, 200K)	29	34
Have mortgage debt >200K	13	31
Own 1–2 homes	98	94
Own 3+ homes	2	6

Source: NYFed survey.

Notes: Mortgage debt is based on the question: "Do you (or your spouse/partner) have any outstanding loans against the value of your home(s), including all mortgages, home equity loans, and home equity lines of credit? If yes: Which category represents the total amount of current outstanding loans against your home(s) (Less than $25,000, $25,000 to $49,999, $50,000 to $99,999, $100,000 to $149,999, $150,000 to $199,999, $200,000 to $299,999, $300,000 to $499,999, $500,000 to $799,999, or $800,000 or more)?"

than renters. Among owners, many saw considerable gains in housing wealth evaporate during the recession, with those who bought their homes after 2005 (on average younger and with lower incomes) and those living in one of the bubble states experiencing the largest nominal losses and most likely to currently be underwater on their mortgage. Ultimately, the impact of the decline in the housing market on a specific household's financial situation and behavior will depend on many factors, including where the house is located, when the house was bought, how it was financed, how much equity was extracted during the housing boom, the owner's ability to make mortgage payments, and on how long the household plans to live in the home.

9.2.2   The Stock Market

In addition to significant losses in housing wealth during the 2007 recession, many households experienced considerable losses in their stock market wealth following the stock market crash in October 2008. As measured by the S&P 500 index, after falling more than 45 percent between the end of 2007 and the beginning of 2009, the stock market has rebounded somewhat, but stocks at the end of 2009 remained approximately 27 percent below their peak values (figure 9.5).

Not all households were directly affected by this drop in stock values, with exposure varying considerably across households. Based on the 2007 Survey of Consumer Finances, stock market participation rates, as measured by the proportion of families holding stocks directly or indirectly (through mutual funds in pension accounts), increases monotonically with income from less than 14 percent for those in the bottom income quintile to 91 percent in the top decile (table 9.3). A similar positive relationship with income is found for the average and median stock value held by stock market participants. The

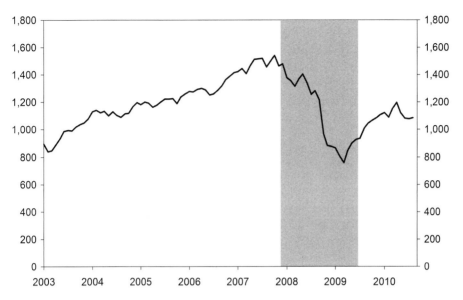

Fig. 9.5   S&P 500 stock market trend

Table 9.3   Stock market participation in 2007

	Families having stock holdings, direct or indirect	Median value among families with holdings (thousands of 2007 dollars)
All families	51.1	35.0
Percentile of income		
Less than 20	13.6	6.5
20–39.9	34.0	8.8
40–59.9	49.5	17.7
60–79.9	70.5	34.1
80–89.9	84.4	62.0
90–100	91.0	219.0
Age of head (years)		
Less than 35	38.6	7.0
35–44	53.5	26.0
45–54	60.4	45.0
55–64	58.9	78.0
65–74	52.1	57.0
75 or more	40.1	41.0
Housing status		
Owner	62.5	41.2
Renter	26.0	8.6

Source: Survey of Consumer Finances 2007. See Bucks, Kennickell, Mach, and Moore (2009).

participation rate, as well as the median stock value held among participants, has a bell-shaped relationship with respect to the age of the household head. Reflecting a lower average income, stock market exposure was also much lower on average for renters.

The same patterns exhibited by the 2007 Survey of Consumer Finances also show up in responses to the 2008 RAND survey shown in table 9.4. In November 2008, 58 percent of households reported to directly or indirectly own stocks at a median value of $40,000. Approximately 90 percent of stockholders reported a loss in the overall value of their stocks since October 1, 2008, with 38 percent reporting losses over 30 percent. Both rates show very little variation across demographic groups. During a period in which, on average, the S&P 500 index fell by 24 percent, those reporting positive stock holdings reported a median 25 percent decline in stock value between October 1, 2008, and the interview date in November 2008, corresponding to a median loss in value of $12,000.[10] Some 38 percent of stockholders reported losses of over 30 percent. While there was little variation in percentage losses across demographic groups, a percentage loss of 25 percent translates into very different dollar values, varying between $4,000 for stockholders under age forty and those with lower incomes (incomes under $30,000), and $25,000 for stockholders over fifty-five and with high incomes (incomes over $75,000).

The patterns for stock ownership found in the RAND survey are consistent with those for pension plan participation in the NYFed survey. Older individuals and higher-income individuals are twice as likely (about 50 percent versus 25 percent) to report that they or their spouse currently are, or ever have been enrolled in a defined-benefit pension plan. Similarly, 86 percent of individuals with household incomes over $75,000 report that they or their spouse currently are or ever have been enrolled in a defined-contribution plan (such as a 401[k], individual retirement account [IRA], tax-deferred annuity or 403[b], 457 thrift savings plan), while only 38 percent reported so for individuals with incomes under $30,000. Across age groups we find an inverted-U pattern, with 56 percent of individuals under age forty having such a pension plan, 78 percent of individuals between age forty and fifty-five, and 65 percent of individuals older than fifty-five ever or currently participating in such a plan. Thus the decline in the stock market is most likely to have affected middle- and older-age individuals and those with higher household incomes.

9.2.3   The Labor Market

Since the recession began, the unemployment rate increased by more than 5 percentage points to 10 percent at the end of 2009, while the proportion of

10. Averaged over all the daily closings during November 2008, the S&P500 had fallen, on average, by 24 percent since October 1, 2008.

Table 9.4   Changes in stock values and retirement savings

	All	Age			Income			College	Bubble states	Home-owner
		<40	40-55	>55	<30K	30-75	>75K			
Nov. 2008										
Percent self/spouse is stock owner	58	47	66	64	27	59	82	80	57	68
Percent with stock value loss since Oct. 1, 2008	52	40	59	58	24	50	75	72	51	61
Percent with more than 30% loss	22	17	28	24	10	20	34	30	24	26
Stock owners										
Median current stock value ($K)*	40	15	50	95	9	20	76	74	36	55
Median reported % change in value*	-25	-24	-25	-22	-20	-20	-26	-25	-25	-25
Median change in value since Oct. 1, 2008 ($K)*	-12	-4	-15	-25	-3	-4	-25	-22	-13	-15
Retirement savings										
Percent with fall in value of retirement savings**	59	48	71	64	37	57	80	79	61	69
Median percentage decline among those with decline+	22	20	25	20	20	20	25	20	25	20
Median $K decline among those reporting decline+	9.5	3	15	15	2	5	15	15	10	10
Nov. 2009–Jan. 2010										
Percent you/spouse currently/ever been enrolled in:										
DB pension plan	37	25	42	49	23	35	52	46	32	46
DC pension plan or IRA	65	56	78	65	38	68	86	79	66	74
Either	74	61	86	78	45	79	92	86	76	82

Source: Nov. 2008 data from RAND survey and Nov. 2009–Jan. 2010 data from NYFed Survey.

Notes: The RAND survey data is based on the following questions: "In the next set of questions we will ask you about stock holdings (including those held by you and your spouse/partner jointly, by you only, or by you and your spouse/partner only). Do you (or your husband/wife/partner) have any shares of stock or stock mutual funds? Please include stocks that you (or your husband/wife/partner) hold in an employer pension account. Thinking back to the time immediately before October 1, 2008, that is, before the large drop in the stock markets, what were your (and your spouse's/partner's) stock holdings worth immediately before then? Please include the value of stocks that you hold directly and the value of stocks that you (and your spouse's/partner's) hold in an employer pension account. And what are your (and your spouse's/partner's) stock holdings worth now?" The NYFed survey data is based on the following questions: "Please indicate whether you (or your spouse/partner) currently are or ever have been enrolled in each of the following types of pension plans: A defined-benefit plan, also known as a traditional employer-provided pension plan, which pays a fixed amount when you retire, where the amount typically depends on your final or average salary.

A defined-contribution plan (such as a 401[k], individual retirement account [IRA], tax deferred annuity or 403[b], 457 thrift savings plan) in which workers and/or their employers make contributions to an account in which money accumulates, and that money can be paid out in a variety of ways depending on the plan or worker's choice."

*among stock holders.

**proportion who answered yes to the question: "Have the recent financial problems in the economy reduced the value of your (and your spouse's/partner's) retirement savings?"

+based on percentage and absolute amount responses to the question: "Thinking of your (and your spouse's/partner's) retirement savings (not including Social Security) how much have they lost in value as a result of the problems in the economy since October 1, 2008?"

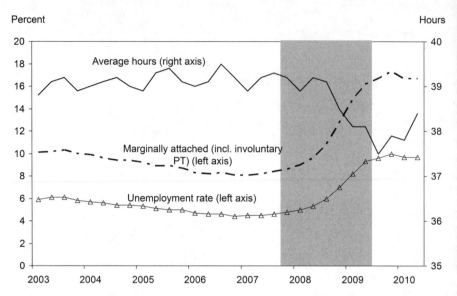

Fig. 9.6   Unemployment rate, proportion marginally attached, and average weekly hours
Source: BLS.

those marginally attached to the labor force (which includes the unemployed as well as those involuntarily working part-time) increased from about 8 percent in 2007 to 17 percent at the end of 2009. As shown in figure 9.6, during the past two years there also was a considerable fall in the average weekly hours of work.

Not surprisingly, these patterns are reflected in the trends for personal income, calculated by the National Income and Product Accounts. As shown in figure 9.7, between the end of 2007 and the end of 2009 per capita real personal income fell by 3.8 percent, with total compensation and wages falling respectively by 5.8 percent and 6.7 percent during this period. However, as also shown in the figure, per capita disposable income remained relatively constant during this period, due to a drop in personal taxes.

Not all households were equally affected by the decline in the labor market. As shown in table 9.5, unemployment rates as reported in the NYFed survey at the end of 2009 varied considerably by age and geography, with younger individuals and those living in the bubble states more likely to be unemployed at the time of the survey.[11] Not surprisingly, unemployment was

11. The lower overall unemployment rate of 7 percent in the NYFed sample compared to a national rate closer to 10 percent at the end of 2009 may be due to a difference between what individuals believe constitutes being unemployed and how unemployment is officially measured. It may also reflect a lower survey response rate among the unemployed.

Per Capita (2005 $)   Per Capita (2005 $)

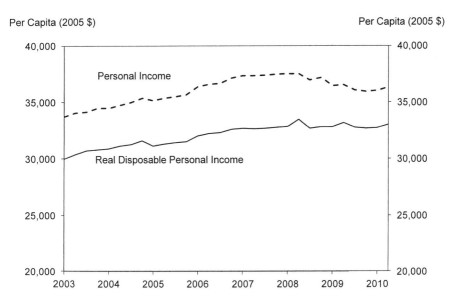

Fig. 9.7   Personal income
Source: BEA, SAAR, in 2005 dollars.

also more prevalent in (and a cause of) lower income households. The same patterns are found for spousal unemployment—8 percent of respondents report a job loss by a spouse during the past twelve months. During the survey period, in 14 percent of households either the respondent was currently unemployed and/or had a spouse who had been laid off during the past year. In addition to losing jobs, significant proportions of respondents reported incurring a pay cut (15 percent), having to take unpaid furlough days off (7 percent), losing 401(k) matching (8 percent), and reductions in health benefits (14 percent) during the last twelve months. Homeowners, individuals over age fifty-five, and those with household incomes over $75,000 were less likely to report pay cuts or reductions in health benefits.

As reported in table 9.5, the combined impact of employment losses and wage cuts led to an overall average decrease in pretax household income of about 3.9 percent during 2009, with 19 percent of individuals reporting losses of 10 percent of income or higher. While all demographic groups suffered income losses during the past year, the losses were greatest among the forty to fifty-five age group (average decline of 5.8 percent) and among individuals living in bubble states (4.7 percent).

9.2.4   Credit Markets

During a recession in which most interest rates on personal loans fell, the most significant change in the credit markets was an overall decline in

Table 9.5   Labor market experiences reported at end of 2009

	All	Age			Income				Bubble states	Home-owner
		<40	40–55	>55	<30K	30–75	>75K	College		
Percent currently unemployed	7	8	6	5	12	6	2	7	9	5
Percent spouse lost job	8	10	9	5	8	12	5	7	11	9
Percent self or spouse unemployed	14	17	14	9	18	17	7	14	18	12
Percent incurred pay cut	15	15	23	8	14	15	16	18	16	15
Percent had to take furlough days	7	9	9	3	7	8	8	8	7	6
Percent lost 401(k) matching	8	9	8	7	8	9	8	10	11	8
Percent lost or had health benefits reduced	14	17	15	10	17	16	11	14	25	11
Know friends/family who lost job	64	65	65	63	59	65	68	69	67	68
Perceived HH pretax income change past yr.:										
Up	27	32	26	22	22	26	33	33	30	25
Down	32	32	38	27	30	36	29	29	28	34
Same	41	36	36	51	48	38	38	38	43	41
Mean % change	-3.9	-2.5	-5.8	-3.9	-5.7	-5.4	-0.8	-2.6	-4.7	-4.2
Percent income loss over 10%	19	19	22	15	19	23	13	17	16	19

Source: NYFed survey.

Note: Survey data is based on the following questions: "During the past twelve months have you (for each answer Y/N): (1) had a spouse/partner who lost a job, (2) taken a cut in pay, (3) lost or had your health benefits reduced, (4) had to take furlough days off from work for which you were not paid, (5) your employer stopped contributing to your 401(k) plan, and (6) known friends or family who lost their jobs? Was the total combined income of all members of your household during the last twelve months higher, lower, or the same as the combined income during the previous twelve months? In percentage terms, by approximately how much was it higher/lower?"

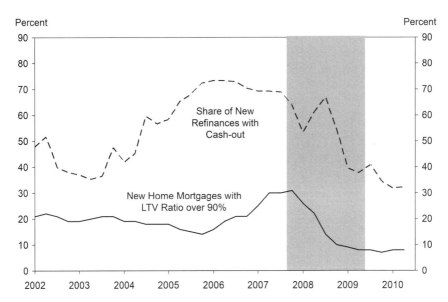

Fig. 9.8   Consumer credit—Mortgage LTVs and cash-outs
Source: FHFA.

demand for and a tightening in the supply of credit.[12] As shown in figure 9.8, reflecting an overall sharp decline in the average loan-to-value ratio of new mortgage loans, the proportion of all mortgage originations with loan/ price ratios over 90 percent dropped steadily from 31 percent in the middle of 2007 to about 7 percent of new mortgages at the end of 2009.[13] At the same time, the proportion of refinances involving a cash-out dropped dramatically from over 70 percent of refinances in early 2006 to 35 percent of refinances at the end of 2009.[14]

Another striking change during the past year has been a decline in the number of loan accounts opened and a sharp increase in the number of accounts closed. As shown in figure 9.9, the FRBNY Consumer Credit Panel indicates that about 319 million accounts were closed during 2009, while just 166 million were opened. Credit cards have been the primary source of these reductions: the number of open credit card accounts fell to 394 million by

12. At the end of 2009, while average rates on credit cards were comparable to those at the end of 2007, interest rates on fixed-rate thirty-year mortgage loans, forty-eight-month new car loans, and twenty-four-month personal loans had, on average, all fallen by a little over 1 percentage point since the end of 2007.

13. After a gradual increase in the average loan-to-value ratio on all mortgage loans, which came to a halt at the end of 2007, by the end of 2009 it had fallen back to 73.9 percent, a level not seen since early 2004 (FHFA).

14. During the same period, total cash-out dollars as a proportion of aggregate refinanced originations dropped from about 30 percent to 6 percent (FHFA).

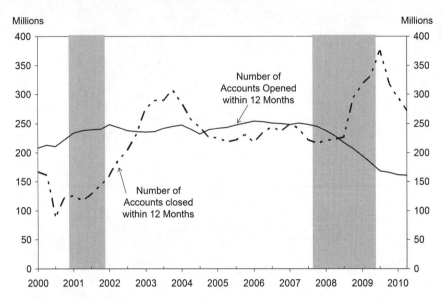

Fig. 9.9   Total number of new and closed accounts
Source: FRBNY Consumer Credit Panel.

the end of December 2009, a decrease of 78 million (16.5 percent) from a year earlier and 20.5 percent from the peak in 2008:Q2.

Additional insight into the apparent tightening of credit and closing of accounts is provided in table 9.6. During the survey period at the end of 2009, 57 percent of respondents perceived that it had become more difficult to obtain credit compared to a year earlier, while only 12 percent thought it had become easier. Little variation shows up in these responses across age and income groups. While 36 percent of respondents reported to have closed a credit card account during the past year at their own request, 13 percent reported to have had one of their credit card accounts closed by the bank or credit card company, with the proportion being highest among younger and lower-income respondents and among those living in one of the bubble states.[15]

Finally, approximately equal proportions of respondents reported increases and decreases in the combined total credit limit on their combined credit cards. Decreases were more prevalent for the highest income group and those living in bubble states, while they were less prevalent among the lowest income group (for whom credit limits are likely to have been low to

15. Additional survey data collected by the FRBNY between December 2009 and January 2010 indicated that about twice as many credit card accounts were closed at the customer's request than were closed at the banks' initiative. Of all cards closed (at own request or not), 43 percent had a zero balance at the time of closing.

Table 9.6   Access to credit

	All	Age			Income			College	Bubble states	Homeowner
		<40	40–55	>55	<30K	30–75	>75K			
Credit access vs. past yr.										
Percent easier	12	11	13	12	12	13	12	9	6	12
Percent tougher	57	61	58	52	55	57	59	63	55	59
Percent same	30	28	29	36	33	30	29	27	39	29
Credit card accounts closed										
Percent closed by self	36	36	34	38	30	37	40	34	42	36
Percent closed by bank	13	16	12	10	16	12	12	10	15	14
Change in total credit limit										
Percent increase	20	28	15	15	14	24	21	21	21	19
Percent decrease	19	20	21	17	15	19	23	18	22	19
Percent stayed same	60	52	64	67	70	56	56	61	56	61

Source: NYFed survey.

Notes: Survey data is based on the following questions: "Do you believe it generally has been easier, harder, or equally difficult to obtain credit or loans during the last year when compared to the year before?" (Answer options: [1] easier, [2] harder, [3] equally difficult.) "During the past twelve months, did you pay off and close any of your credit card accounts?" (Only include accounts that were closed at your request.) "During the past twelve months, were any of your credit card accounts closed by your bank or credit card company?" (Only include accounts that were not explicitly closed at your request.) "During the past twelve months, did the combined total credit limit (the maximum amount you are allowed to borrow on your cards) on all your credit cards that remained open increase, decrease, or stay the same?"

begin with). Increases in credit limits were instead more likely to be reported by those under age forty and with incomes in the $30,000–$75,000 range.

9.2.5   Measures of Overall Distress

The reported microeconomic evidence of considerable declines in housing and stock market wealth is consistent with the large drop in per capita net worth calculated by the Flow of Funds Accounts and shown in figure 9.10. Given the decline in net worth as well as the weak labor market, it is not surprising that since the middle of 2008 a majority of respondents in the Reuters/University of Michigan Survey of Consumers considered themselves to be worse off financially than a year earlier. During the past year only about 20 percent report that they (and their family) are better off financially than they were a year ago (figure 9.11). When differentiating by age (not shown), we find these trends to apply equally to all age groups, except that overall ratings of changes in one's personal financial situation are persistently somewhat higher (less negative) for younger and lower (more negative) for older individuals.

As shown in table 9.7, about 68 percent of consumers in the RAND survey reported in November 2008 that they had been affected "somewhat" or "a lot" by the crisis. The proportion of individuals who reported to have been affected a lot, was greatest among the forty to fifty-five age group and among individuals living in one of the housing crisis states. In the November 2008 survey, a little under half of the respondents reported to be worse off finan-

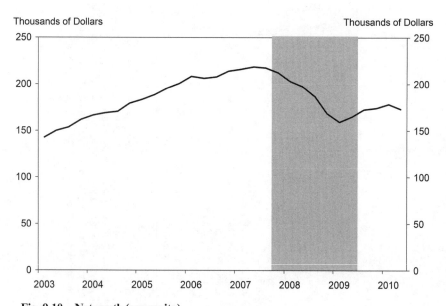

Fig. 9.10   Net worth (per capita)
Source: Flow of Funds Accounts, NSA, and current dollars.

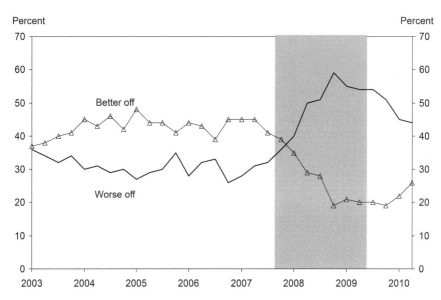

Fig. 9.11   Perceived decline in financial situation (percent worse off compared to year ago)
Source: Reuters/University of Michigan Survey of Consumers.

cially relative to a year ago, with older and lower-income individuals more likely to report to be worse off than younger and higher income individuals.

An alternative and arguably more objective measure of financial stress can be derived based on some of the RAND survey findings discussed earlier. In November 2008, about one-third of all individuals reported at least one of three indicators of financial distress: self or spouse unemployed, have negative equity in their home, or lost more than 30 percent of their retirement savings. While unemployment and negative home equity were more concentrated among younger individuals, large retirement savings losses were more common among those forty years of age or older, and especially among the forty to fifty-five age group. Comparing across income groups, we find that while unemployment was more frequently experienced by individuals in low-income families, negative equity and large retirement savings losses were instead much more common in higher-income households. The same is true when comparing those with and without college degrees. Finally, while individuals living in the bubble states were equally likely to report large retirement savings losses as those in other states, they were much more likely to be unemployed and underwater at the end of 2008.

During the November 2009–January 2010 interview period, large proportions of respondents in the NYFed survey continued to report deteriorating personal financial conditions, with 36 percent reporting being worse off and only 13 percent reporting being better off than a year earlier. As in the

Table 9.7   Measures of overall financial distress

	All	Age			Income			College	Bubble states	Home-owner
		<40	40-55	>55	<30K	30-75	>75K			
As of Nov. 2008*										
Affected by crisis?+										
No	32	35	24	35	40	32	25	25	24	31
Yes, little	49	49	52	45	44	49	53	54	51	50
Yes, a lot	19	16	24	19	16	19	22	21	25	19
Personal fin. situation vs. yr. ago										
Better	10	16	6	6	7	12	12	14	10	10
Same	45	48	41	45	46	42	47	42	44	45
Worse	45	36	53	49	47	46	42	45	46	46
Percent self or spouse unemployed	8	13	7	5	13	8	5	4	12	7
OR underwater	13	18	12	7	17	13	10	8	18	13
OR lost >30% of retirement savings	32	31	36	27	24	30	39	34	37	35
As of Nov. 2009**										
Personal fin. situation vs. yr. ago										
Better	13	16	13	10	11	12	17	17	10	13
Same	51	51	47	55	46	50	56	48	52	51
Worse	36	32	40	36	43	37	28	35	37	36
Percent self or spouse unemployed	14	17	14	9	18	17	7	14	18	12
OR drop household income>10%	27	29	29	21	28	33	18	25	29	26
OR underwater	33	39	34	23	32	37	28	31	36	35

Notes: Survey data is based on the following questions from the RAND survey: "Over the past months there have been reports about the nation's financial problems, including large drops in the stock market and in the housing market and increased rates of foreclosures and joblessness. As this financial crisis unfolds, more and more people have been affected in different ways. Have you (or your husband/wife/partner) been affected by these problems? We are interested in how people are getting along financially these days. Would you say that you (and your household) are better off or worse off financially than you were a year ago?" The proportion of respondents with retirement savings losses over 30 percent is based on answers in the RAND survey to the question: "Thinking of your (and your spouse's/partner's) retirement savings (not including Social Security), how much have they lost in value as a result of the problems in the economy since October 1, 2008?" In the RAND survey, the proportion underwater is calculated based on the perceived current value of a house and the total amount owed on the house. In the NYFed survey, the proportion underwater represents households with a mortgage who answered "no" to the question: "If you sold your home today, would the proceeds be sufficient to pay off all mortgage loans and any costs of completing the sale?" In NYFed survey, the proportion with over 10 percent income drop represents the proportion of respondents who reported drops of over 10 percent in the total combined income of all members of the household during the last twelve months.

*Source: RAND survey.

**Source: NYFed survey.

end-of-2008 RAND survey, a larger fraction of individuals in the forty to fifty-five age range reported worsening conditions. About a third of respondents reported to have experienced one of three types of financial distress: currently unemployed or have a spouse who lost his/her job during the past year, experienced a drop in household income over 10 percent compared to the previous year, or currently being underwater on their mortgage. The proportion reporting at least one of these types of distress is somewhat higher among those younger than forty (39 percent) and with incomes in the $30,000 to $75,000 range (37 percent), and lowest among individuals over age fifty-five (23 percent) and with incomes above $75,000 (28 percent).

All in all, the survey evidence indicates that while different segments of the population were affected in distinct ways depending on whether they owned a home (and when they bought it and where it was located), whether they owned stocks, and whether they had secure jobs, the crisis' impact appears to have been widespread, affecting large shares of households across all age, income, and education groups.

9.3 How Did Households Respond to the Changes in Economic Conditions?

After investigating the nature and prevalence of deteriorating economic conditions during the 2007 recession, we focus next on how households responded to these changing conditions in their financial decision making. We first discuss changes in consumer spending behavior, followed by an analysis of changes in saving behavior. In examining how, at the individual household level, saving behavior may have changed, we consider the extent to which households changed their allocations to retirement accounts and how much they added or withdrew funds from other savings accounts. We also analyze in detail whether and how households reduced or increased their outstanding mortgage and nonmortgage debt.

9.3.1 Consumer Spending

After reaching a peak in the fourth quarter of 2007, ending a long period of steady growth, real personal consumption expenditures were down 3.1 percent by the second quarter of 2009 and remained 2.4 percent below the peak in the fourth quarter of 2009 (figure 9.12). Between the end of 2007 and the second quarter of 2009, real personal expenditures on goods fell by 7.2 percent (with durable goods expenditures falling 9.9 percent), expenditures on services fell by only 1.0 percent, and expenditures on food and beverages purchased for off-premises consumption fell by 3.1 percent.[16]

16. Expenditures on goods, services, and food at the end of 2009 remained, respectively, 5.4 percent, 0.8 percent, and 1.6 percent below their levels attained at the end of 2007 (Bureau of Economic Analysis, NIPA).

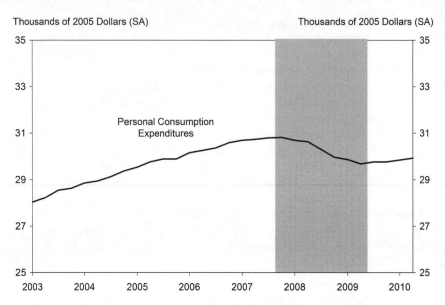

Thousands of 2005 Dollars (SA)   Thousands of 2005 Dollars (SA)

Fig. 9.12   Spending per capita
Source: BEA (NIPA).

Figure 9.13 provides additional information regarding the sharp drop in spending that occurred during the last quarter of 2008 and the first quarter of 2009. Daily discretionary consumer spending as measured by the Gallup daily poll dropped 40 percent during this period.[17] While consumer spending rebounded somewhat after the first quarter of 2009, at the end of 2009 it remained about 28 percent below 3Q 2008 levels. Over the past two-year period, the average percentage change in daily discretionary spending has been very similar for lower- and middle-income individuals (defined by Gallup as incomes below \$90,000) and high-income individuals (incomes above \$90,000).

Evidence from the RAND and NYFed surveys is consistent with these findings. As shown in table 9.8, as stock prices fell sharply, 75 percent of households reduced their monthly spending between October 1, 2008, and the interview date in November 2008, with a median cut reported of 20 percent or about \$200. Spending cuts across demographic groups were similar, except that among individuals fifty-five-years-of-age or older a somewhat smaller share reported reductions in spending, and on average reported smaller spending cuts. Percentage wise, cuts fell with household income,

---

17. Discretionary spending in the Gallup poll is defined as the money spent or charged during the previous day on all types of purchases, such as at a store, restaurant, gas station, online, or elsewhere, excluding purchases of a home, motor vehicle, or normal household bills.

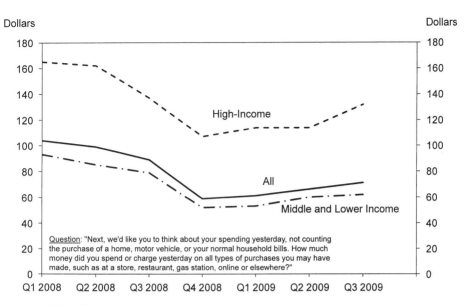

Dollars   Dollars

Fig. 9.13   Daily discretionary consumer spending
Source: Gallup poll.
Note: High income = income over $90,000.

with those with incomes below $30,000 cutting spending by 25 percent, while those with incomes above $75,000 cutting spending by 15 percent.

At the time of the NYFed survey (fielded between November 2009 and January 2010), a slightly higher proportion of individuals reported their current spending to be lower compared to a year ago (27 percent) than the proportion for whom it was higher (22 percent). On average, households reported spending to be 2.2 percent lower at the end of 2009 than it was a year earlier, with those age forty to fifty-five, with incomes under $30,000, and living in a bubble state reporting larger percentage cuts, while older and higher-income individuals making smaller or no spending cuts (see table 9.8). The median change in spending was 0 percent, which is broadly consistent with the relatively flat trend in personal consumer expenditures that followed the large drop in spending at the end of 2008 shown earlier in figure 9.12.

Not surprisingly, spending cuts are strongly related to measures of financial distress. As shown in table 9.9, the large majority of those unemployed at the end of 2009 reported cuts in spending during the year, with spending falling on average by more than 18 percent for this group. Similarly, those who reported household income losses of over 10 percent during 2009 and those who reported to be underwater on their mortgage reported spending approximately 10 percent and 6 percent less on average compared to a year

Table 9.8   Changes in spending behavior

	All	Age			Income				Bubble states	Homeowner
		<40	40–55	>55	<30K	30–75	>75K	College		
As of Nov. 2008+										
Percent cut spending since Oct. 1, 2008	75	77	79	69	76	77	72	71	75	75
Median amount cut ($)	200	200	200	100	100	200	200	250	200	200
Median % cut	20	20	20	15	25	20	15	15	20	20
As of Nov. 2009*										
HH spending vs. year ago										
Up	22	20	18	27	24	22	20	25	19	22
Down	27	29	33	16	33	25	22	23	32	27
Same	52	50	49	56	43	53	59	52	49	51
Average % chg.	-2.2	-2.0	-6.1	1.1	-4.2	-2.0	-0.8	-0.9	-4.6	-2.0

Notes: Survey data is based on the following question: "The next questions are about your household's spending. Please include the spending of everyone who lives with you in your household, as well as your own. Consider household interest payments on mortgages, amount spent on rent, homeowner's or renter's insurance, vehicle taxes and repairs, home repairs, property taxes, utilities, food and groceries, clothing, housekeeping supplies and services, garden/yard services, health insurance, drugs, medical supplies and doctor/hospital visits, gasoline, personal care products and services, trips and vacations, and hobbies and leisure equipment. Also include child support and alimony payments, gifts to anyone outside your household, and losses from a farm, business, or professional practice. Exclude money saved or invested, including real estate investments like home purchases. How does your current monthly household spending compare with your household's monthly spending a year ago?" (Answer options: higher now, about the same, lower now.) "In percentage terms, by how much has your monthly household spending increased (decreased) compared to a year ago?"

+Source: RAND survey.
*Source: NYFed survey.

Table 9.9   **Spending behavior and wealth and income losses**

	All	Unemployed	Lost >10% income	Underwater
As of Nov. 2009*				
HH spending vs. year ago				
Up	22	5	21	18
Down	27	60	48	47
Same	52	35	31	35
Average % chg.	–2.2	–18.2	–9.6	–5.9

*Source: NYFed survey. See notes to table 9.8.

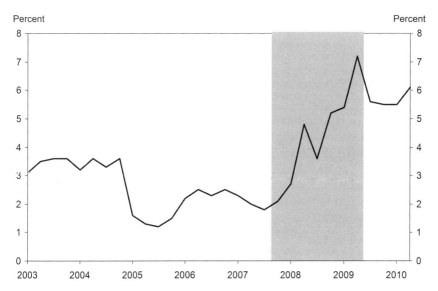

Fig. 9.14   Personal saving rate. Personal saving as percent of disposable personal income
Source: BEA (NIPA).
Note: Personal savings rate = Personal savings/disposable personal income.

earlier, cuts much higher than the 2.2 percent average decline in spending during this period in our sample.

9.3.2   Saving

The relatively stable level of per capita disposable income shown earlier in figure 9.7 combined with what appears to be a persistent drop in personal consumption expenditures has resulted in a significant and widely reported increase in personal saving and in the personal saving rate. As shown in figure 9.14, the National Income and Products Accounts (NIPA) Personal Saving Rate as computed by the Bureau of Economic Analysis increased from historically low levels of around 1 percent in the first quarter of 2008 to recent levels over 6 percent. While the personal saving rate does not directly map into actual household saving,[18] at the microeconomic level an increase in household saving could manifest itself as an increase in allocations to retirement and savings accounts. Alternatively, it could exhibit itself as an increase in allocations used to reduce or pay off debt; this could be mortgage debt or debt on other consumer loans such as auto, student, and credit card loans. In what follows we first present survey evidence on recent changes in allocations to retirement and other savings accounts. This is followed by an analysis of survey and administrative data on changes in consumer debt.

Consumer Allocations to Retirement and Other Savings Accounts

In the NYFed survey conducted during the November 2009–January 2010 period, we asked individuals whether they had made any changes to their retirement account contributions over the past year. As reported in table 9.10, while 11 percent of all individuals increased their contributions and 3 percent started contributing to a retirement account (including defined-contribution accounts and IRAs) for the first time, 12 percent decreased their contributions, 16 percent stopped contributing all together, and 11 percent prematurely withdrew funds from their accounts. Those who increased their allocations did so by a median amount of $100 per month, while those who decreased their allocations did so by a median amount of $150 per month.[19]

Not only did more individuals report reducing their contributions to retirement accounts than increasing their contributions, more individuals also report having withdrawn funds from other savings accounts (including checking, savings, and money market accounts) than having added funds to them. The proportions of individuals who reported that they on net withdrew funds during the past year from their checking, savings, and money market accounts exceeded the proportions of respondents who reported that on net they had added funds to each of these accounts. In contrast, approximately equal proportions reported that they on net had added funds to their stock market accounts as had withdrawn funds from stock market accounts. All together 25 percent of individuals said they had added more than they used up of their total other (nonretirement) savings during the past year, with a median net annual increase of $5,000. However, 38 percent reported that they actually used up more than they added, with a median reduction of $3,500. Therefore, our survey evidence provides little support

18. For example, the NIPA measure includes income and outlays of nonprofit organizations.
19. We also asked individuals for the overall percentage change in the total amount of money in their retirement and other savings accounts over the past year, after including all contributions and withdrawals during the year as well as changes in the value of funds already in their accounts. Overall respondents reported an average 3.2 percent decline in their total retirement account balances and an average 5.1 percent decline in balances of their other savings accounts. Given the slight increase in average stock and bond values during the period considered, this is consistent with an overall net withdrawal of funds from those accounts.

Table 9.10   Changes in contributions to retirement and other savings accounts, Nov. 2008–Nov. 2009

	All	Age			Income			College	Bubble states	Home-owner
		<40	40–55	>55	<30K	30–75	>75K			
Change in retirement account contributions past 12 months										
Percent increased contr.	11	12	13	9	5	11	14	13	13	12
Median increase ($)	100	100	45	300	25	75	150	150	100	100
Percent decreased contr.	12	14	12	8	7	12	13	16	9	12
Median decrease ($)	150	150	160	200	150	100	200	200	150	150
Percent started contr.	3	6	2	1	3	5	2	1	3	3
Percent stopped contr.	16	12	13	24	25	19	10	16	22	15
Percent prematurely withdrew	11	7	13	14	14	17	5	7	12	10
Change in other savings (vs last yr.)										
Checking accounts										
Percent added more/% withdrew more	−8	−7	−15	−3	−15	−10	0	−7	−7	−5
Savings accounts										
Percent added more/% withdrew more	−5	−1	−9	−5	−14	−11	+10	+4	0	−2
Money market										
Percent added more/% withdrew more	−2	1	−2	−5	−5	−2	2	3	0	−2
Stocks										
Percent added more/% withdrew more	1	1	3	1	−3	2	5	2	0	3
Net change in allocations to other saving accounts										
Percent added more than used up	25	27	26	22	13	21	41	36	28	29
Median net addition ($K)	5	2	5	6	0.6	2.5	5.0	6.5	5.0	5.0

(continued)

Table 9.10   (continued)

	All	Age			Income			College	Bubble states	Home-owner
		<40	40–55	>55	<30K	30–75	>75K			
Percent used up more than added	38	32	40	44	44	46	25	36	35	37
Median net withdrawal ($K)	3.5	2.0	3.5	6.0	2.0	3.0	6.0	6.0	3.0	5.0

Source: NYFed survey.

Notes: Survey data is based on the questions: "During the past twelve months have you: (indicate Y/N for each) (1) started putting less of your money in 401(k), IRA, or other retirement accounts, (2) started putting more of your money in 401(k), IRA, or other retirement accounts, (3) stopped putting money in a 401(k), IRA, or other retirement accounts, (4) started saving (for the first time) in a 401(k), IRA, or other retirement account, and (5) prematurely withdrawn money from your retirement savings?

You indicated that you started putting more(less) of your money into your retirement account(s). By how much did you (and your spouse/partner) increase(decrease) your total monthly contribution to your retirement account(s)?" Our next question asks about other savings and investments you may have, excluding those in a retirement account. We first want to know whether you made any contributions and/or withdrawals to your savings and investments over the past year. Please do not consider changes in the market value of the funds in these accounts, only consider the amounts of new money you added and the amounts you took out. "For each of the following would you say that over the past twelve months you (and your spouse/partner) have withdrawn more from your investments or savings than you have added to them in new money, that you have added more to savings and investments than you withdrew, or neither (checking accounts, saving accounts, money market accounts, stocks)? Considering all accounts together, would you say that during the past twelve months you (and your spouse/partner) have used up more of your investments or savings than you have added to them in new money, that you have added more to savings and investments than you used up, or neither?" (Answer options: (1) have used up more than added, (2) have added more than used up, or (3) added about the same as used up.) "During the past twelve months, about how much more did you (and your spouse/partner) use up or withdraw from your investments or savings than you added to it? During the past twelve months, about how much more did you (and your spouse/partner) add to your investments or savings than you used or withdrew from it?"

for the conjecture that households increased their saving by contributing more to their retirement and savings accounts.

Some of the observed changes in allocations to retirement and savings accounts undoubtedly reflect normal life cycle patterns in saving behavior, with retired individuals stopping to contribute and beginning to draw down their savings and younger individuals starting to save or to increase their saving as they advance in their careers. Some of the differences in reported behaviors across age groups in table 9.10 indeed seem to reflect such life cycle effects. However the changes reported in table 9.10, and especially the large proportions of respondents who stopped contributing or who prematurely withdrew funds during 2009 are much higher than one would expect to see in a more typical year.

The impact of the crisis is clearly reflected in the much higher proportion of *lower-income* households who stopped contributing or prematurely withdrew funds from their retirement accounts and the much lower proportion of households that increased contributions. These households were also much more likely to have used up more than they added to their other savings accounts. A higher proportion of higher-income households instead increased their contributions to their retirement account and reported net additions to their other savings account.

More insight into this issue is provided in table 9.11, which shows changes in allocations to retirement and other savings accounts for those unemployed at the end of 2009 and for those who experienced income losses over 10 percent during the past year. Between 90 and 100 percent of individuals belonging to these groups report decreasing or stopping their contributions

Table 9.11   Allocations to savings accounts and wealth and income losses

Change in retirement account contributions over past 12 months	All	Unemployed	Lost >10% income	Underwater
Percent increased contribution	11	0	6	12
Median increase ($)	100	150	80	
Percent decreased contribution	12	28	27	5
Median decrease ($)	150	150	150	50
Percent started contributing	3	0	2	2
Percent stopped contributing	16	41	29	9
Percent prematurely withdrew	11	16	19	9
Net change in allocations to other saving accounts				
Percent added more than used up	25	21	14	16
Median net addition ($K)	5.0	8.0	3.0	3.0
Percent used up more than added	38	45	55	47
Median net withdrawal ($K)	3.5	2.0	3.5	3.6

Source: NYFed survey. See notes to table 9.10.

or report prematurely withdrawing funds from their retirement account. A much higher share of these groups than in the rest of the sample also report having used up funds from their other savings accounts.

Among reasons provided, many respondents mentioned job, salary, and household income changes as playing a role in their decisions to increase or decrease their net contributions to their retirement and other savings accounts (table 9.12). Perhaps not surprisingly, among the reasons for increasing allocations, a desire to increase savings for retirement was the most

Table 9.12   **Reasons provided for changing allocations to savings accounts**

A. Reason for *increase* in contributions to retirement and other savings accounts—proportion who list option as moderately or very important

	Retirement accounts	Other savings accounts
Job change	27	29
Salary change	53	51
Change in other income	29	37
To increase savings for retirement	92	60
Now is a good time to invest	75	40
To be able to leave a bequest	23	19
To make up for decline in value house	19	15
To make up for loss in stocks/investments	33	23
To build cushion for future job loss	n/a	51
To build cushion for future health expenses	n/a	51

B. Reason for *decrease* in contributions to retirement and other savings accounts—proportion who list option as moderately or very important

	Retirement accounts	Other savings accounts
Job change	31	26
Salary change	51	44
Change in other income	39	38
Involuntary job loss	31	22
Voluntarily stopped working	14	13
To pay down/pay debt	43	45
To pay bills	30	41
To pay for general living expenses	48	70

Source: NYFed survey.

Notes: Panel A applies to those who responded that they reduced contributions or stopped contributing to their retirement account, while panel B applies to respondents who indicated that they had started putting money into or had increased contributions into a retirement account. The proportions in the table are based on responses to the following questions: "Please indicate how important each of the following was for the increase/decrease in your monthly contribution." (Answer options: very important, moderately important, not at all important, or not applicable.) "Please indicate how important each of the following was in your decision to withdraw some of your investments or savings (to add more to your investments or savings)." (Answer options: very important, moderately important, not at all important, or not applicable.)

important factor, with "good time to invest" also often listed as motivation. Precautionary savings motives were listed as significant factors as well, while bequest motives and a desire to make up losses in home and stock values were less frequently mentioned. Among those who decreased net contributions to their retirement accounts or who used up funds from other savings accounts, a need or desire to pay for general living expenses, pay bills, and reduce debt were most frequently reported as motivations.

In our survey we also asked respondents to rate the importance to their household of a set of alternative reasons for savings in general. The findings, reported in table 9.13, show saving for retirement, precautionary savings motives, and saving to pay for a child or grandchild's education as the reasons most frequently listed as "very important." Saving for retirement is more frequently mentioned by those in the middle and older age groups and those with household incomes over $75,000. Precautionary savings motives are generally more frequently mentioned by the forty to fifty-five age groups and those with household incomes under $30,000. Saving to pay for the education of children or grandchildren or to buy a house or car is more frequently mentioned as an important reason for saving by younger individuals.

Finally, in addition to measuring changes in net contributions, it is interesting to analyze whether individuals made changes to how new funds or existing funds in their retirement and savings accounts were allocated. As shown in table 9.14, while approximately equal proportions increased and decreased the amount of new allocations used to buy stocks, a larger proportion of respondents rebalanced their stockholding by reducing their exposure to stocks in the first two months immediately following the stock market crash in October 2008, with about 3 percent pulling all funds out of the stock market. Similarly, 18 percent of respondents in the end-of-2009 survey indicated that they moved some of their retirement savings to less risky investments. This survey evidence suggests that a nonnegligible number of households appear to have shifted their allocations away from stocks, implying that not all consumers may have fully benefited from the recent rebound in the stock market.

Recent Changes in Consumer Debt

Before discussing our survey-based evidence on changes in consumer debt, we first describe recent findings based on the FRBNY Consumer Credit Panel, a unique and comprehensive administrative database of credit report records for a large random sample of US individuals and households. As shown in figure 9.15, after reaching a peak at the end of the third quarter of 2008, overall household debt has fallen steadily, declining by about $567 billion (4.5 percent) up to the end of December 2009.

In order to relate the observed change in total consumer debt to the NIPA measure of savings, we first distinguish between mortgage debt (on first mortgages, second mortgages, and home equity lines of credit [HELOCs])

Table 9.13   Saving motives

	All	Age			Income			College	Bubble states	Home-owner
		<40	40–55	>55	<30K	30–75	>75K			
Percent reporting as very important										
Retirement/old age	40	29	50	46	38	34	49	49	35	42
Precautionary reasons										
Job loss	33	35	41	22	34	30	34	33	39	33
Illness	29	24	37	29	38	27	24	24	31	28
General emergencies	33	29	40	31	44	31	26	28	39	32
Bequest/transfers										
Education of (grand)children	38	52	37	20	35	33	45	42	34	37
Gifts to children/family	9	6	12	11	10	11	6	9	10	8
Charitable contr.	11	8	12	14	14	10	10	12	6	11
To make large purchase										
House	17	23	19	8	18	16	17	21	21	12
Car	15	22	14	7	19	13	13	12	16	12

Source: NYFed survey.

Notes: Survey data is based on the following question: "Now we would like to ask you some questions about your household's attitudes toward savings. People have different reasons for saving, even though they may not be saving all the time. For your household, please indicate how important you consider the following reasons for saving to be."

Table 9.14   **Reallocations of savings**

	Proportion among retirement account holders
Between Oct. 2008–May 2009*	
Allocations of *new funds*	
Percent increased amounts to stocks	4.7
Percent decreased amounts to stocks	5.1
Allocation of *balances*	
Percent increased amounts to stocks	6.2
Percent decreased amounts to stocks	15.5
Percent sold all stocks in retirement accounts	2.7
Between end 2008–end 2009+	
Percent moved retirement savings into less risky investments	18

Notes: Survey data is based on the following question: "During the past twelve months have you . . . moved your retirement savings into less risky investments? (Y/N)."
* Hurd and Rohwedder (2010).
+ NYFed survey.

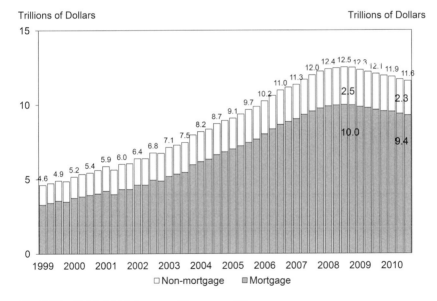

Fig. 9.15   Total debt balance and its composition
Source: FRBNY Consumer Credit Panel.

and nonmortgage debt (on credit card loans, auto loans, student loans, and other personal loans). Second, we exclude from the observed quarter-to-quarter changes in overall mortgage debt all changes in debt associated with home transactions. Third, in computing changes in mortgage and non-mortgage debt, we exclude amounts charged-off by banks. The resulting

Billions of Dollars   Billions of Dollars

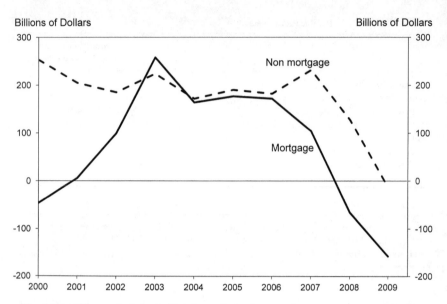

Fig. 9.16   **Changes in household debt available for spending (annual)**
Source: FRBNY Consumer Credit Panel.

measure describes how much individuals on average are paying down or adding to their debts.[20]

The trends in net changes in mortgage and nonmortgage debt, shown in figure 9.16, reveal that until 2008 net pay-down on mortgage debt was actually negative: the increases in debt associated with cash-out refinances, second mortgages, and HELOCs exceeded the total mortgage payments consumers were making to reduce mortgage principals. Since then, consumers have accelerated paying down mortgage debt and, in 2009, mortgage debt was reduced by 140 billion dollars. Similarly, in 2009 consumers on average started paying down their outstanding nonmortgage debt, even though by a much smaller amount. Differentiating by loan type, we find that while consumers were paying down auto loan debt, student loan debt has been growing rapidly.

The evidence from the NYFed survey shown in table 9.15 is broadly consistent with recent trends in the FRBNY Consumer Credit Panel. A considerably larger proportion of respondents report decreasing rather than increasing their mortgage debt, with declines in mortgage debt reported most frequently among the forty to fifty-five age and high-income groups. While most individuals who reduced mortgage debt reported doing so by making their scheduled mortgage payments, about 17 percent mentioned doing so in part by prepaying principal and 11 percent did so in part through

20. For further explanation and details of this analysis see Brown et al. (2010).

Table 9.15   Changes in household debt, end of 2008–end of 2009

	All	Age			Income				Bubble states	Home-owner
		<40	40–55	>55	<30K	30–75	>75K	College		
Change over past year in:										
Mortgage debt										
Percent with increase	**5**	**7**	**6**	**3**	**3**	**5**	**6**	**6**	**1**	**7**
Reason:										
Missed/late payments (%)	31	41	25	10	59	41	8	21	52	31
Added HELOC/2nd mortgage (%)	31	32	27	34	5	24	50	35	48	31
Refinance (%)	28	15	45	42	9	28	39	40	0	28
Percent with decrease	**33**	**31**	**41**	**29**	**13**	**30**	**53**	**39**	**33**	**46**
Reason:										
Paid down regular schedule	69	79	57	71	82	69	66	60	69	69
Prepaid principal	17	12	22	18	6	12	22	25	22	17
Refinance	11	7	16	11	9	13	11	12	6	11
Percent stayed same+	**31**	**17**	**30**	**49**	**31**	**33**	**29**	**32**	**31**	**43**
Percent NA*	31	45	23	19	52	31	12	23	34	3
Nonmortgage debt										
Percent with increase	24	29	22	19	22	30	19	27	26	21
Percent with decrease	30	28	36	27	24	28	37	33	27	32
Percent stayed same	46	42	42	53	53	42	43	40	46	46
Average change ($1,000s)	0.4	1.1	0.3	−0.4	1.6	1.7	−2.0	0.7	0.5	−0.4

Source: NYFed survey.

Notes: Survey data is based on following questions: "During the past twelve months has the total amount you (and your spouse/partner) owe on these mortgages increased, decreased, or stayed the same?" If decreased or increased: "What was the reason for this change in your overall mortgage balance (1) paid down some of the principal on the regular schedule, (2) prepaid (ahead of schedule) some of the principal, (3) refinanced, (4) missed or made late or incomplete payments and fees were added to the mortgage balance, and (5) added an additional mortgage or borrowed on a home equity line of credit?" (Check all that apply.) Next consider all outstanding debt you (and your spouse/partner) have, including balances on credit cards (including retail cards), auto loans, student loans, as well as all other personal loans but excluding all mortgage debt. "During the past twelve months has the total outstanding balance (that is the total amount you owe) of these loans combined increased, decreased, or stayed the same? By how much has the overall combined balance on these debts increased/decreased during the past twelve months?"

* Includes those not currently owning a home or who purchased a home within the past year.

+ Includes those who did not have a mortgage over the past twelve months.

Table 9.16   Changes in household debt for affected subgroups

Change over past year in:	All	Unemployed	Lost >10% income	Under-water
Mortgage debt				
Percent with increase	5	12	10	11
Percent with decrease	33	19	31	45
Percent stayed same+	31	19	33	39
Percent n/a*	31	50	26	5
Nonmortgage debt				
Percent with increase	24	30	31	36
Percent with decrease	30	39	31	34
Percent stayed same	46	31	38	30
Average change ($1,000s)	0.5	2.3	0.5	2.6

Source: NYFed survey. See notes to table 9.15.
* Includes those not currently owning a home or purchased a home within the past year.
+ Includes those who did not have a mortgage over the past twelve months.

a refinance. Prepaying and refinancing were more frequently reported by higher-income individuals and college graduates. These findings suggest that at least a substantial share of households who reduced their outstanding mortgage debt did so voluntarily.

Interestingly, our survey results provide little evidence that households also reduced nonmortgage debt during the past year. While overall a slightly larger share of households reduced than increased such debt, on average, debt increased by about $400 during the past year. Declines in nonmortgage debt were more likely to be reported by older individuals and those with household incomes above $75,000. The latter group of respondents actually reported reducing their nonmortgage debt on average by $2,000 during the past year. Overall, this survey evidence is consistent with the findings of households paying down mortgage debt presented earlier in figure 9.16, but with little if any reductions in outstanding nonmortgage debt.

Not surprisingly, individuals who were unemployed at the end of 2009 were less likely to report reductions in their mortgage debt and more likely to report increases (table 9.16). They were also more likely to report increases in their nonmortgage debt, but a greater share of such individuals also reported decreases in nonmortgage debt.[21] Overall, unemployed individuals reported adding to their nonmortgage debt by $2,300, on average. Similarly, respondents from households that experienced an income drop of more than 10 percent during the year also were more likely to report increases in their mortgage and nonmortgage debt.

21. Unfortunately, we cannot evaluate with our data the extent to which the observed declines in mortgage and nonmortgage debt of individuals were due to lenders tightening standards and reducing limits on revolving credit lines during this period.

Responses in Spending and Savings to Hypothetical Income Shocks

To get an alternative view of household preferences and intentions for saving and spending, we asked respondents about their intended responses to a positive shock in their year-ahead income, as well as a negative income shock, to account for a possible asymmetry in intended response behavior. Responses to both questions are shown in table 9.17. Overall, 99 percent of respondents say they would at least use part of the extra income to save, invest, or pay down debt, with 61 percent of all respondents saying that they would in fact use all the extra income for saving and/or for paying down debt. Only 1 percent of individuals say that they will spend or donate it all, with another 39 percent saying they would spend only some of the extra income. Aggregated across all individuals, on average 41 percent of the extra income would be used for saving/investing, 44 percent for debt payoff, and only 15 percent for spending. Comparing across demographic groups, we find surprisingly little differences in the expected shares of income to be used for consumption.

Faced with an unexpected income drop, respondents instead expect to respond mainly by reducing their spending. Overall, 53 percent of respondents expect to reduce spending by the full amount of the shortfall. Only 13 percent expect to take on some more debt to cover the shortfall, while 41 percent expect to use some of their savings to cover the lost income. On average, individuals expect to cover about 74 percent of the income loss by cutting spending, 20 percent by using some of their savings, and 6 percent by borrowing.

Care must be taken in interpreting stated intentions as actual future behavioral responses to realized income surprises. However, the findings appear to suggest that consumers will be unlikely to increase spending by much if their incomes were to increase by more than expected, while on the other hand, they seem likely to cut spending quite drastically in response to an unexpected future income shortfall.

9.4   Households' Expectations of Future Conditions and Behaviors

In this section we analyze what households are expecting for the future. In the NYFed survey we asked a number of questions eliciting individuals' expectations regarding a variety of outcomes and decisions, including their household's income, spending, saving behavior, and retirement plans.

We first discuss individuals' expectations reported at the end of 2009 about overall economic conditions during the following twelve months. As shown in table 9.18, more respondents expect to see increases than decreases in the unemployment, loan interest, and mortgage rate. However, a slightly higher share expect an increase rather than a decrease in the average house price at the national level, but on average expecting an increase of only

Table 9.17 Reported responses to hypothetical income shocks

		Age			Income					
	All	<40	40–55	>55	<30K	30–75	>75K	College	Bubble states	Homeowner
Surprise 10% extra income next yr.										
Percent save or invest all of it	22	20	19	28	22	19	26	22	22	20
Percent spend or donate all	1	0	0	1	0	1	1	1	1	1
Percent use all to pay down debt	26	31	26	18	29	25	23	21	19	27
Percent spend some, save some	16	12	15	23	17	16	15	16	19	18
Percent spend some, pay some debt	7	7	6	7	8	5	7	6	4	7
Percent save some, pay some debt	13	14	13	13	13	11	15	15	16	14
Percent spend some, save some, pay some debt	16	17	21	11	12	23	12	21	19	14
Percent save/invest	41	37	39	49	39	39	45	44	44	41
Percent spend/donate	15	13	14	18	16	16	12	15	17	14
Percent pay debt	44	50	47	33	44	45	42	41	38	45
Surprise 10% less income next yr.										
Percent cut spending by whole amt.	53	51	53	54	55	54	49	43	52	50
Percent cut savings by whole amt.	4	1	3	8	2	3	5	4	4	4
Percent increase debt by whole amt.	2	4	1	1	4	3	0	1	4	1
Percent cut spending and savings	30	27	30	31	26	26	36	39	28	34
Percent cut spending, increase debt	4	5	4	3	2	6	5	4	2	5
Percent cut savings, increase debt	0	0	1	0	0	1	0	1	0	0
Percent cut spending, savings, and increase debt	7	11	8	2	10	8	5	7	10	6
Percent cut savings	20	17	19	24	18	18	24	24	21	22
Percent cut spending	74	73	76	73	74	75	73	70	72	74
Percent increase debt	6	9	5	3	8	7	3	6	7	4

Source: NYFed survey.

Notes: Survey data is based on the questions: "Suppose next year you were to find your household with 10 percent more income than normal, what would you do with the extra income?" Answer options: (1) save or invest all of it, (2) spend or donate all of it, (3) use all of it to pay down debts, (4) spend and save some, (5) spend some and use part of it to pay down debts, (6) save some and use part of it to pay down debts, or (7) spend some, save some, and use some to pay down debts." For options (4) to (7), follow-up question: "Please indicate what share of the extra income you would use to save or invest, spend or donate, or pay down debts." (Please note that the three proportions need to add up to 100 percent.) "Now imagine that next year you were to find yourself with 10 percent less household income. What would you do?" Answer options: (1) cut spending by the whole amount, (2) not cut spending at all, but cut my savings by the whole amount, (3) not cut spending at all, but increase my debt by borrowing the whole amount, (4) cut spending by some and cut savings by some, (5) cut spending by some and increase debt by some, (6) cut savings by some and increase debt by some, or (7) cut spending by some, cut savings by some, and increase debt some. For options (4) to (7), follow-up question: "Please indicate what share of the lost income you would cover by reduce spending, reduce savings, or increase borrowing." (Please note that the three proportions need to add up to 100 percent.)

Table 9.18   **Expectations of macro measures**

	All	Age			Income			College	Bubble states	Homeowner
		<40	40–55	>55	<30K	30–75	>75K			
Percent expect higher unemployment	37	27	48	41	45	35	33	33	39	37
Percent expect lower unemployment	16	16	15	18	15	15	18	23	16	14
Percent expect higher interest rate	52	50	47	61	52	54	50	53	53	54
Percent expect lower interest rate	8	11	10	5	14	8	5	7	10	6
Percent expect higher mortgage rate	46	39	45	55	42	49	46	53	38	48
Percent expect lower mortgage rate	9	12	9	5	11	9	7	7	9	7
Percent expect higher house prices	31	33	29	32	26	34	34	37	32	32
Percent expect lower house prices	21	23	26	15	30	19	16	14	21	19
Aver. expected % home price change	00.5	0.8	0.2	0.6	0.2	1.0	0.4	1.0	1.3	0.6

Source: NY Fed survey.

Notes: Survey data based on the following questions: "For people out of work during the coming twelve months—Do you think that there will be more unemployment than now, about the same, or less? No one can say for sure, but what do you think will happen to interest rates for borrowing money during the next twelve months—Will they go up, stay the same, or go down? A year from now, do you think interest rates on home mortgages will be higher, lower, or about the same as they are now? One year from now, do you think that the average house price at the national level will be higher, lower, or about the same as today? In percentage terms, how much higher/lower on average do you expect the average house price to be at the national level a year from now?"

Table 9.19   Expectations of macro measures for affected subgroups

	All	Unemployed	Lost >10% income	Underwater
Percent expect higher unemployment	37	30	30	44
Percent expect lower unemployment	16	26	18	8
Percent expect higher interest rate	52	34	49	59
Percent expect lower interest rate	8	5	10	0
Percent expect higher mortgage rate	46	28	51	54
Percent expect lower mortgage rate	9	15	8	5
Percent expect higher house prices	31	19	38	42
Percent expect lower house prices	21	20	17	24
Aver. expected % home price change	0.5	–0.7	1.6	1.9

Source: NYFed survey. See notes to table 9.18.

0.5 percent during 2010. Perhaps not surprisingly, expectations about overall economic conditions vary with experiences of financial distress. As shown in table 9.19, those who are underwater are more likely to expect higher unemployment, interest, and mortgage rates. Expectations for those who are unemployed or those who reported household income losses of over 10 percent during 2009 do not depict the same pessimistic picture. In fact, expectations for this group tend to be more optimistic relative to our sample. It is also notable that those who report to be underwater are more likely to expect home prices to rise in the future, and to expect a higher mean increase in home prices relative to the entire sample.

Tables 9.20 and 9.21 report expectations about a number of personal outcomes and decisions. Considering first year-ahead expectations of household incomes, while there exists considerable heterogeneity in expectations across individuals, overall respondents are reasonably optimistic, expecting an average increase of 4.1 percent in their household income over the next twelve months. Expected increases are higher on average among younger- and lower-income respondents, while older- and higher-income respondents instead on average expect a small decline in their household incomes.[22] Expected increases are highest on average for financially distressed respondents, that is, those who report to be unemployed at the end of 2009 and those who report to have lost over 10 percent of household income in 2009 (table 9.21). This is consistent with respondents anticipating finding a job or experiencing an income rebound in the next twelve months. A similar pattern is found for wage expectations (asked of those who were employed at the

22. Clearly some of these responses reflect expectations of nonlabor income, life cycle behavior (expected retirement) and rebounds in income by the unemployed expecting to find work.

Table 9.20   Expectations of income, saving, debt, and spending

	All	Age			Income			College	Bubble states	Home-owner
		<40	40–55	>55	<30K	30–75	>75K			
Household income										
Percent expect HH income higher	32	43	33	16	30	40	25	32	38	28
Percent expect HH income lower	17	14	18	19	14	12	23	18	16	18
Aver. expected % change in HH income	4.1	7.0	5.1	-0.8	8.6	6.0	-1.8	4.9	6.3	0.7
Aver. expected % wage change+	3.4	4.5	2.9	1.3	5.3	3.1	2.6	2.6	4.4	2.5
Saving										
Percent expect to incr. retirement contributions	13	15	18	5	6	13	20	17	15	13
Percent expect to decr. retirement contributions	4	2	6	5	2	5	5	4	3	4
Percent expect to add more/use less of other savings	29	37	33	15	22	32	31	34	39	27
Percent expect to add less/use more of other savings	24	21	22	29	31	22	19	20	27	22
Debt										
Percent expect to pay down principal*	81	82	82	78	64	84	85	81	80	81
Percent expect to prepay principal*	24	24	25	24	15	21	29	35	30	24
Percent expect to miss mort. payments*	6	11	4	2	22	6	1	3	1	6
Percent expect to add mortgage/heloc*	6	4	8	5	9	7	4	7	7	6
Percent expect to decr. nonmortgage debt	66	70	67	60	61	67	70	63	67	67
Percent expect to incr. nonmortgage debt	4	5	3	4	5	4	4	4	7	3

(continued)

Table 9.20 (continued)

	All	Age			Income			College	Bubble states	Home-owner
		<40	40-55	>55	<30K	30-75	>75K			
Spending										
Higher monthly spending	29	28	24	35	39	25	24	26	28	28
Lower monthly spending	16	16	18	13	15	16	17	16	14	15
Average change in monthly spending	1.7	2.6	0.6	1.7	4.9	0.5	0.2	1.1	1.4	1.4

Source: NYFed survey.

Notes: Survey data based on following questions: "During the next twelve months do you expect the total combined income of all members of your household to increase, decrease, or stay the same? In percentage terms, by approximately how much do you expect it to increase/decrease? Suppose that, twelve months from now, you are actually working in the exact same job, at the same place you currently work, and working the exact same number of hours. Twelve months from now, do you expect that your earnings on this job, before taxes and deductions, to have gone up, or gone down, or stayed where they are now? By about what percent do you expect that your earnings on this job, before taxes and other deductions, will have gone up or down, twelve months from now, in that case? Thinking now about the coming year, do you (and your spouse/partner) expect to make any changes to your contributions to your retirement account(s) during the next twelve months?" Answer options: (1) yes, expect to increase total contribution; (2) yes, expect to decrease total contribution; (3) no, expect to keep total contribution the same. "Thinking now about the coming year, do you (and your spouse/partner) expect to use up more, less, or about the same amount of your savings and investments during the next twelve months than you did in the last year or do you (and your spouse/partner) expect to add more, less, or about the same amount of new money to your savings and investments during the next twelve months than you did in the last year?" "Thinking now about the coming year, do you (and your spouse/partner) (1) expect to pay down some of the principal on the regular schedule; (2) expect to prepay (ahead of schedule) some of the principal; (3) expect to miss payments; (4) expect to add an additional mortgage or borrow on a home equity line of credit; or (5) other (please specify)." (Check all that apply.) "Thinking ahead, one year from now: How do you expect your monthly spending one year in the future to compare to your monthly spending today? In percentage terms, by how much do you expect your average monthly spending to increase or decrease?"

* Among homeowners with a mortgage or a HELOC.

+ Among those currently working.

Table 9.21   **Expectations of income, saving, debt, and spending for affected subgroups**

	All	Unemployed	Lost >10% income	Underwater
Household income				
Percent expect HH income higher	32	41	46	27
Percent expect HH income lower	17	26	21	16
Aver. expected % change in HH income	4.1	11.1	10.5	1.7
Aver. expected % wage change+	3.4	NA	4.5	1.9
Saving				
Percent expect to incr. retirement contributions	13	11	16	8
Percent expect to decr. retirement contributions	4	12	8	4
Percent expect to add more/use less of other savings	29	35	30	32
Percent expect to add less/use more of other savings	24	30	31	30
Debt				
Percent expect to pay down principal*	81	65	81	71
Percent expect to prepay principal*	24	15	24	15
Percent expect to miss mort. payments*	6	30	11	13
Percent expect to add mortgage/heloc*	6	7	5	8
Percent expect to decr. nonmortgage debt	66	51	69	76
Percent expect to incr. nonmortgage debt	4	7	2	10
Spending				
Higher monthly spending	29	30	25	30
Lower monthly spending	16	24	28	16
Average change in monthly spending	1.7	1.9	–1.5	2.3

Source: NYFed survey. See notes to table 9.20.

time of the survey at the end of 2009), with workers expecting an average 3.4 percent increase in their wages.

When asked whether they expect to make any changes to their retirement contributions over the next year, 13 percent report that they expect to increase their contributions, 4 percent expect to decrease contributions, and the remainder expect to keep them unchanged. Older individuals, those with low incomes, and those currently underwater are less likely to expect to increase their retirement account allocations. About 29 percent expect to add more or to use up less of their other savings accounts during the next year, while 24 percent instead expect to add less or use up more of their other savings. Overall, older and lower-income households plan to add less or use more of their other savings than their younger and more affluent counterparts.

While over 80 percent of homeowners with a mortgage expect to pay down some of the principal on their mortgage loans, some 24 percent expect to prepay some of the principal. Low-income individuals and those unemployed at the end of 2009 are least likely to expect to pay down some of the principal (64 percent) and least likely to expect to prepay some of the principal (15 percent). On the other hand, 6 percent of homeowners with mortgages expect to miss payments during the next year, with the rate being as much as 22 percent for those with incomes under $30,000 and 30 percent for those unemployed. Interestingly, the share of households expecting to miss a mortgage payment during the next year is actually smaller (1 percent) in the bubble states than in the nation as a whole. Finally, another 6 percent of homeowners with mortgages are expecting to add an additional mortgage or a home equity line of credit.

Considering nonmortgage debt, we find that 66 percent of respondents expect to decrease their combined debt on credit cards, auto loans, and student loans and only 4 percent expect to increase it. Plans to reduce such debt are slightly more prevalent among younger individuals and higher-income individuals, and are the highest among individuals who report to be underwater on their mortgage.

A greater share of households expects to increase their monthly spending over the next twelve months than to decrease it. On average, household spending is expected to increase by 1.7 percent. Given an average expected increase in pretax household income of 4.1 percent, and assuming a similar increase in disposable income, this implies an average expected increase of 2.4 percent in saving or debt reduction. Closely tracking their expectations of household income increases, younger individuals, those with incomes under $30,000, and those who are underwater expect the greatest increases in spending over the next twelve months.

We also elicited expectations about future retirement, bequests, and personal year-ahead overall financial situation. As shown in tables 9.22 and 9.23, 24 percent reported that they had postponed retirement, while 5 percent now plan to retire earlier. Plans to postpone retirement were most prevalent among workers over age fifty-five and workers with higher household incomes. Perhaps not surprisingly, given the loss of wealth experienced during the recession, more respondents report that the chance that they will leave an inheritance has fallen instead of increased during the past year, with declined chances more likely to be reported by those who are financially distressed.

Asked whether over the next twelve months they expect that it will generally become easier, harder, or equally difficult to obtain credit or loans compared to the past twelve months, about twice as many respondents expect credit conditions to worsen: 39 percent expect credit to become more difficult to obtain (with the rate being as high as 59 percent for those underwater), while 20 percent expect it to become easier.

Finally, significantly more respondents expect to be financially better off than worse off twelve months from now. Comparing across age and income groups, we find that younger individuals are far more optimistic than older individuals, but find little differences across income groups. Individuals who are most financially distressed report the most optimistic expectations.

Table 9.22   Expectations of retirement, bequests, access to credit, and financial well-being

	All	Age			Income			College	Bubble states	Homeowner
		<40	40–55	>55	<30K	30–75	>75K			
Retirement										
Prob. of working FT at/after 62**	62	62	65	57	57	63	65	66	52	64
Prob. of working FT at/after 65**	50	50	52	43	51	49	51	52	44	50
Expected retirement age*	67	66	69	69	70	67	66	67	64	68
Plan to retire later*	24	16	30	32	24	20	27	29	29	25
Plan to retire earlier*	5	6	2	6	5	4	5	2	5	5
Inheritance										
Decreased chance of leaving bequest	18	13	21	24	23	19	14	19	18	19
Increased chance of leaving bequest	7	7	5	8	4	7	8	7	8	7
Credit access										
Credit easier	20	20	18	24	19	20	21	17	14	20
Credit harder	39	41	42	35	43	36	39	37	34	39
Overall financial situation										
Will be better off financially	32	45	29	16	29	35	30	36	31	29
Will be worse off financially	13	6	15	21	16	12	11	13	17	14

Source: NYFed survey.

Notes: Survey data based on the following questions: "Thinking about work in general and not just your present job (if you currently work), what do you think is the percent chance that you will be working full-time after you reach age 62 (65)? Has the age at which you plan to retire changed since last year?" Answer options: (1) I now plan to retire sooner than I did last year, (2) no change in plans, (3) I now plan to retire later than I did last year. "In the past twelve months, have the chances of you (and your spouse/partner) leaving an inheritance increased, decreased, or stayed the same? During the next twelve months, do you expect that it generally will become easier, harder, or equally difficult to obtain credit or loans compared to the past twelve months? Now, looking ahead—Do you think that a year from now you (and your household) will be better off financially, or worse off, or just about the same as now?"

* Among those currently working.

** Among those age 60 or younger.

Table 9.23   Expectations of retirement, bequests, access to credit, and financial well-being for affected subgroups

	All	Unemployed	Lost >10% income	Underwater
Retirement				
Prob. working FT at/after 62**	62	64	69	64
Prob. working FT at/after 65**	50	55	54	57
Expected retirement age*	67	n/a	69	69
Plan to retire later*	24	n/a	25	1
Plan to retire earlier*	5	n/a	11	27
Inheritance				
Decreased chance of leaving bequest	18	32	35	31
Increased chance of leaving bequest	7	20	6	3
Credit access				
Credit easier	20	20	18	12
Credit harder	39	33	41	59
Overall financial situation				
Will be better off financially	32	47	43	34
Will be worse off financially	13	15	13	13

Source: NYFed survey. See notes to table 9.22.

9.5   Conclusion

In this chapter we first documented the extent to which households were affected by the declines in the housing, stock, and labor markets as well as the heterogeneity in the impact of these declines across age, income, education groups, and geographic areas. Next, we analyzed the nature of behavioral responses to the shocks in income and wealth, including changes in spending, contributions to retirement and savings accounts, and changes in household mortgage and nonmortgage debt. Finally, we assessed people's expectations about a large set of behaviors and outcomes going forward, including their expectations about the labor and housing markets, access to credit, their future spending and saving behavior, and expectations for paying down debts.

We found large differences across households in the extent to which they were affected by the recession, especially by income, age, and geography. While considerable proportions of households were not directly affected by declines in the housing, stock, and labor markets, a large share of households were affected by at least one of these. The proportion of households that suffered large declines in housing wealth and in retirement savings, and which experienced large income drops varied across demographic groups, but the proportion that experienced at least one of these was fairly evenly spread across groups.

In response to their deteriorated financial situation, households reduced their average spending. At the same time, they increased their saving, with the personal saving rate as measured by the National Income and Product Accounts (NIPA) increasing considerably from historically low prerecession levels. Survey data suggest that if there indeed was a recent increase in household saving, this increase—at least in 2009—did not materialize through an increase in contributions to retirement and savings accounts. If anything, such contributions actually declined on average during the past year. Instead, the higher saving rate appears to reflect a considerable decline in household debt, particularly mortgage debt. This suggests that rebuilding net wealth was an important driver of household decisions. Unlike the period leading up to the recent recession, during which the average mortgage debt pay-down rate was negative (increases in debt associated with second mortgages, cash-out refinances, and home equity lines of credit exceeded regular principal pay-downs on existing mortgages), since 2008 it has turned positive. Similarly, the steady annual increase in outstanding nonmortgage debt (also referred to as consumer debt) came to a halt in 2009. However, unlike mortgage debt, consumers made little headway in 2009 in actually *lowering* total nonmortgage debt, with some debt such as that associated with student loans continuing to grow steadily.

Regarding individuals' expectations about the future, we find that individuals across all demographic groups had moderately optimistic expectations about income and earnings in 2010. At the end of 2009, consumers expected to increase spending in 2010 by less than perceived increases in earnings and income, and expected to pay down debt and increase savings, suggesting a shift in attitudes regarding saving and consumption. The implied moderate increase in saving during 2010 is in fact consistent with what we have observed so far in 2010. While consumers were moderately optimistic about their income prospects, they were pessimistic about the availability of credit, with access to credit expected to become even more difficult during 2010.

Appendix

The RAND American Life Panel

The survey data used in this chapter were collected through two survey modules administered over the Internet to participants in RAND's American Life Panel (ALP). The ALP is an Internet panel of respondents age eighteen and over. Respondents in the panel either use their own computer to log on to the Internet or they were provided a small laptop or a WebTV, which allows them to access the Internet using their television and a telephone line. The technology allows respondents who did not have previous Internet access or a computer to participate in the panel and furthermore use the WebTVs for browsing the Internet or use email.

The first survey module we analyze, referred to in the chapter as the RAND survey, was designed by Michael Hurd and Susann Rohwedder to evaluate the effects of the financial crisis. The survey was fielded from November 2008 to February 2009, with the vast majority of respondents completing the survey in November 2008. The NYFed survey on saving behavior was fielded between the end of October 2009 and January 2010, with the vast majority again responding in November 2009. Respondents were paid an incentive of about $20 per thirty minutes of interviewing. Although respondents were allowed to skip questions, those who tried to do so received a prompt encouraging them to provide an answer.

Most of the participants in both ALP surveys were randomly selected among participants in the Reuters/University of Michigan Survey of Consumers at the University of Michigan's Survey Research Center. An additional group of respondents were recruited through a snowball sample, through referrals of friends and acquaintances. While all ALP members were invited to participate in the RAND survey on the effects of the financial crisis, the NYFed survey on saving behavior was restricted to a subset of newer ALP members—those who participated in the Michigan Survey after December 2006.

A total of 900 ALP participants completed the NYFed survey, while 2,057 members completed the RAND survey. Respondents in the NYFed survey reported an average age of 50.5, with a median of 51. In total, 58 percent were female, 66 percent were married or living with a partner, 52 percent had at least a bachelor's degree, 81 percent owned a home, and 89 percent were white. Twenty-one percent lived in one of the five states that experienced the greatest housing bubble and/or bust, which were Arizona, California, Florida, Michigan, and Nevada. The median reported income range was $60,000–$75,000, with 43 percent of the respondents reporting incomes over $75,000.

Respondents in the RAND survey reported an average age of 50.0, with a median age of 51. In total, 57 percent were female, 65 percent were married or living with a partner, 45 percent had at least a bachelor's degree, 78 percent owned a home, and 90 percent were white. Twenty-two percent lived in one of the five bubble/bust states. The median reported income range was $60,000–$75,000, with 37 percent of the respondents reporting incomes over $75,000. For a more detailed description of the sample, see Hurd and Rohwedder (2010).

In all the analyses reported in this chapter, sample weights were applied to make the two samples representative of the US population. The weights were computed to equate sample proportions to those in the 2009 Current Population Survey for all population subgroups defined by homeownership, living in a bubble state, income under $30,000, age under forty, and having a college degree.

The FRBNY Consumer Credit Panel

Some of the analyses in this study are based on credit report data from the FRBNY Consumer Credit Panel. The panel comprises a nationally representative 5 percent random sample of US individuals with credit files, and all of the household members of those 5 percent. In all, the data set includes files on more than 15 percent of the adult population (age eighteen or older), or approximately 37 million individuals in each quarter from 1999 to the present. The underlying sampling approach ensures that the panel is dynamically updated in each quarter to reflect new entries into and exits out of the credit markets, with young individuals and immigrants entering the sample and deceased individuals and emigrants leaving the sample at the same rate as in the population of individuals with credit files. In each quarter, the records of all other household members who shared a primary individual's mailing address were also included. Even though all individuals included in the database are anonymous, the panel allows one to track individuals and households consistently over time. In addition to the computation of nationally representative estimates of individual and household-level debt and credit in each quarter, the panel therefore permits a rich analysis of the dynamics of consumer debt and related policy issues at both the individual and household levels.

Since the FRBNY Consumer Credit Panel data are collected at the borrower level, they offer a more comprehensive perspective on mortgage debt than is available in standard loan-level data sets. In addition to detailed data on all debts secured by residential real estate, the panel includes information on individuals' and households' other loans, such as credit cards, auto loans, and student loans. More general information available in the panel include the residential location of the borrower at the census block level, the individual's year of birth, the individual's credit experience such as foreclosure, bankruptcy, and collection, as well as a consumer credit score that is comparable to the well known FICO score. More details regarding the sample design and data content can be found in Lee and van der Klaauw (2010).[23]

References

Bruine de Bruin, Wändi, Simon Potter, Robert Rich, Giorgio Topa, and Wilbert van der Klaauw. 2010. "Improving Survey Measures of Household Inflation Expectations." *Current Issues in Economics and Finance* 16(7). http://www.newyorkfed.org/research/current_issues/ci16-7.html.

23. Lee and van der Klaauw (2010).

Brown, Meta, Andrew Haughwout, Donghoon Lee, and Wilbert van der Klaauw. 2010. "The Financial Crisis at the Kitchen Table: Trends in Household Debt and Credit." Staff Report no. 480, Federal Reserve Bank of New York, December.

Bucks, Brian K., Kennickell, Arthur B., Mach, Traci L., and Kevin B. Moore. "Changes in US Family Finances from 2004 to 2007: Evidence from the Survey of Consumer Finances." Federal Reserve Bulletin, vol. 95, Board of Governors of the Federal Reserve System. February.

Haughwout, Andrew, Richard Peach, and Joseph Tracy. 2010. "The Homeownership Gap." Current Issues in Economics and Finance 16 (5). http://www.newyorkfed.org /research/staff_reports/sr418.html.

Hurd, Michael D., and Susann Rohwedder. 2010. "Effects of the Financial Crisis and Great Recession on American Households." NBER Working Paper no. 16407, Cambridge, MA.

Lee, Donghoon, and Wilbert van der Klaauw. 2010. "An Introduction to the FRBNY Consumer Credit Panel." Staff Report no. 479, Federal Reserve Bank of New York, November.

10

Drowning or Weathering the Storm?
Changes in Family Finances
from 2007 to 2009

Jesse Bricker, Brian Bucks, Arthur Kennickell,
Traci Mach, and Kevin Moore

The aggregate effects of the recent financial downturn were often starkly apparent and readily measured, but the microeconomic consequences were more difficult to gauge. To fill this gap, the Federal Reserve Board (FRB) designed and implemented in 2009 a follow-up survey of households that completed the 2007 Survey of Consumer Finances (SCF). The 2007 SCF was the most recent source of detailed information of families' finances, conducted just as the economy started to turn down, so reinterviewing participants in that survey provides a unique basis for measuring how the financial crisis affected families.

This chapter provides the first look at changes in families' finances captured in the 2007–2009 SCF panel. The panel data allow us to examine how the effects of changes in the value of specific types of assets and debts and other economic disturbances played out at the household level. The data also allow us to consider the potential longer-term consequences of the financial crisis on families' decisions and expectations.

The broad contours of changes in households' assets, debts, and net worth align with changes in the corresponding aggregate measures, but the microdata available in the 2007–2009 SCF panel highlight the substantial

Jesse Bricker is an economist at the Board of Governors of the Federal Reserve System. Brian Bucks is an economist at the Consumer Financial Protection Bureau. Arthur Kennickell is assistant director of the Board of Governors of the Federal Reserve System. Traci Mach is senior economist at the Board of Governors of the Federal Reserve System. Kevin Moore is senior economist at the Board of Governors of the Federal Reserve System.

Opinions expressed in this chapter are those of the authors alone, and they do not necessarily reflect the views of the Board of Governors of the Federal Reserve System or its staff. For acknowledgments, sources of research support, and disclosure of the authors' material financial relationships, if any, please see http://www.nber.org/chapters/c12526.ack.

variation in families' experiences over this two-year period. Although over 60 percent of families saw their wealth decline over the two-year period, a sizable fraction of households experienced gains in wealth, and some families' financial situation changed little, at least on net, between 2007 and 2009. The shifts in wealth do not appear to be correlated in a simple way with families' characteristics; instead, the pattern of mixed losses, gains, and modest shifts in wealth across families generally holds within groups defined by demographic characteristics or by 2007 net worth or income.

On the whole, changes in net worth appear to stem from changes in asset values rather than changes in debt, though, again, the results vary across households. As might be expected, changes in the values of homes, stock, and business equity appear to have been important determinants of changes many families' wealth. The economic experiences of families that might have been seen as financially vulnerable in 2007, by and large, did not differ dramatically from those of other families, except for families with high debt payments relative to income, who were more likely to have comparatively large declines in wealth. Finally, at least in the aggregate, households appear more cautious in 2009 than two years earlier, as most households increased their desired level of buffer savings and many expressed concern over future income and employment.

The first section of the chapter surveys macroeconomic changes over the 2007–2009 period and offers an overview of key technical aspects of the design and execution of the 2009 survey. The chapter then examines in greater depth the changes in household wealth, shifts in portfolio composition, changes in net worth over selected demographic groups, the relationship between wealth changes and potential economic vulnerability, and a variety of measures that may point toward the future evolution of both the economy as a whole and the household sector in particular.

10.1   Background

10.1.1   Economic Background

The 2007 to 2009 period covered by the SCF panel was a time of extraordinary economic upheaval and crisis most families had never experienced. As the field period for the 2007 SCF concluded in the beginning of 2008, the economic downturn was in its early stages. In the fourth quarter of 2007, the growth in real gross domestic product (GDP) was still 2.9 percent and the unemployment rate remained relatively low at 5 percent. However, house prices, as measured by the CoreLogic national index, fell about 9 percent during 2007, and the major stock market indices that peaked in October 2007 began to trend downward. Real GDP was essentially steady for the first half of 2008 and fell by 4.0 and 6.8 percent in the third and fourth quarters, respectively. Unemployment rose to 7.4 percent by the end of 2008, and over the course of the year, house prices declined 17 percent and the Wilshire 5000 index of publicly traded equities fell 39 percent.

In the first half of 2009, the economic contraction continued as real GDP declined, unemployment continued to rise, and housing and equity prices continued to fall. However, in the second half of 2009, some aspects of the economy started to improve, with strong growth in real GDP of 5 percent in the final quarter of 2009, sizeable gains in the equity market, and a slowing of the decline in house prices. Despite these positive signs, the labor market continued to struggle as the unemployment rate rose to 10 percent by the end of 2009. The 2009 reinterviews took place between July of 2009 and January of 2010, and despite the signs of the nascent recovery, the economic downturn was likely still very present for many families.

10.1.2   SCF 2007 Cross-Section and 2009 Reinterview

The SCF is normally conducted by the FRB as a triennial cross-sectional survey, but there is an earlier history of the collection of panel data. The collection of wealth data at the FRB began with the 1962 Survey of Financial Characteristics of Consumers and the 1963 Survey of Changes in Financial Characteristics of Consumers, which reinterviewed the earlier survey participants. The current SCF series was started in 1983, and respondents to that survey were reinterviewed briefly in 1986 and more extensively in 1989. Until the reinterview in 2009 with the participants of the 2007 SCF, no further SCF panel interviews were conducted.

The 2007 and 2009 Survey Instruments

The triennial cross-sectional SCF surveys, of which the 2007 is the most recently completed, provide detailed information on all aspects of household finances, and most of this information is collected at the level of individual items. For example, the survey covers up to three mortgages (aside from home equity lines of credit) on a primary residence, with questions on all aspects of the mortgage terms. The typical interview time is between seventy-five and ninety minutes, but the distribution of interview length is skewed, with interviews for some participants with complicated finances requiring up to four hours and sometimes several sessions.

The 2009 SCF focused on a smaller set of variables that were most useful for understanding the nature of the changes experienced by families during the financial crisis. To maximize comparability of data between the original and follow-up interviews, the 2009 questionnaire maintained as much as possible the ordering and systematic framing of concepts as in the 2007 questionnaire. In the great majority of cases, the 2009 reinterview retained virtually identical text for the highest-level questions that determine the logical flow of the interview through each of the wealth categories. To reduce the response burden, less detail was typically collected on the components of net worth. In a few important instances—particularly mortgages on primary residences and components of income—the survey retained the full detail of the 2007 survey.[1] As a consequence of the panel questionnaire design, it is possible to construct parallel estimates for all of the most important aspects of wealth in both 2007 and 2009. In addition, a few new questions were introduced, most notably a sequence targeting owners of small businesses and a series of questions on mortgage refinancing and modification. The 2009 reinterview also collected information about changes in families' portfolios and about key positive and negative events for the family between 2007 and 2009. The typical panel interview required about forty-five to sixty minutes.

SCF Sample Design and Unit of Observation

The SCF employs a dual-frame sample design, including a multistage area probability (AP) sample and a list sample. The AP sample, which comprises roughly 60 percent of the total sample, provides broad national coverage and a sample of households selected with equal probability. The AP sample for 2007 was selected by NORC at the University of Chicago (see Tourangeau et al. 1993). The list sample is selected from statistical records derived from individual income tax returns by the Statistics of Income (SOI) division of the Internal Revenue Service. The list sample oversamples households that are predicted to be relatively wealthy based on a model of wealth estimated using variables available in the SOI data (see Kennickell and McManus 1993; Kennickell 1998, 2001). The two samples are combined to represent the population of households.

In 2007, the eligible respondent in a given household was the economically dominant single individual or the most financially knowledgeable member of the economically dominant couple.[2] Most of the questions in the interview of that sample were focused on the "primary economic unit" (PEU), a concept that includes the core individual or couple and any other people in the household (or away at school) who were financially interdependent with that person or couple.[3] Detailed information on employment and pensions was collected on only the respondent and, as relevant, that person's spouse or partner.[4]

---

1. Because of the perceived sensitivity of the information in the survey, dependent interviewing (that is, the carrying over of information from the 2007 interview to frame the changes) was limited to two narrow sets of information: housing tenure and date the household moved into their residence, and ownership or partial ownership of a privately held business. This information was necessary to assess changes as accurately as possible for these key variables.

2. Where no one was knowledgeable or where the respondent was too busy or disabled to be able to participate, it was possible to use a proxy for the respondent if the person would be able to answer the questions on behalf of the respondent. Usually, the proxy would be an accountant, a business manager, a legal guardian, or an adult child.

3. We use the term "family" throughout this chapter to mean the PEU.

4. The SCF cross-sections include a highly summarized set of questions at the end of the interview to obtain rough information about the finances of people in the household that are not in the PEU. The panel questionnaire did not collect this information on anyone in the household outside the PEU.

For the 2009 panel survey, a concerted effort was made to track every 2007 household and to conduct an interview with the original respondent or an eligible alternate, as defined below. Even over the roughly two years between the 2007 and 2009 surveys, there were large changes in the structure of some households, so it is important to be clear about who in the original households were followed in the 2009 survey. For both the AP and list samples, the target household at the time of the 2009 survey was defined as follows:

1. If the 2007 respondent was alive and not living permanently outside the United States, the target household in 2009 was the one that contained that person.

2. If (a) the 2007 respondent was either deceased or living permanently outside the United States and if (b) the 2007 respondent had a spouse or partner who was a part of the PEU as defined in the 2007 survey and who lived permanently in the United States, the target household in 2009 was the one that contained the 2007 spouse or partner of the 2007 respondent.

3. Where (a) the 2007 respondent was either deceased or living permanently outside the United States in 2009 and (b) either there was no spouse or partner who was a part of the 2007 primary economic unit or there was such a spouse or partner but that person was either deceased or living permanently outside the United States, then the case was considered to be out of scope for the 2009 survey.

Note that each household interviewed in 2007 corresponds to at most one household in the panel. To maximize the comparability of answers in the two interviews, whenever possible the same person who was interviewed in 2007 was reinterviewed in 2009. When that person was not available and there was a financially knowledgeable spouse or partner of that person in an eligible 2009 household, that person was allowed to serve as the respondent in 2009.[5]

The FRB gave approval for the 2009 reinterview in April of 2009. The first interviews were conducted in July of that year, and nearly all interviews were completed before January 2010, when data collection stopped. When the field work ended, almost 89 percent of the eligible 2007 SCF participants had been reinterviewed, and the panel response rate based on the eligible cases was at least 87 percent in every sample group.[6] Analysis of nonresponse to the 2009 interview suggests that there is little relationship between response and the most important characteristics in the panel.

There was some change in the composition of the survey households over

---

5. As in the 2007 cross-section, a knowledgeable proxy was allowed to complete the interview on behalf of the respondent if the respondent was disabled, too busy, or not knowledgeable about the finances of the household.

6. See Kennickell (2010) for an analysis of nonresponse in the 2009 panel. The response rate relative to the full sample of households selected for the 2007 SCF was, of course, lower due to nonresponse in the 2007 survey.

the 2007–2009 period. For example, in 5 percent of households there was a spouse or partner of the respondent in 2009 where there had been no such person in 2007, and in 4.7 percent of households there was no spouse or partner in 2009 where there had been such a person in 2007. Deleting families with such large compositional changes does not affect the qualitative findings reported in this chapter.

Data Processing

The SCF data are carefully edited to incorporate information reported by the interviewer about problems in the data and to address inconsistencies in reporting. Although the data editing for the panel focused most directly on the 2009 data, the process was organized around comparisons of the 2007 and 2009 data for each cases. Sometimes information in the panel was sufficient to cause a review of an original editing decision made for the 2007 data. Changes observed in panel data are virtually always subject to compounding of error from multiple measurements, but in general, the inspection of the SCF data during the editing process suggests that there is a relatively high level of comparability between the two years. Missing data in the combined 2007–2009 data set were imputed using a multiple imputation routine developed for the SCF. Data originally missing in 2007 were reimputed conditional on the 2009 data. Weights for the panel were constructed using a procedure comparable to that applied to generate the original 2007 cross-sectional weights. As noted above, the samples of eligible respondents for the original 2007 and 2009 panel differ slightly. Even allowing for this difference, estimates of 2007 characteristics may differ from previously published estimates as a consequence of additional editing, differences in imputation, or differences in weighting.

10.2   Wealth Change and Its Decomposition

This section describes key dimensions of wealth change for families from 2007 to 2009. We first look at of the changes in the overall wealth distribution. Next we consider the changes in wealth for selected demographic groups and look at the role of housing, stocks and business equity, and debt in those changes. We then focus on families that experienced shocks or that might have been considered financially vulnerable. The final subsection presents behavioral and attitudinal shifts that we believe point to factors that may influence the path of families' finances and the economy.

We use the term "wealth" here to mean net worth, or total assets less total liabilities.[7] Assets include a main residence, other real estate holdings, net business equity, vehicles, trusts in which the family has an equity interest, annuities with a cash value, other financial assets, pension accounts that the

---

7. See Bucks, Kennickell, Mach, and Moore (2009) for a detailed discussion of the wealth measure used here. All dollar values reported are given in 2009 dollars.

family can withdraw from or take loans against, and miscellaneous assets. Defined-benefit pensions and other assets where there is no equity interest are not included here as assets. Liabilities include mortgages on primary and secondary residences, lines of credit, credit card debt, installment loans, loans against pension accounts or life insurance, and all other types of personal debt. Debt held by a family's business or nonresidential real estate is netted against the value of those assets.

10.2.1   Changes in the Distribution of Wealth

The distribution of wealth for the population covered by the SCF panel shifted downward across the entire range from 2007 to 2009. Comparison of the cumulative distributions of wealth for 2007 and for 2009 given in figure 10.1 shows a broad downward slide in the mass of the distribution. The mean (median) fell from $595,000 ($125,000) in 2007 to $481,000 ($96,000) in 2009. The quantile-difference plot given in figure 10.2 breaks out the shifts across the full range of the wealth distribution. In dollar terms, there were substantial absolute increases in the level of negative wealth at the bottom of the distributions, about no change just above the 10th percentile, and progressively larger decreases at the higher percentiles.

10.2.2   Changes in Wealth within Families

The simple comparisons discussed above take the wealth distributions in the two years as independent. A key virtue of the panel data is that it is possible to look directly at the range of changes for all types of families.

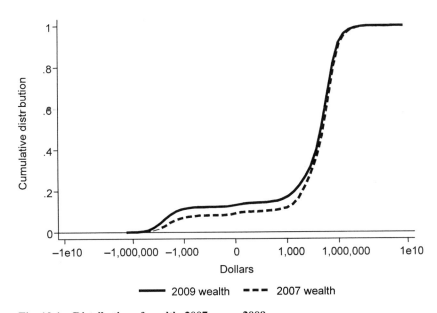

Fig. 10.1   **Distribution of wealth: 2007 versus 2009**

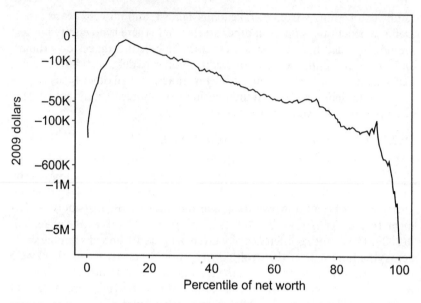

Fig. 10.2   Quantile-difference: 2009 wealth–2007 wealth

Table 10.1   Joint distribution of 2007 and 2009 wealth

	Percentile of 2009 wealth				
Percentile of 2007 wealth	Less than 25	25–49.9	50–74.9	75–89.9	90–100
Less than 25	19.6	5.4	0.7	0.1	0.0
25–49.9	4.8	15.0	4.8	0.2	0.0
50–74.9	1.1	4.1	15.2	4.0	0.2
75–89.9	0.2	0.3	3.6	8.9	1.8
90–100	0.0	0.1	0.4	1.7	7.9

In contrast to the declines in wealth at each percentile of the overall wealth distribution, changes in the wealth of individual families were more mixed. Table 10.1 uses wealth percentile groups in 2007 and 2009 to summarize the joint distribution of wealth in the two years. As evidenced by the two-thirds of families along the main diagonal, the most common single outcome was relatively small or no change in a family's relative position in the distribution. This stability is, of course, in part a function of the coarse wealth categories used in the table. The fraction of families that do not move across wealth ranges falls to 43 percent if households are classified into a 10 × 10 table based on deciles of wealth for each year and to 26 percent for a 20 × 20 table of 5-percentile-point wealth ranges for each year (not shown).

The level of wealth fell between 2007 and 2009 for 63 percent of families, and the median decline was 18 percent of 2007 wealth (table 10.2). The first and third quartiles illustrate just how diverse families' financial experiences were over the two-year period; wealth fell by over 50 percent for a quarter of families, but at the opposite extreme, wealth increased by just over 25 percent for another quarter. The kernel density estimate of changes for the panel members was bimodal: most families experienced losses, and a smaller fraction realized gains (figure 10.3). The histogram also shows that a noticeable

Table 10.2   **Changes in family wealth between 2007 and 2009 and share of families with wealth declines (by selected characteristics of families)**

Family characteristic	Percent change (%)			Share with decline in wealth (%)
	Median	25th percentile	75th percentile	
All families	−18.1	−56.9	26.9	62.5
Percentile of 2007 income				
Less than 20	−18.3	−67.6	39.7	60.7
20–39.9	−15.7	−62.8	41.3	57.8
40–59.9	−20.6	−63.7	33.7	60.9
60–79.9	−18.5	−51.5	19.9	64.8
80–89.9	−18.5	−46.5	16.9	66.1
90–100	−18.2	−44.2	3.4	71.1
Percentile of 2007 wealth				
Less than 25	0.0	−98.8	161.0	49.3
25–49.9	−18.1	−66.6	32.7	59.8
50–74.9	−17.2	−46.9	12.4	66.5
75–89.9	−21.6	−43.5	1.3	74.0
90–100	−23.8	−46.7	−2.2	76.9
Region				
Northeast	−9.5	−45.7	26.7	58.7
North central	−17.5	−54.8	27.7	62.7
South	−17.7	−58.1	32.7	61.5
West	−27.7	−62.6	16.1	67.5
Age of head (2007)				
Less than 35	−25.5	−86.9	69.1	59.5
35–44	−19.5	−64.3	37.0	58.7
45–54	−19.6	−51.1	16.8	67.0
55–64	−15.2	−46.6	20.5	61.8
65–74	−13.9	−38.8	16.5	62.7
75 or more	−20.4	−43.5	11.9	68.7
Change in wealth percentile, 2007–2009				
Less than −10	−86.8	−115.9	−67.5	100.0
−10 to −3.1	−48.2	−70.9	−38.6	100.0
−3–2.9	−22.4	−40.3	−12.8	92.7
3–9.9	15.9	1.6	38.3	18.0
10 or more	160.1	86.3	417.5	0.0

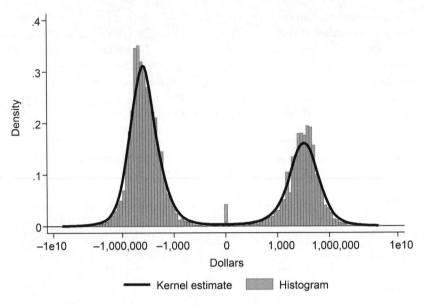

Fig. 10.3   Density of changes in wealth

share of families had essentially no change in their wealth. As a result, there was a substantial reshuffling of families across the wealth distribution.

The wealth losses and gains were generally shared across demographic groups (table 10.2). The median percent change in wealth was similar—between 16 and 21 percent—across groups of families classified by 2007 income. There was greater variation in wealth changes for lower-income families, at least as measured by the interquartile range of percent changes in wealth.[8] The narrower range of wealth changes in percentage terms is also reflected in shares of households whose wealth fell between 2007 and 2009; roughly 60 percent of families in the first three income quintiles experienced a drop in wealth, but this fraction rises to 71 percent of families in the top decile of 2007 income.

The pattern is similar when families are arrayed by their 2007 wealth. The greatest dispersion in wealth changes was among the least-wealthy quarter of families in 2007, and the interquartile range generally narrows across the groups as 2007 wealth increases.[9] The experiences of families in the bottom quartile of 2007 wealth varied most widely, but the median change was

8. A persistent problem in analyzing lower-income families is that some part of the group is quite wealthy but has either realized substantial losses or otherwise has transitorily low income and another part of the group has wealth that is negative or close to zero.

9. Part of the spread in percentage change for the least wealth group is attributable to the fact that the 2007 base for measuring percentage change was quite small in absolute terms for many families.

roughly zero. By comparison, the median change for other wealth groups was relatively similar.

Across the four census regions, median wealth was highest in 2007 for families living in the Northeast or in the West, and the variation in wealth within regions was also somewhat larger in those areas.[10] In percentage terms, losses tended to be greatest for families living in the West, a reflection in large part of the relatively greater declines in real estate prices in that region.

When classified by the age of the household "head," the variation of percent changes in wealth, as captured by the interquartile range, was greatest for the youngest group, which had the lowest median wealth and the smallest median absolute change in wealth (table 10.3).[11] The largest median absolute losses were for families headed by persons in the four oldest age groups, which also have progressively greater median wealth. The variation in absolute wealth changes was greatest for the fifty-five to sixty-four group.

There are limitations to any common measure of change and, as illustrated by the discussion of wealth changes by age above, the choice of measure can alter conclusions regarding the relative magnitude of changes for different groups. As is apparent from comparing median wealth and absolute wealth changes in the first four columns of table 10.3, changes in absolute, dollar terms tend to follow the distribution of baseline 2007 wealth too closely to be separately informative. But percentage changes, shown in the next three columns, tend to show very large changes from low levels of baseline wealth as a consequence of quite small absolute changes or as a reflection of measurement error.

Much of the remainder of the chapter classifies families by the difference in their percentile rank in the wealth distribution in each of the two years. As may be seen from the final three columns of table 10.3, this measure shares some of the shortcomings of percentage changes, but the effects of these limitations tend to be more muted. The first shortcoming is that, due to the high degree of skewness in the wealth distribution, extremely large nominal changes at the top of the distribution can correspond to small shifts in terms of percentiles. Second, because the distribution of wealth is fairly flat around zero wealth, small nominal changes can imply substantial movements in terms of percentiles, but the effect is generally not as strong as for percentage changes.

It is important to emphasize that this measure of wealth change is a measure of relative change that may not correspond to changes in levels. By

10. See Bucks, Kennickell, Mach, and Moore (2009, table 4).
11. If a couple is economically dominant in the PEU, the head is the male in a mixed-sex couple or the older person in a same-sex couple. If a single person is economically dominant, that person is designated as the family head. This concept of household "head" is chosen only to provide a consistent arrangement of the data and it does not imply any judgment about actual economic relationships within a household.

Table 10.3 Change in wealth by 2007 wealth percentile and age of household head (thousands of 2009 dollars unless specified)

Family characteristic	Median 2007 wealth	Absolute change			Percent change (%)			Change in wealth percentile (percentage points)		
		Median	25th	75th	Median	25th	75th	Median	25th	75th
Percentile of 2007 wealth										
Less than 25	1.7	0.0	−6.6	8.5	0.0	−98.8	161.0	4.0	−0.4	10.6
25–49.9	61.3	−10.7	−36.3	18.1	−18.1	−66.6	32.7	1.4	−7.3	8.1
50–74.9	237.5	−40.1	−108.3	27.7	−17.2	−46.9	12.4	0.6	−8.1	6.6
75–89.9	616.0	−134.1	−261.8	7.7	−21.6	−43.5	1.3	−0.8	−6.6	3.2
90–100	2,039.2	−449.3	−1,216.2	−36.4	−23.8	−46.7	−2.2	−0.3	−2.4	0.5
Age of head (2007)										
Less than 35	14.2	−4.9	−34.3	9.5	−25.5	−86.9	69.1	1.5	−5.4	8.3
35–44	97.1	−6.8	−91.1	17.4	−19.5	−64.3	37.0	1.0	−7.6	7.1
45–54	203.0	−23.9	−134.3	10.7	−19.6	−51.1	16.8	0.4	−6.0	5.4
55–64	257.7	−13.7	−154.3	29.3	−15.2	−46.6	20.5	0.9	−3.7	5.9
65–74	232.7	−18.2	−118.0	16.2	−13.9	−38.8	16.5	0.9	−2.0	5.7
75 or more	228.9	−20.5	−123.2	13.8	−20.4	−43.5	11.9	0.3	−4.6	5.3

Table 10.4   Wealth percentiles and share of families by change in wealth percentile

Percentile point change in 2007–2009 in wealth	Percentiles of wealth (thou. of 2009 dollars)			Share of families (%)
	Median	25th	75th	
Less than –10	168.0	58.7	349.2	15.7
–10 to –3.1	191.9	38.2	478.2	15.0
–3 to 2.9	248.2	27.8	941.4	29.8
3 to 9.9	73.9	5.1	284.2	23.2
10 or more	30.8	1.4	146.8	16.3

definition, the net change over all families under this measure is zero. When most families experienced wealth declines, as is the case in the SCF panel, even a household whose relative rank improved by this measure may have lost ground in dollar terms. For example, 18 percent of families whose rank in the wealth distribution improved by 3–10 percentile points, in fact, had a decline in their wealth. Similarly, over 90 percent of families whose rank in the wealth distribution shifted only modestly—an absolute change of no more than 3 percentile points—experienced declines in wealth between 2007 and 2009 (table 10.2).

Families that moved up the wealth distribution by 3 or more percentiles tended to have lower wealth than other families (table 10.4). Almost 30 percent of families experienced absolute change of less than 3 percentile points. The fact that this group has the highest median and 75th percentile for wealth of any of the groups and a 25th percentile wealth level within the range of values for the other percentile-point-change groups suggests this middle group includes families located throughout the wealth distribution. Just less than a quarter of families moved up in the wealth distribution by between 3 and 10 percentile points, and roughly 15 percent of families fell into each of the other three groups.

10.2.3   Shifts in Portfolio Composition

Underlying the changes in family wealth over the 2007–2009 period were shifts in the composition of assets and debts in families' portfolios. Some of these portfolio shifts were the result of active decisions by families to restructure their balance sheets and others were the result of changes in asset prices over the period. We focus on three key portfolio items: home equity, stock equity and business equity, and total debt.

Most asset values fell over the 2007–2009 period. Two important components of this decline were drops in the value of home equity and the value of stock and business equity.[12] The aggregate share of the primary residence

---

12. The definition of business equity also includes the net value of nonresidential real estate.

Table 10.5   Ownership of selected assets and of debt, all families and by 2007 wealth
                    and 2007–2009 change in wealth percentile

Family characteristic	2007 percent of families with any (%)			2007–2009 change (percentage points)		
	Home equity*	Businesses and equity	Debt	Home equity	Businesses and equity	Debt
All families	68.9	58.7	79.7	1.4	1.9	–2.2
	Percentile of 2007 wealth					
Less than 25	15.5	20.5	72.8	5.5	5.3	–3.3
25–49.9	73.8	51.7	84.8	2.0	4.4	3.4
50–74.9	93.0	69.8	82.1	–2.2	0.8	–3.3
75–89.9	95.4	92.7	80.3	0.3	–3.9	–4.2
90–100	96.8	97.9	77.7	–0.2	–2.2	–7.5
	Change in wealth percentile, 2007–2009					
Less than –10	78.3	64.1	88.7	–6.1	–7.7	0.6
–10 to –3.1	76.6	65.9	80.1	–2.1	–0.9	0.3
–3 to 2.9	74.5	63.5	76.2	1.4	0.2	–1.0
3 to 9.9	61.6	50.6	72.5	2.7	3.8	–3.4
10 or more	53.0	49.8	87.0	10.2	14.1	–7.7
MEMO						
Aggregate value as a share of assets	19.8	41.4	14.7	–1.5	–4.7	3.1

* Ownership of home equity is identical to homeownership.

as a fraction of total assets declined 1.5 percentage points, and the share of
stock and business equity fell by nearly 5 percentage points (table 10.5). The
ratio of total debt to assets, the leverage ratio, rose by about 3 percentage
points to nearly 18 percent over the period, primarily due to a decline in the
value of assets rather than an increase in debt, as shown below. Mortgage
debt as a share of total assets rose 1.9 percentage points (not shown).

Housing is a key part of the portfolio for many families. Among the least
wealthy quarter of families, the homeownership rate is less than 20 percent,
but it rises to nearly 100 percent among the wealthiest.[13] Declines in home
equity were an important driver of decreases in wealth. Among families
that moved down the wealth distribution by more than 10 percentile points,
the value of home equity as a share of 2007 assets declined by about 13 percentage points at the median; among families who moved down 3–10 per-

13. The ownership rate for home equity shown in table 10.5 treats all homeowners as having
home equity, including those with zero or negative equity, so that the homeownership rate is
identical to the share of families with home equity. The 2009 SCF panel indicates that homeownership increased slightly between 2007 and 2009. This is in contrast to cross-sectional census
data on homeownership that shows a decline over the same period. The modest difference is
likely attributable to aging or cohort effects in the panel.

Table 10.6   Changes in home equity and businesses and equity as a share of 2007 assets, by changes in wealth percentile (percentage points)

	Change in home equity as a share of 2007 assets			Change in businesses and equity as a share of 2007 assets		
Change in wealth percentile	Median	25th percentile	75th percentile	Median	25th percentile	75th percentile
Less than −10	−13.1	−30.4	0.0	−0.4	−15.8	0.0
−10 to −3.1	−6.0	−19.3	0.0	0.0	−12.2	0.0
−3 to 2.9	−1.6	−9.3	0.0	0.0	−8.5	0.0
3 to 9.9	0.0	−2.2	2.9	0.0	0.0	5.0
10 or more	0.0	0.0	20.2	0.3	0.0	31.3

centile points the median decline in the share was 6 percentage points (table 10.6). The median share was little changed for the remaining groups. The change in the share showed the most variation among the groups of families with the largest increases or decreases in their percentile rank, which were also the groups with the largest changes in homeownership rates, shown in table 10.5.[14]

Stock and businesses equity are less widely held among families than are houses, but they account for roughly 40 percent of families' assets overall. Ownership of stocks and business equity rises with wealth, but does so more gradually across 2007 wealth groups than homeownership (table 10.5). Measured as a share of 2007 assets, the value of stock and business equity increased for families with below-median wealth in 2007 and declined for families in the top wealth quintile in 2007 (not shown).

These changes in holdings of stock or business equity from 2007 to 2009 appear to explain some of the observed wealth shifts over that time, particularly for families with the largest increases or decreases in their rank in the wealth distribution. The share of families with stock or business equity increased among families that moved up the wealth distribution by 3 or more percentiles, and the share declined for families that moved down the distribution by 10 or more percentiles (table 10.5). Although there was little change in the median of families' holdings of these assets as a ratio of their total 2007 assets, the interquartile ranges across the wealth-change groups indicate that, for those families that did experience a change, the share of total assets fell for families that moved down the wealth distribution and increased for families that moved up the wealth distribution (table 10.6). A

14. The homeownership rate declined from 78 percent to 72 percent for families in the bottom percentile-change group, and the rate rose from 53 percent to 63 percent for families whose rank in the wealth distribution improved by at least 10 percentile points. In contrast, the changes in the homeownership rate for the other percentile-change groups ranged from −2 percent to 3 percent.

Table 10.7   Changes in leverage ratio and in debt as a share of 2007 assets, by change
                    in wealth percentile (percentage points)

Change in wealth percentile	Change in leverage ratio			Change in debt as share of 2007 assets		
	Median	25th percentile	75th percentile	Median	25th percentile	75th percentile
Less than –10	29.7	13.8	59.9	0.2	–4.6	10.7
–10 to –3.1	10.6	0.3	22.6	0.0	–2.2	7.6
–3 to 2.9	0.5	–0.4	7.8	0.0	–3.0	4.0
3 to 9.9	–1.2	–8.2	0.0	0.0	–8.5	0.8
10 or more	–16.0	–47.3	–2.0	–3.1	–28.5	6.0

comparison of the quartiles in the table suggests that, on the whole, changes in home equity likely played a greater role in the evolution of families' wealth between 2007 and 2009 than did changes in business and equity.

Debt is an important element of the portfolios of many families, particularly when they purchase capital assets. Indeed, in 2007 nearly 80 percent of families held some kind of debt. Mortgage debt is by far the largest component of family debt—nearly three-quarters of the total reported in the SCF in 2007.[15] Installment loans and debt on residential real estate other than the primary residence each make up about one tenth of total debt, and most of the remaining debt—3 to 4 percent of all debt in recent SCF surveys—is owed on credit cards. These proportions changed little between the two waves of the SCF panel.

When viewed across the wealth-change categories, families that moved down the wealth distribution from 2007 to 2009 by more than 3 percentile points tended to become more highly leveraged over this period (table 10.7). The median leverage ratio for families who moved down by more than 10 percentile points rose nearly 30 percentage points. For families who moved up by 10 or more percentile points, the median decrease was more than 15 percentage points, a drop that is due in part to the nearly 8 percentage point decline in the fraction of these families that had any debt (table 10.5). However, when debt is viewed relative to 2007 assets, the changes across the change groups tend to cluster more closely around zero, suggesting that it is variation in asset values rather than debt values that is the dominant factor (table 10.7).

Figure 10.4 reinforces this conclusion. Families who moved up by 3 or more percentile points had a positive change in assets relative to 2007 wealth, while families who either stayed in place or moved down saw a negative change in assets relative to 2007 wealth. These positive (negative) changes

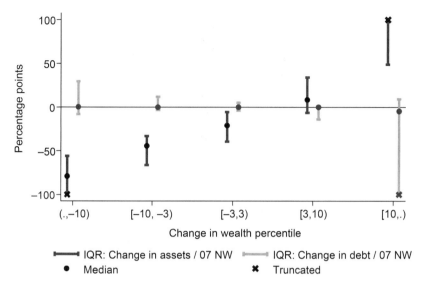

Fig. 10.4   Change in assets and debt as a share of 2007 wealth, by change in wealth percentile

in assets were largest for those families who moved up (down) the most. In contrast, the median change in debt relative to 2007 wealth was zero for each group, though the interquartile ranges suggest that families who moved up (down) were more likely to have a decrease (increase) in debt.

To complete the picture of shifts in households' portfolios between 2007 and 2009, Figure 10.5 presents the portfolio shares for mortgage debt and nonmortgage debt separately, as well as the share of assets other than net home equity and holdings of businesses and stock equity.[16] Nonmortgage debt is shown as a negative fraction of assets; to ease interpretation of home equity, mortgage debt is shown overlaid on the share of principal residences.[17]

The overall portfolio share of homes increased for both groups that moved down the wealth distribution by more than 3 percentile points, but the increase was more than offset by a larger rise in the share of mortgage debt. The share of business and equity holdings also declined for these groups, the share of other assets was slightly lower, and the share of nonmortgage debt increased. For families that moved up the distribution by 3 or more percentile points, the shares of homes and mortgage debt both declined, but the share of principal residences declined more, resulting in a

16. In the figure, "other assets" includes residential real estate other than a principal residence, financial assets, pension accounts, vehicles, and miscellaneous assets.
17. Thus, the portfolio share of principal residences is given by the sum of home equity and mortgage debt.

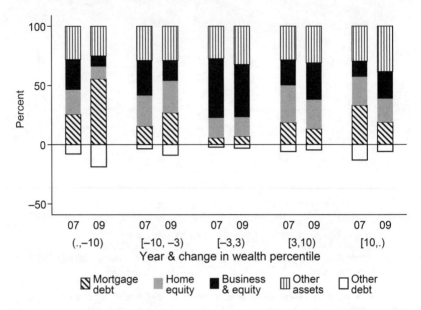

Fig. 10.5   Portfolio shares relative to assets (by year and change in wealth percentile)

decline in the share of home equity. The shares of businesses and equity and of other assets rose, while the share of other debt fell. Families that roughly maintained their place in the wealth distribution saw little change in their portfolio shares.

10.2.4   Shock, Vulnerability, and Wealth Change

In this section, we narrow our attention to families that might have been considered financially vulnerable in 2007 or who faced an unemployment spell. These are groups that might be considered likely to have experienced deterioration in their financial condition over the period covered by the panel.

Families that suffer a job loss may, in response, draw down their savings or increase their borrowing; in one extreme, the consequences of an unemployment spell could include mortgage default and foreclosure. Both the 2007 and 2009 waves of the SCF panel contain information on the current employment status of the household head and that person's spouse/partner (if applicable) as well as data on any other spells of unemployment in the twelve months prior to the interview.

In general, the relationship between unemployment spells and shifts of families within the wealth distribution appears weak. Three points stand out. First, families where at least the head or the spouse or partner of that person was unemployed in 2007 but not in 2009 were the most likely to move up the wealth distribution by 10 or more percentile points (table 10.8). It may

Table 10.8   **Distribution of unemployment status, high payment-to-income ratio, high leverage, and late debt payments by change in wealth percentile**

Family characteristic	Both 2007 and 2009	2007 but not 2009	2009 but not 2007	Neither 2007 nor 2009	Leverage >75	PIR > 40	Late 60 days
	Unemployment				High debt burden		
All families	7.4	7.7	13.9	71.0	16.1	11.5	5.9
	Change in wealth percentile						
Less than –10	7.9	8.4	18.1	65.6	15.3	24.5	7.1
–10 to –3.1	7.0	6.6	17.0	69.4	9.3	11.2	4.0
–3 to 2.9	6.4	7.1	12.6	73.9	11.5	7.9	4.1
3 to 9.9	8.4	7.5	12.4	71.6	13.5	8.8	6.3
10 or more	7.7	9.4	11.7	71.2	35.4	9.8	9.1

be that return to employment allowed these families to rebuild their assets. Second, families where at least the head or the spouse or partner of that person was unemployed in 2009, but not in 2007, were most likely to move down the wealth distribution by 3 or more percentile points. For example, among families that fell 10 or more percentile points in the wealth distribution, 18.1 percent were unemployed in 2009, but were not unemployed in 2007. Third, families that did not have an unemployment spell in either year were the most likely of any group to have only a small change in their relative wealth position.

We also consider three sets of families that showed signs of having high debt burdens in 2007. The first group comprises families whose ratio of total debt payments in 2007 to their total income (payment-to-income ratio [PIR]) exceeded 40 percent of their prior year's income (about 11 percent of all families). The second set is families that had high debt relative to assets, namely a leverage ratio greater than 75 percent (about 16 percent of all families). The final group includes families that had missed a debt payment by sixty days or more in the year prior to the 2007 SCF interview (about 6 percent of all families).[18]

The clearest correlation between these measures of financial vulnerability in 2007 and subsequent wealth changes is for the group with a PIR of 40 percent or more. Families with regular debt payments greater than 40 percent of income were more than twice as likely as other families to have moved down the wealth distribution by more than 10 percentile points. This relationship may indicate a greater rate of dissaving among the group, or the loss of a leveraged asset with positive net value in 2007. In contrast, families with a comparatively high leverage ratio in 2007 were disproportionately

18. Roughly 6 percent of all families met two of these criteria, while only about 1 percent met all three.

represented in the group of families that moved up within the wealth distribution by at least 10 percentile points; thus, it appears that some of these families may have made a successful leveraged bet.[19] Families that reported having missed a debt payment in the 2007 SCF were slightly more likely than families as a whole to have fallen in the wealth distribution by more than 10 percentile points, but they are even more likely than others to have moved up, especially by at least 10 percentile points.

10.2.5   Attitudes, Expectations, and Wealth Change

The potential longer-term economic consequences of the most recent recession depend, in part, on the extent to which the downturn and financial crisis led to changes in families' expectations and behavior. The two waves of the SCF panel provide direct evidence on several of these factors: changes in families' saving intentions or behavior, their tolerance for financial risk, and their retirement planning. The 2009 survey collected a variety of attitudinal data on the economic downturn and on how families had changed or intended to change their financial decisions as a consequence. Overall, the data suggest a shift toward caution: most families—especially those whose position in the wealth distribution improved—reported a desire for less risk and for higher reserve savings. Further, in most cases, heads of households that were working full-time planned on extending their working lives.

The SCF asks families the savings they need for emergencies and other contingencies—a measure of desired savings for precautionary purposes.[20] Families' desired level of precautionary savings tends to increase over wealth groups.[21] Most families in each of the relative wealth change categories reported greater desired precautionary savings in 2009 than they had in 2007 (table 10.9), as might be expected if families generally believed they were exposed to a higher level of risk than they were previously. Some families reported much higher preferred buffer savings: nearly 30 percent of families who moved up by 3 or more percentile points and nearly a quarter of all other families reported desired precautionary savings that were at least 200 percent higher in 2009 than in 2007. Nonetheless, a substantial minority of families reported either no change or a decrease in their precautionary savings in 2009.

An analysis of families' reported willingness to take financial risk in investing and saving suggests that the recession and other economic developments may have led families to become somewhat more cautious. Across the array of relative wealth changes, except for families in the highest percentile-

19. This group might also include families whose principal residence had a mortgage that exceeded its value in 2007 and who had lost that home by 2009; however, the data show that this situation is a negligible element in the observed outcomes.
20. See Kennickell and Lusardi (2004) for an analysis of the SCF measure of desired precautionary savings.
21. See Bucks, Kennickell, Mach, and Moore (2009, table 3.1).

Table 10.9   **Changes in desired precautionary savings level, expected retirement, and attitude toward financial risk**

| Change in wealth percentile | Percentiles of change in desired precautionary savings (%) | | | Unwilling to take financial risk (%) | | Change in age at which stop full-time work* (years) | | |
	Median	25th	75th	2007 level	2007–2009 change	Median	25th	75th
Less than –10	24.4	–29.7	189.7	40.8	11.8	0	0	5
–10 to –3.1	18.6	–45.5	189.7	38.1	5.7	0	–1	4
–3 to 2.9	28.8	–35.6	189.7	35.2	4.9	0	0	3
3 to 9.9	54.5	–21.9	262.1	45.9	6.0	0	–1	5
10 or more	60.9	–3.4	286.3	45.8	–0.5	0	–2	3

*For household heads age sixty-three or younger working full-time at the time of the 2007 and 2009 surveys who either reported a stopping age in both surveys or said they would never stop full-time work in both surveys.

change group, more families were unwilling to take any financial risk in 2009 (table 10.9). The increases in this proportion were roughly 5 to 6 percent for families whose rank rose or fell by no more than 10 percentile points, but the shift in the proportion of families unwilling to take risk was twice as large for families that moved down the wealth distribution by more than 10 percentile points.

Working families that experienced negative wealth shocks from 2007 to 2009 might be expected to plan to work longer to recoup savings for retirement, and others might plan to work longer to hedge against future uncertainties. For families headed by a full-time worker age sixty-three or younger in 2007 who was still working full-time in 2009, the median change in the worker's anticipated retirement age was zero across all wealth change groups (table 10.9).[22] But those workers who did shift their anticipated retirement date tended to report that they would stop working full-time at a date later than what they had reported in 2007. At least 25 percent of full-time household heads reported postponing retirement by two years. Not surprisingly, the largest fraction of household heads who plan to stop working two years *earlier* than planned in 2007 are the heads of households who moved up the wealth distribution by 10 or more percentile points.

Generally, specifications of the wealth effect in macroeconomic analysis assume that responses to upturns and downturns are symmetrical. The SCF offers some evidence on how individual families respond to wealth changes.

22. Table 10.9 shows the difference in the reported ages at which household heads reportedly planned to stop working full-time as reported in the 2007 and 2009 surveys. These differences are calculated only for those heads who worked full-time in 2007 and 2009, who were in the household in both survey years, and who were younger than sixty-three at the time of the 2007 interview.

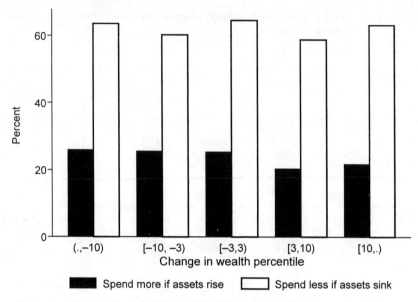

Fig. 10.6   **2009 share that spend more (less) if value of assets goes up (down)**

For a number of surveys, the SCF has included a question asking respondents whether (and to what extent) they agreed or disagreed that they would increase their spending if the value of their assets rose; the history of the question suggests that the overall response patterns are stable. For the 2009 panel interview, a new question was added using parallel language to ask about whether the family would decrease their spending if the value of their assets declined. When families are classified by their wealth changes from 2007 to 2009, the proportion agreeing with these two questions is fairly flat. However, the proportion agreeing that they would spend more if their assets rose is markedly lower than the fraction agreeing they would spend less if their assets declined in value (figure 10.6). This outcome suggests that such asymmetrical spending responses could be a factor in retarding economic recovery.

10.2.6   Future Expectations and Between-Survey Events

The SCF respondents in 2007 and 2009 were asked about their expectations of the economy over the next five years relative to the last five years—specifically, if they expected the economy would be worse, better, or about the same. In addition, in 2009 the respondents were also asked whether they thought the economy next year would be "better than now." Across the wealth-change groups, the most striking result is the greater optimism for all groups in 2009 in the five-year economic outlook (figure 10.7). Because the overall economic situation at the time of the 2009 interview was sub-

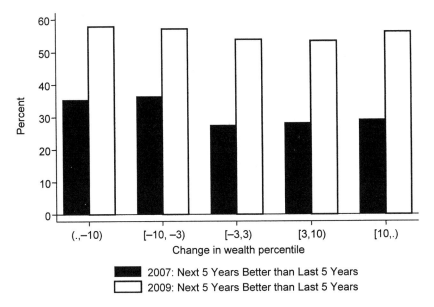

Fig. 10.7   Economic expectations by change in wealth percentile

stantially worse than at the time of the 2007 interview, this result might be taken to reflect a tendency to believe in mean reversion. The outlook over the next year after the panel interview is less optimistic, and it is similar to the five-year outlook from 2007.

In addition to these questions about the economic outlook, at the conclusion of the 2009 panel interview, respondents were asked open-ended questions about their experiences over the preceding two years, their reactions to those experiences, and their plans looking forward. We examine several of these questions in turn, classifying the distributions of responses by the changes in wealth the families experienced.

In all the wealth-change groups, most families found at least something positive in their experience, and the most common response was an answer that indicated a recognition that the workers in the family had managed to keep or get a job or that their income had somehow otherwise been maintained at an adequate level (table 10.10).[23] Nonetheless, substantial fractions of families reported that there had been no positive events, and unsurprisingly the group most likely to report this answer was the one that had moved furthest down the wealth distribution.

23. Although some respondents provided more than one answer in their open-ended response, in this and the remaining figures we have included only the answer the respondent deemed most important. Including all the answers in the analysis does not qualitatively change these results, but it would complicate the interpretation, since the sum of the shares of each answer category would exceed 100 percent.

Table 10.10   Positive and negative financial events in 2007–2009 period and biggest financial challenges by change in wealth percentile

Change in wealth percentile	Income/ employment	Portfolio	Economy	Long-term saving	Other	None
Most important positive event for family's finances						
Less than –10	40.0	12.6	0.9	n/a	10.7	35.9
–10 to –3.1	43.8	11.3	2.0	n/a	12.2	30.7
–3 to 2.9	43.4	14.6	1.6	n/a	11.5	28.9
3 to 9.9	46.2	11.7	1.0	n/a	11.1	30.0
10 or more	47.6	14.5	0.9	n/a	11.5	25.5
Most important negative event for family's finances						
Less than –10	34.1	18.5	16.2	n/a	23.1	8.0
–10 to –3.1	28.7	15.7	18.3	n/a	28.9	8.4
–3 to 2.9	24.7	24.0	17.1	n/a	24.7	9.5
3 to 9.9	29.1	17.3	15.9	n/a	24.4	13.2
10 or more	27.4	15.7	15.2	n/a	26.9	14.9
Biggest financial challenge						
Less than –10	37.8	27.5	n/a	23.1	7.1	4.5
–10 to –3.1	33.7	20.4	n/a	30.0	9.5	6.5
–3 to 2.9	29.8	17.7	n/a	31.6	13.5	7.4
3 to 9.9	34.0	18.9	n/a	30.6	10.8	5.7
10 or more	30.7	24.3	n/a	29.3	8.9	6.9

As might also be expected, far fewer families reported that there were no negative events. Families' perceptions of negative events affecting their finances varied more. Though a substantial fraction of families reported negative income- or job-related events, a nearly equivalent-sized group reported a range of outcomes classified as "other," a category that includes perceptions of recent political events, the international situation, family problems, and a broad miscellany of other answers.

Finally, the most common concern among families' future financial challenges was maintaining income or employment. Portfolio management was also a key challenge for the groups with the largest positive or negative changes in their relative wealth position.

10.3   Conclusions

From 2007 to 2009, wealth declined for most families across the initial 2007 wealth spectrum, and it declined very substantially for some. Yet many families saw only small changes and a nonnegligible group of families saw substantial increases in their wealth. This diversity of outcomes is pervasive in the data. For that reason, in this chapter we use distributions to describe as clearly as possible the central tendencies and dispersions of outcomes or changes.

By definition, changes in families' portfolios underlay the observed wealth shifts, but it is sometimes not directly obvious from the data whether the changes were driven by portfolio rebalancing or by revaluation of portfolio items. Responses to direct questioning on general portfolio changes made during the interval between the 2007 SCF and the 2009 panel interview indicate that the large majority of families passively accepted changes in portfolio shares driven by changes in asset prices. Unemployment spells are also associated with wealth declines, whether because of the necessity of dissaving or because cumulated late payments might have caused the loss of an asset, such as a home, through foreclosure. Although continued saving might also account for some marginal differences, it appears that the major shifts were driven by revaluation of assets. As expected, changes in the values of principal residences and of stock and businesses equity appear to have played a substantial part in explaining the observed changes in wealth. Shifts in leverage that took place over the period are largely explained by the general decline in the value of assets.

The data show signs that families' behavior may act in some ways as a brake on reviving the economy in the short run. Two things stand out in this regard. First, a large proportion of families in all wealth groups and across the range of changes in wealth expressed the need for greater precautionary savings. The perceived desire for additional savings is further amplified by answers to open-ended questions about recent and future adjustments to family finances. Second, the data show a tendency for families to respond asymmetrically to changes in wealth. Overall, it appears that families may be relatively reluctant to spend more when assets prices rise and may more readily reduce spending when asset prices fall. In general, the families with relative gains appeared more pessimistic and cautious before the crisis than the families with relative losses, and families with gains still appeared more cautious and less likely to spend as the economy enters a recovery

This chapter has provided only a basic outline of the results from 2007–2009 SCF panel data. Subsequent research will explore more detailed behavioral responses and consider more deeply the implications of the data for the future.

References

Bucks, Brian K., Arthur B. Kennickell, Traci L. Mach, and Kevin B. Moore. 2009. "Changes in US Family Finances from 2004 to 2007: Evidence from the Survey of Consumer Finances." *Federal Reserve Bulletin* 95:A1–A55.

Kennickell, Arthur B. 1998. "List Sample Design for the 1998 Survey of Consumer Finances." Working Paper, Board of Governors of the Federal Reserve System, Washington, DC. http://www.federalreserve.gov/pubs/oss/oss2/papers/listsample .pdf.

————. 2001. "Modeling Wealth with Multiple Observations of Income: Redesign of the Sample for the 2001 Survey of Consumer Finance." Working Paper, Board of Governors of the Federal Reserve System, Washington, DC. http://www.fed eralreserve.gov/pubs/oss/oss2/papers/scf2001.list.sample.redesign.9.pdf.

————. 2010. "Try, Try Again: Response and Nonresponse in the 2009 SCF Panel." Proceedings of the Section on Survey Research Methods, American Statistical Association.

Kennickell, Arthur B., and Annamaria Lusardi. 2004. "Disentangling the Importance of the Precautionary Saving Motive." NBER Working Paper no. 10888, Cambridge, MA.

Kennickell, Arthur B., and Douglas A. McManus. 1993. "Sampling for Household Financial Characteristics Using Frame Information on Past Income." Proceedings of the Section on Survey Research Method, American Statistical Association.

Tourangeau, Roger, Robert A. Johnson, Jiahe Qian, Hee-Choon Shin, and Martin R. Frankel. 1993. "Selection of NORC's 1990 National Sample." Working Paper, National Opinion Research Center at the University of Chicago.

11

The Misfortune of Nonfinancial Firms in a Financial Crisis
Disentangling Finance and Demand Shocks

Hui Tong and Shang-Jin Wei

[George Soros] noted, the financial crisis is beginning to have serious effects on the real economy, adding: The extent of that is not, in my opinion, yet fully recognised.
—Reuters (New York), April 9, 2008

The claim that disruptions to the banking system necessarily destroy the ability of nonfinancial businesses to borrow from households is highly questionable.
—Chari, Christiano, and Kehoe (2008)

11.1 Introduction

The subprime crisis that began in August 2007 has been called the worst financial crisis since the Great Depression by George Soros, Joseph Stiglitz, the International Monetary Fund, and other commentators.[1] While headline news tends to be dominated by the plight of investment and commercial banks and insurance companies, nonfinancial firms have also experienced economic difficulties. Figure 11.1 shows that their stock prices have exhibited a dramatic decline since the crisis broke out in August 2007.

Hui Tong is an economist at the International Monetary Fund. Shang-Jin Wei is the N. T. Wang Professor of Chinese Business and Economy, Professor of Finance and Economics and of International and Public Affairs, and director of the Jerome A. Chazen Institute of International Business at Columbia University and research associate and director of the Chinese Economy Working Group at the National Bureau of Economic Research.

We thank Tamim Bayoumi, Stijn Claessens, Marcello Estevao, Charles Hulten, Laura Kodres, Luc Laeven, Deborah Lucas, Michael Palumbo, Marshall Reinsdorf, Neng Wang, Toni Whited, Yishay Yafeh, and seminar and conference participants at the IMF, HKMA, NBER Conference on Research in Income and Wealth, and the International Finance Conference sponsored by Bank of Canada and Queen's University for helpful comments, and John Klopfer, Andrew Swiston, and Natalia Barrera Tovar for excellent research assistance. The views in the chapter are those of the authors, and do not necessarily reflect those of the IMF. For acknowledgments, sources of research support, and disclosure of the authors' material financial relationships, if any, please see http://www.nber.org/chapters/c12536.ack.

1. See http://www.thisismoney.co.uk/investing-and-markets/article.html?in_article_id =437212&in_page_id =3&ct=5; http://economictimes.indiatimes.com/International_Business /Financial_crisis_worst_since_1930s/articleshow/2881608.cms; http://www.guardian.co.uk /business/2008/apr/10/useconomy.subprimecrisis.

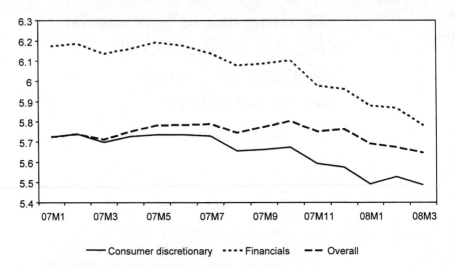

Fig. 11.1   The log of stock index during the subprime crisis

It is not self-evident, however, that the real economy suffers from a nega-tive finance shock. The fall in the stock prices of nonfinancial firms could be explained by a fall in the demand for their output. Indeed, those firms that produce consumer discretionary and leisure products, and hence are more sensitive to a change in aggregate demand, tend to experience a greater decline in their stock prices. Furthermore, as Bates, Kahle, and Stulz (2009, 1986) document, nonfinancial firms held an abundance of cash prior to the crisis. According to them, "the net debt ratio (defined as debt minus cash, divided by book assets), a common measure of leverage for practi-tioners, exhibits a sharp secular decrease. Most of this decrease in net debt is explained by the increase in cash holdings. The fall in net debt is so dramatic that the average net debt for U.S. firms is negative in 2004, 2005, and 2006." Given the apparent secular upward trend in cash holdings, the net debt ratio was likely even further into the negative territory by mid-2007, right before the start of the full-blown subprime crisis. This at least suggests the possi-bility of no serious liquidity tightening outside the financial sector. Prob-ably out of this belief, Federal Reserve Chairman Ben S. Bernanke called strong corporate balance sheets "a bright spot in the darkening forecast" during his testimony at the US Congress on monetary policy on February 27, 2008.[2] Finally, as recently as mid-October 2008, Chari, Christiano, and Kehoe (2008) suggest that the data do not support the view that the supply of financing to nonfinancial firms had declined significantly in terms of either bank lending or issuance of commercial papers.[3]

---

2. Ben S. Bernanke, Semiannual Monetary Policy Report to the Congress, February 27. http://www.federalreserve.gov/newsevents/testimony/bernanke20080227a.htm.
    3. See Cohen-Cole et al. (2008) for a rebuttal.

Disentangling finance and demand shocks is difficult in the aggregate as they are observationally equivalent. They also feed on each other as a crisis unfolds. To make progress, we propose a simple framework that explores heterogeneity across nonfinancial firms based on their differential ex ante vulnerability to each of the shocks. If there is a supply-of-finance shock, the effect is likely to be more damaging to those firms that are relatively more financially constrained to start with. Similarly, if there is an aggregate demand shock, it is likely to affect more of those firms that are intrinsically more sensitive to a demand contraction. Exploring variations across firms may thus open a window into the respective roles of the two shocks in the fortune (or misfortune) of nonfinancial firms.

To determine cross-firm heterogeneity in the sensitivity to an aggregate demand contraction, we propose a measure of (sector-level) sensitivity to a demand shock, based on the stock price response to the September 11, 2001, terrorist attack. (We exclude firms in the airline, insurance, and defense industries because they were directly affected by the 9/11 attack.) To determine cross-firm vulnerability to a supply-of-finance shock, we construct a firm-level index on the degree of ex ante financial constraint, following Whited and Wu (2006). We further use an index of intrinsic dependence on external finance developed by Rajan and Zingales (1998) as a robustness check. It is important to note that financial constraint refers to difficulties in raising external finance of all kinds, not merely in borrowing from banks.

As control variables, we add beta, firm size, and book/market ratio from the Fama and French (1992) three-factor model, and the fourth factor of momentum suggested by Lakonishok, Shleifer, and Vishny (1994). These factors are often, but not always, statistically significant. However, our two key regressors, financial constraint and consumer demand sensitivity, are always statistically significant with a correct sign. Our interpretation is that when the financial crisis hits, our two variables may reflect aspects of firm risks that are not completely captured by the three-factor, or the four-factor, model. As an extension, we further control for exposure to exchange rates and commodity prices.

To address concerns about possible endogeneity of the two key regressors, we make sure that our measures, the degree of a firm's liquidity constraint, and its sensitivity to demand shock, are predetermined with respect to the financial crisis. In other words, our thought experiment is this: If we classify nonfinancial firms into different baskets based on their ex ante degree of liquidity constraint and ex ante sensitivity to demand shocks, would this classification help us to forecast the ex post stock price performance of these firms? If there is forecasting ability associated with these classifiers, would it carry over beyond what can be explained by the three Fama-French factors and the momentum factor?

We find that the answer to each question is yes. An increase in liquidity constraint by one standard deviation is associated with an additional decline in the stock price of 12.4 percentage points from July 31, 2007, to March 31,

2008. In comparison, an increase in sensitivity to consumer confidence by one standard deviation is associated with a contraction in stock price of 3.4 percentage points during the same period. We can also form four portfolios based on these two dimensions. The portfolio analysis suggests that a supply-of-finance shock is more important quantitatively than a contraction of demand in understanding the plight of nonfinancial firms.

This chapter is linked to the literature on credit crunches (e.g., Bernanke and Lown 1991; Borensztein and Lee 2002; Dell'Ariccia, Detragiache, and Rajan 2008; Mian, forthcoming, among others). We differ from the earlier literature by considering demand sensitivity together with liquidity constraint. While our use of the Whited-Wu index as a measure of vulnerability to a finance shock is new, our measure of sensitivity to a demand shock is more novel. This chapter is also related to a small but growing literature on the origin and consequences of the subprime problem as a *financial crisis*, including recent work by Mian and Sufi (2008), Reinhart and Rogoff (2008), Dell'Ariccia, Igan, and Laeven (2008), and Greenlaw et al. (2008). As of now, we have not come across a paper that disentangles the mechanisms by which the subprime financial crisis spills over from the financial sector to the real economy. In this sense, this chapter fills an important void.

The chapter proceeds as follows. Section 11.2 presents our key specification, construction of key variables, and sources of data. Section 11.3 discusses the main empirical results and a slew of robustness checks and extensions. Section 11.4 offers concluding remarks.

11.2   Specification and Key Variables

11.2.1   Basic Specification

Our basic strategy is to check whether a classification of firms by their ex ante vulnerability to a supply-of-finance shock and ex ante sensitivity to a contraction of demand helps to predict the ex post magnitude of their relative stock price movement during the crisis. To be precise, our basic specification is given by the following equation:

(1) $Stockreturn_{it} = \alpha_0 + \beta_1 DemandSensitivity_i$
$$+\beta_2 FinancialConstraint_{i,t-1} + \varepsilon_{it}.$$

Note that this is a purely cross-sectional regression, and the key regressors are predetermined (in 2006). By construction, our specification avoids the complication associated with possible two-way feedbacks between the finance and demand shocks as a crisis progresses. As a basic robustness check, we also add the three factors from Fama and French (1992): firm size (log of assets), the ratio of the market to book values, and beta (the correlation of the firm's stock return with the overall market). In some specifications, we also add a fourth control variable: a momentum factor from Lakonishok, Shleifer, and Vishy (1994). The expanded specification is:

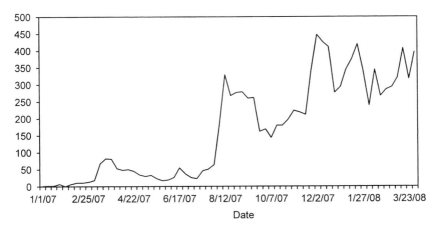

Fig. 11.2   News count of "subprime" and "crisis"

Source: Factiva.

Notes: This graph reports a weekly count of news articles containing the words "subprime" and "crisis" in all US newspapers, excluding republished news, recurring pricing, and market data. A week is defined as from Sunday to Saturday. The count was 64 for the week of July 29th, 189 for the week of August 5th, and 329 for the week of August 12, 2007, respectively.

(2)
$$Stockreturn_{it} = \alpha_0 + \beta_1 DemandSensitivity_i$$
$$+ \beta_2 FinancialConstraint_{i,t-1} + \gamma_1 Size_{i,t}$$
$$+ \gamma_2 Market / Book_{i,t-1} + \gamma_3 Beta_{i,t-1}$$
$$+ \gamma_4 Momentum_{i,t-1} + \varepsilon_{it}.$$

We follow Whited and Wu (2006) and incorporate the four factors by entering the relevant firm characteristics directly in our regressions rather than entering them indirectly by going through a factor model first. As control variables, these two ways of incorporating the four factors should be equivalent. Entering firm characteristics directly is easier to implement, though the interpretation of the coefficients on these factors is less straightforward.

While subprime loans were sporadically reported as problematic in late 2006 and early 2007, it began to be widely recognized as a crisis in August 2007. We conduct a search of news articles that contain the words "subprime" and "crisis" in all newspapers in the United States, excluding pricing and market data and republished news, and report the results in figure 11.2. There was a clear spike in such news in early August 2007. The International Monetary Fund also clearly thought of August 2007 as the starting date of a serious crisis[4]. We therefore implement our main regressions for the period

4. International Monetary Fund, *World Economic Outlook*, April 2008.

from early August 2007 to the end of March 2008. We will also consider other sample periods as extensions or placebo tests.

11.2.2   Key Data

Percentage Change in Stock Price

The stock price data is from Datastream, with adjustments for dividends and capital actions such as stock splits and reverse splits. Figure 11.1 presents the stock price index for the S&P 500 and its subcomponents over the period from January 2007 to March 2008. From there, we see that the cumulative decline of stock price index was approximately 14 percent, with the largest drop coming from the financial sector. However, many nonfinancial firms also lost value, such as "consumer discretionary" firms.

Financial Constraint Index

There is an active literature on measuring liquidity constraint. One popular measure is given by Kaplan and Zingales (1997). They use ex ante information to judge which firms are liquidity constrained, and then use a regression framework to see which variables can best forecast whether a firm is liquidity constrained. This procedure leads them to define an index of liquidity constraint based on five variables: the ratio of cash flow to capital, Tobin's q, the ratio of debt to capital, the ratio of dividends to capital, and the ratio of cash to capital.

The most up-to-date and theoretically consistent measure is provided by Whited and Wu (2006). They cast the liquidity constraint faced by a firm as the shadow value of raising one extra dollar of external financing—the value of a Lagrange multiplier associated with a lower bound on dividend payouts in a firm's optimization problem. They assume a functional relationship between the shadow value and a set of nine variables that the existing literature has suggested to be relevant for liquidity constraint. After a generalized method of moments (GMM) estimation, they determine that the following six variables are statistically significant at the 10 percent: (a) the ratio of cash flow to assets; (b) a dummy that takes the value of one if the firm issues positive dividend in that period, and zero otherwise; (c) the ratio of long-term debt to total assets; (d) the natural log of total assets; (e) the firm's three-digit industry sales growth; and (f) the firm's sales growth. The other variables are judged to be insignificant by both individual t-tests and a joint significance test. Reassuringly, the signs of the first six coefficients are also consistent with economic theory and intuition. Whited and Wu define a firm's financial constraint as the shadow value of external financing as predicted by these six variables.

We take the coefficient estimates from Whited and Wu's preferred specification (i.e., column [4] in table 1 of their paper), use the values of the six variables at the end of 2006, and compute the fitted value of the shadow value equation firm by firm. To be more precise, a firm's financial constraint index is given by the following equation:

$$(3) \quad FinancialConstraint_{it} = -0.091(CashFlow / Asset)_{it}$$
$$-0.062DividendDummy_{it}$$
$$+0.021(Debt / Asset)_{it} - 0.044\ln(Asset)_{it}$$
$$+0.102IndustryGrowth_{it}$$
$$-0.035FirmGrowth_{it}.$$

Firm-level balance sheet data come from Compustat USA. By construction, they are predetermined with respect to the onset of the subprime crisis in the summer of 2007.

Whited and Wu compare their index with another popular measure of financial constraint given by Kaplan and Zingales (1997). In simulated data, they find that the Kaplan-Zingales index does not perform well in selecting firms that are financially constrained by design. In a sense, this is not surprising as Whited and Wu could be regarded as a generalization of the Kaplan-Zingales index, but with a better grounding in the theory and in a more sound structural estimation from the data. As a result, we make the Whited-Wu index our primary measure of financial constraint.

As a robustness check, we also employ an alternative measure proposed by Rajan and Zingales (1998). The RZ index gives a sector-level approximation of a firm's intrinsic demand for external finance. Following Rajan and Zingales (1998), we define a firm's intrinsic demand for external financing by:

$$(4) \quad \text{Dependence on external finance} =$$
$$\frac{[\text{capital expenditures} - \text{cash flow}]}{\text{capital expenditures}},$$

where cash flow = cash flows from operations + decreases in inventories + decreases in receivables + increases in payables. All the numbers are based on US firms, which are judged to be least likely to suffer from financing constraints relative to firms in other countries. The original Rajan and Zingales (1998) paper covers only forty (mainly two-digit) sectors. Here, we expand the number of sectors to around 400 four-digit sectors.

To calculate the demand for external financing for US firms, we take the following steps: First, every firm is sorted into one of the four-digit sectors. Second, we calculate the ratio of dependence on external finance for each firm from 1990–2006. Third, we calculate the sector-level median from firm ratios for each four-digit sector that contains at least five firms, and the median value is then chosen as the index of demand for external financing in that sector.

Conceptually, the Rajan-Zingales (RZ) index measures something related to but not identical to the Whited-Wu index. The RZ index aims to identify sector-level features, that is, which sectors are intrinsically more dependent on external financing for their business operation. It ignores the question of which firms within a sector are more liquidity constrained. What the RZ index measures could be regarded as a "technical feature" of a sector, almost like a part of the production function. Of course, the RZ and WW indices should also be related: firms located in a sector that is naturally more dependent on external finance are also more likely to be liquidity constrained. Conversely, in a sector that does not need external finance, firms are less likely to be liquidity constrained. The simple correlation between the WW and RZ indices is 0.26.

Demand Sensitivity Index

A second key regressor is an index of a firm's sensitivity to a contraction in consumer demand. There are no existing measures in the literature, so we have to invent one. Ideally, we want this index to reflect the sensitivity of a firm's stock price to a sudden, unexpected change in future consumer demand. At the same time, we do not want the index to be contaminated by a firm's sensitivity to a liquidity shock or other factors.

We propose an index at the sector level based on the stock price reactions of the firms in that sector to the terrorist attack in 2001 (from September 10, 2001, to September 28, 2001). The 9/11 shock was large and unexpected. We can verify that there was a big downward shift in consumer confidence and expected future demand, as reflected by a downward adjustment in the forecast of subsequent US gross domestic product (GDP) growth by the International Monetary Fund and other professional forecasters in the aftermath of the shock.[5] Figure 11.3 shows that the consensus forecast for the 2002 US GDP growth rate also declined sharply by 1.5 percent after the 9/11 shock, and stayed low for at least three months. Figure 11.4 further shows a sharp drop in consumer confidence right after September 11th, which stayed low for the subsequent four months. The International Monetary Fund, in its special December 2001 issue of the *World Economic Outlook*, asserted that "the main impact [of the 9/11 shock] is likely to depend primarily on the fall in demand generated by the loss in confidence about the economy."[6] We therefore conclude the changes in stock price from September 10, 2001, to September 28, 2001, capture firms' vulnerability to a perceived contraction in consumer demand.

At the same time, because the Federal Reserve took timely and decisive actions, it may be argued that the effect of the 9/11 shock on firms' financial constraint was small, or at most, short lived. In fact, the Federal Reserve an-

5. The consensus forecast for the year of 2001 real GDP growth rate dropped from 1.6 percent to 1 percent after the September 11, 2001, attack. Meanwhile, the consensus forecast for the year of 2002 dropped from 2.7 percent to 1.2 percent.
6. http://www.imf.org/external/pubs/ft/weo/2001/03/index.htm.

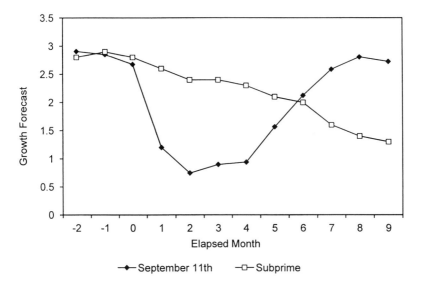

Fig. 11.3   Consensus forecast of US real GDP growth
Note: The two lines trace the forecast of annual GDP growth for the calendar years 2002 and 2008, respectively.

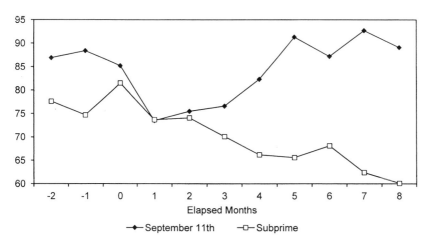

Fig. 11.4   Consumer confidence around September 11th and the subprime crisis
Source: University of Michigan Consumer Expectation Survey.

nounced on September 17, 2001: "The Federal Reserve will continue to supply unusually large volumes of liquidity to the financial markets, as needed, until more normal market functioning is restored." This is particularly true when comparing the interest rate spread between the period of the 2001 terrorist attack and the corresponding period in 2007. Figure 11.5 plots

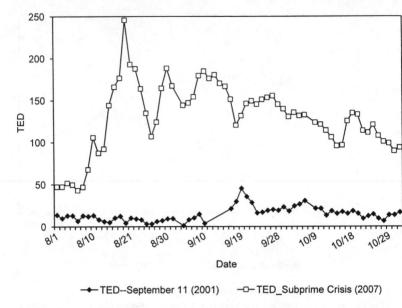

Fig. 11.5   TED (Eurodollar bond over Treasury bond) spread around September 11th and the subprime crisis

the spread between the three-month interest rate banks charge each other (in the Eurodollar market) over the three-month Treasury bills (TED spread) from early August to the end of October in both 2001 and 2007. In the first episode, both the level of the real interest rate and the spread (risk premium) returned quickly to a level that was only moderately higher than the pre-9/11 level after an initial spike. This suggests that the market likely regarded the Federal Reserve's actions in the first few days following the terrorist attack as sufficient to restore the market's desired level of liquidity. Indeed, the International Monetary Fund, in its December 2001 supplemental issue of the *World Economic Outlook*, declared that "concerted policy responses by the US and other authorities to provide such liquidity were effective in quickly restoring market stability and heading off systemic concerns."[7] We therefore conclude that the cumulative stock price change over the period September 10–28, 2001, is unlikely to also reflect a firm's reaction to a deterioration of credit availability. (In contrast, the subprime crisis news is associated with a much greater increase in the TED spread.)

We further examine the impacts of uncertainty on the stock price. Bloom (2009) argue that the uncertainty component increases significantly right after the 9/11 shock. We hence examine the measure of market uncertainty as used in Bloom (2009): the VIX index. The VIX index has been the ticker

7. http://www.imf.org/external/pubs/ft/weo/2001/03/index.htm.

symbol for the Chicago Board Options Exchange Volatility Index since 1987, a popular measure of the implied volatility of S&P 500 index options. A high value corresponds to a more volatile market and, therefore, more costly options. We find that after 9/11 the VIX index increased from 31.84 on 9/10 to 43.71 on 9/20, but that the index declined after 9/20. By 9/28 it reached 31.93, similar to the pre-crisis level. That is, by 9/28 the uncertainty factor due to the 9/11 shock has significantly subdued. Hence, when we compare the stock price from September 10 to 28, 2001, to derive the demand sensitivity, the uncertainty is unlikely to be a major driver.

To construct the index of demand sensitivity, we first compute the change in log stock price for each US firm from September 10 to 28, 2001. We then look at the mean of log stock price change for each four-digit standard industrial classification (SIC) sector and use it as the sector-level demand sensitivity. In this exercise, we drop the airlines, defense, and insurance sectors, which were affected directly by the terrorist attack. We also exclude financial sector firms and are left with 759 four-digit sectors in total. We choose our window deliberately. If the window is too short, the index may also reflect a firm's reaction to a perceived tightening of liquidity. If the window is too long, the prospect for US GDP growth might be revised upward so that the index may no longer capture a firm's reaction to a perceived economic downturn.

We perform two additional sniff tests to check if the index is sensible. First, we pick out a sector that intuitively should be relatively sensitive to a demand contraction ("consumer discretionary" such as leisure goods), and another sector that intuitively should be much less so ("consumer staples" such as food and nondurable household goods). We check if the 9/11 index produces values that are consistent with this classification. The 9/11 index indeed yields a larger value for "consumer discretionary" sector, which is consistent with the notion that the 9/11 index reflects sensitivity to a demand contraction.

As a second sniff test, we compute a revision in analyst forecasts of a firm's earnings for the following year in the months immediately before and after the 9/11 terrorist attack (typically August and October of that year), and check to see if the revisions of earnings forecast are related to our proposed index for sensitivity to a demand contraction. When the proposed demand contraction index is regressed on the revision in earnings forecast, the slope coefficient is positive (0.17) with a t-statistic of 13.5. The exact point estimate may not be that useful, but the positive sign of the coefficient that is statistically significant shows that the 9/11 index is plausibly a measure of sensitivity to a demand contraction.

Other Variables and Summary Statistics

In subsequent statistical analyses, we sometimes add other control variables, such as the three factors from the Fama-French (1992) model, and the momentum factor. The underlying data come from the Center for Research in Security Prices (CRSP) database including firm-level market beta.

Table 11.1A reports summary statistics of the key variables. Demand sensitivity, liquidity constraint (the Whited-Wu index), and intrinsic dependence on external finance (the Rajan-Zingales index) are all standardized to facilitate interpretation of subsequent regression coefficients. They all have a unitary standard deviation by construction. Table 11.1B reports pair-wise correlations among the variables. It is particularly noteworthy that the correlation between the two key regressors, demand sensitivity and financial constraint, is as low as 0.01. Hence they are virtually orthogonal to each other.

Table 11.1A   Summary statistics

Variable	No. obs.	Median	Mean	Std. Dev.	Min.	Max.
Percentage change in stock price *(July 31, 2007–March 31, 2008)*	2,760	–22.2	–30.1	44.7	–180.7	48.6
Demand sensitivity *(Reaction to the 9/11 news)*	2,789	1.42	1.56	1.00	–0.83	4.10
Financial constraint *(Whited-Wu index)*	2,789	–2.31	–2.24	1.00	–4.19	0.21
External finance dependence *(Rajan-Zingales index)*	2,687	0.17	0.54	1.00	–0.39	3.55
Constraint (WW) * dependence (RZ)	2,687	–0.35	–0.96	2.11	–14.88	1.63
Firm size (log assets)	2,789	5.81	5.77	2.16	–1.89	13.45
Book-to-market ratio	2,722	0.76	1.20	2.54	0.01	76.5
Beta	2,495	1.03	1.08	0.74	–2.54	4.27
Momentum	2,506	4.54	2.58	30.88	–162.09	306.95

Table 11.1B   Correlation among variables

	Stock return	Demand sensitivity	Financial constraint	External finance	WW* RZ	Firm size	Book/ market	Beta
Demand sensitivity	–0.07							
Financial constraint– WW	–0.26	0.01						
External finance dependence (RZ)	–0.07	–0.09	0.26					
Constraint (WW) * dependence (RZ)	–0.02	0.07	0.02	–0.85				
Firm size	0.22	0.00	–0.92	–0.21	–0.02			
Book/market	–0.15	0.05	–0.11	–0.15	0.11	0.17		
Beta	0.11	0.09	–0.27	–0.04	0.01	0.30	–0.05	
Momentum	0.17	0.03	–0.10	–0.12	0.08	0.07	0.03	0.03

11.3   Empirical Analysis

11.3.1   Basic Results

We examine percentage change in stock price (or more precisely, difference in log stock price) from July 31, 2007, to March 31, 2008, for US nonfinancial firms. In column (1) of table 11.2, we have the demand sensitivity index and the liquidity constraint (Whited-Wu) index as the only regressors. Both variables have a negative coefficient and are statistically significant: across firms, those that are more sensitive to a loss in consumer confidence, or were more liquidity constrained before the subprime crisis, experienced a greater fall in stock price during the subprime crisis. Since both variables are standardized, we can read off the point estimates directly: an increase in ex ante sensitivity to demand contraction by one standard deviation is associated with an extra drop in stock price by 3.7 percent. In comparison, an increase in ex ante liquidity constraint by one standard deviation is associated with an extra drop in stock price by 11.7 percent. As far as variation across firms is concerned, liquidity constraint appears to be a quantitatively more important explanation than an expected contraction of demand. (The relatively

Table 11.2   **Change in stock price during the subprime crisis (July 31, 2007–March 31, 2008)**

	1	2	3
Demand sensitivity	−3.69***	−3.27***	−3.37***
	[0.85]	[0.88]	[0.87]
Financial constraint–WW	−11.67***	−13.72***	−12.35***
	[0.82]	[2.33]	[2.32]
Firm size		−0.31	0.10
		[1.15]	[1.14]
Book-to-market ratio		−6.24***	−6.37***
		[0.64]	[0.63]
Beta		3.13**	3.01**
		[1.25]	[1.24]
Momentum			0.20***
			[0.03]
Constant	−52.35***	−52.75***	−51.93***
	[2.48]	[3.13]	[3.10]
Observations	2,761	2,410	2,410
R-squared	0.07	0.12	0.14

Notes: Stock return, financial constraint, and demand sensitivity are winsorized at the 2 percent level.
***Significant at the 1 percent level.
**Significant at the 5 percent level.
*Significant at the 10 percent level.

low R-squared does not overly bother us as this is a pure cross-sectional regression, and changes in stock prices are likely to be difficult to explain if the efficient market hypothesis is approximately correct.)

In column (2) of table 11.2, we add the three factors from the Fama-French model as controls. Two of them are statistically significant. Firms with a high book-to-market ratio experience a greater decline in price. This is consistent with the idea that a higher ratio of this type represents a greater risk, and a riskier stock will exhibit a bigger price fall in bad times. (If we take the inverse of the book-to-market ratio as a measure of investment opportunities, this means that firms with fewer investment opportunities lose more in stock value.) The firm size variable is not significant. This pattern is also present in the original Whited and Wu (2006) paper. According to their interpretation, liquidity constraint is the underlying reason why size matters for stock returns. Once we properly control for a theory-consistent measure of liquidity constraint, firm size no longer matters. The coefficient on the "beta" variable is positive and significant. Somewhat surprisingly, it says that firms with a larger beta experience a smaller reduction in stock price, other things being equal. In any case, even with the three Fama-French factors controlled for, both demand sensitivity and financial constraint factors are still statistically significant. In column (3), we add a momentum variable as an additional control. This variable is statistically significant. Stocks that have experienced a fall in price in the recent past are more likely to continue to fall in price in the subsequent periods. Again, controlling these four factors makes little difference to the statistical significance level or the size of the point estimates for demand sensitivity and liquidity constraint. Hence, our key conclusion appears robust: initially, more financially constrained firms suffered a larger drop in stock price. The same is true for relatively more demand-sensitive firms[8].

If the financial crisis disproportionately harm those nonfinancial firms that are more liquidity constrained and/or more sensitive to a consumer demand contraction, could financial investors earn excess returns by betting against these stocks (relative to other stocks)? This is essentially another way to gauge the quantitative importance of these two factors. We now turn to a "portfolio approach," and track the effects of the two factors over time. Specifically, we follow three steps. First, we classify each nonfinancial stock (other than airlines, defense, and insurance firms) along two dimensions: whether its degree of liquidity constraint at the end of 2006 (per the value of the Whited-Wu index) is above or below the median in the sample, and whether its sensitivity to a consumer demand contraction is above or below

8. Ex ante, financial constraint and demand sensitivity could be related. In the data, however, the correlation between the two is relatively low (at 0.01). In any case, we have tried a regression that extends the specification in the last column of table 11.2 by adding an interaction term between the two indices. The coefficient on the interaction term turns out to be statistically insignificant.

the median. Second, we form four portfolios on July 31, 2007, and fix their compositions in the subsequent periods: the HH portfolio is a set of equally weighted stocks that are highly liquidity constrained by the end of 2006 and highly sensitive to consumer demand contraction; the HL portfolio is a set of stocks that are highly liquidity constrained, but relatively not sensitive to a change in consumer demand; the LH portfolio consist of stocks that are relatively not liquidity constrained but highly sensitive to consumer confidence; and finally, the LL portfolio consists of stocks that are neither liquidity constrained nor sensitive to consumer confidence. Third, we track the cumulative returns of these four portfolios over time and plot the results in figure 11.6.

Several interesting patterns can be discerned from the graph. First, the HH portfolio clearly has the largest cumulative decline in stock prices over time, whereas the LL portfolio has the smallest. Second, the cumulative returns lines for the HH and HL portfolios are close to each other at the bottom of the group, whereas those for LL and LH are next to each other, on top of the group. This means the quantitative effect of liquidity constraint (in explaining cross-firm difference in stock price declines) is much bigger than that of a loss in consumer confidence. Third, if one were to have formed a megaportfolio at the beginning of August 2007 that shorted the HH portfolio and longed the LL portfolio, one would have earned a return on the order of 30 percent by the end of March 2008.

We cannot say that the quantitative effect of demand contraction on the market as a whole is small because it could reduce the stock prices of all firms in a proportional fashion. However, the difference between the HH and

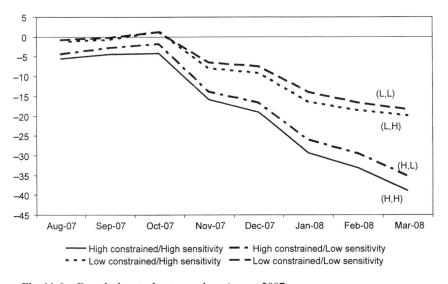

Fig. 11.6   **Cumulative stock returns since August 2007**

LL portfolios in terms of the percentage fall in stock price is approximately half of the unconditional fall in the overall stock price (about 20 percentage points out of 40 percentage points from early August 2007 to the end of March 2008). A conservative estimate is that at least half of the overall price decline is due to a negative shock to the finance supply (for those stocks that were liquidity constrained to start with).

11.3.2   Evolving Roles of Finance and Demand Shocks

Our primary regressions reported in table 11.2 are conducted on the sample period from July 31, 2007, to March 31, 2008. They look into the separate roles of a reduction in the supply of finance and a contraction of the aggregate demand in explaining the cumulative stock price decline during the period. As an alternative, we can trace the roles of these two factors over time by conducting the same regressions over a set of gradually expanding sample periods, adding one month each time to the sample, but always controlling for size, book-to-market ratio, beta, and momentum. Specifically, we perform the first regression on the period from July 31, 2007, to August 31, 2007, the second regression from July 31, 2007, to September 30, 2007, and so on, until the eighth regression from July 31, 2007, to March 31, 2008. The specification is always the same as in column (3) of table 11.2. A major difference between this exercise and the analysis of the four portfolios discussed above is the control for the three Fama-French factors and momentum. Instead of reporting the detailed results of the eight regressions, we summarize the coefficients on the two key regressors, liquidity constraint and demand sensitivity, in figure 11.7. While the point estimates (and the corresponding standard errors in parenthesis) for demand sensitivity are 0.33 (0.23), –0.01 (0.34), –0.12 (0.45), –0.38 (0.57), –0.61 (0.65), –2.03 (0.65), –2.65 (0.73), and –2.72 (0.80), respectively, the point estimates for financial constraint are –1.98 (0.62), –0.07 (0.91), –1.22 (1.23), –2.84 (1.54), –4.84 (1.75), –7.55 (1.76), –8.26 (1.98), and –12.50 (2.18), respectively.

Several features of the data are worth noting. First, in the first month of the sample (July 31, 2007–August 31, 2007), the coefficient on liquidity constraint is negative, but the coefficient on demand sensitivity is zero. By searching news reports, we find that this was the time when the subprime woes were first thought of as a widespread crisis. American Home Mortgage filed for bankruptcy on August 6, 2007. The news broke on August 16 that Countrywide Financial Corporation had to take out an emergency loan of $11 billion to narrowly escape bankruptcy. Financial institutions outside the United States such as BNP Paribas started to reveal large exposure to US subprime losses. A major presidential candidate, Hillary Clinton, proposed a bailout fund for homeowners at risk of foreclosure on August 7, 2007. Perhaps more significantly, the Federal Reserve Board lowered the discount rate by 50 basis points to 6.25 percent, while President Bush announced a limited bailout of homeowners on August 31, 2007. However, there was only

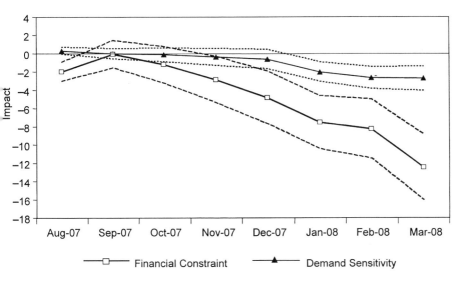

Fig. 11.7   Key regression coefficients from successively expanding samples

a very modest adjustment in the consensus forecast of US GDP growth rate in that month (see figure 11.3). Apparently, while the subprime woes were recognized as a shock to the financial system, it was not widely expected then that they would have a major negative impact on the US economy.

Curiously, during the second sample period (July 31, 2007–September 30, 2007) neither coefficient is different from zero. It is possible that market participants interpreted the actions taken by the Federal Reserve and the president as being sufficient to prevent a spillover of the crisis from the financial sector to the real economy, given what market participants thought they knew about the extent of the subprime problem. However, bad news did not stop coming in August. The British bank Northern Rock experienced a bank run in mid-September 2007. Former Federal Reserve Chairman Alan Greenspan joined the fray by declaring that the fall of housing prices was likely going to be "larger than most people expect." More and more financial institutions started to reveal bad news about exposure to subprime loan products in September, November, and the first quarter of 2008. The Federal Reserve took a succession of actions, including lowering policy interest rates and expanding liquidity provisions over this period. The federal government also took several initiatives (e.g., the creation of the Hope Now Alliance, the announcement to encourage a voluntary and temporary freeze of mortgage payments, and the attempt to modernize the Federal Housing Authority). At the same time, the market began to reassess the seriousness of the subprime problem and its impact on the real economy. In figure 11.7, the market reaction to these developments manifests itself in incrementally more negative coefficients on the key regressors over time. This is shown most clearly in the case of liquidity constraint. The coefficient became –1.2 in October and increased in absolute value steadily month by month until reaching –12.5 by the end of March 2008. In relative terms, a loss of consumer confidence was not perceived to be a major factor until December 2007. Even then, the coefficient on sensitivity to demand contraction was always smaller than that on liquidity constraint in every subsequent sample period, reaching –2.72 by the end of March 2008.

A deterioration of financial constraint faced by nonfinancial firms in the first quarter of 2008 is consistent with a Senior Loan Officer Survey conducted in April 2008.[9] About 55 percent of domestic US banks, up from about 30 percent in the January survey, reported to have tightened lending standards on loans to large- and medium-sized (nonfinancial) firms over the preceding three months. Moreover, about 70 percent of the banks—up from about 45 percent in the January survey—indicated that they had increased the spread of loan rates over their cost of funds. They noted that concerns about their current or expected capital positions had contributed to more stringent lending policies over the preceding three months.

To summarize, the realization that credit crunch and demand contraction could damage the real economy outside the financial sector looks like a gradually unfolding drama. Throughout the sample period, tightening liquidity constraints are a leading actor, always perceived to be more important, while demand contraction is a supporting actor, playing a quantitatively smaller role in explaining cross-firm differences in stock performance.

11.3.3   Alternative Measure of Financial Dependence

For our story to be persuasive, we have to make sure that the key measure of liquidity constraint is valid and informative. We therefore conduct several additional checks. The Whited-Wu index has been used as a measure of liquidity constraint at the firm level in all the regressions so far. As an alternative, we follow Rajan and Zingales (1998) and adopt a sector-level measure of a firm's intrinsic demand for external finance. As noted in the data section, the underlying idea behind Rajan and Zingales (1998) is different from Whited-Wu (2006); the simple correlation between the Rajan-Zingales (RZ) index and the Whited-Wu (WW) index is 0.26. This means that the RZ index can potentially provide an informative and independent check on the notion that financial constraint plays a major role in explaining the effect of the subprime crisis on nonfinancial firms. While the original RZ index was constructed for some forty sectors at the SIC two-digit level, we expand it to cover about 400 sectors at the SIC four-digit level (following the same conceptual framework).

In column (1) of table 11.3, we report the regression in which the WW index is replaced by the RZ index. As we can see, both the RZ index and the demand sensitivity index have negative coefficients that are statistically significant at the 1 percent level. In particular, those firms that naturally rely

Table 11.3   Alternative measure of financial dependence

	1	2	3	4
Demand sensitivity	−4.00***	−3.87***	−3.30***	−3.41***
	[0.92]	[0.89]	[0.91]	[0.90]
External finance dependence	−3.03***	−3.18*	−6.55***	−5.74***
(RZ index, based on 1990–2006)	[0.90]	[1.84]	[2.02]	[2.00]
Financial constraint		−10.94***	−11.81***	−10.81***
(WW index, 2006 value)		[0.98]	[2.53]	[2.51]
Financial constraint		−1.60**	−2.66***	−2.56***
* external finance dependence		[0.81]	[0.86]	[0.85]
Firm size			−0.17	0.15
			[1.18]	[1.17]
Book-to-market ratio			−6.48***	−6.53***
			[0.65]	[0.64]
Beta			3.25**	3.11**
			[1.28]	[1.26]
Momentum				0.19***
				[0.028]
Constant	−23.07***	−50.33***	−48.00***	−47.92***
	[1.80]	[3.01]	[3.56]	[3.52]
Observations	2,660	2,660	2,327	2,327
R-squared	0.01	0.08	0.13	0.15

Notes: LHS variable = change in stock price during the subprime crisis (7/31/07–3/31/08). Stock return, financial constraint, external finance dependence and demand sensitivity are winsorized at the 2 percent level.
***Significant at the 1 percent level.
**Significant at the 5 percent level.
*Significant at the 10 percent level.

more on external finance for business operation experience a bigger fall in stock prices during the financial crisis period. An increase in the RZ index by one standard deviation is associated with a bigger decline in stock price, by 3 percentage points.

Because the RZ and the WW indices measure somewhat different aspects of a firm's dependence on external finance, we can also include both in a regression and explore the role of their interaction. This is done in column (2) of table 11.3. It turns out that each of the two indices, and an interaction term between the two, all produce negative coefficients that are significant at least at the 5 percent level. In other words, firms that were liquidity constrained at the beginning of the sample period fared worse in their stock prices following the outbreak of the subprime crisis. This effect is magnified for firms that were both liquidity constrained and located in sectors that are naturally more dependent on external finance.

In columns (3) and (4) of table 11.3, we add the three Fama-French factors (firm size, book-to-market ratio, and beta) and the momentum factors, respectively, to the above regression. Clearly, even after controlling for these four factors, liquidity constraint, intrinsic dependence on external finance, and their interactions (as well as sensitivity to demand shock) continue to have negative coefficients that are significant at the 1 percent level. This provides some additional support for our contention that there really was a serious financial shock that negatively impacted nonfinancial firms in a statistically and economically significant way.

11.3.4   Placebo Tests

We use firm-level stock price reaction to the September 11, 2001, terrorist attack (the change in log stock price from September 10 to September 28, 2001) as a measure of a firm's sensitivity to demand contraction in the subsequent subprime period. We cited evidence that there was an expectation of recession after the attack as indicated by a sharply more pessimistic forecast of US GDP growth by the International Monetary Fund and by professional commercial forecasters subsequent to the 9/11 shock that lasted well beyond September 28, 2001. Since the 9/11 attack directly and physically affected many Wall Street financial institutions and the New York Stock Exchange was closed for a few days, it is reasonable to ask whether our 9/11 index could also partly reflect a firm's sensitivity to a tightening liquidity constraint. If it is, then this could contaminate our interpretation of the results reported in table 11.2. We previously argued in the data section that any effect on cost of capital and availability of external finance from the 9/11 attack was temporary and short-lived (as shown in figure 11.5). By the choice of our time window (September 10–28, 2001), the 9/11 index (or the variation across firms in stock price responses) is not likely to be severely contaminated by firms' sensitivity to financial constraint.

We now perform a placebo test that examines this directly. Specifically, we measure a firm's liquidity constraint by the Whited-Wu index, using the values of the constituent variables at the end of 2000. (This is exactly parallel to the index used in table 11.2, except that the constituent variables of the Whited-Wu index in that case are based on their end-of-2006 values.) We ask whether this direct measure of liquidity constraint helps to explain the magnitude of stock price declines from September 10, 2001, to September 28, 2001, the period used to construct the index for demand sensitivity. The results are presented in table 11.4. We find that financial constraint is not statistically significant: differential degrees of liquidity constraint across firms (in 2000) do not explain cross-firm differences in stock price reactions after the 9/11 shock. This increases our confidence that the 9/11 index is not likely to be contaminated by firms' sensitivity to liquidity constraint itself.

Our principal claim is that the subprime crisis affects the real sectors in the economy through a combination of a tightening liquidity constraint and a contraction of consumer demand. How do we know these two factors only became important after the subprime trouble began to be recognized as a large-scale crisis in August 2007?

We now conduct a different placebo test, replicating the key regressions

Table 11.4   Placebo tests—Does liquidity constraint explain changes in stock prices from September 10 to 28, 2001?

	1	2
Firm size	−0.17	−0.45
	[0.13]	[0.34]
Book-to-market ratio	−0.38***	−0.38***
	[0.074]	[0.08]
Firm beta	−5.49***	−5.33***
	[0.48]	[0.49]
Momentum	2.57***	2.51***
	[0.54]	[0.55]
Financial constraint		−0.59
(Whited-Wu index, 2000 value)		[0.68]
Constant	−7.21***	−7.14***
	[0.82]	[0.83]
Observations	4,678	4,563
R-squared	0.04	0.04

Notes: Stock return, financial constraint, external finance dependence and demand sensitivity are winsorized at the 2 percent level.
***Significant at the 1 percent level.
**Significant at the 5 percent level.
*Significant at the 10 percent level.

in table 11.2, but on a sample period prior to the subprime trouble being recognized as a generalized crisis. Table 11.5 reports these regressions for the period June 30 to July 31, 2007 (firm-level financial constraints are still measured based on end-2006 values of the Whited-Wu index). Neither financial constraint nor demand sensitivity is statistically significant. A lack of statistical significance on the Whited-Wu index suggests that it was not a general predictor of future firm value before August 2007. A lack of statistical significance on the demand sensitivity variable confirms the information in figures 11.6 and 11.7: As there was no general expectation of a demand contraction, there was no reason then for stocks that were more sensitive to a demand contraction to do worse than other stocks. This also reinforces our confidence that the 9/11 index appears to capture firms' sensitivity to a change in consumer demand. We replicate the same exercise for an earlier period (January 1, 2007–May 31, 2007), and find the same pattern (of no statistical significance for demand sensitivity or liquidity constraints). This leads us to conclude that the data patterns in table 11.2 are really those associated with the subprime crisis period, and not with other factors present in earlier periods.

11.3.5   Exposures to Exchange Rate and Commodity Price Movements

Since the subprime crisis broke out in August 2007, there have been other developments in the economy that could affect stock prices ex post. Most

Table 11.5   Placebo tests—Stock price changes before the subprime crisis (June 30–July 31, 2007)

	1	2	3
Demand sensitivity	−0.26	0.03	0.05
	[0.22]	[0.23]	[0.23]
Financial constraint	0.06	−0.56	−0.37
(Whited-Wu index)	[0.22]	[0.62]	[0.62]
Firm size		−0.06	−0.01
		[0.31]	[0.30]
Book-to-market ratio		−0.95***	−1.00***
		[0.17]	[0.17]
Beta		−1.03***	−1.04***
		[0.33]	[0.33]
Momentum			0.02***
			[0.01]
Constant	−5.15***	−4.69***	−4.72***
	[0.64]	[0.82]	[0.82]
Observations	2,760	2,409	2,409
R-squared	0	0.02	0.02

***Significant at the 1 percent level.
**Significant at the 5 percent level.
*Significant at the 10 percent level.

prominently, the US dollar depreciated against the euro and the Japanese yen by 15 and 18 percent, respectively, from July 31, 2007, to March 31, 2008; the world oil price increased by close to 40 percent during the same period. The dollar depreciation would presumably increase the profit of export-oriented firms but reduce that of those that rely heavily on imported inputs. Similarly, the energy price hike would likely increase the profit of energy producers but reduce that of most other companies.

Recall that both the liquidity constraint and demand sensitivity indices are measured using data collected prior to the subprime crisis period. Since we are interested in understanding whether an ex ante classification of firms by their degree of liquidity constraint and sensitivity to demand contraction could help predict their ex post stock price movement during the subprime crisis period, we may argue that the three Fama-French factors plus the momentum factor have already summarized all the other ex ante information relevant for stock returns. In other words, the specifications in tables 11.2 and 11.3 are already sufficient; there is no need to incorporate ex post firm exposures to exchange rate and commodity price movements as additional controls.

Nonetheless, there could be coincidental correlations between our ex ante measure of liquidity constraint (or demand sensitivity) and the ex post realized movement in exchange rates and commodity prices. As another robustness check, we now attempt to control for a firm's exposures to currency and commodity price movement. An immediate difficulty that we face is a lack of systematic information on firm revenue and cost by currency, or on a firm's exposure to commodity price movement. We follow Adler and Dumas (1984) and Dominguez and Tesar (2001, 2006) by constructing our own indices for exposure to exchange rates and commodity prices, based on a three-step procedure. In step 1, we measure the relationship between weekly stock prices and major exchange rates and commodity prices in the three calendar years prior to the subprime crisis. More precisely, for each firm, we regress its weekly stock returns on the S&P 500 market return, percentage changes in the euro-dollar exchange rate and the yen-dollar exchange rate, and percentage changes in three commodity groups' spot price indices (energy, agricultural products, and metals) during the period from 2004 to 2006.[10] We collect the five estimated coefficients on the exchange rates and the commodity prices for each firm. In step 2, we multiply these coefficients individually with the realized percentage changes for these exchange rates and commodity price indices over the period July 31, 2007, to March 31, 2008.[11] These are firm-level ex post exposures to major currencies and commodity prices. In step 3, we add these five exposure variables as additional controls in our main regressions. Note that in the first step, an oil producer would likely have a positive coefficient on the energy price index, whereas a firm that uses oil as an input would likely have a negative coefficient. As a result, all exposure variables are expected to enter step 3 with a positive sign.

We report the regression result (step 3, above) in the first column of table 11.6. Of the five new control variables, the coefficient on energy price exposure is positive and statistically significant: energy producers, relative to energy users, experienced a smaller drop in stock prices (or even an increase in stock prices) from July 31, 2007, to March 31, 2008. The coefficients on the two exchange rates and the agriculture price exposure are not different from zero statistically. This could mean that most firms in the sample did not have much exposure to these factors. Alternatively, it could mean that most firms had already undertaken adequate hedging strategies, including buying currency futures and options, so that ex post realized movements in exchange rates and agricultural prices did not have a material impact on their profit. The coefficient on metal price exposure has a negative sign. We do not have a good explanation except to note that this turns out not to be robust in subsequent specifications (reported in the last two columns of table 11.6).

We now come to our two key regressors: liquidity constraint and demand sensitivity. Both continue to have a negative coefficient that is statistically significant at the 1 percent level. In fact, the size of the point estimates is

9. http://www.federalreserve.gov/boarddocs/snloansurvey/200805/.

10. For more details on the S&P commodity spot price indices, see http://www2.goldman sachs.com/services/ securities/products/ sp-gsci-commodity-index/tables.html.

11. From July 31, 2007, to March 31, 2008, the price of agriculture and energy rose by 36 percent and 29 percent, respectively, while the price of metal declined by 0.7 percent.

Table 11.6   Adding exposures to exchange rate and commodity price movement (Stock price change during the subprime crisis, 7/31/07–3/31/08)

	1	2	3	4
Demand sensitivity	-3.02***	-2.98***	-3.22***	-3.18***
	[0.87]	[0.90]	[0.87]	[0.90]
Financial constraint (WW index)	-12.01***	-10.75***	-12.40***	-11.06***
	[2.31]	[2.51]	[2.31]	[2.51]
Firm size	0.27	0.24	-0.08	-0.09
	[1.13]	[1.16]	[1.13]	[1.16]
Book-to-market ratio	-6.32***	-6.42***	-6.39***	-6.50***
	[0.63]	[0.64]	[0.63]	[0.64]
Beta	1.10	1.32	1.51	1.64
	[1.29]	[1.32]	[1.30]	[1.32]
Momentum	0.19***	0.18***	0.20***	0.19***
	[0.03]	[0.03]	[0.03]	[0.03]
Exposure to euro	16.46	16.95	-10.6	-7.87
	[12.0]	[12.2]	[18.5]	[18.9]
Exposure to yen	2.30	-0.37	4.65	-1.55
	[10.6]	[10.8]	[18.1]	[18.5]
Exposure to energy	0.67***	0.65***	0.82***	0.83***
	[0.15.]	[0.15]	[0.19]	[0.19]
Exposure to metal	-15.23**	-14.13**	-4.87	-3.52
	[6.12]	[6.27]	[8.68]	[8.91]
Exposure to agriculture	-0.16	-0.18	-0.38**	-0.42**
	[0.11]	[0.11]	[0.19]	[0.19]
Financial constraint (RZ index)		-5.01**		-5.21***
		[1.99]		[1.99]
Financial constraint * external finance dependence		-2.49***		-2.53***
		[0.84]		[0.84]
Constant	-51.47***	-48.22***	-50.31***	-46.89***
	[3.15]	[3.57]	[3.12]	[3.54]
Observations	2,408	2,325	2,408	2,325
R-squared	0.15	0.16	0.15	0.16

Note: The exposures to exchange rates and commodity prices are constructed following a two-step procedure. In step 1, for each firm, we regress its weekly stock returns on the S&P 500 market return, percentage changes in the euro-dollar exchange rate and the yen-dollar exchange rate, and percentage changes in three commodity groups' spot price indexes (energy, agriculture, and metal) during 2004 to 2006. We collect the five estimated coefficients on the exchange rates and the commodity prices for each firm. In step 2, we multiple these coefficients individually with the realized percentage changes for these exchange rates and commodity price indexes over July 31, 2007–March 31, 2008. These are firm-level ex post exposures to major currencies and commodity prices used in columns (1) and (2). In columns (3) and (4), we use an alternative definition of exposures in which all statistically insignificant coefficients in step 1 are assigned a zero value.

virtually unaffected by the inclusion of the exposures to major exchange rates and commodity prices.

In column (2) of table 11.6, we add the Rajan-Zingales measure of intrinsic dependence on external finance, and its interaction with the Whited-Wu measure of liquidity constraint. As in table 11.3, liquidity-constrained firms experienced a bigger fall in stock prices, especially for those located in sectors that are intrinsically more reliant on external finance.

In constructing our firm-level exposures to major exchange rates and commodity prices, we notice that some of the coefficients in firm-by-firm regressions (in step 1, discussed above) are not different from zero statistically. As an alternative way to construct our exposure variables, we assign these coefficients to be zero and redo our regressions. The regressions with the alternative definition of the exposures are reported in columns (3) and (4) of table 11.6. The coefficient on the energy exposure variable is still positive and significant, with the point estimate 20 percent larger than before. The two exchange rate exposures are still insignificant. This time, the metal price exposure becomes insignificant but the agriculture price exposure becomes negative and significant. Other than these, there are no material changes to the regression results. In particular, firms that are more liquidity constrained or more sensitive to demand contraction continue to exhibit a larger decline in their stock prices during the subprime crisis period.

As an extension, we have also attempted to control for firm-level exposure to interest rate changes. It is possible that different firms may respond differently to a given rise in the interest rate, for reasons unrelated to their liquidity constraints. We account for this using a methodology similar to the approach to control for a firm's exposure to exchange rates and commodity prices. Specifically, we first estimate a firm-level sensitivity to these factors by regressing weekly stock returns on the market return, changes in the two exchange rates, changes in the three commodity price indices, and then changes in the interest rate (proxied by three-month Treasury bills) during the period from 2004 to 2006. Using the estimated coefficients and the actual realized change in the interest rate from July 31, 2007, to March 31, 2008, we can compute a firm-specific exposure to interest rate change (and similarly, exposures to changes in exchange rates and commodity prices). Incorporating the interest rate exposure in specifications like those in table 11.6 reveals no material effect on the estimates or the significance levels of the coefficients on either the demand elasticity or the liquidity constraint variable (regression results not reported to save space).

11.3.6   Additional Robustness Checks and Extensions

We construct an alternative index of sensitivity to a demand shock that purges the influence of the four factors: firm size, book/market, beta, and momentum. In other words, we first regress change in log stock prices from September 10 to 28, 2001, on the four factors (which is reported in the first column of table 11.4). We then use the residual to construct an alternative index of a firm's sensitivity to demand shocks. We redo all the regressions in tables 11.2 and 11.3, but find the results to be virtually unaffected. To be precise, the coefficients on demand sensitivity and financial constraint are negative and statistically significant at the 1 percent level. The point estimates are slightly smaller than, but not statistically different from, those in tables 11.2 and 11.3.

We vary the time window used to construct the demand sensitivity index from September 10–28, 2001, to September 10–October 12, 2001. With this modified index, the coefficient on demand sensitivity in a specification similar to column (3) in table 11.2 becomes smaller in absolute value (from –3.37 to –2.58), but it does not materially affect the estimate on the liquidity constraint measure (not reported).

The demand sensitivity index is measured at the four-digit sector level. As a robustness check, we also construct it at the three- and two-digit levels, respectively. The three-digit level index is constructed as the mean of the index at the four-digit level, and the two-digit level index as the mean of the index at the three-digit level. Because different sectors have uneven numbers of subsectors, these alternative constructions also effectively reassign weights to the firms. We rerun all regressions in table 11.2 and find similar results. For example, when using the three-digit level index in a regression similar to that in the last column of table 11.2, the estimated coefficient on demand sensitivity is –2.21, with a standard error of 0.84. In other words, the point estimate is a bit smaller, but still significant at the 1 percent level.

We note in the introduction that many firms had larger cash holdings in recent years than in the past. Some may point to this and argue that a liquidity constraint is not likely to be a significant factor during the current subprime crisis. However, the level of cash holding is, in principle, endogenous. For example, it could be a response to increased risk associated with more volatile cash flows (as pointed out by Bates, Kahle, and Stulz [2009]). We add a firm's "cash and short-term investments" as an additional control to a specification otherwise identical to column [3] of table 11.2. The associated coefficient turns out to be negative and statistically significant at the 1 percent level, with a point estimate of –12.8 and a standard error of 3.90. In other words, those firms with a higher cash stock actually experienced a larger drop in stock prices. This is consistent with the view that a higher level of cash holding is a sign of a riskier cash flow: when a crisis hits, these firms are likely to fare worse. Reassuringly, the coefficients on both liquidity constraint and demand sensitivity continue to be negative and statistically significant at the 1 percent level. In fact, the point estimates are very close to those in table 11.2.

11.4   Conclusion

In this chapter, we propose a methodological framework to study the underlying mechanisms by which a financial-sector crisis may affect the real sector and apply it to the case of the current financial crisis. In particular, we are interested in documenting and quantifying the importance of tightening liquidity constraints and the deterioration of consumer confidence on nonfinancial firms. We ask the question: Could an ex ante classification of the firms based on their degrees of liquidity constraint and sensitivity to demand contraction *prior to* the subprime crisis help to predict their ex post stock price performance *during* the crisis period? We find the answer to be a resounding yes. Both channels are at work; liquidity constraints appear to be more significant quantitatively in explaining cross-firm differences in the magnitude of stock price declines. A conservative estimate is that a tightening supply of financing is likely to explain at least half of the actual drop in stock prices for firms that were liquidity constrained to start with.

In order to reach these conclusions, we propose a novel methodology that distinguishes a shock to the supply of finance from a firm sensitivity to demand contraction. We measure a firm's sensitivity to demand contraction by its stock price reaction to the September 11, 2001, terrorist attack (change in log stock price from September 10, 2001, to September 28, 2001). We measure a firm's liquidity constraint by the Whited-Wu (2006) index, valued at the end of 2006. We conduct extensive robustness checks to ensure that these indicators are valid and informative. For example, we verify that the 9/11 index is not contaminated by the impact of a liquidity constraint itself. While liquidity constraint and demand sensitivity, as measured by these two indicators, have statistically significant power in predicting stock price movement during the subprime crisis period, placebo tests suggest that they do not predict stock price movement in a period shortly before the subprime crisis broke out. An alternative measure of a firm's dependence on external finance proposed by Rajan and Zingales (1998) and valued based on information from 1990 to 2006 also has predictive power about stock price movement during the subprime crisis period.

Correctly diagnosing the transmission channels for a financial crisis to affect the real economy has implications for designing appropriate policy responses to the crisis. For the subprime mortgage crisis, our analysis suggests that policies that aim primarily at restoring consumer confidence and increasing demand, such as a tax rebate to households, will probably be insufficient to help the real economy; policies that could relax liquidity constraints faced by nonfinancial firms are likely to have larger effects and the economy is unlikely to rebound without them. Our methodology should also be useful in other contexts where effects of a financial shock to the real economy need to be measured. We leave these applications for future work.

References

Adler, Michael, and Bernard Dumas. 1984. "Exposure to Currency Risk: Definition and Measurement." *Financial Management* 13:41–50.

Bates, Thomas W., Kathleen M. Kahle, and René M. Stulz. 2009. "Why Do US Firms Hold So Much More Cash Than They Used To?" *Journal of Finance*:1985–2021.

Bernanke, Ben S., and Cara S. Lown. 1991. "The Credit Crunch." *Brookings Papers on Economic Activity* 2:205–47.

Bloom, Nicholas. 2009. "The Impact of Uncertainty Shocks." *Econometrica* 77 (3): 623–85.

Borensztein, Eduardo, and Jong-Wha Lee. 2002. "Financial Crisis and Credit Crunch in Korea: Evidence from Firm-Level Data." *Journal of Monetary Economics* 49: 853–75.

Chari, V. V., Lawrence Christiano, and Patrick J. Kehoe. 2008. "Facts and Myths about the Financial Crisis of 2008." Working Paper no. 666, Federal Reserve Bank of Minneapolis, October.

Cohen-Cole, Ethan, Burcu Duygan-Bump, Jose Fillat, and Judit Montoriol-Garriga. 2008. "Looking Behind the Aggregates: A Reply to 'Facts and Myths about the Financial Crisis of 2008'." Working Paper no. QAU08–5, Federal Reserve Bank of Boston.

Dell'Ariccia, Giovanni, Enrica Detragiache, and Raghuram Rajan. 2008. "The Real Effect of Banking Crises." *Journal of Financial Intermediation* 17:89–112.

Dell'Ariccia, Giovanni, Deniz Igan, and Luc Laeven. 2008. "Credit Booms and Lending Standards: Evidence from the Subprime Mortgage Market." CEPR Discussion Paper no. DP6683, Centre for Economic Policy Research.

Dominguez, Kathryn, and Linda L. Tesar. 2001. "A Reexamination of Exchange Rate Exposure." *American Economic Review* 91 (2): 396–99.

———. 2006. "Exchange Rate Exposure." *Journal of International Economics* 68: 188–218.

Fama, Eugene F., and Kenneth R. French. 1992. "The Cross-Section of Expected Stock Returns." *Journal of Finance* 47:427–65.

Greenlaw, David, Jan Hatzius, Anil K Kashyap, and Hyun Song Shin. 2008. "Leveraged Losses: Lessons from the Mortgage Market Meltdown." Draft paper, US Monetary Policy Forum Conference. http://research.chicagobooth.edu/igm/docs/USMPF_FINAL_Print.pdf.

Kaplan, Steven, and Luigi Zingales. 1997. "Do Financing Constraints Explain Why Investment is Correlated with Cash Flow?" *Quarterly Journal of Economics* 112:169–216.

Lakonishok, Josef, Andrei Shleifer, and Robert W. Vishny. 1994. "Contrarian Investment, Extrapolation and Risk." *Journal of Finance* 49:1541–78.

Mian, Atif. Forthcoming. "The Case for a Credit Registry." In *Risk Topography: Systemic Risk and Macro Modeling*, edited by Markus K. Brunnermeier and Arvind Krishnamurthy. Chicago: University of Chicago Press.

Mian, Atif, and Amir Sufi. 2008. "The Consequences of Mortgage Credit Expansion: Evidence from the 2007 Mortgage Default Crisis." Working Paper, Graduate School of Business, University of Chicago.

Rajan, Raghuram, and Luigi Zingales. 1998. "Financial Dependence and Growth." *American Economic Review* 88:559–86.

Reinhart, Carmen, and Kenneth Rogoff. 2008. "Is the 2007 US Sub-Prime Financial Crisis So Different? An International Historical Comparison." Working Paper, University of Maryland and Harvard University.

Whited, Toni, and Guojun Wu. 2006. "Financial Constraints Risk." *Review of Financial Studies* 19:531–59.

Contributors

Barry Bosworth
The Brookings Institution
1775 Massachusetts Avenue
Washington, DC 20036

Jesse Bricker
Board of Governors of the Federal
  Reserve System
20th Street and Constitution Avenue,
  NW
Washington, DC 20551

Brian Bucks
Consumer Financial Protection Bureau
1700 G Street, NW
Washington, DC 20552

Rajashri Chakrabarti
Federal Reserve Bank of New York
33 Liberty Street
New York, NY 10045

Carol A. Corrado
The Conference Board
845 Third Avenue
New York, NY 10002

Stephanie E. Curcuru
Board of Governors of the Federal
  Reserve System
20th Street and Constitution Avenue,
  NW
Washington, DC 20551

Dominique Durant
Banque de France, Autorité de contrôle
  prudential et de résolution 66-2700
61 rue Taitbout
75009 Paris, France

Matthew J. Eichner
Board of Governors of the Federal
  Reserve System
20th Street and Constitution Avenue,
  NW
Washington, DC 20551

Joshua Gallin
Board of Governors of the Federal
  Reserve System
20th Street and Constitution Avenue,
  NW
Washington, DC 20551

Christopher A. Gohrband
Bureau of Economic Analysis
1441 L Street, NW
Washington, DC 20230

Kristy L. Howell
Bureau of Economic Analysis
1441 L Street, NW
Washington, DC 20230

Charles R. Hulten
Department of Economics
University of Maryland
Room 3114, Tydings Hall
College Park, MD 20742

Arthur Kennickell
Board of Governors of the Federal
   Reserve System
20th Street and Constitution Avenue,
   NW
Washington, DC 20551

Donald L. Kohn
The Brookings Institution
1775 Massachusetts Avenue, NW
Washington, DC 20036

Donghoon Lee
Federal Reserve Bank of New York
33 Liberty Street
New York, NY 10045

David Lenze
Bureau of Economic Analysis
1441 L Street, NW
Washington, DC 20230

Traci Mach
Board of Governors of the Federal
   Reserve System
20th Street and Constitution Avenue,
   NW
Washington, DC 20551

Kevin Moore
Board of Governors of the Federal
   Reserve System
20th Street and Constitution Avenue,
   NW
Washington, DC 20551

Leonard Nakamura
Economic Research
Federal Reserve Bank of Philadelphia
10 Independence Mall
Philadelphia, PA 19106-1574

Michael G. Palumbo
Board of Governors of the Federal
   Reserve System
20th Street and Constitution Avenue,
   NW
Washington, DC 20551

Marshall B. Reinsdorf
Statistics Department, Real Sector
   Division
International Monetary Fund
700 19th Street, NW
Washington, DC 20431

Charles P. Thomas
Board of Governors of the Federal
   Reserve System
20th Street and Constitution Avenue,
   NW
Washington, DC 20551

Hui Tong
Research Department
International Monetary Fund
700 19th Street, NW
Washington, DC 20431

Wilbert van der Klaauw
Microeconomic Studies Function
Federal Reserve Bank of New York
33 Liberty Street
New York, NY 10045

Shang-Jin Wei
Graduate School of Business
619 Uris Hall
Columbia University
3022 Broadway
New York, NY 10027

Basit Zafar
Microeconomic Studies Function
Federal Reserve Bank of New York
33 Liberty Street
New York, NY 10045

Author Index

Subject Index